Religion and the American
Experience, 1620-1900

Religion and the American Experience, 1620-1900

A Bibliography of Doctoral Dissertations

Compiled by **Arthur P. Young** and **E. Jens Holley**
with the assistance of Annette Blum

Bibliographies and Indexes in Religious Studies, Number 24

Greenwood Press
Westport, Connecticut • London

Library of Congress Cataloging-in-Publication Data

Young, Arthur P.
  Religion and the American experience, 1620-1900: a bibliography
of doctoral dissertations/compiled by Arthur P. Young and E. Jens
Holley; with the assistance of Annette Blum.
    p. cm.—(Bibliographies and indexes in religious studies,
ISSN 0742-6836;no. 24)
  Includes bibliographical references and indexes.
  ISBN 0-313-27747-8 (alk. paper)
  1. United States—Religion—Bibliography. 2. Dissertations,
Academic—United States—Bibliography. I. Holley, E. Jens.
II. Blum, Annette. III. Title. IV. Series.
Z7757.U5Y68 1992
[BL2424]
016.2'00973—dc20   92-28450

British Library Cataloguing in Publication Data is available.

Library of Congress Catalog Card Number: 92-28450
ISBN: 0-313-27747-8
ISSN: 0742-6836

First published in 1992

Greenwood Press, 88 Post Road West, Westport, CT 06881
An imprint of Greenwood Publishing Group, Inc.

Printed in the United States of America

The paper used in this book complies with the
Permanent Paper Standard issued by the National
Information Standards Organization (Z39.48-1984).

10 9 8 7 6 5 4 3 2 1

To

Selby U. Gration

Donald W. Krummel

James F. Wyatt

For Their Friendship

CONTENTS

PART TWO
Topical Studies

PREFACE

From the Puritan theocracy to televangelist Pat Robertson, religion has touched nearly every facet of American life. The impact of religion on the nation has been chronicled since the seventeenth century with Cotton Mather's *Magnolia Christi Americana* and continues in this century with Martin E. Marty's 23-volume series, *Chicago Studies in the History of American Religion*. Early research centered on Puritan themes and assumed a Protestant hegemony. More recently, scholars have expanded their horizon to address the full spectrum of denominations and social characteristics such as class, ethnic origin, and gender. We invoke Mather's timeless observation about the study and value of religion for the appearance of this compilation: "But of all *History* it must be confessed, that *Palm* is to be given unto *Church History*; wherein the *Dignity*, the *Suavity*, and the *Utility* of the *Subject* is transcendent."

To facilitate advanced scholarly inquiry, the large body of graduate-level research on the American religious experience is assembled in this bibliography of doctoral dissertations. Divided into two main sections, citations in Part One are arrayed alphabetically by sixty-five denominations and movements. Those listings with more than twenty-five dissertation titles are further subdivided by broad subject descriptor. Thematic studies and those titles covering more than one denomination are organized under twenty topical headings located in Part Two.

The 4,240 citations were drawn from *Dissertation Abstracts International* through June 1991. This compilation incorporates titles pertaining to the historical dimension of the nation's religious experience. More than 500 subject terms and 1,000 personal names were used to search the CD-ROM version of the dissertation database. Both titles and associated abstracts were searched to determine relevancy and to assign index terms. Order numbers are furnished for all doctoral dissertations which are available from University Microfilms, Inc.

Beyond the expected denominational and biographical studies, *Religion and the American Experience* includes citations relating to such important collateral areas as communal societies, fraternal orders, literature, pragmatism, science, slavery, and temperance. The bibliography also includes titles pertaining to church-affiliated institutions of higher education. Studies which summarize contemporary activities or otherwise omit an historical orientation are not eligible. General theological treatments unrelated to a specific denomination are excluded. The detailed subject index furnishes access to personal names, titles of publications, specific subjects, broad terms, states, and geographic regions. All post-1980 abstracts were electronically searched for supplemental terms, and the print version of numerous pre-1980 abstracts was screened for names and terms to enhance the subject index.

Individual denominations and movements with the most entries are Catholic, 410; Congregational, 368; Baptist, 220; Puritan, 185; Presbyterian, 179; Transcendentalism, 175; Methodist, 170; Latter-Day Saints, 141; Judaism, 116; and Society of Friends, 100. The top degree-granting institutions are the University of Chicago, Columbia University, Yale University, Harvard University, Catholic University, University of Pennsylvania, New York University, University of Michigan, Southern Baptist Theological Seminary, University of Iowa, University of Wisconsin, and Duke University. Seventy-five percent of the authors are men and twenty-five percent are women.

Special appreciation is owed to Virginia Sue Cary, Barbara George, Jennifer Merkel, Reda Rietveld, and Roberta Taylor for record input and proofreading. Phyllis Watts rendered invaluable assistance with the formatting and verification phases. Annette Blum joined the project at the outset and contributed so much that her name appears on the title page.

Arthur P. Young
E. Jens Holley
Columbia, South Carolina

PART ONE

DENOMINATIONS AND MOVEMENTS

ADVENTIST

General Studies

1 Arthur, David T. "Come out of Babylon": A Study of Millerite Separatism and Denominationalism, 1840-1865. Ph.D., University of Rochester, 1970. 397p. UMI# 71-01367.

2 Baum, Ruth E. The Ethnohistory of Law: The Hutterite Case. Ph.D., State University of New York, 1977. 444p. UMI# 7804545.

3 Deets, Lee E. The Hutterites; A Study in Social Cohesion. Ph.D., Columbia University, 1940.

4 Dick, Everett N. The Adventist Crisis, 1843-1844. Ph.D., University of Wisconsin, 1930.

5 Doan, Ruth A. The Miller Heresy, Millennialism and American Culture. Ph.D., University of North Carolina-Chapel Hill, 1984. 293p. UMI# 8508576.

6 Harkness, Reuben E.E. The Social Origins of the Millerite Movement. Ph.D., University of Chicago, 1927.

7 McCumber, Harold O. Beginnings of the Seventh-Day Adventist Church in California. Ph.D., University of California-Berkeley, 1934.

8 Peter, Karl A. Factors of Social Change and Social Dynamics in the Communal Settlements of Hutterites: 1527-1967. Ph.D., University of Alberta, 1968.

9 Reid, George W. The Foundations and Early Development of the Health Emphasis Among Seventh-Day Adventists. Th.D., Southwestern Baptist Theological Seminary, 1976.

10   Rowe, David L. Thunder and Trumpets: The Millerite Movement and Apocalyptic Thought in Upstate New York, 1800-1845. Ph.D., University of Virginia, 1974. 384p. UMI# 7423325.

11   Serl, Vernon C. Stability and Change in Hutterite Society. Ph.D., University of Oregon, 1964. 177p. UMI# 6502481.

12   Tumangday, Miriam S. Albert Bandura and Ellen G. White: A Comparative Study of Their Concepts of Behavior Modification Through Modeling. Ed.D., Andrews University, 1977. 250p. UMI# 7727584.

Art and Architecture

13   Thompson, William P. Hutterite Community: Artefact Ark; An Historical Study of the Architecture and Planning of a Communal Society. Ph.D., Cornell University, 1977. 317p. UMI# 7728388.

Biography

14   Bean, Raymond J. The Influence of William Miller in the History of American Christianity. Ph.D., Boston University, 1949. 175p.

15   Bermeo, Franklin H. Ellen G. White's Theory of Character Development With Inferences Suggested by Selected Contemporary Psychologists. Ph.D., New York University, 1979. 305p. UMI# 7918834.

16   Bissell, Ronald D. The Background, Formation, Development, and Presentation of Ellen White's Concept of Forgiveness From Her Childhood to 1864. Ph.D., Andrews University, 1990. 387p. UMI# 9031250.

17   Daily, Steven G. The Irony of Adventism: The Role of Ellen White and Other Adventist Women in Nineteenth Century America. D.Min., School of Theology-Claremont, 1985. 361p. UMI# 8516134.

18   Fowler, John M. The Concept of Character Development in the Writings of Ellen G. White. Ed.D., Andrews University, 1977. 268p. UMI# 7727581.

19   Graybill, Ronald D. The Power of Prophecy: Ellen G. White and the Women Religious Founders of the Nineteenth Century. Ph.D., Johns Hopkins University, 1983. 242p. UMI# 8316961.

20   Irwin, Bernadine L. A Psychohistory of the Young Ellen White: A Founder of the Seventh-Day Adventist Church. Ph.D., United States International University, 1984. 192p. UMI# 8419894.

21   Lesher, William R. Ellen G. White's Concept of Sanctification. Ph.D., New York University, 1970. 324p. UMI# 7113651.

22   Lindsay, Allan G. Goodloe Harper Bell: Pioneer Seventh-Day Adventist Christian Educator. Ed.D., Andrews University, 1982. 472p. UMI# 8320337.

23   Navarro, Juan. Major Contextual Dimensions and Dynamic Factors in the Transmission of the Judeo-Christian Religious Heritage According to Selected Writings of Ellen G. White. Ed.D., Andrews University, 1979. 335p. UMI# 8008641.

24   Teesdale, William H. Ellen G. White: Pioneer, Prophet. Ph.D., University of California-Berkeley, 1933.

25   Valentine, Gilbert M. William Warren Prescott: Seventh-Day Adventist Educator. Ph.D., Andrews University, 1982. 687p. UMI# 8318624.

26   Waters, John F. Warren Eugene Howell: Seventh-Day Adventist Educational Administrator. Ed.D., Andrews University, 1988. 524p. UMI# 8907849.

27   Whidden, Woodrow W., II. The Soteriology of Ellen G. White: The Persistent Path to Perfection, 1836-1902. Ph.D., Drew University, 1989. 462p. UMI# 9014373.

28   Winslow, Guy H. Ellen Gould White and Seventh-Day Adventism. Ph.D., Clark University, 1933.

29   Yamagata, Masao. Ellen G. White and American Premillennialism. Ph.D., Pennsylvania State University, 1983. 345p. UMI# 8312684.

Education

30   Ashworth, Warren S. Edward Alexander Sutherland and Seventh-Day Adventist Educational Reform: The Denominational Years, 1890-1904. Ph.D., Andrews University, 1986. 471p. UMI# 8624220.

31   Burton, Wilbur A. A History of the Mission of Seventh-Day Adventist Education, 1844-1900. Ph.D., Kansas State University, 1987. 425p. UMI# 8715196.

32   Cadwallader, Edward M. Educational Principles in the Writings of Ellen G. White. Ph.D., University of Nebraska, 1949. 675p.

33   Coy, Gerald W. Manual Training: Its Role in the Development of

the Seventh-Day Adventist Educational System. D.I.T., University of Northern Iowa, 1987. 230p. UMI# 8811277.

34   Harris, Daniel S., Jr. Activism and Adventist Higher Education. Ed.D., University of Southern California, 1974. 313p. UMI# 74-14444.

35   Rogers, Bruce C. Impact of Writings of Ellen G. White on Work and Education for Work in Seventh-Day Adventist Academies. Ed.D., North Carolina State University-Raleigh, 1984. 106p. UMI# 8506975.

Missions and Missionaries

36   Brown, Walton J. The Foundations of the Seventh-Day Adventist Church in Austral South America, 1785-1912. Ph.D., University of Southern California, 1953.

Organizational Structure

37   Anderson, Carl D. The History and Evolution of Seventh-Day Adventist Church Organization. Ph.D., American University, 1960. 635p. UMI# 60-02950.

38   Mustard, Andrew G. James White and the Development of Seventh-Day Adventist Organization, 1844-1881. Ph.D., Andrews University, 1987. 334p. UMI# 8725223.

39   Oliver, Barry D. Principles for Reorganization of the Seventh-Day Adventist Administrative Structure, 1888-1903: Implications for an International Church. Ph.D., Andrews University, 1989. 449p. UMI# 8922841.

Preaching

40   Shaw, Horace J. A Rhetorical Analysis of the Speaking of Mrs. Ellen G. White, a Pioneer Leader and Spokeswoman of the Seventh-Day Adventist Church. Ph.D., Michigan State University, 1959. 684p. UMI# 61-01149.

41   Turner, R. Edward. A Critical Analysis of the Concept of Preaching in the Thought of Ellen G. White. Ph.D., School of Theology-Claremont, 1979. 230p. UMI# 7919931.

Social Programs

42   Wilson, Norman C. A Study of Ellen G. White's Theory of Urban Religious Work as It Relates to Seventh-Day Adventist Work in

New York City. Ph.D., New York University, 1981. 213p. UMI# 81-28240.

Theology

43   Damsteegt, Pieter G. Toward the Theology of Mission of the Seventh-Day Adventist Church. Ph.D., Free University, 1977. 363p. UMI# 8107820.

44   Harder, Frederick E.J. Revelation, a Source of Knowledge, as Conceived by Ellen G. White. Ph.D., New York University, 1960. 526p. UMI# 6001919.

45   Lee, Jairyong. Faith and Works in Ellen G. White's Doctrine of the Last Judgment. Th.D., Andrews University, 1985. 419p. UMI# 8624223.

46   McGarrell, Roy I. The Historical Development of Seventh-Day Adventist Eschatology, 1884-1895. Ph.D., Andrews University, 1990. 468p. UMI# 9106809.

47   Moore, Arthur L. Ellen G. White's Concept of Righteousness by Faith as It Relates to Contemporary SDA Issues. Ph.D., New York University, 1980. 451p. UMI# 8027470.

AFRICAN AMERICAN

General Studies

48   Adefila, Johnson A. Slave Religion in the Antebellum South: A Study of the Role of Africanisms in the Black Response to Christianity. Ph.D., Brandeis University, 1975. 196p. UMI# 75-24796.

49   Baldwin, Lewis V. "Invisible" Strands in African Methodism: A History of the African Union Methodist Protestant and Union American Methodist Episcopal Churches, 1805-1980. Ph.D., Northwestern University, 1980. 349p. UMI# 8104686.

50   Cheaney, Henry E. Attitudes of the Indiana Pulpit and the Press Toward the Negro, 1860-1880. Ph.D., University of Chicago, 1961.

51   Daniel, Vattel E. Ritual in Chicago's South Side Churches for Negroes. Ph.D., University of Chicago, 1941.

52   Earnest, Joseph B. The Religious Development of the Negro in Virginia. Ph.D., University of Virginia, 1914. 233p.

53   Factor, Robert L. The Archdiocese of Color: Cause, Casuistry and

Organization in Black America. Ph.D., University of Wisconsin, 1968. 840p. UMI# 69-00905.

54   Fordham, Monroe. Major Themes in Northern Black Religious Thought, 1800-1860. Ph.D., State University of New York-Buffalo, 1973. 264p. UMI# 74-04396.

55   Hall, Robert L. "Do, Lord, Remember Me:" Religion and Cultural Change Among Blacks in Florida, 1565-1906. Ph.D., Florida State University, 1984. 485p. UMI# 8419215.

56   Knighton, Stanley A. A Study of Congregationalism Among Black People in the Southern Part of the United States of America, 1861-1926. D.Min., Howard University, 1974. 209p.

57   Lawton, Samuel M. The Religious Life of South Carolina Coastal and Sea Island Negroes. Ph.D., George Peabody College for Teachers of Vanderbilt University, 1939.

58   Montgomery, William E. Negro Churches in the South, 1865-1915. Ph.D., University of Texas-Austin, 1975. 362p. UMI# 75-16711.

59   Raboteau, Albert J. "The Invisible Institution:" The Origins and Conditions of Black Religion Before Emancipation. Ph.D., Yale University, 1974. 320p. UMI# 7515350.

60   Rankin-Hill, Lesley M. Afro-American Biohistory: Theoretical and Methodological Considerations. Ph.D., University of Massachusetts, 1990. 344p. UMI# 9035390.

61   Roth, Donald F. "Grace Not Race." Southern Negro Church Leaders, Black Identity, and Missions to West Africa, 1865-1919. Ph.D., University of Texas-Austin, 1975. 419p. UMI# 75-16728.

62   Suttles, William C., Jr. A Trace of Soul: The Religion of Negro Slaves on the Plantations of North America. Ph.D., University of Michigan, 1979. 213p. UMI# 79-16825.

63   Touchstone, Donald B. Planters and Slave Religion in the Deep South. Ph.D., Tulane University, 1973. 269p. UMI# 74-00323.

64   Watson, James J. The Religion of the Negro. Ph.D., University of Pennsylvania, 1912.

Biography

65   Angell, Stephen W. Henry McNeal Turner and Black Religion in the

South, 1865-1900. Ph.D., Vanderbilt University, 1988. 670p. UMI# 8815715.

66   Burke, Ronald K. Samuel Ringgold Ward: Christian Abolitionist. Ph.D., Syracuse University, 1975. 215p. UMI# 76-18498.

67   Dean, David M. James Theodore Holly, 1829-1911, Black Nationalist and Bishop. Ph.D., University of Texas-Austin, 1972. 243p. UMI# 73-00423.

68   Earl, Riggins R., Jr. Toward a Black Christian Ethic: A Study of Alexander Crummell and Albert Cleage. Ph.D., Vanderbilt University, 1978. 441p. UMI# 7819527.

69   George, Carol A. Richard Allen and the Independent Black Church Movement, 1787-1831. Ph.D., Syracuse University, 1970. 382p. UMI# 70-24078.

70   Hunter, Carol M. To Set the Captives Free: Reverend Jermain Wesley Loguen and the Struggle for Freedom in Central New York, 1835-1872. Ph.D., State University of New York-Binghamton, 1985. 387p. UMI# 8926260.

71   Miller, George M. *A This Worldly Mission*: The Life and Career of Alexander Walters (1858-1917). Ph.D., State University of New York-Stony Brook, 1984. 488p. UMI# 8416628.

72   Mitchell, James N. Nat Turner: Slave, Preacher, Prophet, and Messiah, 1800-1831: A Study of the Call of a Black Slave to Prophethood and to the Messiahship of the Second Coming of Christ. D.Min., Vanderbilt University Divinity School, 1975. 159p. UMI# 76-16670.

73   Swan, Robert J. Thomas McCants Stewart and the Failure of the Mission of the Talented Tenth in Black America, 1880-1923. Ph.D., New York University, 1990. 346p. UMI# 9025148.

74   Thomas, Herman E. An Analysis of the Life and Work of James W.C. Pennington, a Black Churchman and Abolitionist. Ph.D., Hartford Seminary Foundation, 1978. 370p. UMI# 7923560.

Clergy

75   Dennard, David C. Religion in the Quarters: A Study of Slave Preachers in the Antebellum South, 1800-1860. Ph.D., Northwestern University, 1983. 340p. UMI# 8403407.

76   Goode, Gloria D. Preachers of the Word and Singers of the Gospel:

The Ministry of Women Among Nineteenth Century African-Americans. Ph.D., University of Pennsylvania, 1990. 456p. UMI# 9112565.

77   Wheeler, Edward L. Uplifting the Race: The Black Minister in the New South, 1865-1902. Ph.D., Emory University, 1982. 273p. UMI# 82-21542.

Education

78   Brown, Herman. Origin, Development and Contributions of Negro Colleges and Universities as Institutions of Higher Education in the United States, 1776-1890. Ph.D., Catholic University of America, 1972. 261p. UMI# 73-14323.

79   McMillan, Joseph T., Jr. The Development of Higher Education for Blacks During the Late Nineteenth Century: A Study of the African Methodist Episcopal Church; Wilberforce University; the American Missionary Association; Hampton Institute; and Fisk University. Ed.D., Columbia University Teachers College, 1986. 535p. UMI# 8612271.

80   Sims, Charles F. The Religious Education of the Southern Negroes. Ph.D., Southern Baptist Theological Seminary, 1926.

Missions and Missionaries

81   De Boer, Clara M. The Role of Afro-Americans in the Origin and Work of the American Missionary Association: 1839-1877. Ph.D., Rutgers University, 1973. 844p. UMI# 73-27914.

82   Williams, Walter L. Black American Attitudes Toward Africa: The Missionary Movement, 1877-1900. Ph.D., University of North Carolina-Chapel Hill, 1974. 349p. UMI# 75-15723.

Music

83   Clark, Roy L. A Fantasy Theme Analysis of Negro Spirituals. Ph.D., Southern Illinois University-Carbondale, 1979. 157p. UMI# 7926299.

84   Davis, Henderson S. The Religious Experience Underlying the Negro Spiritual. Ph.D., Boston University, 1950. 176p.

85   Maultsby, Portia K. Afro-American Religious Music: 1619-1861. Part I-Historical Development. Part II-Computer Analysis of One Hundred Spirituals. Ph.D., University of Wisconsin-Madison, 1974. 460p. UMI# 7507597.

86   Odum, Howard W. Religious Folk-Songs of the Southern Negroes. Ph.D., Clark University, 1909.

87   Taylor, John E. The Sociological and Psychological Implications of the Texts of the Antebellum Negro Spirituals. Ed.D., University of Northern Colorado, 1971. 218p. UMI# 7120727.

Preaching

88   Pipes, William H. An Interpretative Study of Old-Time Negro Preaching. Ph.D., University of Michigan, 1943.

AMANA CHURCH SOCIETY

89   Andelson, Jonathan G. Communalism and Change in the Amana Society, 1855-1932. Ph.D., University of Michigan, 1974. 479p. UMI# 7510124.

90   Duval, Francis A. Christian Metz, German-American Religious Leader and Pioneer. Ph.D., University of Iowa, 1949. 271p.

91   Rettig, Lawrence L. Grammatical Structures in Amana German. Ph.D., University of Iowa, 1970. 136p. UMI# 7015638.

92   Moore, Frank M. The Amana Society, 1867-1932: Accommodation of Old World Beliefs in a New World Frontier Setting. Ph.D., Vanderbilt University, 1988. 276p. UMI# 8815735.

AMISH

93   Landing, James E. The Spatial Development and Organization of an Old Order Amish-Beachy Amish Settlement: Nappanee, Indiana. Ph.D., Pennsylvania State University, 1967. 230p. UMI# 6808716.

94   Madeira, Sheldon. A Study of the Education of the Old Order Amish Mennonites of Lancaster County, Pennsylvania. Ph.D., University of Pennsylvania, 1955. 184p. UMI# 13407.

95   Smith, Elmer L. A Study of Acculturation in an Amish Community. D.S.S., Syracuse University, 1956. 282p. UMI# 16663.

ANABAPTIST

96   Bauman, Harold E. The Believers' Church and the Church College. Ed.D., Columbia University, 1972. 248p. UMI# 72-19508.

ANGLICAN

General Studies

97 Austin, Alan K. The Role of the Anglican Church and Its Clergy in the Political Life of Colonial Virginia. Ph.D., University of Georgia, 1969. 258p. UMI# 70-01136.

98 Bolton, Sidney C. The Anglican Church of Colonial South Carolina, 1704-1754: A Study in Americanization. Ph.D., University of Wisconsin-Madison, 1973. 425p. UMI# 73-20237.

99 Cooksey, Ronald L. The Americanization of the Anglican Church in Northern Colonies During the Eighteenth Century. Ph.D., University of Toronto, 1977.

100 Gage, Thomas E. The Established Church in Colonial Virginia, 1689-1785. Ph.D., University of Missouri-Columbia, 1974. 232p. UMI# 75-15994.

101 Goodwin, Gerald J. The Anglican Middle Way in Early Eighteenth-Century America: Anglican Religious Thought in the American Colonies, 1702-1750. Ph.D., University of Wisconsin, 1965. 376p. UMI# 65-05125.

102 Gough, Deborah M. Pluralism, Politics, and Power Struggles: The Church of England in Colonial Philadelphia, 1695-1789. Ph.D., University of Pennsylvania, 1978. 631p. UMI# 78-16307.

103 Hooker, Richard J. The Anglican Church and the American Revolution. Ph.D., University of Chicago, 1944. 378p.

104 Jones, Jerome W. The Anglican Church in Colonial Virginia, 1690-1760. Ph.D., Harvard University, 1960.

105 Kantrow, Alan M. Jacob's Ladder: Anglican Traditionalism in the New England Mind. Ph.D., Harvard University, 1979.

106 Mappen, Marc A. Anatomy of a Schism: Anglican Dissent in the New England Community of Newtown, Connecticut, 1708-1765. Ph.D., Rutgers University, 1976. 217p. UMI# 77-07253.

107 Percy, David O. The Anglican Interest in Early Eighteenth-Century New England: A Political Analysis. Ph.D., University of Nebraska-Lincoln, 1973. 242p. UMI# 74-13009.

108 Seiler, William H. The Anglican Parish in Tidewater Virginia, 1607-1776. Ph.D., University of Iowa, 1948.

109   Whiting, Marvin Y. Virginia's Experiment With Religious Uniformity: A Study of a Major Aspect of Anglican and Evangelical Ideology, 1699-1786. Ph.D., Columbia University, 1971.

Art and Architecture

110   Friary, Donald R. The Architecture of the Anglican Church in the Northern American Colonies: A Study of Religious, Social, and Cultural Expression. Ph.D., University of Pennsylvania, 1971. 1237p. UMI# 71-26101.

Biography

111   Metz, Wayne N. The Reverend Samuel Peters (1735-1826): Connecticut Anglican, Loyalist, Priest. Ph.D., Oklahoma State University, 1974. 324p. UMI# 76-09724.

112   Mohler, Samuel R. Commissary James Blair: Churchman, Educator, and Politician of Colonial Virginia. Ph.D., University of Chicago, 1941. 389p.

113   Motley, Daniel E. Life of Commissary James Blair, Founder of William and Mary College. Ph.D., Johns Hopkins University, 1899.

Clergy

114   Gundersen, Joan R. The Anglican Ministry in Virginia 1723-1776: A Study of Social Class. Ph.D., University of Notre Dame, 1972. 336p. UMI# 72-26805.

115   Kinloch, Hector G.L.M. Anglican Clergy in Connecticut, 1701-1785. Ph.D., Yale University, 1960.

116   Van Voorst, Carol L. The Anglican Clergy in Maryland, 1692-1776. Ph.D., Princeton University, 1978. 332p. UMI# 78-18359.

Liturgy

117   Hatchett, Marion J. The Making of the First American Prayer Book. Th.D., General Theological Seminary, 1972. 572p. UMI# 73-16708.

Missions and Missionaries

118   Gifford, Frank D. The Church of England in Colonial Westchester: A Study of the Work of the S.P.G. Missionaries in the Parishes of West Chester, Rye, and New Rochelle. Ph.D., New York University, 1942. 957p.

119   King, Irving H. The S.P.G. in New England, 1701-1784. Ph.D., University of Maine, 1968. 324p. UMI# 6818067.

120   Lewis, Norman. English Missionary Interest in the Indians of North America, 1578-1700. Ph.D., University of Washington, 1968. 503p. UMI# 6907064.

121   Nelson, John K. Anglican Missions in America, 1701-1725: A Study of the Society for the Gospel in Foreign Parts. Ph.D., Northwestern University, 1962. 770p. UMI# 63-01324.

122   Newcombe, Alfred W. The Organization and Procedure of the S.P.G. With Special Reference to New England. Ph.D., University of Michigan, 1934. 245p.

Music

123   Clark, John B. Organ Accompaniments to Seventeenth Century Anglican Church Music With Emphasis on the *Adrian Batten Organ Book*. Ph.D., University of Michigan, 1964. 585p. UMI# 65-05285.

124   Wilson, Ruth M. Anglican Chant and Chanting in England and America, 1660-1811. Ph.D., University of Illinois at Urbana-Champaign, 1988. 424p. UMI# 8823292.

Organizational Structure

125   Cross, Arthur L. The Anglican Episcopate and the American Colonies. Ph.D., Harvard University, 1899.

126   Hartdagen, Gerald E. The Anglican Vestry in Colonial Maryland. Ph.D., Northwestern University, 1965. 281p. UMI# 65-12092.

127   Jordan, Jean P. The Anglican Establishment in Colonial New York, 1693-1783. Ph.D., Columbia University, 1971. 724p. UMI# 74-08187.

128   Mills, Frederick V. Anglican Resistance to an American Episcopate 1761-1769. Ph.D., University of Pennsylvania, 1967. 362p. UMI# 67-12783.

129   Owen, James K. The Virginia Vestry: A Study in the Decline of a Ruling Class. Ph.D., Princeton University, 1947. 306p. UMI# 10987.

130   Painter, Borden W., Jr. The Anglican Vestry in Colonial America. Ph.D., Yale University, 1965. 266p. UMI# 65-15095.

Social Programs

131   Peters, Peter W. The Doctrine of the Church in Relation to Moral Action: A Study in Nineteenth Century Anglican Social Ethics. Ph.D., Vanderbilt University, 1979. 350p. UMI# 7922184.

Theology

132   Smith, William H. The Influence of Bishop Butler's *Analogy* in American Apologetic Thinking. Ph.D., University of Chicago, 1925.

BAPTIST

General Studies

133   Anderson, Henry L. The Ecclesiology of Ante-Bellum Baptist Churches in the South. Ph.D., New Orleans Baptist Theological Seminary, 1960.

134   Baxter, Norman A. History of the Freewill Baptists: A Study in New England Separatism. Ph.D., Harvard University, 1954.

135   Brame, Webb. Baptists' Struggles for Religious Liberty From 1523 to 1789. Ph.D., Southern Baptist Theological Seminary, 1914.

136   Brooks, Evelyn. The Women's Movement in the Black Baptist Church, 1880-1920. Ph.D., University of Rochester, 1984. 351p. UMI# 8416581.

137   Brown, Archie E. The History of the Baptist Brotherhood of the South. Ph.D., Southwestern Baptist Theological Seminary, 1950. 256p.

138   Carter, James E. The Southern Baptist Convention and Confessions of Faith, 1845-1945. Ph.D., Southwestern Baptist Theological Seminary, 1965.

139   Carter, Terry G. Baptist Participation in Anti-Catholic Sentiment and Activities, 1830-1860. Ph.D., Southwestern Baptist Theological Seminary, 1983.

140   Cheatham, Thomas R. The Rhetorical Structure of the Abolitionist Movement Within the Baptist Church: 1833-1845. Ph.D., Purdue University, 1969. 225p. UMI# 70-03867.

141   Coleman, Leslie H. A History of the Baptists in Shelby County, Tennessee, 1818-1950. Ph.D., Southwestern Baptist Theological Seminary, 1959.

142   Dalton, Jack P. A History of Florida Baptists. Ph.D., University of Florida, 1952. 175p.

143   Davidson, James A. Baptist Beginnings in Western Pennsylvania. Ph.D., University of Pittsburgh, 1941. 300p.

144   Davidson, William F. The Original Free Will Baptists in America: A Continuing Witness From Infancy to Identity (1727-1830). Ph.D., New Orleans Baptist Theological Seminary, 1972.

145   Dillow, Myron D. A History of Baptists in Illinois, 1786-1845. Ph.D., Southwestern Baptist Theological Seminary, 1965.

146   Duncan, Curtis D. A Historical Survey of the Development of the Black Baptist Church in the United States and a Study of Performance Practices Associated With Dr. Watts Hymn Singing: A Source Book for Teachers. Ed.D., Washington University, 1979. 286p. UMI# 79-18594.

147   Duncan, Pope A. A History of Baptist Thought, 1600-1660. Ph.D., Southern Baptist Theological Seminary, 1948. 234p.

148   Ehren, Ralph E. Connectionalism in Baptist Life Before 1826. Ph.D., Southwestern Baptist Theological Seminary, 1966.

149   Elliott, Nelson R. A History of the General Six Principle Baptists in America. Ph.D., Southwestern Baptist Theological Seminary, 1956. 172p.

150   Fish, Roy J. The Awakening of 1858 and Its Effects on Baptists in the United States. Ph.D., Southwestern Baptist Theological Seminary, 1963.

151   Fletcher, Jesse C. The Interaction Between English and American Baptists From 1639 to 1689. Ph.D., Southwestern Baptist Theological Seminary, 1959.

152   Ford, Glen R. The Baptist District Associations of Virginia, 1766-1950. A Study in Baptist Ecclesiology. Ph.D., Southern Baptist Theological Seminary, 1961.

153   Haines, Stephen M. Church Discipline as Practiced by Representative Southern Baptist Churches, 1880-1939. Ph.D., Southwestern Baptist Theological Seminary, 1984. UMI# 0558637.

154   Hamilton, Robert S., Jr. The History and Influence of the Baptist Church in California, 1849-1899. Ph.D., University of Southern California, 1953.

155   Harvey, Sam A. The Roots of California Southern Baptists. Ph.D.,
       Golden Gate Baptist Theological Seminary, 1973.

156   Haynes, Julietta. A History of the Primitive Baptists. Ph.D.,
       University of Texas-Austin, 1959. 410p. UMI# 59-06711.

157   Hudson, Clement W. American Baptists in Bible Revision. Ph.D.,
       Southern Baptist Theological Seminary, 1906.

158   Hudson, Esper V. A History of the Baptists in North Carolina From
       1690-1830. Ph.D., Southern Baptist Theological Seminary, 1922.

159   Hughes, John E. A History of the Southern Baptist Convention's
       Ministry to the Negroes: 1845-1904. Th.D., Southern Baptist
       Theological Seminary, 1971. 315p. UMI# 71-28964.

160   Humphrey, James E. Baptist Discipline in Kentucky, 1781-1860.
       Ph.D., Southern Baptist Theological Seminary, 1960.

161   Juster, Susan M. Sinners and Saints: The Evangelical Construction
       of Gender and Authority in New England, 1740-1830. Ph.D.,
       University of Michigan, 1990. 465p. UMI# 9034450.

162   Kroll-Smith, Jack S. In Search of Status Power: The Baptist Revival
       in Colonial Virginia, 1760-1776. Ph.D., University of Pennsylvania,
       1982. 256p. UMI# 8227287.

163   Maring, Norman H. A Denominational History of the Maryland
       Baptists, 1742-1882. Ph.D., University of Maryland, 1948. 228p.

164   Marshall, David W. Southern Baptist Patriots: Religion, Revolution
       and Nationalism, 1776-1876. Ph.D., Texas Tech University, 1989.
       328p. UMI# 9023316.

165   Martin, Patricia S. Hidden Work: Baptist Women in Texas,
       1880-1920. Ph.D., Rice University, 1982. 310p. UMI# 8216341.

166   Meroney, W.P. The Old Church in the New Era. Ph.D., Southern
       Baptist Theological Seminary, 1919.

167   Miller, Clifford R. Baptist Beginnings in Oregon. Ph.D., University
       of Oregon, 1955.

168   Mitchell, Carlton T. Baptist Worship in Relation to Baptist Concepts
       of the Church, 1608-1865. Ph.D., New York University, 1952. 296p.
       UMI# 63-05359.

169   Moreland, Marion. Development of the Concept of Individualism

With Reference to the Work of Roger Williams. Ph.D., University of Toronto, 1937.

170   Murray, Thomas. A History of Baptists in Washington State: 1853-1931. Ph.D., Yale University, 1947.

171   Neely, H.K., Jr. The Territorial Expansion of the Southern Baptist Convention. Ph.D., Southwestern Baptist Theological Seminary, 1964.

172   Norberg, Janet L. From Opposition to Appropriation: The Resolution of Southern Baptist Conflict With Dramatic Forms, 1802-1962. Ph.D., University of Iowa, 1964. 453p. UMI# 64-07937.

173   Norfleet, Frank F. A History of Arkansas Baptist to 1900. Ph.D., Southern Baptist Theological Seminary, 1950. 256p.

174   Olsen, Olaf S. A History of the Baptists of the Rocky Mountain Region, 1849-1890. Ph.D., University of Colorado, 1953.

175   Olson, Robert W. Southern Baptists' Reactions to Millerism. Th.D., Southwestern Baptist Theological Seminary, 1972.

176   Rodgerson, Phillip E. A Historical Study of Alien Baptism Among Baptists Since 1640. Ph.D., Southern Baptist Theological Seminary, 1952.

177   Rogers, Robert C. From Alienation to Integration: A Social History of Baptists in Antebellum Natchez, Mississippi. Th.D., New Orleans Baptist Theological Seminary, 1990. 123p. UMI# 9026810.

178   Russell, Charles A. A History of the Regular Baptists in Rhode Island, 1825-1931. Ph.D., Boston University, 1959. 399p. UMI# 59-03474.

179   Satterfield, James H. The Baptists and the Negro Prior to 1863. Ph.D., Southern Baptist Theological Seminary, 1919.

180   Seat, William R., Jr. A History of Tennessee Baptists to 1820-25. Ph.D., Southern Baptist Theological Seminary, 1931.

181   Storey, John W. The Negro in Southern Baptist Thought, 1865-1900. Ph.D., University of Kentucky, 1968. 280p. UMI# 69-15519.

182   Stringfellow, Denver C., Jr. Candidates for Baptism: A Study in Southern Baptist History. Ph.D., Southwestern Baptist Theological Seminary, 1961.

183   Stripling, Paul W. The Negro Excision From Baptist Churches in Texas (1861-1870). Ph.D., Southwestern Baptist Theological Seminary, 1968.

184   Thom, William T. The Struggle for Religious Freedom in Virginia: The Baptists. Ph.D., Johns Hopkins University, 1899.

185   Tiffany, Henry W. The History of Arminianism and Calvinism Among Baptists in America. Ph.D., Southern Baptist Theological Seminary, 1920.

186   Towell, Sherman E. The Features of Southern Baptist Thought, 1845-1879. Ph.D., Southern Baptist Theological Seminary, 1956.

187   Tresch, John W., Jr. Evangelism Among Churches Affiliated With the Nashville Baptist Association: An Historical Study of Methodology. D.Div., Vanderbilt University, 1970. 148p. UMI# 71-07893.

188   Tull, James E. A Study of Southern Baptist Landmarkism in the Light of Historical Baptist Ecclesiology. Ph.D., Columbia University, 1960. 727p. UMI# 6003152.

189   Turner, James B. The Historical Development of Calvinism Among American Baptists. Ph.D., Southern Baptist Theological Seminary, 1916.

190   Washington, James M. The Origins and Emergence of Black Baptist Separatism, 1863-1897. Ph.D., Yale University, 1979. 295p. UMI# 79-26854.

Art and Architecture

191   Nichols, J.B. A Historical Study of Southern Baptist Church Architecture. Ph.D., Southwestern Baptist Theological Seminary, 1954. 185p.

Biography

192   Allen, Crawford L. *The Restauration of Zion*: Roger Williams and the Quest for the Primitive Church. Ph.D., University of Iowa, 1984. 418p. UMI# 8423528.

193   Backman, Milton V., Jr. Isaac Backus: A Pioneer Champion of Religious Liberty. Ph.D., University of Pennsylvania, 1959. 411p. UMI# 59-04593.

194   Barron, James R. The Contributions of John A. Broadus to

Southern Baptists. Th.D., Southern Baptist Theological Seminary, 1972. 264p. UMI# 72-30185.

195   Brockunier, Sam H. Roger Williams: A Study of His Life and Career to 1657. Ph.D., Harvard University, 1937.

196   Brumberg, Joan J. A Mission for Life: The Judson Family and American Evangelical Culture, 1790-1850. Ph.D., University of Virginia, 1978. 331p. UMI# 79-16231.

197   Calamandria, Mauro. Theology and Political Thought of Roger Williams. Ph.D., University of Chicago, 1954.

198   Cates, John D. B.H. Carroll: The Man and His Ethics. Ph.D., Southwestern Baptist Theological Seminary, 1962.

199   Coyle, Edward W. From Sinner to Saint: A Study of the Critical Reputation of Roger Williams With an Annotated Bibliography of Writings About Him. Ph.D., University of Massachusetts, 1974. 221p. UMI# 75-06006.

200   Creed, John B. John Leland, American Prophet of Religious Individualism. Ph.D., Southwestern Baptist Theological Seminary, 1986. 230p. UMI# 8705900.

201   Crichton, Robert J. Roger Williams on Church and State. Ph.D., Columbia University, 1962.

202   Cunningham, James L. The Contributions of Jeremiah Bell Jeter to Southern Baptists. Th.D., New Orleans Baptist Theological Seminary, 1987. 212p. UMI# 8810249.

203   Diemer, Carl J., Jr. A Historical Study of Roger Williams in the Light of the Quaker Controversy. Ph.D., Southwestern Baptist Theological Seminary, 1972.

204   Dilday, Russell H., Jr. The Apologetic Method of E.Y. Mullins. Ph.D., Southwestern Baptist Theological Seminary, 1961.

205   Ellis, William E. Edgar Young Mullins: Southern Baptist Theologian, Administrator, and Denominational Leader. Ph.D., University of Kentucky, 1974. 288p. UMI# 75-18479.

206   Ernst, James E. The Political Thought of Roger Williams. Ph.D., University of Washington, 1926. 229p.

207   Fry, Russell R. Theological Principles of Isaac Backus and the Move From Congregationalism to Baptist Leadership in New England.

Ph.D., Drew University, 1988. 266p. UMI# 8817733.

208   Gardner, Robert G. John Leadley Dagg: Pioneer American Baptist Theologian. Ph.D., Duke University, 1957.

209   Gibson, L. Tucker. Luther Rice's Contribution to Baptist History. S.T.D., Temple University, 1944.

210   Gilpin, W. Clark. The Way to Lost Zion: Millenarian Piety and Religious Controversy in the Career of Roger Williams. Ph.D., University of Chicago, 1974.

211   Halbrooks, Guy T. Francis Wayland: Contributor to Baptist Concepts of Church Order. Ph.D., Emory University, 1971. 291p. UMI# 71-27781.

212   Havins, Thomas R. Noah T. Byars: A Study in Baptist Missionary Effort on the Frontier. Ph.D., University of Texas-Austin, 1941. 203p.

213   Holmes, Bernard G. The Contribution of John Lightfoot Waller to Kentucky Baptists 1830-1854. Th.D., Southwestern Baptist Theological Seminary, 1975.

214   Honeycutt, Dwight A. A Study of the Life and Thought of Henry Clay Vedder. Th.D., New Orleans Baptist Theological Seminary, 1984. 235p. UMI# 8509621.

215   Houghton, George G. The Contributions of Adoniram Judson Gordon to American Christianity. Ph.D., Dallas Theological Seminary, 1970.

216   Huber, Paul. A Study of the Rhetorical Theories of John A. Broadus. Ph.D., University of Michigan, 1956. 206p. UMI# 18611.

217   Jackson, Herbert C. Henry Lyman Morehouse, Statesman of the Baptist Denomination in the North. Ph.D., Yale University, 1954.

218   James, Robert A. A Study of the Life and Contributions of Henry Allen Tupper. Th.D., New Orleans Baptist Theological Seminary, 1989. 257p. UMI# 9020106.

219   Jennings, Helen L. John Mason Peck and the Impact of New England on the Old Northwest. Ph.D., University of Southern California, 1961. 326p. UMI# 6409621.

220   Johnson, Lee S. An Examination of the Role of John Gano in the Development of Baptist Life in North America, 1750-1804. Ph.D.,

Southwestern Baptist Theological Seminary, 1986. 249p. UMI# 8614899.

221   Jonas, William G., Jr. A Critical Evaluation of Albert Henry Newman, Church Historian. Ph.D., Baylor University, 1990. 273p. UMI# 9027783.

222   Jordan, Clifford F. Thomas Treadwell Eaton: Pastor, Editor, Controversialist, and Denominational Servant. Ph.D., New Orleans Baptist Theological Seminary, 1965.

223   Kennedy, Larry W. The Fighting Preacher of the Army of Tennessee: General Mark Perry Lowrey. Ph.D., Mississippi State University, 1976. 213p. UMI# 7711754.

224   Martin, Donald L., Jr. The Thought of Amzi Clarence Dixon. Ph.D., Baylor University, 1989. 288p. UMI# 8919929.

225   Maston, Thomas B. The Ethical and Social Attitudes of Isaac Backus. Ph.D., Yale University, 1939.

226   McKibbens, Thomas R., Jr. A Study of the Life and Work of Morgan Edwards. Ph.D., Southern Baptist Theological Seminary, 1976. 239p. UMI# 7619836.

227   Mills, Reginald S. Robert Baylor Semple: A Study in Baptist Denominational Development, 1790-1831. Ph.D., Southern Baptist Theological Seminary, 1986. 239p. UMI# 8628708.

228   Mondy, Robert W. Jesse Mercer: A Study in Frontier Religion. Ph.D., University of Texas-Austin, 1950.

229   Mortensen, Joseph I. The Career of the Reverend George Dana Boardman. Th.D., Boston University, 1966. 212p. UMI# 66-11535.

230   Paris, Ricky. The Contributions of J.B. Gambrell to the Development of Denominational Consciousness Among Southern Baptists. Ph.D., Baylor University, 1988. 414p. UMI# 8811284.

231   Reed, John W. The Rhetoric of a Colonial Controversy: Roger Williams Versus the Massachusetts Bay Colony. Ph.D., Ohio State University, 1966. 205p. UMI# 6615124.

232   Reynolds, J. Alvin. Richard Furman, A Study of His Life and Work. Ph.D., New Orleans Baptist Theological Seminary, 1962.

233   Roddy, Clarence S. The Religious Thought of Roger Williams. Ph.D., New York University, 1948.

234   Searles, Joan C. The Worlds of Roger Williams. Ph.D., Pennsylvania State University, 1971. 219p. UMI# 7213931.

235   Skaggs, Donald. Roger Williams in History: His Image in the American Mind. Ph.D., University of Southern California, 1972. 263p. UMI# 7226055.

236   Snowden, Gary L. An Historical Study of the Life and Times of R.E.B. Baylor: His Contributions to Texas and Texas Baptist. Ph.D., Southwestern Baptist Theological Seminary, 1986. 260p. UMI# 8614905.

237   Spurgin, Hugh D., II. Roger Williams and the Separatist Tradition: English Origins of His Religious and Political Thought. Ph.D., Columbia University, 1985. 272p. UMI# 8511554.

238   Sweeney, Kevin M. River Gods and Related Minor Deities: The Williams Family and the Connecticut River Valley, 1637-1790. Ph.D., Yale University, 1986. 813p. UMI# 8701094.

239   Wacker, Grant A., Jr. Augustus H. Strong: A Conservative Confrontation With History. Ph.D., Harvard University, 1979.

240   West, Earle H. The Life and Educational Contributions of Barnas Sears. Ph.D., George Peabody College for Teachers, 1961. 664p. UMI# 61-05832.

241   Withers, Richard E. Roger Williams and the Rhode Island Colony: A Study in Leadership Roles. Ph.D., Boston University, 1966. 432p. UMI# 6611338.

242   Wright, Paul O. Roger Williams: God's Swordsman in Searching Times. Ph.D., Dallas Theological Seminary, 1968.

Church and State

243   Joiner, Edward E. Southern Baptists and Church-State Relations, 1845-1954. Ph.D., Southern Baptist Theological Seminary, 1960.

244   Slatton, James H. A Study of Early American Baptist Concepts of Separation of Church and State. Ph.D., Southwestern Baptist Theological Seminary, 1965.

Clergy

245   Allen, William L. Spirituality Among Southern Baptist Clergy as Reflected in Selected Autobiographies. Ph.D., Southern Baptist Theological Seminary, 1984. 284p. UMI# 8429158.

246   Corkern, Randall A. A Study of the Education, Morals, Salary, and Controversial Movements of the Frontier Baptist Preacher in Kentucky From Its Settlement Until 1830. Ph.D., Southern Baptist Theological Seminary, 1954.

247   Loftis, John F. Factors in Southern Baptist Identity as Reflected by Ministerial Role Models, 1750-1925. Ph.D., Southern Baptist Theological Seminary, 1987. 319p. UMI# 8712818.

Education

248   Batts, Henry L. The Historical and Educational Development of the Lake Avenue Memorial Baptist Church of Rochester, New York. Ph.D., Hartford Seminary Foundation, 1935.

249   Beasley, Steven D. The Development of the Church Training Program of the Southern Baptist Convention: A Historical Review. Ed.D., Southern Baptist Theological Seminary, 1988. 222p. UMI# 8810926.

250   Buller, Francis P. A History of Ministerial Education in the Baptist Churches of the United States to 1845. Ph.D., Yale University, 1927.

251   Epting, James B. A Chronological Review of the Development of Judson College, Marion, Alabama, 1838-1978. Ed.D., University of Alabama, 1978. 159p. UMI# 79-05404.

252   Flowers, John W. A Study of the Religious Educational Philosophy of J.M. Frost as Reflected in the Birth and Growth of the Sunday School Board of the Southern Baptist Convention. Ph.D., New Orleans Baptist Theological Seminary, 1962.

253   James, William C. A History of the Western Baptist Theological Institution, Covington, Kentucky. Ph.D., Southern Baptist Theological Seminary, 1905.

254   Keyser, Bernard D. A History of Baptist Higher Education in the South to 1865. Ph.D., Southern Baptist Theological Seminary, 1956.

255   Kinlaw, Howard M. Richard Furman as a Leader in Baptist Higher Education. Ph.D., George Peabody College for Teachers, 1960. 228p. UMI# 60-05865.

256   Magruder, Edith M.C. A Historical Study of the Educational Agencies of the Southern Baptist Convention, 1845-1945. Ph.D., Columbia University, 1951. 161p.

257   McGlon, Charles A. Speech Education in Baptist Theological

Seminaries in the United States, 1819-1943. Ph.D., Columbia University, 1951. 484p. UMI# 02837.

258   McManus, Harold L. The American Baptist Home Mission Society and Freedmen Education in the South, With Special Reference to Georgia: 1862-1897. Ph.D., Yale University, 1953. 323p.

259   Moore, Leroy, Jr. The Rise of American Religious Liberalism at the Rochester Theological Seminary, 1872-1928. Ph.D., Claremont Graduate School, 1966. 329p. UMI# 67-09520.

260   Moore, Ralph R. History of Baptist Theological Education in South Carolina and Georgia. Ph.D., Southwestern Baptist Theological Seminary, 1949. 175p.

261   Pate, James A. The Development of the Instructional Program at Howard College, 1842-1957. Ed.D., University of Alabama, 1959. 608p. UMI# 60-00282.

262   Potts, David B. Baptist Colleges in the Development of American Society, 1812-1861. Ph.D., Harvard University, 1967.

263   Rouse, Roscoe, Jr. A History of the Baylor University Library, 1845-1919. Ph.D., University of Michigan, 1962. 390p. UMI# 62-3257.

264   Tyms, James D. The History of Religious Education Among Negro Baptists. Ph.D., Boston University, 1942.

265   Vandever, William T., Jr. An Educational History of the English and American Baptists in the Seventeenth and Eighteenth Centuries. Ph.D., University of Pennsylvania, 1974. 523p. UMI# 75-14633.

266   Walker, Thomas T. Mary Hardin-Baylor College, 1845-1937. Ed.D., George Peabody College for Teachers, 1962. 241p. UMI# 63-01901.

267   Wilson, Carl B. A History of Baptist Educational Efforts in Texas, 1829-1900. Ph.D., University of Texas-Austin, 1934.

268   Winegarden, Neil A. A Historical Survey of Homiletical Education in the United States. Ph.D., Northern Baptist Theological Seminary, 1953. 323p.

Ethnic Groups

269   Eller, David B. The Brethren in the Western Ohio Valley, 1790-1850: German Baptist Settlement and Frontier

Accommodation. Ph.D., Miami University, 1976. 250p. UMI# 76-24469.

270   Flory, John S. The Literary History of the German Baptists in America. Ph.D., University of Virginia, 1907.

Evangelism

271   Harris, Thomas B., III. American Baptists and Various Forms of Revival, 1726-1860. Th.D., Southwestern Baptist Theological Seminary, 1974.

272   O'Kelly, Steve. The Influence of the Separate Baptists on Revivalistic Evangelism and Worship. Th.D., Southwestern Baptist Theological Seminary, 1978.

Missions and Missionaries

273   Baker, Robert A. The American Baptist Home Mission Society and the South, 1832-1894. Ph.D., Yale University, 1947. 318p. UMI# 80-16284.

274   Carroll, B.H., Jr. The Reflex Effect of the Foreign Mission Movement Among American Baptists. Ph.D., Southern Baptist Theological Seminary, 1901.

275   Carroll, Daniel M., Jr. The Development of Religious Education in the Baptist Work of Argentina. Ph.D., Southwestern Baptist Theological Seminary, 1960.

276   Coughlin, Margaret M. Strangers in the House: J. Lewis Shuck and Issachar Roberts, First American Baptist Missionaries to China. Ph.D., University of Virginia, 1972. 341p. UMI# 77-22632.

277   Crawley, James W. The Call to Foreign Missions Among Southern Baptists, 1845-1945. Ph.D., Southern Baptist Theological Seminary, 1947. 171p.

278   Greer, Harold E., Jr. History of Southern Baptist Mission Work in Cuba, 1886-1916. Ph.D., University of Alabama, 1965. 334p. UMI# 66-02937.

279   Hites, Laird T. An Investigation of Southern Baptist Mission Work in Rio de Janeiro. Ph.D., University of Chicago, 1925.

280   Hobart, Kenneth G. A Comparative History of the East and South China Missions of the American Baptist Foreign Missions Society, 1833-1935. Ph.D., Yale University, 1937.

281   Martin, Sandy D. The Growth of Christian Missionary Interest in West Africa Among Southeastern Black Baptists, 1880-1915. Ph.D., Columbia University, 1981. 292p. UMI# 81-13539.

282   Moffit, James W. A History of Early Baptist Missions Among the Five Civilized Tribes. Ph.D., University of Oklahoma, 1947.

283   Nash, Robert N., Jr. The Influence of American Myth on Southern Baptist Foreign Missions, 1845-1945. Ph.D., Southern Baptist Theological Seminary, 1989. 304p. UMI# 9004719.

284   Niederer, Albert R. Baptist Missionary Activity Among the German People in Texas, 1850-1950. Ph.D., Baylor University, 1976. 170p. UMI# 77-03071.

285   Ohlmann, Eric H. The American Baptist Mission to German-Americans: A Case Study of Attempted Assimilation. Th.D., Graduate Theological Union, 1973. 276p. UMI# 73-23128.

286   Ray, Stanley E. The History and Evaluation of Baptist Mission Policy in Nigeria, 1850-1960. Ph.D., Southwestern Baptist Theological Seminary, 1970.

287   Schultz, George A. An Indian Canaan: Isaac McCoy, Baptist Missions, and Indian Reform. Ph.D., University of Iowa, 1963. 415p. UMI# 64-03426.

288   Shank, Oliver. The Aims and Ideals of the Foreign Mission Board of the Southern Baptist Convention as Reflected in Their Annual Reports. Ph.D., Southern Baptist Theological Seminary, 1915.

289   Smith, Larry D. The Historiography of the Origins of Anti-Missionism Examined in Light of Kentucky Baptist History. Ph.D., Southern Baptist Theological Seminary, 1982. 268p. UMI# 8212717.

290   Stuart, Charles H. The Lower Congo and the American Baptist Mission to 1910. Ph.D., Boston University, 1969. 440p. UMI# 69-18749.

291   Tonks, Alfred R. A History of the Home Mission Board of the Southern Baptist Convention: 1845-1882. Th.D., Southern Baptist Theological Seminary, 1968. 261p. UMI# 68-07826.

292   Tumblin, John A., Jr. The Southern Baptist Missionary: A Study in the Sociology of the Professions. Ph.D., Duke University, 1956.

293   Tunnell, Gene V. The Role of Christian Social Ministries in

Southern Baptist Foreign Missions. Ph.D., University of Texas-Arlington, 1978. 221p. UMI# 78-21203.

294   Wiggins, Lexie O., Jr. A Critical History of the Southern Baptist Indian Mission Movement, 1855-1861. Ph.D., University of Alabama, 1980. 226p. UMI# 8100597.

Music

295   Measels, Donald C. A Catalog of Source Readings in Southern Baptist Church Music: 1818-1890. D.M.A., Southern Baptist Theological Seminary, 1986. 581p. UMI# 8704380.

296   Murrell, Irvin H., Jr. An Examination of Southern Ante-Bellum Baptist Hymnals and Tunebooks as Indicators of the Congregational Hymn and Tune Repertories of the Period With an Analysis of Representative Tunes. D.M.A., New Orleans Baptist Theological Seminary, 1984. 146p. UMI# 8509624.

Newspapers and Periodicals

297   Crook, Roger H. The Ethical Emphases of the Editors of Baptist Journals Published in the Southern Region of the United States up to 1865. Ph.D., Southern Baptist Theological Seminary, 1947. 295p.

298   English, Carl D. The Ethical Emphases of the Editors of Baptist Journals Published in the Southeastern Region of the United States, 1865-1915. Ph.D., Southern Baptist Theological Seminary, 1949. 308p.

299   Sumerlin, Claude W. A History of Southern Baptist State Newspapers. Ph.D., University of Missouri-Columbia, 1968. 437p. UMI# 6903415.

Organizational Structure

300   Allison, William H. Baptist Councils in America. Ph.D., University of Chicago, 1905.

301   Bruner, Weston. A Query in Baptist History: The Philadelphia Association: Was It in Its Organization and Early History Strictly Calvinistic? Ph.D., Southern Baptist Theological Seminary, 1894.

302   Clossman, Richard H. A History of the Organization and Development of the Baptist Churches in Ohio From 1789 to 1907, With Particular Reference to the Ohio Baptist Convention. Ph.D., Ohio State University, 1971. 352p. UMI# 71-17448.

303   Deweese, Charles W. The Origin, Development, and Use of Church Covenants in Baptist History. Th.D., Southern Baptist Theological Seminary, 1973. 386p. UMI# 74-02178.

304   Hand, Walter R. A History of the Background, Development, and Programs of the Pittsburgh Baptist Association. Ph.D., University of Pittsburgh, 1944. 152p.

305   Harrison, Paul M. Authority and Power in the American Baptist Convention. Ph.D., Yale University, 1958. 172p.

306   Johnson, Roy L. History of Rehoboth Baptist Association of Texas, 1856 to 1940. Ph.D., Southwestern Baptist Theological Seminary, 1949. 215p.

307   Jones, Charles A. A Historical Study of the Salem Association of Kentucky Baptist, 1837-1950. Ph.D., Southern Baptist Theological Seminary, 1951.

308   Kelly, Ernest E. A History of the Mississippi Baptist State Convention From Its Conception to 1900. Ph.D., Southern Baptist Theological Seminary, 1953.

309   Kerstan, Reinhold J. Historical Factors in the Formation of the Ethnically Oriented North American Baptist General Conference. Ph.D., Northwestern University, 1971. 296p. UMI# 71-30855.

310   Lee, Walter M. A History of the Elkhorn Association of Baptists in Kentucky. Ph.D., Southern Baptist Theological Seminary, 1905.

311   Lewis, Walter O. A History of the Baptists in St. Louis Association to 1849. Ph.D., Southern Baptist Theological Seminary, 1904.

312   Moore, David O. The Landmark Baptists and Their Attack Upon the Southern Baptist Convention Historically Analyzed. Ph.D., Southern Baptist Theological Seminary, 1950. 256p.

313   Ridenour, George L. An Historical and Social Study of Salem Association of Baptists in Kentucky, 1785-1837. Ph.D., Southern Baptist Theological Seminary, 1931.

314   Semple, James H. A History of the Florida Baptist Convention From 1865 to 1918. Ph.D., Southwestern Baptist Theological Seminary, 1962.

315   Shamburger, William M. A History of Tarrant County Baptist Association, 1886-1922. Ph.D., Southwestern Baptist Theological Seminary, 1953.

316   Shotwell, Malcolm G. Renewing the Baptist Principle of Associations. D.Min., Eastern Baptist Theological Seminary, 1990. 388p. UMI# 9026404.

317   Taylor, Raymond H. The Triennial Convention, 1814-1845: A Study of Baptist Cooperation and Conflict. Ph.D., Southern Baptist Theological Seminary, 1961.

318   Thomas, Frank H., Jr. The Development of Denominational Consciousness in Baptist Historical Writings, 1783-1886. Ph.D., Southern Baptist Theological Seminary, 1975. 320p. UMI# 76-0438.

319   Tidwell, Donavon D. History of West Fork Baptist Association. Ph.D., Southwestern Baptist Theological Seminary, 1949. 229p.

320   Todd, Willie G. The Slavery Issue and the Organization of a Southern Baptist Convention. Ph.D., University of North Carolina-Chapel Hill, 1964. 373p. UMI# 65-09067.

321   Torbet, Robert G. A Social History of the Philadelphia Baptist Association, 1707-1940. Ph.D., University of Pennsylvania, 1945. 247p.

Preaching

322   Ashby, Jerry P. John Albert Broadus: His Theory and Practice of Preaching. Ph.D., New Orleans Baptist Theological Seminary, 1968.

323   Echols, Steven F. An Investigation of Selected Factors of Communication in the Preaching of George Herbert Morrison. Th.D., New Orleans Baptist Theological Seminary, 1983. 201p. UMI# 8414078.

324   Insko, Chester A. The Biblical Preaching of Alexander MacLaren. Ph.D., Southern Baptist Theological Seminary, 1950.

325   Jones, George A. Richard Fuller and His Preaching. Ph.D., Southern Baptist Theological Seminary, 1954.

326   Owens, Raymond E. Preaching in a Revivalist Tradition: The Influence of Revivalism on Southern Baptist Preaching, 1845-1877. Th.D., Union Theological Seminary, 1967. 348p. UMI# 67-12175.

327   Patterson, Farrar. A History of Representative Southern Baptist Preaching From 1845 to 1895. Ph.D., Southwestern Baptist Theological Seminary, 1967.

328   Renaker, David W. The Biographical Sermon as a Biblical Method

in the Preaching of F.B. Meyer. Ph.D., Southwestern Baptist Theological Seminary, 1968.

329   Robinson, Robert J. The Homiletical Method of Benajah Harvey Carroll. Ph.D., Southwestern Baptist Theological Seminary, 1957.

330   Sherman, Cecil E. A History of Baptist Preaching in the South Before 1845. Ph.D., Southwestern Baptist Theological Seminary, 1960.

Social Programs

331   McClatchy, Ricky J. The Demise of the Antislavery Movement Among Baptists in America, 1783-1830. Ph.D., Southwestern Baptist Theological Seminary, 1990. 251p. UMI# 9026799.

332   McPherson, John T. John Mason Peck: A Conversionist Methodology for Social Transformation on the American Frontier. Ph.D., Southern Baptist Theological Seminary, 1985. 275p. UMI# 8515000.

333   Richards, Walter W. Theological Roots of Social Inaction in the Southern Baptist Convention. Ph.D., Florida State University, 1984. 282p. UMI# 8505317.

334   Yance, Norman A. Southern Baptists and Social Action: An Historical Interpretation of the Christian Life Commission and Its Denominational Role. Ph.D., George Washington University, 1973. 443p. UMI# 73-25098.

Theology

335   Allen, Arthur L. A Comparative Study of the Person of Christ in Selected Baptist Theologians: Augustus H. Strong, William N. Clarke, Edgar Y. Mullins, and Walter T. Conner. Th.D., New Orleans Baptist Theological Seminary, 1979.

336   Basden, Paul A. Theologies of Predestination in the Southern Baptist Tradition: A Critical Evaluation. Ph.D., Southwestern Baptist Theological Seminary, 1986. 339p. UMI# 8623458.

337   Cochran, Bernard H. William Newton Clarke: Exponent of the New Theology. Ph.D., Duke University, 1962. 336p. UMI# 6300865.

338   Englerth, Gilbert R. American Baptists and Their Confessions of Faith. Ph.D., Temple University, 1969. 446p. UMI# 69-19953.

339   Gates, Errett. The Early Relation and Separation of Baptists and

Disciples. Ph.D., University of Chicago, 1902.

340   Houghton, Myron J. The Place of Baptism in the Theology of James Robinson Graves. Th.D., Dallas Theological Seminary, 1971.

341   Mask, E. Jeffrey. At Liberty Under God: A Baptist Ecclesiology. Ph.D., Emory University, 1990. 294p. UMI# 9106728.

342   Matheson, Mark E. Religious Knowledge in the Theologies of John Leadley Dagg and James Petigru Boyce: With Special Reference to the Influence of Common Sense Realism. Ph.D., Southwestern Baptist Theological Seminary, 1984.

343   Mixon, Forest O. A Historical Survey of Baptist Beliefs and Some Important Reformation Principles. Ph.D., Southern Baptist Theological Seminary, 1932.

344   Moody, Dwight A. Doctrines of Inspiration in the Southern Baptist Theological Tradition. Ph.D., Southern Baptist Theological Seminary, 1982. 239p. UMI# 8217989.

345   Patterson, T.A. Theology of J.R. Graves and Its Influence on Southern Baptist Life. Ph.D., Southwestern Baptist Theological Seminary, 1949. 293p.

346   Priestley, David T.D. From Theological Polemic to Nonpolemical Theology: The Absence of Denominational Apology in Systematic Theologies by Nineteenth-Century American Baptists. Th.D., Lutheran School of Theology, 1986. 317p. UMI# 8621953.

347   Renault, James O. The Development of Separate Baptist Ecclesiology in the South, 1755-1976. Ph.D., Southern Baptist Theological Seminary, 1978. 314p. UMI# 78-21380.

348   Smith, Harold S. A Critical Analysis of the Theology of J.R. Graves. Th.D., Southern Baptist Theological Seminary, 1966. 429p. UMI# 6611262.

349   Stewart, Wilson L. Ecclesia: The Motif of B.H. Carroll's Theology. Ph.D., Southwestern Baptist Theological Seminary, 1960.

350   Thomas, Bill C. Edgar Young Mullins: A Baptist Exponent of Theological Restatement. Ph.D., Southern Baptist Theological Seminary, 1963.

351   Thompson, Luther J. A Study of Roger Williams' Religious Thought, With Special Reference to His Conception of Religious Liberty. Ph.D., University of Edinburgh, 1952. 245p.

352   Williams, Daniel D. The Andover Liberals: A Study in American Theology. Ph.D., Columbia University, 1942. 203p.

BISHOP HILL

353   Mikkelsen, Michael A. The Bishop Hill Colony: A Religious Communistic Settlement in Henry County, Illinois. Ph.D., Johns Hopkins University, 1892.

BRETHREN

General Studies

354   Alderfer, Owen H. The Mind of the Brethren in Christ: A Synthesis of Revivalism and the Church Conceived as Total Community. Ph.D., Claremont Graduate School, 1964. 331p. UMI# 6603323.

355   Becktel, Russell G. The Backgrounds and Origins of the United Brethren in Christ Church in Lancaster County Prior to 1800. S.T.D., Temple University, 1939. 245p.

356   Bemesderfer, James O. Pietism and Its Influence Upon the Evangelical United Brethren Church. S.T.D., Temple University, 1951. 227p. UMI# 64-11255.

357   Dove, Frederick D. Cultural Changes in the Church of the Brethren: A Study in Cultural Sociology. Ph.D., University of Pennsylvania, 1932. 246p.

358   Eshleman, Robert F. A Study of Changes in the Value Patterns of the Church of the Brethren. Ph.D., Cornell University, 1948.

359   Frantz, Clair G. The Religious Teachings of the German Almanacs Published by the Sauers in Colonial Pennsylvania. Ed.D., Temple University, 1955. 150p. UMI# 15318.

360   Gillin, John L. The Dunkers; A Sociological Interpretation. Ph.D., Columbia University, 1906.

361   Henry, J. Maurice. History of the Church of the Brethren (Dunkers) in Maryland. Ph.D., George Washington University, 1924.

362   Keller, Charles H. A History of the Allegheny Conference of the Church of the United Brethren in Christ. Ph.D., University of Pittsburgh, 1943.

363   Maxwell, Harold H. The History of the Rocky Mountain

Conference, Evangelical United Brethren Church, 1869-1951. Ph.D., Iliff School of Theology, 1965.

364   Porte, Robert F. The Pietistic Tradition in the Brethren Church. Th.D., Drew University, 1933.

365   Robertson, John D. Christian Newcomer, (1749-1830), Pioneer of Church Discipline and Union Among the United Brethren in Christ, the Evangelical Association, and the Methodist Episcopal Church. Ph.D., George Washington University, 1973. 293p. UMI# 73-17017.

366   Rupel, Esther F. An Investigation of the Origin, Significance, and Demise of the Prescribed Dress Worn by Members of the Church of the Brethren. Ph.D., University of Minnesota, 1971. 366p. UMI# 7214366.

367   Schrag, Martin H. The Brethren in Christ Attitude Toward the "World": A Historical Study of the Movement From Separation to an Increasing Acceptance of American Society. Ph.D., Temple University, 1967. 392p. UMI# 68-04521.

368   Shinn, Robert W. The Plymouth Brethren and Ecumenical Protestantism. Th.D., Union Theological Seminary, 1968. 225p. UMI# 68-13612.

369   Stein, Kenneth J. Church Unity Movements in the Church of the United Brethren in Christ Until 1946. Th.D., Union Theological Seminary, 1965. 344p. UMI# 65-09651.

370   Stoffer, Dale R. The Background and Development of Thought and Practice in the German Baptist Brethren (Dunker) and the Brethren (Progressive) Churches (c.1650-1979). Ph.D., Fuller Theological Seminary, 1980. 815p. UMI# 80-20942.

Clergy

371   Riley, Jobie E. An Analysis of the Debate Between Johann Conrad Beissel and Various Eighteenth-Century Contemporaries Concerning the Importance of Celibacy. Ph.D., Temple University, 1974. 349p. UMI# 7428365.

Education

372   Boyer, John N. The Functional Development of Christian Education in the Church of the United Brethren in Christ. Ph.D., University of Pittsburgh, 1947.

373   Boyers, Auburn A. Changing Conceptions of Education in the

Church of the Brethren. Ed.D., University of Pittsburgh, 1969. 214p. UMI# 70-04542.

374 Fisher, Paul G. Music: A Dominant Force in the First Century of Lebanon Valley College. Ed.D., University of Michigan, 1969. 251p. UMI# 70-4023.

375 Hanle, Robert V. A History of Higher Education Among German Baptist Brethren, 1708-1908. Ph.D., University of Pennsylvania, 1974. 345p. UMI# 75-14569.

376 Henkel, Julia S. An Historical Study of the Educational Contributions of the Brethren of the Common Life. Ph.D., University of Pittsburgh, 1962. 301p. UMI# 63-02428.

377 Henry, Tobias F. The Development of Religious Education in the Church of the Brethren in the United States. Ph.D., University of Pittsburgh, 1938.

378 Lansman, Quentin C. An Historical Study of the Development of Higher Education and Related Theological and Educational Assumptions in the Evangelical United Brethren Church: 1800-1954. Ph.D., Northwestern University, 1969. 418p. UMI# 70-00102.

379 Wilkins, Martha H. Education for Freedom: The Noble Experiment of Sarah A. Dickey and the Mount Hermon Seminary. Ph.D., University of Mississippi, 1985. 162p. UMI# 8603331.

Missions and Missionaries

380 Brandauer, Frederick W. The History and Development of the Central China Mission of the Evangelical United Brethren Church. Ph.D., Temple University, 1953.

381 Moyer, Elgin S. Missions in the Church of the Brethren: Their Development and Effect Upon the Denomination. Ph.D., Yale University, 1929. 301p.

382 Roberts, Walter N. The Development of the Indigenous Evangelical Church in the Philippine Islands as Revealed in the Work of the Church of the United Brethren in Christ. Ph.D., Hartford Seminary Foundation, 1932.

BROOK FARM

383 Crowe, Charles R. George Ripley, Transcendentalist and Utopian Socialist. Ph.D., Brown University, 1955. 338p. UMI# 13164.

384   Riggs, Lisette. George and Sophia Ripley. Ph.D., University of Maryland, 1942.

385   Rittenhouse, Caroline S. The Testimony of Man's Inward Nature: A Study of George Ripley's Transcendentalism. Ph.D., Harvard University, 1965.

386   Wilson, Howard A. George Ripley: Social and Literary Critic. Ph.D., University of Wisconsin-Madison, 1942.

BUDDHIST

387   Prothero, Stephen R. Henry Steel Olcott (1832-1907) and the Construction of "Protestant Buddhism". Ph.D., Harvard University, 1990. 333p. UMI# 9035616.

388   Tweed, Thomas A. The American Encounter With Buddhism, 1844-1912: Responses to Buddhism, Dissent and Consent, and Victorian Religious Culture. Ph.D., Stanford University, 1989. 294p. UMI# 8919485.

BURNED OVER DISTRICT

389   McElroy, James L. Social Reform in the Burned-Over District: Rochester, New York, as a Test Case, 1830-1854. Ph.D., State University of New York-Binghamton, 1974. 278p. UMI# 7420690.

390   Wellman, Judith M. The Burned-Over District Revisited: Benevolent Reform and Abolitionism in Mexico, Paris, and Ithaca, New York, 1825-1842. Ph.D., University of Virginia, 1974. 502p. UMI# 7429206.

CATHOLIC

General Studies

391   Baeszler, St. Alfred. The Congregation of Notre Dame in Ontario and the United States: The History of Holy Angels' Province. Ph.D., Fordham University, 1944. 251p.

392   Barrett, John D.M. A Comparative Study of the Councils of Baltimore and the Code of Canon Law. Ph.D., Catholic University of America, 1932.

393   Bartlett, Chester J. Jural Personality and Church Property Tenure in the United States. Ph.D., Catholic University of America, 1926.

394   Beaman, Warren J. From Sect to Cult to Sect: The Christian

Catholic Church in Zion. Ph.D., Iowa State University, 1990. 198p. UMI# 9110482.

395   Becker, Martin J. A History of Catholic Life in the Diocese of Albany, 1609-1864. Ph.D., Fordham University, 1973. 369p. UMI# 74-02727.

396   Beckman, Peter. The Catholic Church on the Kansas Frontier. Ph.D., Catholic University of America, 1943.

397   Bisson, Wilfred J. Some Conditions for Collective Violence: The Charlestown Convent Riot of 1834. Ph.D., Michigan State University, 1974. 157p. UMI# 74-27386.

398   Bracco, Theodore G. The Pastoral Theology, Problems, and Practice of John Carroll, First Catholic Bishop of the United States, as Related in His Letters to Rome. Ph.D., Saint Louis University, 1990. 358p. UMI# 9102893.

399   Brown, Gayle K.P. A Controversy Not Merely Religious: The Anti-Catholic Tradition in Colonial New England. Ph.D., University of Iowa, 1990. 348p. UMI# 9103195.

400   Browne, Henry J. The Catholic Church and the Knights of Labor. Ph.D., Catholic University of America, 1949. 342p.

401   Burich, Keith R. The Catholic Church and American Intellectuals: From Cooper to Santayana. Ph.D., University of North Carolina-Chapel Hill, 1979. 380p. UMI# 80-13915.

402   Campbell, Frances M. American Catholicism in Northern New Mexico: A Kaleidoscope of Development, 1840-1885. Ph.D., Graduate Theological Union, 1986. 330p. UMI# 8617052.

403   Campbell, James H. New Parochialism: Change and Conflict in the Archdiocese of Cincinnati, 1878-1925. Ph.D., University of Cincinnati, 1981. 371p. UMI# 81-23743.

404   Campbell, Jefferson H. Orestes Brownson's Doctrine of Communion. Ph.D., Duke University, 1963. 250p. UMI# 6304370.

405   Carthy, Mary P. English Influences on Early American Catholicism. Ph.D., Catholic University of America, 1960.

406   Casas, Myrna. Theatrical Production in Puerto Rico From 1700-1824: The Role of the Government and of the Roman Catholic Church. Ph.D., New York University, 1974. 272p. UMI# 74-17133.

407　　　　Cross, Robert D. Liberal Catholicism in America: 1885-1900. Ph.D., Harvard University, 1955.

408　　　　Daily, Maria R. The Connecticut Mind and Catholicism, 1829-1860. Ph.D., Yale University, 1939.

409　　　　Derrig, James R. The Political Thought of the Catholic Press, 1880 to 1920. Ph.D., Saint Louis University, 1980. 420p. UMI# 61-00736.

410　　　　Dignan, Patrick J. Catholic Church Property in the United States (1784-1832). Ph.D., Catholic University of America, 1933.

411　　　　Dolan, Jay P. Urban Catholicism: New York City, 1815-1865. Ph.D., University of Chicago, 1971.

412　　　　Donnelly, James F. Catholic New Yorkers and New York Socialists, 1870-1920. Ph.D., New York University, 1982. 439p.

413　　　　Duke, Keith E. Geographical Factors in the Location of Church Sites in Urban Los Angeles. Ph.D., University of California-Los Angeles, 1965. 384p. UMI# 6506040.

414　　　　Duratschek, Mary C. Beginnings of Catholicism in South Dakota. Ph.D., Catholic University of America, 1943.

415　　　　Fitzmorris, Mary A. Four Decades of Catholicism in Texas, 1820-1860. Ph.D., Catholic University of America, 1926. 109p.

416　　　　Foik, Paul J. Pioneer Efforts of Catholic Journalism in the United States. Ph.D., Catholic University of America, 1913.

417　　　　Franchot, Jenny. Roads to Rome: Catholicism in Antebellum America. Ph.D., Stanford University, 1986. 625p. UMI# 8700750.

418　　　　Garraghan, Gilbert J. The Beginnings of Catholicity in Kansas City, MO. Ph.D., Saint Louis University, 1919.

419　　　　Gibson, Laurita. American Catholic Converts to 1829. Ph.D., Catholic University of America, 1943.

420　　　　Goodrow, Esther M. Catholic Participation in the Diplomacy of the American Civil War. Ph.D., Saint Louis University, 1954.

421　　　　Green, James J. The Impact of Henry George's Theories on American Catholics. Ph.D., University of Notre Dame, 1956. 377p. UMI# 18454.

422　　　　Griffin, Joseph A. The Contribution of Belgium to the Catholic

Church in America (1523-1857). Ph.D., Catholic University of America, 1932.

423   Guerrieri, Dora A. Catholic Thought in the Age of Jackson. Ph.D., Boston College, 1960.

424   Harlan, Rolvix. The Christian Catholic Church in Zion. Ph.D., University of Chicago, 1906.

425   Harney, Loyola. The Defensive Action of the Right Reverend Benedict J. Fenwick, S.J., to Anti-Catholicism in New England, 1829-1845. Ph.D., Boston University, 1936.

426   Harris, Innis D. Anti-Roman Catholic Movements in the United States From 1800 to 1900. Th.D., Drew University, 1923.

427   Hastings, Martin F. United States-Vatican Relations: Policies and Problems. Ph.D., University of California-Berkeley, 1952. 247p.

428   Hayman, Robert W. Catholicism in Rhode Island the Diocese of Providence, 1780-1886. Ph.D., Providence College, 1977.

429   Hinrichsen, Carl D. The History of the Diocese of Newark, 1873-1901. Ph.D., Catholic University of America, 1963. 453p. UMI# 63-08062.

430   Kelly, Mary G. A History of Catholic Immigration Colonization Projects in the United States, 1815-1860. Ph.D., University of Illinois at Urbana-Champaign, 1939.

431   Langlois, Edward R. The Formation of American Catholic Political Thought: Isaac Hecker's Political Theory. Ph.D., Cornell University, 1977. 280p. UMI# 78-07787.

432   Lebuffe, Leon A. Tensions in American Catholicism, 1820-1870, An Intellectual History. Ph.D., Catholic University of America, 1973. 173p. UMI# 74-03502.

433   Lundy, Edward J. The Transcendental Roots of Isaac Hecker's Vision for the American Catholic Church. Ph.D., University of Texas-Austin, 1985. 325p. UMI# 8527609.

434   Martin, M. Aquinata. The Catholic Church on the Nebraska Frontier, 1854-1885. Ph.D., Catholic University of America, 1937.

435   Mattingly, M. Ramona. The Catholic Church on the Kentucky Frontier (1785-1812). Ph.D., Catholic University of America, 1936.

436   McAvoy, Thomas F. The Catholic Church in Indiana, 1789-1834. Ph.D., Columbia University, 1941. 226p.

437   McCarthy, Charles R. The Political Philosophy of Orestes A. Brownson. Ph.D., University of Toronto, 1962. 274p. UMI# 6306990.

438   McConville, Mary S.P. Political Nativism in the State of Maryland, 1830-1860. Ph.D., Catholic University of America, 1928. 133p.

439   McEniry, Blanche M. American Catholics in the War With Mexico. Ph.D., Catholic University of America, 1937.

440   McGloin, John B. The Influence of James Chrysostom Bouchard, S.J., on Catholicism in the Far West, 1861-1889. Ph.D., Saint Louis University, 1948.

441   McLaughlin, Katherine A. The Role of the Laity in the Thought of John Ireland. Ph.D., Marquette University, 1990. 189p. UMI# 9101418.

442   McManamin, Francis G. The American Years of John Boyle O'Reilly, 1870-1890. Ph.D., Catholic University of America, 1959.

443   McNally, Michael J.T. Cross in the Sun: The Growth and Development of Catholicism in South Florida, 1868-1968. Ph.D., University of Notre Dame, 1982. 508p. UMI# 8305878.

444   McNamara, William. The Catholic Church on the Northern Indiana Frontier, 1789-1844. Ph.D., Catholic University of America, 1931. 84p.

445   Moffit, Robert E. Metaphysics and Constitutionalism: The Political Theory of Orestes Brownson. Ph.D., University of Arizona, 1975. 934p. UMI# 7519583.

446   Mulvey, Anita M. The Catholic Church in New York: Its Historical Development. Ph.D., St. John's University, 1959.

447   Murphy, John C. An Analysis of the Attitudes of American Catholic Toward the Immigrant and the Negro, 1825-1925. Ph.D., Catholic University of America, 1941. 499p.

448   Noone, Bernard J. A Critical Analysis of the American Catholic Response to Higher Criticism as Reflected in Selected Catholic Periodicals 1870 to 1908. Ph.D., Drew University, 1976. 457p. UMI# 76-26250.

449   Nordbeck, Elizabeth C. The New England Diaspora: A Study of the

Religious Culture of Maine and New Hampshire, 1613-1763. Ph.D., Harvard University, 1978.

450   Osborne, William A. The Race Problem in the Catholic Church in the United States Between the Time of the Second Plenary Council (1866) and the Founding of the Catholic Interracial Council of New York (1934). Ph.D., Columbia University, 1954. 248p. UMI# 10223.

451   Prosen, Anthony J. A History of the Catholic Church in Lafayette Diocese in Indiana. Ph.D., Ball State University, 1977. 308p. UMI# 78-03671.

452   Ray, Mary A. American Opinion of Roman Catholicism in the Eighteenth Century. Ph.D., Columbia University, 1937. 457p.

453   Reher, Margaret M. The Church and the Kingdom of God in America: The Ecclesiology of the Americanists. Ph.D., Fordham University, 1972. 331p. UMI# 7301492.

454   Rice, Madeleine H. American Catholic Opinion in the Slavery Controversy. Ph.D., Columbia University, 1944. 177p.

455   Riley, Arthur J. Catholicism in Colonial New England: 1620-1788. Ph.D., Catholic University of America, 1936.

456   Robichaud, Paul G. The Resident Church: Middle Class Catholics and the Shaping of American Catholic Identity, 1889 to 1899. Ph.D., University of California-Los Angeles, 1989. 357p. UMI# 9000820.

457   Robinson, Samuel W. The Modernist Movement in the Catholic Church. Ph.D., Boston University, 1912.

458   Ryan, Leo R. Old St. Peter's: The Mother Church of Catholic New York, 1785-1935. Ph.D., Fordham University, 1936.

459   Ryan, Mary T. An Analysis of Modern Socialism by Catholic Journalists, 1848-1914. Ph.D., Saint Louis University, 1952. 382p. UMI# 60-02035.

460   Sanfilippo, Mary H. The New England Transcendentalists' Opinions of the Catholic Church. Ph.D., University of Notre Dame, 1972. 339p. UMI# 72-26819.

461   Schroeder, M. Carol. The Catholic Church in the Diocese of Vincennes, 1847-1877. Ph.D., Catholic University of America, 1946.

462   Sewrey, Charles L. The Alleged "Un-Americanism" of the Church as a Factor in Anti-Catholicism in the United States, 1860-1914.

Ph.D., University of Minnesota, 1955. 412p. UMI# 13793.

463   Shannon, James P. Colonization by Catholic Immigrants in Minnesota, 1876-1881. Ph.D., Yale University, 1955. 367p.

464   Shaughnessy, Gerald. A Study of Immigration and Catholic Growth in the United States: 1790-1920. Ph.D., Catholic University of America, 1925. 289p.

465   Shearer, Donald C. Pontificia Americana: A Documentary History of the Catholic Church in the United States, 1784-1884. Ph.D., Catholic University of America, 1933.

466   Shuell, Noel B. American Catholic Responses to the Religious Philosophy of William James: The Neo-Traditionalist Responses. Ph.D., Marquette University, 1985. 517p. UMI# 8516284.

467   Simpson, Eleanor E. The Conservative Heresy: Yankees and the "Reaction in Favor of the Roman Catholics." Ph.D., University of Minnesota, 1974. 465p. UMI# 74-17280.

468   Stauffer, Alvin P., Jr. Anti-Catholicism in American Politics, 1865-1900. Ph.D., Harvard University, 1933.

469   Taves, Ann. Relocating the Sacred: Roman Catholic Devotions in Mid-Nineteenth-Century America. Ph.D., University of Chicago, 1983.

470   Taylor, Mary C. A History of the Foundations of Catholicism in Northern New York. Ph.D., Saint Louis University, 1967. 455p. UMI# 68-01300.

471   Thomas, M. Evangeline. Nativism in the Old Northwest, 1850-1860. Ph.D., Catholic University of America, 1936.

472   Thomas, M. Ursula. The Catholic Church on the Oklahoma Frontier 1824-1907. Ph.D., Saint Louis University, 1938. 392p. UMI# 00205.

473   Walker, Fintan G. The Catholic Church in the Meeting of Two Frontiers: The Southern Illinois Count (1763-1893). Ph.D., Catholic University of America, 1935.

474   Wallace, Leslie G. The Rhetoric of Anti-Catholicism: The American Protective Association, 1887-1911. Ph.D., University of Oregon, 1973. 212p. UMI# 7406913.

475   Westhues, Kenneth L. The American Catholic World: Its Origins

and Prospects. Ph.D., Vanderbilt University, 1970. 159p. UMI# 70-24898.

476   Wimmer, Judith C. American Catholic Interpretations of the Civil War. Ph.D., Drew University, 1980. 369p. UMI# 80-21087.

477   Worland, Carr E. American Catholic Women and the Church to 1920. Ph.D., Saint Louis University, 1982. 261p. UMI# 82-23752.

478   Yocum Mize, Sandra A. The Papacy in Mid-Nineteenth Century American Catholic Imagination. Ph.D., Marquette University, 1987. 344p. UMI# 8811065.

Art and Architecture

479   Strong, Janet A. The Cathedral of Saint John the Divine in New York: Design Competitions in the Shadow of H.H. Richardson, 1889-1891. Ph.D., Brown University, 1990. 971p. UMI# 9101841.

Biography

480   Agonito, Joseph A. The Building of an American Catholic Church: The Episcopacy of John Carroll. Ph.D., Syracuse University, 1972. 335p. UMI# 72-20305.

481   Ahern, Patrick H. The Life of Archbishop John J. Keane, 1839-1918. Ph.D., Catholic University of America, 1954.

482   Andrews, Rena M. Archbishop Hughes and the Civil War. Ph.D., University of Chicago, 1934.

483   Barcio, Robert G. Tobias Mullen and the Diocese of Erie, 1868-1899. Ph.D., Case Western Reserve University, 1965. 298p. UMI# 66-05178.

484   Barger, Robert N. John Lancaster Spalding: Catholic Educator and Social Emissary. Ph.D., University of Illinois at Urbana-Champaign, 1976. 271p. UMI# 77-08930.

485   Bartsch, Arthur H. Spalding and the Enlightenment. Ph.D., University of Chicago, 1979.

486   Bennett, Spencer C. Orestes Brownson: On Civil Religion. Conflicts in the Evolution of a Concept of National Faith. Ph.D., Case Western Reserve University, 1973. 170p. UMI# 74-02491.

487   Boever, Richard A. The Spirituality of St. John Neumann, C.SS.R.

Fourth Bishop of Philadelphia. Ph.D., Saint Louis University, 1983. 188p. UMI# 8325333.

488   Brokhage, Joseph D. Francis Patrick Kenrick's Opinion on Slavery. Ph.D., Catholic University of America, 1955.

489   Butler, Gregory S. In Search of the American Spirit: The Political Thought of Orestes Brownson. Ph.D., Catholic University of America, 1989. 274p. UMI# 8919393.

490   Carey, Patrick W. John England and Irish American Catholicism 1815-1842. Ph.D., Fordham University, 1975. 444p. UMI# 76-04111.

491   Conroy, Paul R. Orestes A. Brownson: American Political Philosopher. Ph.D., Saint Louis University, 1937. 399p. UMI# 195.

492   Corrigan, M. Felicia. Some Social Principles of Orestes A. Brownson. Ph.D., Catholic University of America, 1939.

493   Curran, Robert E. Michael Augustine Corrigan and the Shaping of Conservative Catholicism in America, 1878-1895. Ph.D., Yale University, 1974. 496p. UMI# 7515298.

494   Daly, John E. Orestes A. Brownson and Transcendentalism. Ph.D., Fordham University, 1956.

495   Deye, Anthony H. Archbishop John Baptist Purcell of Cincinnati: Pre-Civil War Years. Ph.D., University of Notre Dame, 1959. 478p. UMI# 65-04709.

496   Easterly, Frederick J. The Life of Rt. Rev. Joseph Rosati, C.M., First Bishop of St. Louis, 1789-1843. Ph.D., Catholic University of America, 1943.

497   Faddoul, Germain A. The Harmonizing of Faith and Reason in Brownson's Pre-Catholic Experience. Ph.D., University of Notre Dame, 1963. 410p. UMI# 6307325.

498   Farrell, Bertin B. Orestes Brownson and the Existence of God. Ph.D., Catholic University of America, 1950. 176p.

499   Farry, Joseph P. Themes of Continuity and Change in the Political Philosophy of Orestes Brownson: A Comparative Study. Ph.D., Fordham University, 1968. 293p. UMI# 6811014.

500   Flanagan, Mary K. The Influence of John Henry Hobart on the Life of Elizabeth Ann Seton. Ph.D., Union Theological Seminary, 1978. 252p. UMI# 7919322.

501   Fogarty, Gerald P. Denis J. O'Connell: Americanist Agent to the Vatican, 1885-1903. Ph.D., Yale University, 1969. UMI# 70-2731.

502   Fox, Columba. The Life of Rt. Rev. John Baptist Mary David (1761-1841): Bishop of Bardstown and Founder of the Sisters of Charity of Nazareth. Ph.D., Catholic University of America, 1925. 251p.

503   Frawley, Mary A. Patrick Donahoe. Ph.D., Catholic University of America, 1946.

504   Gaffey, James P. The Life of Patrick William Riordan, Second Archbishop of San Francisco, 1841-1914. Ph.D., Catholic University of America, 1965. 612p. UMI# 65-09209.

505   Geiger, John O. H.J. Desmond, Catholic, Citizen, Reformer: The Quest for Justice Through Educational and Social Reform. Ph.D., Marquette University, 1972. 347p. UMI# 73-27503.

506   Gilhooley, Leonard. Orestes Brownson and the American Idea, 1838-1860. Ph.D., Fordham University, 1961. 341p. UMI# 6201026.

507   Gilmore, William J. Orestes Brownson and New England Religious Culture, 1803-1827. Ph.D., University of Virginia, 1971. 503p. UMI# 7522124.

508   Godecker, Mary S. Right Reverend Simon William Gabriel Brute de Remur, First Bishop of Vincennes, Indiana. Priestly Career in Maryland, 1810-1834. Ph.D., Catholic University of America, 1929. 125p.

509   Grozier, Richard J. The Life and Times of John Bernard Fitzpatrick: Third Roman Catholic Bishop of Boston. Ph.D., Boston College, 1966.

510   Hallinan, Paul J. Life of Richard Gilmour, Second Bishop of Cleveland, 1872-1891. Ph.D., Case Western Reserve University, 1963.

511   Henthorne, Mary E. The Career of the Right Reverend John Lancaster Spalding, Bishop of Peoria, as President of the Irish Catholic Colonization Association of the United States, 1879-1892. Ph.D., University of Illinois at Urbana-Champaign, 1930. 191p.

512   Holden, Vincent F. The Early Years of Isaac Thomas Hecker (1819-1844). Ph.D., Catholic University of America, 1939.

513   Hovarter, Nancy C. The Social and Political Views of Orestes

Augustus Brownson. Ed.D., Ball State University, 1974. 247p. UMI# 7508525.

514   Kearney, Anna R. James A. Burns, C.S.C.: Educator. Ph.D., University of Notre Dame, 1975. 216p. UMI# 75-19940.

515   Killen, David P. John Spalding's American Understanding of the Church. Ph.D., Marquette University, 1970. 305p. UMI# 71-20736.

516   Kirk, Martin J. The Spirituality of Isaac Thomas Hecker Reconciling the American Character and the Catholic Faith. Ph.D., Saint Louis University, 1980. 402p. UMI# 8100495.

517   Kline, Omer U. The Public Address of James Cardinal Gibbons as a Catholic Spokesman on Social Issues in America. Ed.D., Columbia University, 1963. 480p. UMI# 6401486.

518   Lackner, Joseph H. Bishop Ignatius F. Horstmann and the Americanization of the Roman Catholic Church in the United States. Ph.D., Saint Louis University, 1978. 499p. UMI# 78-22083.

519   Lannie, Vincent P. Archbishop John Hughes and the Common School Controversy, 1840-1842. Ed.D., Columbia University, 1963. 612p. UMI# 64-04323.

520   Lee, Chang S. Political Thought of Archbishop John Ireland. Ph.D., Aquinas Institute, 1972.

521   Lenk, Edward A. Mother Marianne Cope (1838-1918): The Syracuse Franciscan Community and Molokai Lepers. Ph.D., Syracuse University, 1986. 227p. UMI# 8716935.

522   Lipcomb, Oscar H. The Administration of Michael Portier, Vicar Apostolic of Alabama and the Floridas, 1826-1829, and First Bishop of Mobile, 1829-1859. Ph.D., Catholic University of Alabama, 1963. 381p. UMI# 64-06566.

523   Lothamer, James W. Communion as an Ecclesiological Theme in the Writings of Orestes A. Brownson (A Study of Brownson's Doctrine of Communion in His Ecclesiological Writings From 1842-1844 and a Review of His Revival of the Doctrine in 1857). Ph.D., University of St. Michael's College, 1980. 348p. UMI# 8304981.

524   Lyons, Mary E. A Rhetoric for American Catholicism: The Transcendental Voice of Isaac T. Hecker. Ph.D., University of California-Berkeley, 1983. 263p. UMI# 8413485.

525   Magaret, Helene. Father De Smet, Pioneer Priest of the Rockies. Ph.D., University of Iowa, 1941.

526   Malone, Michael T. Levi Silliman Ives: Priest, Bishop, Tractarian, and Roman Catholic Convert. Ph.D., Duke University, 1970. 393p. UMI# 71-11640.

527   Marotti, Frank, Jr. Juan Baptista de Segura and the Failure of the Florida Jesuit Mission (1566-1572). D.A., University of Miami, 1984. 158p. UMI# 8425898.

528   Marschall, John P. Francis Patrick Kenrick, 1851-1863: The Baltimore Years. Ph.D., Catholic University of America, 1965. 427p. UMI# 6513023.

529   Marshall, Hugh. Orestes Brownson and the American Civil War. Ph.D., Catholic University of America, 1962. 325p. UMI# 6304089.

530   McCann, Mary A. Archbishop Purcell and the Archdiocese of Cincinnati: A Study Based on Original Sources. Ph.D., Catholic University of America, 1918. 108p.

531   McGrath, James W. The Catholicism of Orestes A. Brownson. Ph.D., University of New Mexico, 1961. 396p. UMI# 61-05274.

532   Melville, Annabelle M. The Life of Elizabeth Bayley Seton, 1774-1821. Ph.D., Catholic University of America, 1950.

533   Murphy, Cecilia. A Reevaluation of the Episcopacy of Michael Domenac, 1860-1877, Second Bishop of Pittsburgh and Only Bishop of Allegheny. Ph.D., Saint Louis University, 1974. 374p. UMI# 75-26293.

534   Murphy, Mary C. Bishop Joseph Rosati, C.M., and the Diocese of New Orleans, 1824-1830. Ph.D., Saint Louis University, 1960. 245p. UMI# 61-00673.

535   Murtha, Ronin J. The Life of the Most Reverend Ambrose Marechal, Third Archbishop of Baltimore, 1768-1828. Ph.D., Catholic University of America, 1965. 326p. UMI# 65-07862.

536   Neri, Michael C. Hispanic Catholicism in Transitional California: The Life of Jose Gonzalez Rubio, O.F.M. (1804-1875). Ph.D., Graduate Theological Union, 1974. 243p. UMI# 74-23192.

537   Nolan, Hugh J. Francis Patrick Kenrick, Bishop of Philadelphia (1830-1851). Ph.D., Catholic University of America, 1944. 93p.

538   Nugent, Mary F. Sister Louise (Josephine van der Schrieck) (1813-1886) American Foundress of the Sisters of Notre Dame de Namur. Ph.D., Catholic University of America, 1931. 352p.

539   O'Toole, James M. Militant and Triumphant: William Henry O'Connell and Boston Catholicism, 1859-1944. Ph.D., Boston College, 1987. 358p. UMI# 8807552.

540   Padovano, Rose M.B. The Influence of Elizabeth Seton Reflected in Dimensions of Her Charism and Educational Ministry: A Renewal Program. D.Min., Drew University, 1984. 111p. UMI# 8418042.

541   Perschbacher, Susan J. Journey of Faith: The Conversion and Reconversions of Isaac Hecker. Ph.D., University of Chicago, 1981. UMI# 0535149.

542   Peterman, Thomas J. Thomas Andrew Becker, the First Catholic Bishop of Wilmington, Delaware and Sixth Bishop of Savannah, Georgia, 1831-1899. Ph.D., Catholic University of America, 1982. 619p. UMI# 82-21443.

543   Portier, William L. Providential Nation: An Historical-Theological Study of Isaac Hecker's Americanism. Ph.D., University of St. Michael's College, 1980. 709p. UMI# 8212169.

544   Quinn, Joseph L. Unrepresentative Man: The Significance of Orestes Brownson's Year of Self-Assessment. Ph.D., Harvard University, 1976.

545   Raemers, Sidney A. A Critical Examination Into the Alleged Ontologism of Orestes A. Brownson. Ph.D., University of Notre Dame, 1929.

546   Riedl, John O. The Life and Philosophy of Orestes A. Brownson. Ph.D., Marquette University, 1930.

547   Roemer, Lawrence J. The Political Philosophy of Orestes Brownson. Ph.D., Loyola University of Chicago, 1947.

548   Schroll, Agnes C. The Social Thought of John Lancaster Spalding. Ph.D., Catholic University of America, 1944.

549   Seddon, John T., III. The Spirituality of the Reverend Thomas Frederick Price, M.M. Ph.D., Fordham University, 1989. 284p. UMI# 8918643.

550   Sheridan, Mary B. Bishop Odin and the New Era of the Catholic

Church in Texas, 1840-1860. Ph.D., Saint Louis University, 1937. 119p. UMI# 00204.

551   Spalding, Thomas W. Martin John Spalding: Bishop of Louisville and Archbishop of Baltimore, 1810-1872. Ph.D., Catholic University of America, 1971. 528p. UMI# 71-25029.

552   Steckler, Gerard G. Charles John Seghers: Missionary Bishop in the American Northwest, 1839-1886. Ph.D., University of Washington, 1963. 636p. UMI# 64-04533.

553   Steurer, Justin C. The Impact of Katharine Tekakwitha on American Spiritual Life. Ph.D., Catholic University of America, 1958.

554   Sweeney, David F. The Life of John Lancaster Spalding, First Bishop of Peoria, 1840-1916. Ph.D., Catholic University of America, 1963. 527p. UMI# 63-06827.

555   Szarnicki, Henry A. The Episcopate of Michael O'Connor, First Bishop of Pittsburgh, 1843-1860. Ph.D., Catholic University of America, 1971. 414p. UMI# 7120095.

556   Weber, Ralph E. The Life of Reverend John A. Zahm, C.S.C.: American Catholic Apologist and Educator. Ph.D., University of Notre Dame, 1956. 522p. UMI# 16546.

557   Whalen, Mary R.G. Some Aspects of the Influence of Orestes A. Brownson on His Contemporaries. Ph.D., University of Notre Dame, 1934.

558   Yeager, H. Hildegarde. The Life of James Roosevelt Bayley, First Bishop of Newark and Eighth Bishop of Baltimore. Ph.D., Catholic University of America, 1948.

Church and State

559   Nary, Ralph W. Church, State, and Religious Liberty: The Views of the American Catholic Bishops of the 1890's in Perspective. Ph.D., Georgetown University, 1966. 324p. UMI# 67-05227.

560   Reuter, Frank T. Church and State in the American Dependencies, 1898-1904: A Study of Catholic Opinion and the Formation of Colonial Policy. Ph.D., University of Illinois at Urbana-Champaign, 1960. 248p. UMI# 61-00191.

Clergy

561   Feely, Thomas F. Leadership in the Early Colorado Catholic

Church. Ph.D., University of Denver, 1973. 610p. UMI# 73-28528.

562   Germain, Aidan H. Catholic Military and Naval Chaplains, 1776-1917. Ph.D., Catholic University of America, 1929. 165p.

563   Merwick, Donna J. Changing Thought Patterns of Three Generations of Catholic Clergymen of the Boston Archdiocese From 1850 to 1910. Ph.D., University of Wisconsin, 1968. 374p. UMI# 68-09104.

564   O'Neill, Daniel P. St. Paul Priests, 1851-1930: Recruitment, Formation and Mobility. Ph.D., University of Minnesota, 1979. 165p. UMI# 8011864.

565   Ruskowski, Leo F. French Emigre Priests in the United States, 1791-1815. Ph.D., Catholic University of America, 1940.

Education

566   Abonyi, Malvina H. The Role of Ethnic Church Schools in the History of Education in the United States: The Detroit Experience, 1850-1920. Ed.D., Wayne State University, 1987. 166p. UMI# 8714526.

567   Balmain, Alexander F. The History of Catholic Education in the Diocese of Brooklyn. Ph.D., Fordham University, 1935.

568   Bernad, Miguel A. The Faculty of Arts in the Jesuit Colleges in the Eastern Part of the United States: Theory and Practice (1782-1923). Ph.D., Yale University, 1951. 483p. UMI# 8507574.

569   Bernert, Roman A. A Study of the Responses of Jesuit Educators in Theory and Practice to the Transformation of Curricular Patterns in Popular Secondary Education Between 1880 and 1920. Ph.D., University of Wisconsin-Madison, 1963. 436p. UMI# 6307578.

570   Bigney, John W. A Study of the Jesuits as Educators. Ph.D., Boston University, 1886.

571   Blom, Mary C. Educational Supervision in our Catholic Schools; A Study of the Origin, Development, and Technique of Supervision by Our Teaching Communities. Ph.D., Catholic University of America, 1926.

572   Bollig, Richard. History of Catholic Education in Kansas (1836-1931). Ph.D., Catholic University of America, 1934.

573   Bowler, M. Mariella. Catholic Higher Education for Women in the

United States. Ph.D., Catholic University of America, 1934.

574   Brewer, Eileen M. Beyond Utility: The Role of the Nun in the Education of American Catholic Girls, 1860 to 1920. Ph.D., University of Chicago, 1984.

575   Buttell, Mary F. A History of Catholic Colleges for Women in the United States of America. Ph.D., Catholic University of America, 1934.

576   Cassidy, Francis P. Catholic College Foundations and Development in the United States (1677-1850). Ph.D., Catholic University of America, 1924.

577   Chase, Cornelius T. Roman Catholic Education in the United States. Ph.D., Hartford Seminary Foundation, 1938.

578   Colasuonno, Michael L. Early Franciscanism as a Prophetic Educational Movement. Ph.D., New York University, 1974. 419p. UMI# 7508536.

579   Condon, M. Andree. The Development of the Financial Procedures for the Establishment and Maintenance of Catholic Schools in the Archdiocese of New Orleans, 1727-1958. Ph.D., Louisiana State University, 1959. 421p. UMI# 59-03072.

580   Connaughton, Edward A. A History of Educational Legislation and Administration in the Archdiocese of Cincinnati. Ph.D., Catholic University of America, 1947. 271p.

581   Costello, William J. The Chronological Development of the Catholic Secondary School in the Archdiocese of Philadelphia. Ed.D., Temple University, 1957. 267p. UMI# 24858.

582   Curry, Catherine A. Shaping Young San Franciscans: Public and Catholic Schools in San Francisco, 1851-1906. Ph.D., Graduate Theological Union, 1987. 391p. UMI# 8802867.

583   Daley, John M. Georgetown College: The First Fifty Years. Ph.D., Georgetown University, 1953.

584   Dalton, M. Arthemise. The History and Development of the Catholic Secondary School System in the Archdiocese of Detroit, 1701-1961. Ed.D., Wayne State University, 1962. 225p. UMI# 62-00906.

585   Di Michele, Charles C. The History of the Roman Catholic Educational System in Mississippi. Ed.D., Mississippi State

University, 1973. 217p. UMI# 74-02915.

586   Diederich, Alphonsus F. A History of Accreditation, Certification and Teacher Training in Catholic Institutions of Higher Learning in California. Ph.D., University of California-Los Angeles, 1958.

587   Diffley, Jerome E. Catholic Reaction to American Public Education, 1792-1852. Ph.D., University of Notre Dame, 1959. 354p. UMI# 59-03658.

588   Dixon, Henry W. An Historical Survey of Jesuit Higher Education in the United States With Particular Reference to the Objectives of Education. Ed.D., Arizona State University, 1974. 196p. UMI# 74-19282.

589   Doherty, M. Michael. History of Catholic Secondary Education in California. Ph.D., University of California-Berkeley, 1940. 190p.

590   Dunigan, David R. A History of Boston College. Ph.D., Fordham University, 1945. 411p.

591   Dunn, William K. The Decline of the Teaching of Religion in the American Public Elementary School, 1776-1861. Ph.D., Johns Hopkins University, 1956.

592   Eftink, Edward M. The Development of the Legal Status of Catholic Education in Missouri. Ph.D., Catholic University of America, 1971. 268p. UMI# 7114079.

593   Erbacher, Sebastian A. Catholic Higher Education for Men in the United States, 1850-1866. Ph.D., Catholic University of America, 1931. 143p.

594   Flynn, Austin. The School Controversy in New York, 1840-1842, and Its Effect on the Formulation of Catholic Elementary School Policy. Ph.D., University of Notre Dame, 1962. 263p. UMI# 63-01063.

595   Francis De Sales, Brother. The Catholic High School Curriculum, Its Development and Present Status. Ph.D., Catholic University of America, 1930.

596   Gillis, Herbert R. The History, Theory and Practice of Speech Education at Georgetown, 1789 to 1890, First Jesuit College in the United States. Ph.D., Western Reserve University, 1958. 172p.

597   Goebel, Edmund J. A Study of Catholic Secondary Education During the Colonial Period up to the First Plenary Council of Baltimore, 1852. Ph.D., Catholic University of America, 1936.

598   Goodchild, Lester F. The Mission of the Catholic University in the Midwest, 1842-1980: A Comparative Case Study of the Effects of Strategic Policy Decisions Upon the Mission of the University of Notre Dame, Loyola University of Chicago, and DePaul University. Ph.D., University of Chicago, 1986.

599   Gorka, Ronald R. Establishing Catholic Collegiate Education in America: Georgetown College, 1784-1832. Ph.D., Harvard University, 1964.

600   Grollmes, Eugene E. The Educational Theory of John Lancaster Spalding: The Ideal of Heroism. Ph.D., Boston College, 1969. 295p. UMI# 7002453.

601   Harney, Paul J. A History of Jesuit Education in American California. Ph.D., University of California-Berkeley, 1944. 184p.

602   Heffernan, Arthur J. A History of Catholic Education in Connecticut. Ph.D., Catholic University of America, 1936. 132p.

603   Jones, Thomas P. The Development of the Office of Prefect of Religion at the University of Notre Dame From 1842 to 1952. Ph.D., Catholic University of America, 1960.

604   Jones, William H. The History of Catholic Education in the State of Colorado. Ph.D., Catholic University of America, 1955. 105p.

605   Kaiser, M. Laurina. Development of the Concept and Function of the Catholic Elementary School in the American Parish. Ph.D., Catholic University of America, 1955. 105p.

606   Kearns, Geraldine A. St. Mary's Training School (1882-1930): The Function of Education in Society as Reflected in a Catholic Institution. Ph.D., Loyola University of Chicago, 1988. 210p. UMI# 8817931.

607   Kegress, M. St. Laure. A History of Catholic Education in New Hampshire. Ph.D., Boston University, 1955. 105p.

608   Kenneally, F. The Catholic Seminaries of California as Educational Institutions, 1840-1950. Ph.D., University of Toronto, 1956.

609   Kennelly, Edward F. A Historical Study of Seton Hall College. Ph.D., New York University, 1944. 246p. UMI# 73-08627.

610   Klein, Christa R. The Jesuits and Catholic Boyhood in Nineteenth-Century New York City: A Study of St. John's College and the College of St. Francis Xavier, 1846-1912. Ph.D., University

of Pennsylvania, 1976. 410p. UMI# 77-10180.

611   Kunkel, Norlene M. Bishop Bernard J. McQuaid and Catholic
       Education. Ph.D., University of Notre Dame, 1974. 283p. UMI#
       74-20588.

612   Lafferty, James K. The Development of Clerical Latin Pedagogy and
       the American Four-Year Seminary High School. Ph.D., Saint Louis
       University, 1965. 186p. UMI# 6507052.

613   Lamonte, Ruth B. Early Maryland Education: The Colonials, the
       Catholics, and the Carrolls. Ph.D., Ohio State University, 1976. 238p.
       UMI# 76-18001.

614   Leary, Mary A. The History of Catholic Education in the Diocese
       of Albany. Ph.D., Catholic University of America, 1957.

615   Linehan, Joseph A. The History of the Augustinians in the Middle
       West as a Teaching Order. Ph.D., Loyola University of Chicago,
       1965.

616   Lucey, Michael H. The Catholic Parish Schools in New York City;
       Their Principles, Origin and Establishment. Ph.D., New York
       University, 1909. 169p. UMI# 7322246.

617   Luetmer, Nora. The History of Catholic Education in the Present
       Diocese of St. Cloud, Minnesota, 1855-1965. Ph.D., University of
       Minnesota, 1970. 561p. UMI# 71-08180.

618   Mattice, Howard L. The Growth and Development of Roman
       Catholic Education in New York City: 1842-1875. Ed.D., New York
       University, 1979. 261p. UMI# 79-11276.

619   McDermott, Maria C. A History of Teacher Education in a
       Congregation of Religious Women: 1843-1964, Sisters of the Holy
       Cross. Ph.D., University of Notre Dame, 1964. 365p. UMI# 65-1133.

620   McDonald, Lloyd P. The Seminary Movement in the United States:
       Projects, Foundations, and Early Development. Ph.D., Catholic
       University of America, 1927.

621   McDonnell, James M., Jr. Orestes A. Brownson and
       Nineteenth-Century Catholic Education. Ph.D., University of Notre
       Dame, 1975. 392p. UMI# 76-02334.

622   McGucken, William J. Jesuit Secondary Education in the United
       States. Ph.D., University of Chicago, 1927.

623   McKevitt, Gerald. The History of Santa Clara College, a Study of Jesuit Education in California, 1851-1912. Ph.D., University of California-Los Angeles, 1972. 372p. UMI# 72-25811.

624   McLaughlin, Raymond. A History of State Legislation Affecting Private Elementary and Secondary Schools in the United States, 1840-1945. Ph.D., Catholic University of America, 1945.

625   McNeil, Teresa B. A History of Catholic School Education in San Diego County, California, From 1850 to 1936. Ed.D., University of San Diego, 1986. 416p. UMI# 8614588.

626   McNulty, Helen P. One Hundred and Ten Years of Education at Xavier. Ph.D., Fordham University, 1958.

627   Meade, Francis L. Progressive Education and Catholic Pedagogy. Ph.D., Niagara University, 1935.

628   Meagher, Walter J. History of the College of the Holy Cross, 1843-1901. Ph.D., Fordham University, 1944. 149p.

629   Meighan, Cecilia. Nativism and Catholic Higher Education, 1840-1860. Ed.D., Columbia University, 1972. 138p. UMI# 72-30340.

630   Meiring, Bernard J. Educational Aspects of the Legislation of the Councils of Baltimore, 1829-1884. Ph.D., University of California-Berkeley, 1963. 320p. UMI# 6405264.

631   Miller, Francis J. A History of the Athenaeum of Ohio, 1829-1960. Ed.D., University of Cincinnati, 1964. 468p. UMI# 64-11973.

632   Montay, M. Innocenta. The History of Catholic Secondary Education in the Archdiocese of Chicago. Ph.D., Catholic University of America, 1953.

633   Morrissey, Timothy H. Archbishop John Ireland and the Faribault-Stillwater School Plan of the 1890's: A Reappraisal. Ph.D., University of Notre Dame, 1975. 354p. UMI# 75-18720.

634   Mundie, Catherine E. Diocesan Organization of Parochial Schools. Studies in Catholic Educational History of the United States. Ph.D., Marquette University, 1936.

635   Murphy, M. Benedict. Pioneer Roman Catholic Girl's Academies: Their Growth, Character, and Contribution to American Education. A Study of Roman Catholic Education for Girls From Colonial Times to the First Plenary Council of 1852. Ph.D., Columbia University, 1958. 337p. UMI# 58-02541.

636   Murphy, Thomas J. History of Catholic Education in Cleveland. Ph.D., Case Western Reserve University, 1944. 93p.

637   Murray, Teresa G. Vocational Guidance in Catholic Secondary Schools; A Study of Development and Present Status. Ph.D., Columbia University, 1939.

638   North, William E. Catholic Education in Southern California. Ph.D., Catholic University of America, 1936.

639   O'Breza, John E. Philadelphia Parochial School System From 1830-1920: Growth and Bureaucratization. Ed.D., Temple University, 1979. 200p. UMI# 80-14554.

640   O'Brien, John J. A History of Catholic Education in the Mississippi Valley, 1704-1866. Ph.D., Saint Louis University, 1951. 134p.

641   O'Brien, M. Agnes. History and Development of Catholic Secondary Education in the Archdiocese of New York. Ph.D., Columbia University, 1950. 242p.

642   O'Connell, Margaret M. The Educational Contributions of the School Sisters of Notre Dame in America for the Century, 1847-1947. Ph.D., Johns Hopkins University, 1950.

643   Paul, Norma A. Catholic Schools and the Religious Teaching Orders in the State of Illinois From 1834 to 1939. Ph.D., Loyola University of Chicago, 1940. 526p.

644   Power, Edward J. The Educational Views and Attitudes of Orestes A. Brownson. Ph.D., University of Notre Dame, 1949.

645   Price, John M. The Catholic Parish School in the United States. Ph.D., Southern Baptist Theological Seminary, 1930.

646   Redden, John D. The History and Development of the Parochial Schools in the Diocese of Manchester, New Hampshire. Ph.D., Fordham University, 1935.

647   Redmond, Catharine F. The Convent School of French Origin in the United States, 1727-1843. Ph.D., University of Pennsylvania, 1936.

648   Rouse, Michael F. A Study of the Development of Negro Education Under Catholic Auspices in Maryland and the District of Columbia. Ph.D., Johns Hopkins University, 1933. 125p.

649   Sanders, James W. The Education of Chicago Catholics: An Urban History. Ph.D., University of Chicago, 1971.

650   Schaefer, M. Luella. The Sources and Development of John Lancaster Spalding's Educational Theory. Ph.D., Saint Louis University, 1962. 397p. UMI# 6403768.

651   Schier, H. Tracy. History of Higher Education for Women at Saint Mary-of-the-Woods: 1840-1980. Ph.D., Boston College, 1987. 294p. UMI# 8807559.

652   Sohn, Frederick H. The Evolution of Catholic Education in the Diocese of Rochester, New York, 1868 to 1970. Ed.D., Indiana University, 1972. 234p. UMI# 73-10785.

653   Steinhauer, Arthur. A History of Parochial Elementary Education in the Diocese of Trenton, New Jersey. Ph.D., Fordham University, 1945. 274p.

654   Sullivan, Daniel C. A History of Catholic Elementary Education in the Archdiocese of Newark, New Jersey. Ph.D., Fordham University, 1942. 89p.

655   Sullivan, M. Xaveria. The History of Catholic Secondary Education in the Archdiocese of Boston. Ph.D., Catholic University of America, 1945. 317p.

656   Tlochenska, Mary S. The American Hierarchy and Education: Studies in Catholic Educational History of the United States (1493-1920). Ph.D., Marquette University, 1934.

657   Vosper, James M. A History of Selected Factors in the Development of Creighton University. Ph.D., University of Nebraska-Lincoln, 1976. 278p. UMI# 77-00955.

658   Wack, John T. The University of Notre Dame du Lac: Foundation, 1842-1857. Ph.D., University of Notre Dame, 1967. 378p. UMI# 67-13606.

659   Walch, Timothy G. Catholic Education in Chicago and Milwaukee, 1840-1890. Ph.D., Northwestern University, 1975. 249p. UMI# 76-12170.

660   White, Elizabeth L. Adult Education and Cultural Invasion: A Case Study of the Salish and the Jesuits. Ed.D., Montana State University, 1990. 187p. UMI# 9103074.

661   Wilson, M. Debora. Benedictine Higher Education and the Development of American Higher Education. Ph.D., University of Michigan, 1969. 353p. UMI# 69-18138.

662   Wohlwend, Mary V. The Educational Principles of Dr. Thomas E. Shields and Their Impact on His Teacher Training Program at the Catholic University of America. Ph.D., Catholic University of America, 1968. 160p. UMI# 69-08902.

663   Yeakel, Mary A. The Nineteenth Century Educational Contribution of the Sisters of Charity of Saint Vincent de Paul in Virginia. Ph.D., Johns Hopkins University, 1938.

Ethnic Groups

664   Alexander, Sylvia J.G. The Immigrant Church and Community: The Formation of Pittsburgh's Slovak Religious Institutions, 1880-1914. Ph.D., University of Minnesota, 1980. 696p. UMI# 8102061.

665   Barry, Colman J. The Catholic Church and German Americans. Ph.D., Catholic University of America, 1953. 348p.

666   Beadles, John A. The Syracuse Irish, 1812-1928: Immigration, Catholicism, Socioeconomic Status, Politics, and Irish Nationalism. Ph.D., Syracuse University, 1974. 508p. UMI# 76-07881.

667   Cross, Lawrence J. The Catholics of Norristown, Pennsylvania. Ph.D., University of Pennsylvania, 1962. 338p. UMI# 62-04273.

668   Grummer, James E. The Parish Life of German-Speaking Roman Catholics in Milwaukee, Wisconsin, 1840-1920. Ph.D., University of Notre Dame, 1989. 286p. UMI# 8901491.

669   Liptak, Dolores A. European Immigrants and the Catholic Church in Connecticut, 1870-1920. Ph.D., University of Connecticut, 1979. 459p. UMI# 79-14170.

670   Niehaus, Juliet A. Ethnic Formation and Transformation: The German-Catholics of Dubois County, Indiana 1838-1979. Ph.D., New School for Social Research, 1981. 240p. UMI# 8202145.

671   Rothan, Emmet H. The German Catholic Immigrant in the United States, 1830-1860. Ph.D., Catholic University of America, 1947. 202p.

672   Russo, Nicholas J. The Religious Acculturation of the Italians in New York City. Ph.D., St. John's University, 1968. 349p. UMI# 69-04141.

673   Sable, Thomas F. Lay Initiative in Greek Catholic Parishes in Connecticut, New York, New Jersey, and Pennsylvania (1884-1909). Ph.D., Graduate Theological Union, 1985. 261p. UMI# 8513080.

674   Saueressig, Yda. Emigration, Settlement, and Assimilation of Dutch
        Catholic Immigrants in Wisconsin, 1850-1905. Ph.D., University of
        Wisconsin, 1982. 286p. UMI# 8306694.

675   Shanabruch, Charles H. The Catholic Church's Role in the
        Americanization of Chicago's Immigrants: 1833-1928. Ph.D.,
        University of Chicago, 1975.

676   Tomasi, Silvano M. Assimilation and Religion: The Role of the
        Italian Ethnic Church in the Metropolitan New York Area,
        1880-1930. Ph.D., Fordham University, 1972. 445p. UMI# 73-04305.

677   Young, John H. The Acadians and Roman Catholicism: In Acadia
        From 1710 to the Expulsion, in Exile, and in Louisiana From the
        1760's Until 1803. Ph.D., Southern Methodist University, 1988. 453p.
        UMI# 8815648.

Evangelism

678   Jonas, Thomas J. The Divided Mind: American Catholic Evangelists
        in the 1890s. Ph.D., University of Chicago, 1980.

679   Kennedy, John H. New France and the European Conscience. Ph.D.,
        Yale University, 1942. 360p. UMI# 7010719.

680   Mentag, John V. Catholic Spiritual Revivals: Parish Missions in the
        Midwest to 1865. Ph.D., Loyola University of Chicago, 1957.

Historiography

681   Cadden, John P. The Historiography of the American Catholic
        Church, 1785-1943. Ph.D., Catholic University of America, 1943.

Literature

682   Barnes, Daniel R. An Edition of the Early Letters of Orestes
        Brownson. Ph.D., University of Kentucky, 1970. 412p. UMI#
        7119353.

683   Bochen, Christine M. Personal Narratives by Nineteenth-Century
        American Catholics: A Study in Conversion Literature. Ph.D.,
        Catholic University of America, 1980. 438p. UMI# 8018511.

684   Drummond, Edward J. Catholic Criticism in America: Studies of
        Brownson, Azarias, and Egan, With an Essay for Catholic Critics.
        Ph.D., University of Iowa, 1942.

685   Durick, Jeremiah K. Catholicism and the Literature of New England

(1815-1865). Ph.D., University of Ottawa, 1943.

686   Gower, Joseph F., Jr. The *New Apologetics* of Isaac Thomas Hecker (1819-88): Catholicity and American Culture. Ph.D., University of Notre Dame, 1978. 281p. UMI# 77-28177.

687   Hollis, Charles C. The Literary Criticism of Orestes Brownson. Ph.D., University of Michigan, 1954. 482p. UMI# 8321.

688   Litz, Francis E.A. Father Tabb; A Study of His Poetry. Ph.D., Johns Hopkins University, 1921.

689   McCarthy, Leonard J. Rhetoric in the Works of Orestes Brownson. Ph.D., Fordham University, 1961. 279p. UMI# 6101576.

690   McInnis, Mary A. The Contribution of Catholic Women to Catholic Thought in the Catholic Literary Periodicals of the United States in the Nineteenth Century. Ph.D., Boston College, 1939.

691   Messbarger, Paul R. American Catholic Dialogue, 1884-1900: A Study of Catholic Fiction. Ph.D., University of Minnesota, 1969. 325p. UMI# 69-18464.

692   Muller, Herman J. Jesuit Writings of the 17th and 18th Centuries and British-American Trade. Ph.D., Loyola University of Chicago, 1950.

693   Panchok, Frances. The Catholic Church and the Theatre in New York, 1890-1920. Ph.D., Catholic University of America, 1976. 606p. UMI# 76-19372.

694   Vollmar, Edward R. Publications on United States Catholic Church History, 1850-1950. Ph.D., Saint Louis University, 1955.

695   White, James A. The Era of Good Intentions: A Survey of American Catholics' Writing Between the Years 1880-1915. Ph.D., University of Notre Dame, 1957. 377p. UMI# 22143.

Liturgy

696   Carmody, Charles J. The Roman Catholic Catechesis in the United States 1784-1930: A Study of Its Theory, Development, and Materials. Ph.D., Loyola University of Chicago, 1975. 606p. UMI# 75-14504.

Missions and Missionaries

697   Donohue, Arthur T. The History of the Early Jesuit Missions in

Kansas. Ph.D., University of Kansas, 1940. 256p. UMI# 00160.

698   Donohue, John A. Jesuit Missions in Northwestern New Spain, 1711-1767. Ph.D., University of California-Berkeley, 1957.

699   Downey, Mary M. The Expulsion of the Jesuits From Baja California. Ph.D., University of California-Berkeley, 1940. 239p.

700   Dunne, Peter M. The Four Rivers: Early Jesuit Missions on the Pacific Coast. Ph.D., University of California-Berkeley, 1935.

701   Farnsworth, Paul. The Economics of Acculturation in the California Missions: A Historical and Archaeological Study of Mission Nuestra Senora de la Soledad. Ph.D., University of California-Los Angeles, 1987. 683p. UMI# 8720008.

702   Fitzgerald, Mary P. Beacon on the Plains. Ph.D., Saint Mary College, 1939. 297p.

703   Geary, Gerald J. The Secularization of the California Missions (1810-1846). Ph.D., Catholic University of America, 1934.

704   Geiger, Maynard. The Franciscan Conquest of Florida, 1573-1618. Ph.D., Catholic University of America, 1937.

705   Gradie, Charlotte M. Jesuit Missions in Spanish North America, 1566-1623. Ph.D., University of Connecticut, 1990. 292p. UMI# 9109848.

706   Hanzeli, Victor E. Early Descriptions by French Missionaries of Algonquian and Iroquoian Languages: A Study of Seventeenth- and Eighteenth-Century Practice in Linguistics. Ph.D., Indiana University, 1961. 274p. UMI# 6104443.

707   Hickey, Edward J. The Society for the Propagation of the Faith: Its Foundation, Organization and Success. Ph.D., Catholic University of America, 1922.

708   Hogue, Harland E. A History of Religion in Southern California: 1846-1880. Ph.D., Columbia University, 1958. 386p. UMI# 58-02687.

709   Kessell, John L. Mission Los Santos Angeles de Guevavi: Jesuits on the Pima Frontier, 1691-1797. Ph.D., University of New Mexico, 1969. 295p. UMI# 70-16386.

710   Lee, Frederic E. The Influence of the Jesuits on the Social Organization of the North American Indians. Ph.D., Yale University, 1916.

711   Leger, Mary C. The Catholic Indian Missions in Maine (1611-1820). Ph.D., Catholic University of America, 1929. 184p.

712   Lyons, Letitia M. Francis Norbert Blanchet and the Founding of the Oregon Missions (1838-1848). Ph.D., Catholic University of America, 1940. 239p.

713   Matter, Robert A. The Spanish Missions of Florida: The Friars Versus the Governors in the "Golden Age" 1606-1690. Ph.D., University of Washington, 1972. 439p. UMI# 72-28631.

714   Moore, James T. The Amerind-Jesuit Encounter: A Study in Cultural Adaptation in Seventeenth Century French North America. Ph.D., Texas A&M University, 1980. 321p. UMI# 8023055.

715   Mulvey, M. Doris. French Catholic Missionaries in the Present United States (1604-1791). Ph.D., Catholic University of America, 1936.

716   Nieser, Albert B. The Dominican Mission Foundations in Baja, California, 1769-1822. Ph.D., Loyola University of Chicago, 1960.

717   Norton, Mary A. Catholic Missionary Activities in the Northwest, 1818-1864. Ph.D., Catholic University of America, 1930. 154p.

718   O'Rourke, Thomas P. The Franciscan Missions in Texas (1690-1793). Ph.D., Catholic University of America, 1927. 107p.

719   Owens, Mary L. The History of the Sisters of Loretto in the Trans-Mississippi West: An Historical Study of Origins and Westward Expansion From 1812 to 1935. Ph.D., Saint Louis University, 1935. 647p. UMI# 186.

720   Padden, Robert C. The Colonial Church in New Spain: Era of Establishment. Ph.D., University of California-Berkeley, 1959.

721   Phelps, Jamie T. The Mission Ecclesiology of John R. Slattery: A Study of an African-American Mission of the Catholic Church in the Nineteenth Century. Ph.D., Catholic University of America, 1989. 404p. UMI# 8917035.

722   Polzer, Charles W. The Evolution of the Jesuit Mission System in Northwestern New Spain, 1600-1767. Ph.D., University of Arizona, 1972. 278p. UMI# 7306731.

723   Rahill, Peter J. The Catholic Indian Missions and Grant's Peace Policy. Ph.D., Catholic American University, 1954.

724   Roemer, Theodore. The Ludwig-Missionsverein and the Church in the United States (1838-1918). Ph.D., Catholic University of America, 1934.

725   Schuetz, Mardith K. The Indians of the San Antonio Missions, 1718-1821. Ph.D., University of Texas-Austin, 1980. 411p. UMI# 80-21509.

726   Thomas, George L. Catholics and the Missions of the Pacific-Northwest, 1826-1853. Ph.D., University of Washington, 1986. 258p. UMI# 8706683.

727   White, Mary A. Catholic Indian Missionary Influence in the Development of Catholic Education in Montana, 1840-1903. Ph.D., Saint Louis University, 1940. 238p. UMI# 00482.

Newspapers and Periodicals

728   Beiser, J. Ryan. The American Secular Newspapers and the Vatican Council, 1869-1870. Ph.D., Catholic University of America, 1942. 154p.

729   Connaughton, Mary S. The Opinion of the *Catholic Telegraph* on Contemporary Affairs, 1871-1921. Ph.D., Catholic University of America, 1943.

730   Hueston, Robert F. The Catholic Press and Nativism, 1840-1860. Ph.D., University of Notre Dame, 1972. 361p. UMI# 72-26807.

731   Huger, Gregory C. The Catholic Press of the United States on Church and State Relationship 1865-1895. Ph.D., Saint Louis University, 1950. 227p.

732   Kulas, John S. *Der Wanderer* of St. Paul, the First Decade, 1867-1877: A Mirror of the German-Catholic Immigrant Experience in Minnesota. Ph.D., University of Minnesota, 1988. 363p. UMI# 8900545.

733   Thomas, Samuel J. The Response of the Periodical Press in the United States to the Intervention of Pope Leo XIII (1878-1903) Into Major Episodes of American Catholic History. Ph.D., Michigan State University, 1971. 242p. UMI# 72-16525.

Organizational Structure

734   Ayers, Robert C. The Americanists and Franz Xaver Kraus: An Historical Analysis of an International Liberal Catholic Combination, 1897-1898. Ph.D., Syracuse University, 1981. 345p. UMI# 82-06965.

735   Bailey, James H., II. A History of the Diocese of Richmond From Its Erection, 1820, to the Coming of Bishop Gibbons, 1872. Ph.D., Georgetown University, 1953.

736   Casey, Thomas F. The Sacred Congregation de Propaganda Fide and the Revision of the First Provincial Council of Baltimore, 1829-1830. Ph.D., Apud Aedes Universitatis Gregorianae, 1957. 233p.

737   Ciesluk, Joseph E. National Parishes in the United States. Ph.D., Catholic University of America, 1944.

738   Harte, Thomas J. Catholic Organizations Promoting Negro-White Relations in the United States. Ph.D., Catholic University of America, 1947. 202p.

739   Hennesey, James J. The Bishops of the United States at the First Vatican Council. Ph.D., Catholic University of America, 1963. 562p. UMI# 63-06822.

740   Jaeger, Leo A. The Administration of Vacant and Quasi-Vacant Dioceses in the United States; Historical Synopsis of General Legislation and Commentary. Ph.D., Catholic University of America, 1932.

741   Manfra, Jo Ann. The Catholic Episcopacy in America, 1789-1852. Ph.D., University of Iowa, 1975. 292p. UMI# 75-23064.

742   Misner, Barbara. A Comparative Social Study of the Members and Apostolates of the First Eight Permanent Communities of Women Religious Within the Original Boundaries of the United States 1790-1850. Ph.D., Catholic University of America, 1981. 323p. UMI# 8111639.

743   O'Donnell, John H. The Catholic Hierarchy of the United States, 1790-1922. Ph.D., Catholic University of America, 1922. 223p.

744   Schafer, Marvin R. The Catholic Church in Chicago, Its Growth and Administration. Ph.D., University of Chicago, 1929.

Preaching

745   Connors, Joseph M. Catholic Homiletic Theory in Historical Perspective. Ph.D., Northwestern University, 1962. 495p. UMI# 63-01277.

746   Martin, Albert T. Pulpit and Platform Speaking of Thomas N. Burke. Ph.D., University of Wisconsin, 1956. 408p. UMI# 19118.

747 O'Fahey, Charles J. Gibbons, Ireland, Keane: The Evolution of a Liberal Catholic Rhetoric in America. Ph.D., University of Minnesota, 1980. 165p. UMI# 8102141.

Religious Orders

748 Barnhiser, Judith A. A Study of the Authority Structures of Three Nineteenth-Century Apostolic Communities of Religious Women in the United States. J.C.D., Catholic University of America, 1975. 252p. UMI# 75-21259.

749 Berg, Carol J. Climbing Learners' Hill: Benedictines at White Earth, 1878-1945. Ph.D., University of Minnesota, 1981. 225p. UMI# 8206328.

750 Cooke, M. Francis. History of the Hospital Sisters of the Third Order of St. Francis. Ph.D., Marquette University, 1943. [Springfield(IL)].

751 Deacon, Florence J. Handmaids or Autonomous Women: The Charitable Activities, Institution Building and Communal Relationships of Catholic Sisters in Nineteenth Century Wisconsin. Ph.D., University of Wisconsin-Madison, 1989. 420p. UMI# 9013338.

752 Delanglez, Jean. The French Jesuits in Lower Louisiana (1700-1763). Ph.D., Catholic University of America, 1935.

753 Dennis, Alfred P. Lord Baltimore's Struggle With the Jesuits. Ph.D., Princeton University, 1901.

754 Ewens, Mary. The Role of the Nun in Nineteenth-Century America: Variations on the International Theme. Ph.D., University of Minnesota, 1971. 434p. UMI# 71-22272.

755 Fallon, Mary L. Early New England Nuns. Ph.D., Boston University, 1936.

756 Finck, Mary H. The Congregation of the Sisters of Charity of the Incarnate Word of San Antonio, Texas. A Brief Account of Its Origin and Its Work. Ph.D., Catholic University of America, 1925. 232p.

757 Heaney, Jane F. A Century of Pioneering: A History of the Ursuline Nuns in New Orleans. Ph.D., Saint Louis University, 1949. 542p.

758 Hebard, Roger D. A Nunnery Movement in Oklahoma. Ph.D., Southwestern Baptist Theological Seminary, 1949. 258p.

759   Jarvis, William. Mother Seton's Sisters of Charity. Ph.D., Columbia University, 1984. 335p. UMI# 8412992.

760   Keefe, St. Thomas A. The Congregation of the Grey Nuns (1737-1910). Ph.D., Catholic University of America, 1943.

761   Maher, Mary D. "To Do With Honor": The Roman Catholic Sister Nurse in the United States Civil War. Ph.D., Case Western Reserve University, 1988. 384p. UMI# 8811189.

762   Mannard, Joseph G. "Maternity of the Spirit": Women Religious in the Archdiocese of Baltimore, 1790-1860. Ph.D., University of Maryland, 1989. 392p. UMI# 9021542.

763   Ochs, Stephen J. Deferred Mission: The Josephites and the Struggle for Black Catholic Priests, 1871-1960. Ph.D., University of Maryland, 1985. 578p. UMI# 8614263.

764   Palm, Mary B. The Jesuit Missions of the Illinois Country, 1673-1763. Ph.D., Saint Louis University, 1931.

765   Renz, Jan E. The Role of the A.S.C. Ministry of Education in the United States (1870-1989) and Its Relation to the Congregation's Mission. Ph.D., Saint Louis University, 1990. 240p. UMI# 9102925.

766   Savage, Mary L. The Congregation of Saint Joseph of Carondelet: A Brief Account of Its Origin and Its Work in the United States, 1650-1922. Ph.D., Catholic University of America, 1923.

767   Scatena, Maria. Educational Movements That Have Influenced the Sister Teacher Education Program of the Congregation of the Sisters of Providence 1840-1940. Ph.D., Loyola University of Chicago, 1987. 317p. UMI# 8718294.

768   Schintz, Mary A. An Investigation of the Modernizing Role of the Maryknoll Sisters in China. Ph.D., University of Wisconsin-Madison, 1978. 571p. UMI# 7815070.

769   Treutlein, Theodore E. Jesuit Travel to America (1678-1756) as Recorded in the Travel Diaries of German Jesuits. Ph.D., University of California-Berkeley, 1934.

770   Vogel, Claude L. The Capuchins in French Louisiana (1722-1766). Ph.D., Catholic University of America, 1928.

771   Winthrop, Robert H. Norm and Tradition in American Benedictine Monasticism. Ph.D., University of Minnesota, 1981. 395p. UMI# 8206437.

Social Programs

772   Bland, Joan. The Catholic Total Abstinence Union of America, 1872-1918. Ph.D., Catholic University of America, 1952.

773   Brophy, Mary L. Social Thought of the Central Verein. Ph.D., Catholic University of America, 1942.

774   Donohoe, Joan M. The Irish Catholic Benevolent Union, 1869-1893. Ph.D., Catholic University of America, 1954.

775   Gannon, Michael V. Augustin Verot and the Emergence of American Catholic Social Consciousness. Ph.D., University of Florida, 1962. 248p. UMI# 63-02668.

776   Hoffman, George J. Catholic Immigrant Aid Societies in New York City From 1880 to 1920. Ph.D., St. John's University, 1947. 193p.

777   Holland, Timothy J. The Catholic Church and the Negro in the United States Prior to the Civil War. Ph.D., Fordham University, 1950. 404p.

778   Jacoby, George P. Catholic Child Care in the Nineteenth Century New York With a Correlated Summary of Public and Protestant Child Welfare. Ph.D., Catholic University of America, 1941. 499p.

779   Miceli, Mary V. The Influence of the Roman Catholic Church on Slavery in Colonial Louisiana Under French Domination, 1718-1763. Ph.D., Tulane University, 1979. 233p. UMI# 79-28726.

780   Nuesse, Celestine J. The Social Thought of the American Catholic, 1634-1829. Ph.D., Catholic University of America, 1944. 346p.

781   Roohan, James E., Jr. American Catholics and the Social Question, 1865-1900. Ph.D., Yale University, 1952. 215p.

782   Schuller, M. Viatora. A History of Catholic Orphan Homes in the United States From 1727 to 1884. Ph.D., Loyola University of Chicago, 1954.

783   Tarbox, Mary P. The Origins of Nursing by the Sisters of Mercy in the United States: 1843-1910. Ed.D., Columbia University Teachers College, 1986. 275p. UMI# 8704315.

784   Walton, Susan S. To Preserve the Faith: Catholic Charities in Boston, 1870 to 1930. Ph.D., Boston University, 1983. 271p. UMI# 8320022.

785   Webster, Anne K. The Impact of Catholic Hospitals in St. Louis. Ph.D., Saint Louis University, 1968. 442p. UMI# 68-14087.

786   Weitzman, Louis G. One Hundred Years of Catholic Charities in the District of Columbia. Ph.D., Catholic University of America, 1931. 161p.

Theology

787   Appleby, Robert S. American Catholic Modernism at the Turn of the Century. Ph.D., University of Chicago, 1985.

788   Dease, Dennis J. The Theological Influence of Orestes Brownson and Isaac Hecker on John Ireland's Americanist Ecclesiology. Ph.D., Catholic University of America, 1978. 371p. UMI# 78-16947.

789   Farina, John E. Isaac Hecker and the Holy Spirit. Ph.D., Columbia University, 1979. 357p. UMI# 82-04478.

790   Griffioen, Arie J. Orestes Brownson's Synthetic Theology of Revelation (1826-1844). Ph.D., Marquette University, 1988. 228p. UMI# 8904255.

791   Haggerty, William J., Jr. Realism in the Philosophy of Orestes A. Brownson. Ph.D., Boston University, 1960. 253p. UMI# 6003452.

792   Hennessy, Paul K. The Theological Influence of the Declaration of Papal Infallibility on the Church in the United States. Ph.D., Catholic University of America, 1977. 376p. UMI# 77-27715.

793   Kaib, Virginia L. The Ecclesiology of John England, The First Bishop of Charleston, South Carolina (1821-1842). Ph.D., Marquette University, 1968. 172p. UMI# 69-03317.

794   Kenny, Gregory D. An Historical Theological Study of Orestes Brownson's Thought on the Church and the Progress of Civil Society. S.T.D., Catholic University of America, 1966. 229p. UMI# 67-06852.

795   Killen, Patricia O. Critique and Conversion: Orestes A. Brownson's Catholic Critique of Industrialization. Ph.D., Stanford University, 1987. 419p. UMI# 8720408.

796   Leliaert, Richard M. Orestes A. Brownson (1803-1876): Theological Perspectives on His Search for the Meaning of God, Christology, and the Development of Doctrine. Ph.D., Graduate Theological Union, 1974. 277p. UMI# 74-23191.

797   Micek, Adam A. The Apologetics of Martin John Spalding. Ph.D.,
           Catholic University of America, 1951.

798   Michel, Virgil G. The Critical Principles of Orestes A. Brownson.
           Ph.D., Catholic University of America, 1918.

799   Newman, Josephine K. Changing Perspectives in Brownson's
           Philosophical Thought. Ph.D., University of Toronto, 1971.

800   Wangler, Thomas E. The Ecclesiology of Archbishop John Ireland:
           Its Nature, Development, and Influence. Ph.D., Marquette
           University, 1968. 270p. UMI# 70-17412.

CHRISTIAN CHURCH

801   Dunnavant, Anthony L. Restructure: Four Historical Ideals in the
           Campbell-Stone Movement and the Development of the Policy of
           the Christian Church. Ph.D., Vanderbilt University, 1984. 678p.
           UMI# 8522468.

802   Hanchett, William F., Jr. Religion and the Gold Rush, 1849-1854:
           The Christian Churches in the California Mines. Ph.D., University
           of California-Berkeley, 1952.

803   Paddick, Kenneth L. Union Christian College: 1858-1924. Ph.D.,
           Southern Illinois University-Carbondale, 1986. 182p. UMI# 8623003.

CHRISTIAN REFORMED

804   Goris, George. Puritan Legalism as a Method of Moral and
           Religious Reform in the Christian Reformed Church. Th.D., Union
           Theological Seminary, 1930.

805   Kromminga, John H. The Christian Reformed Church: A Study in
           Orthodoxy. Ph.D., Princeton Theological Seminary, 1948. 301p.

CHURCH OF CHRIST

806   Campbell, Thomas L. The Contributions of David Lipscomb and the
           Gospel Advocate to Religious Education in the Churches of Christ.
           D.R.E., Southern Baptist Theological Seminary, 1968. 232p. UMI#
           68-14919.

807   Eckstein, Stephen D. History of Churches of Christ in Texas,
           1824-1950. Ph.D., Texas Tech University, 1960.

808   Hooper, Robert E. The Political and Educational Ideas of David
           Lipscomb. Ph.D., George Peabody College for Teachers of

Vanderbilt University, 1965. 259p. UMI# 6610702.

809   Morrison, Matthew C. Daniel Sommer's Seventy Years of Religious
           Controversy. Ph.D., Indiana University, 1972. 291p. UMI# 72-18533.

810   Poyner, Barry C. Role Duality as Represented in the
           Anti-Abolitionist Speeches of James Shannon. Ph.D., Louisiana State
           University, 1990. 198p. UMI# 9104164.

811   Scarboro, Charles A. A Sectarian Religious Organization in
           Heterogeneous Society: The Churches of Christ and the Plain-Folk
           of the Transmontane Mid-South. Ph.D., Emory University, 1976.
           198p. UMI# 7712157.

812   Ulrey, Evan A. The Preaching of Barton Warren Stone. Ph.D.,
           Louisiana State University, 1955. 352p. UMI# 12533.

CHURCH OF CHRIST, SCIENTIST

813   Gottschalk, Stephen. The Emergence of Christian Science in
           American Religious Life, 1885-1910. Ph.D., University of
           California-Berkeley, 1969. 595p. UMI# 70-06109.

814   Hansen, Penny. Woman's Hour: Feminist Implications of Mary
           Baker Eddy's Christian Science Movement, 1885-1910. Ph.D.,
           University of California, 1981. 484p. UMI# 8118470.

815   Lamme, Ary J., III. The Spatial and Ecological Characteristics of the
           Diffusion of Christian Science in the United States: 1875-1910.
           D.S.S., Syracuse University, 1968. 212p. UMI# 69-08633.

816   Twitchell, Remington E. An Analysis of the Published Writings of
           Mary Baker Eddy to Determine Metaphysical Concepts That
           Christian Scientists Might Apply to Selected Business and Personal
           Financial Problems. Ph.D., New York University, 1977. 305p. UMI#
           78-08494.

CHURCH OF GOD

817   Clear, Valorous B. The Church of God: A Study in Social
           Adaptation. Ph.D., University of Chicago, 1954.

818   Forrest, Aubrey L. A Study of the Development of the Basic
           Doctrines and Institutional Patterns in the Church of God. Ph.D.,
           University of Southern California, 1948.

819   Strege, Merle D. "Where Scandinavian Is Spoken": Ethnic Identity
           and Assimilation Among Scandinavian Immigrants in the Church of

God. Th.D., Graduate Theological Union, 1982. 335p. UMI# 82-19273.

CONGREGATIONAL

General Studies

820   Akin, M. Barbara. The Standing Order: Congregationalism in Connecticut 1708-1818. Ph.D., University of Chicago, 1971.

821   Boaz, Roy D. The First Congregational Church of West Haven, Connecticut. Ph.D., Yale University, 1938.

822   Broadbent, Charles D. A Time to Be Born...And to Die: Plymouth Church of Rochester in Retrospect. Ph.D., Colgate Rochester Divinity School/Bexley Hall/Crozer Theological Seminary, 1978.

823   Bryant, Marcus D. History and Eschatology in Jonathan Edwards: A Critique of the Heimert Thesis. Ph.D., University of St. Michael's College, 1976.

824   Bumsted, John M. The Pilgrims Progress: The Ecclesiastical History of the Old Colony, 1620-1775. Ph.D., Brown University, 1965. 485p. UMI# 65-13635.[Plymouth(MA)].

825   Canup, John L. American Nature, English Culture: Environmental Thought and the Emergence of a Provincial Mentality in Colonial New England, 1620-1730. Ph.D., University of North Carolina-Chapel Hill, 1986. 674p. UMI# 8711091.

826   Chatfield, Donald F. The Congregationalism of New England and Its Repercussions in England and Scotland, 1641-1662. Ph.D., University of Edinburgh, 1964. 347p.

827   Crosby, Donald A. Horace Bushnell's Theory of Language: A Historical and Philosophical Study. Ph.D., Columbia University, 1963. 391p. UMI# 6405542.

828   Dailey, Barbara R. Root and Branch: New England's Religious Radicals and Their Transatlantic Community, 1600-1660. Ph.D., Boston University, 1984. 362p. UMI# 8724708.

829   Davidson, James W. Eschatology in New England: 1700-1763. Ph.D., Yale University, 1973. 292p. UMI# 7410663.

830   Davis, Margaret H. "Thy Maker Is Thy Husband": The Espousal Metaphor in Seventeenth Century New England. Ph.D., University of Alabama, 1990. 265p. UMI# 9028299.

831   Ehalt, David R. The Development of Early Congregational Theory of the Church, With Special Reference to the Five "Dissenting Brethren" at the Westminster Assembly. Ph.D., Claremont Graduate School, 1969. 324p. UMI# 6914598.

832   Englizian, H. Crosby. Park Street Church: Citadel of New England Orthodoxy. Ph.D., Dallas Theological Seminary, 1966.

833   Goulding, James A. The Controversy Between Solomon Stoddard and the Mathers: Western Versus Eastern Massachusetts Congregationalism. Ph.D., Claremont Graduate School, 1971. 837p. UMI# 71-29653.

834   Grossbart, Stephen R. The Revolutionary Transition; Politics, Religion, and Economy in Eastern Connecticut, 1765-1800. Ph.D., University of Michigan, 1989. 406p. UMI# 9013913.

835   Guelzo, Allen C. The Unanswered Question: The Legacy of Jonathan Edwards's *Freedom of the Will* in Early American Religious Philosophy. Ph.D., University of Pennsylvania, 1986. 485p. UMI# 8614807.

836   Haskell, George W. Formative Factors in the Life and Thought of Southern California Congregationalism, 1850-1908. Ph.D., University of Southern California, 1947.

837   Haycox, Stephen W. Jeremy Belknap and Early American Nationalism: A Study in the Political and Theological Foundations of American Liberty. Ph.D., University of Oregon, 1971. 267p. UMI# 71-23113.

838   Husband, Paul E. Church Membership in Northampton: Solomon Stoddard Versus Jonathan Edwards. Ph.D., Westminster Theological Seminary, 1990. 299p. UMI# 9026392.

839   Langdon, George D., Jr. New Plymouth: A History of the Old Colony. Ph.D., Yale University, 1961. 361p.

840   Marsh, Roger A. Diminishing Respect for the Clergy and the First Great Awakening: A Study in the Antecedents of Revival Among Massachusetts Congregationalists, 1630-1741. Ph.D., Baylor University, 1990. 492p. UMI# 9027784.

841   Miller, Glenn T. The Rise of Evangelical Calvinism: A Study in Jonathan Edwards and the Puritan Tradition. Th.D., Union Theological Seminary, 1971. 552p. UMI# 71-23419.

842   Oberholzer, Emil, Jr. Saints in Sin: A Study of the Disciplinary

Action of the Congregational Churches of Massachusetts in the Colonial and Early National Periods. Ph.D., Columbia University, 1954. 474p. UMI# 08748.

843   Oh, Deok K. The Churches Resurrection: John Cotton's Eschatological Understanding of the Ecclesiastical Reformation. Ph.D., Westminster Theological Seminary, 1987. 260p. UMI# 8720642.

844   Pearson, Samuel C., Jr. The Growth of Denominational Self-Consciousness Among American Congregationalists, 1800-1852. Ph.D., University of Chicago, 1965.

845   Pope, Robert G. The Half-Way Covenant: Church Membership in the Holy Commonwealths: 1648-1690. Ph.D., Yale University, 1967. 297p. UMI# 68-05204.[Connecticut, Massachusetts].

846   Post, Stephen G. Love and Eudaemonism: A Study in the Thought of Jonathan Edwards and Samuel Hopkins. Ph.D., University of Chicago, 1983.

847   Rankin, Samuel H. Conservatism and the Problem of Change in the Congregational Churches of Connecticut, 1660-1760. Ph.D., Kent State University, 1971. 368p. UMI# 72-09279.

848   Rossi, Maryann. The Congregational Church Membership of Westport, Connecticut: 1835-1880, vs. the Land Structure in a Nineteenth Century New England Town. Ph.D., Saint Louis University, 1983. 228p. UMI# 83-25423.

849   Schafer, Thomas A. The Concept of Being in the Thought of Jonathan Edwards. Ph.D., Duke University, 1951.

850   Schimmelpfeng, Hans. The Conception of Church in Earliest American Congregationalism, 1620-1650. Ph.D., Hartford Seminary Foundation, 1928.

851   Schlaeger, Margaret C. Jonathan Edwards' Theory of Perception. Ph.D., University of Illinois at Urbana-Champaign, 1964. 234p. UMI# 6500900.

852   Shimo, Mochinobu. New England Congregationalism and Modernization of Japan in the Period of the Meiji, 1868-1912. Th.D., Boston University, 1970. 398p. UMI# 71-03957.

853   Steece, Arvel M. A Century of Minnesota Congregationalism. Ph.D., Harvard University, 1957.

854   Swift, David E. The Future Probation Controversy in American Congregationalism, 1866-1893. Ph.D., Yale University, 1947. 321p. UMI# 65-09092.

855   Wainger, Bertrand M. Liberal Currents in Provincial Massachusetts, 1692-1766. Ph.D., Cornell University, 1934. 277p.

856   Wood, William P. A Comparison of the Political Philosophies of John Winthrop and John Wise. Ph.D., Westminster Theological Seminary, 1989. 245p. UMI# 8919580.

857   Wortley, George F. The Status of the Child in New England Congregationalism From Jonathan Edwards to Horace Bushnell. Ph.D., Hartford Seminary Foundation, 1927.

Biography

858   Adams, Howard C. Benjamin Colman: A Critical Biography. Ph.D., Pennsylvania State University, 1976. 762p. UMI# 7629612.

859   Adamson, William R. Bushnell Rediscovered: Pioneer Educator, Champion of Children, Provocative Theologian. Ph.D., Pacific School of Religion, 1960.

860   Aijian, Paul M. The Relation of the Concepts of Being and Value in Calvinism to Jonathan Edwards. Ph.D., University of Southern California, 1950.

861   Akers, Charles W. The Life of Jonathan Mayhew, 1720-1766. Ph.D., Boston University, 1952.

862   Allison, Oscar E. Jonathan Edwards (A Study in Puritanism). Ph.D., Boston University, 1916.

863   Anderson, Glenn P. Joseph Bellamy (1719-1790): The Man and His Work. Ph.D., Boston University, 1971. 956p. UMI# 7126383.

864   Anderson, Michael P. The Pope of Litchfield County: An Intellectual Biography of Joseph Bellamy, 1719-1790. Ph.D., Claremont Graduate School, 1980. 315p. UMI# 8119916.

865   Arkin, Marc M. Edward Beecher: The Development of an Ecclesiastical Career, 1803-1844. Ph.D., Yale University, 1983. 489p. UMI# 8411506.

866   Barnes, Howard A. Horace Bushnell: An American Christian Gentleman. Ph.D., University of Iowa, 1970. 394p. UMI# 7023861.

867   Beall, Otho T., Jr. Cotton Mather's Knowledge of Medicine. Ph.D., University of Pennsylvania, 1952. 279p. UMI# 4895.

868   Becker, William H. The Distinguishing Marks of the Christian Man in the Thought of Jonathan Edwards. Ph.D., Harvard University, 1964.

869   Berk, Stephen E. The Church Militant: Timothy Dwight and the Rise of American Evangelical Protestantism. Ph.D., University of Iowa, 1971. 510p. UMI# 71-22004.

870   Bernhard, Harold E. Charles Chauncy: Colonial Liberal, 1705-1787. Ph.D., University of Chicago, 1945.

871   Birney, George H., Jr. The Life and Letter of Asahel Nettleton, 1783-1844. Ph.D., Hartford Seminary Foundation, 1943.

872   Blight, James G. Gracious Discoveries: Toward an Understanding of Jonathan Edwards' Psychological Theory, and an Assessment of His Place in the History of American Psychology. Ph.D., University of New Hampshire, 1974. 325p. UMI# 7427976.

873   Bohi, Mary J. Nathaniel Ward, Pastor Ingeniosus, 1580?-1652. Ph.D., University of Illinois at Urbana-Champaign, 1959. 386p. UMI# 5904493.

874   Bosco, Ronald A. An Edition of *Paterna*, Cotton Mather's Previously Unpublished Autobiography, Complete, With Introduction and Notes. Ph.D., University of Maryland, 1975. 450p. UMI# 7528732.

875   Brockway, Robert W. The Significance of James Davenport in the Great Awakening. Ph.D., Columbia University, 1951. 169p. UMI# 03100.

876   Brown, Ira V. Lyman Abbott, Christian Evolutionist: A Study in Religious Opinion. Ph.D., Harvard University, 1947.

877   Buchanan, John G. The Pursuit of Happiness: A Study of the Reverend Doctor Samuel Cooper, 1725-1783. Ph.D., Duke University, 1971. 386p. UMI# 72-11072.

878   Buchanan, Lewis E. Timothy Dwight, Man-of-Letters: His Ideas and Art. Ph.D., University of Wisconsin, 1941.

879   Calhoun, George N. Colonel William Bradford. Ph.D., Temple University, 1941.

880   Campbell, Philip S. Cotton Mather. Ph.D., Brown University, 1955. 240p. UMI# 13162.

881   Carafiol, Peter C. James Marsh: Transcendental Puritan. Ph.D., Claremont Graduate School, 1974. 237p. UMI# 75-12741.

882   Carr, James V. Solomon Stoddard: An American Way of Religion. Ph.D., Hartford Seminary Foundation, 1977. 388p. UMI# 78-14097.

883   Caskey, Marie C. Faith and Theology in the Beecher Family (1775-1907). Ph.D., Yale University, 1974. 543p. UMI# 75-15293.

884   Clark, Clifford E., Jr. Henry Ward Beecher: Revivalist and Anti-Slavery Leader, 1813-1867. Ph.D., Harvard University, 1968.

885   Clark, Gregory D. Timothy Dwight's *Travels in New England and New York* and the Rhetoric of Puritan Public Discourse. Ph.D., Rensselaer Polytechnic Institute, 1985. 274p. UMI# 8528655.

886   Clark, Stephen M. Jonathan Edwards: The History of Redemption. Ph.D., Drew University, 1986. 429p. UMI# 8702256.

887   Cogley, Richard W. The Millenarianism of John Eliot, "Apostle" to the Indians. Ph.D., Princeton University, 1983. 188p. UMI# 8309608.

888   Colbert, Thomas B. Prophet of Progress: The Life and Times of Elias Cornelius Boudinot. Ph.D., Oklahoma State University, 1982. 448p. UMI# 8300146.

889   Come, Donald R. John Cotton, Guide of the Chosen People. Ph.D., Princeton University, 1949. 547p. UMI# 10873.

890   Conforti, Joseph A. Samuel Hopkins and the New Divinity Movement, 1740-1820: A Study in the Transformation of Puritan Theology and the New England Social Order. Ph.D., Brown University, 1975. 359p. UMI# 76-15620.

891   Cook, George A. John Wise: Early American Democrat. Ph.D., Columbia University, 1952. 246p.

892   Corrigan, John A., Jr. Religion and the Social Theories of Charles Chauncy and Jonathan Mayhew. Ph.D., University of Chicago, 1982. UMI# 366674.

893   Crocco, Stephen D. American Theocentric Ethics: A Study in the Legacy of Jonathan Edwards. Ph.D., Princeton University, 1986. 208p. UMI# 8603731.

894   Cross, Barbara M. Horace Bushnell, 1802-1876. Ph.D., Radcliffe
           College, 1956.

895   Dahlquist, John T. Nathanael Emmons: His Life and Work. Ph.D.,
           Boston University, 1963. 346p. UMI# 6306646.

896   Daniels, Vincent H. Nature and the Supernatural; A Study in the
           Development of the Thought of Horace Bushnell. Ph.D., Yale
           University, 1939.

897   Delattre, Roland A. Beauty and Sensibility in the Thought of
           Jonathan Edwards: An Essay in Aesthetics and Ethics. Ph.D., Yale
           University, 1966. 349p. UMI# 6614967.

898   Denholm, Andrew T. Thomas Hooker: Puritan Teacher, 1586-1647.
           Ph.D., Hartford Seminary Foundation, 1961. 544p. UMI# 64-08970.

899   Dillon, Timothy L. Jedidiah Morse's Christian Republicanism:
           Reform   and   the   Young   Nation.   Ph.D.,   University   of
           Wisconsin-Madison, 1987. 415p. UMI# 8800704.

900   Dollar, George W. The Life and Works of the Reverend Samuel
           Willard (1640-1707). Ph.D., Boston University, 1960. 221p. UMI#
           60-02720.

901   Duduit, James M. Henry Ward Beecher and the Political Pulpit.
           Ph.D., Florida State University, 1983. 194p. UMI# 8317369.

902   Dunn, Richard S. John Winthrop, John Winthrop, Jr., and the
           Problem of Colonial Dependency in New England, 1630-1676: A
           Study in Contrasts. Ph.D., Princeton University, 1955. 507p. UMI#
           13686.

903   Eller, Gary S. Jonathan Edwards: A Study in Religious Experience
           and Eriksonian Psychobiography. Ph.D., Vanderbilt University, 1988.
           413p. UMI# 8815722.

904   Ellis, C.G. Ethics of Jonathan Edwards. Ph.D., New York University,
           1910.

905   Ellis, Joseph J-M., III. The Puritan Mind in Transition: The
           American Samuel Johnson (1696-1772). Ph.D., Yale University,
           1969. 264p. UMI# 70-16261.

906   Engle, Peter G. Jonathan Edwards as Historiographer: An Analysis
           of His Schema of Church History, Focusing on Period III of His
           History of Redemption. Ph.D., Westminster Theological Seminary,
           1985. 295p. UMI# 8516528.

907   Ericson, Jon M. John Wise: Colonial Conservative. Ph.D., Stanford University, 1961. 225p. UMI# 6104129.

908   Ewert, Wesley C. Jonathan Edwards the Younger: A Biographical Essay. Ph.D., Hartford Seminary Foundation, 1953.

909   Ferm, Jules R.L. Jonathan Edwards the Younger and the American Reformed Tradition. Ph.D., Yale University, 1958. 371p. UMI# 73-10954.

910   Fitzmier, John R. The Godly Federalism of Timothy Dwight, 1752-1817: Society, Doctrine, and Religion in the Life of New England's "Moral Legislator." Ph.D., Princeton University, 1986. 261p. UMI# 8621704.

911   Forde, Lois E. Elias Cornelius Boudinot. Ph.D., Columbia University, 1951. 269p. UMI# 2812.

912   Fraser, James W. Pedagogue for God's Kingdom: Lyman Beecher and the Second Great Awakening. Ph.D., Columbia University, 1975. 532p. UMI# 75-27407.

913   Freiberg, Malcolm. Prelude to Purgatory: Thomas Hutchinson in Provincial Massachusetts Politics, 1760-1770. Ph.D., Brown University, 1951.

914   Gibbs, Norman B. The Problem of Revelation and Reason in the Thought of Charles Chauncy. Ph.D., Duke University, 1953.

915   Giles, Charles B. Benjamin Colman: A Study of the Movement Toward Reasonable Religion in the 17th Century. Ph.D., University of California-Los Angeles, 1963. 259p. UMI# 6404772.

916   Giltner, John H. Moses Stuart: 1780-1852. Ph.D., Yale University, 1956. 600p. UMI# 6502021.

917   Goodell, John. The Triumph of Moralism in New England Piety: A Study of Lyman Beecher, Harriet Beecher Stowe, and Henry Ward Beecher. Ph.D., Pennsylvania State University, 1976. 490p. UMI# 76-29639.

918   Gossard, John H. The New York City Congregational Cluster, 1848-1871: Congregationalism and Antislavery in the Careers of Henry Ward Beecher, George B. Cheever, Richard S. Storrs, and Joseph P. Thompson. Ph.D., Bowling Green State University, 1986. 237p. UMI# 8628836.

919   Greenwood, Douglas M. James Marsh and the Transcendental

Temper. Ph.D., University of North Carolina-Chapel Hill, 1979. 206p. UMI# 7925924.

920   Griffin, Edward M. A Biography of Charles Chauncy (1705-1787). Ph.D., Stanford University, 1966. 353p. UMI# 6704354.

921   Harding, Vincent G. Lyman Beecher and the Transformation of American Protestantism, 1775-1863. Ph.D., University of Chicago, 1966.

922   Harley, Carol S. Cotton Mather, Puritan Enigma. Ph.D., University of South Carolina, 1982. 409p. UMI# 8228515.

923   Harling, Frederick F. A Biography of John Eliot, 1604-1690. Ph.D., Boston University, 1965. 288p. UMI# 6511229.

924   Holmes, Clement E. Philosophy of Jonathan Edwards and Its Relation to His Theology. Ph.D., Boston University, 1904.

925   Johnson, Thomas H. Jonathan Edwards as a Man of Letters. Ph.D., Harvard University, 1934.

926   Jones, Barney L. Charles Chauncy and the Great Awakening in New England. Ph.D., Duke University, 1958. 543p. UMI# 5802737.

927   Jones, David A. The Social and Political Thought of Horace Bushnell: An Interpretation of the Mid-Nineteenth Century American Mind. Ph.D., Northwestern University, 1973. 158p. UMI# 7330625.

928   Kirkpatrick, John E. Timothy Flint, 1780-1840: Minister, Missionary, Litterateur. Ph.D., Hartford Seminary Foundation, 1908.

929   Knoepp, Walther T. Jonathan Edwards: The Way of Sanctification. Ph.D., Hartford Seminary Foundation, 1937.

930   Laird, James H. The Influence of John Cotton in the Massachusetts Bay Colony. Ph.D., Boston University, 1974. 283p.

931   Laurence, David E. Religious Experience in the Biblical World of Jonathan Edwards: A Study in Eighteenth-Century Supernaturalism. Ph.D., Yale University, 1976. 191p. UMI# 76-30253.

932   Lee, Sang H. The Concept of Habit in the Thought of Jonathan Edwards. Ph.D., Harvard University, 1972.

933   Lippy, Charles H. Seasonable Revolutionary: Charles Chauncy and

the Ideology of Liberty. Ph.D., Princeton University, 1972. 337p. UMI# 7229799.

934   Magdol, Edward. Owen Lovejoy: Abolitionist in Congress. Ph.D., University of Rochester, 1971.

935   Manierre, William R., I. Cotton Mather and the Plain Style. Ph.D., University of Michigan, 1958. 292p. UMI# 5803708.

936   May, Sherry P. Asahel Nettleton: Nineteenth Century American Revivalist. Ph.D., Drew University, 1969. 457p. UMI# 69-18626.

937   McColgan, Daniel T. Joseph Tuckerman, Pioneer in American Social Work. Ph.D., Catholic University of America, 1940.

938   Merideth, Robert D. Edward Beecher, the Deacon of the Civil War Generation: A Biographical Study of the Conflict Between Orthodox Theology and Radical Politics. Ph.D., University of Minnesota, 1963. 380p. UMI# 64-10869.

939   Minkema, Kenneth P. The Edwardses: A Ministerial Family in Eighteenth Century New England. Ph.D., University of Connecticut, 1988. 690p. UMI# 8901521.

940   Morison, William J. George Frederick Wright: In Defense of Darwinism and Fundamentalism, 1838-1921. Ph.D., Vanderbilt University, 1971. 462p. UMI# 72-03226.

941   Morris, William S. The Young Jonathan Edwards: A Reconstruction. Ph.D., University of Chicago, 1956.

942   Murdock, Kenneth B. The Life and Works of Increase Mather. Ph.D., Harvard University, 1923.

943   Murray, Sean C. The Reverend Samuel Johnson, 1696-1772: Anglican Protagonist in Colonial America. Ph.D., State University of New York-Buffalo, 1975. 506p. UMI# 76-09091.

944   Myres, William V. The Private and Public Thought of Ezra Stiles, 1760-1795. Ph.D., University of Dallas, 1973. 381p. UMI# 7418753.

945   Pang, Patrick. A Study of Jonathan Edwards as a Pastor-Preacher. D.Min., Fuller Theological Seminary, 1991. 183p. UMI# 9110940.

946   Pellman, Hubert R. Thomas Hooker, a Study in Puritan Ideals. Ph.D., University of Pennsylvania, 1958. 276p. UMI# 58-01862.

947   Peterson, Edward R. The Horace Bushnell Controversy: A Study of

Heresy in Nineteenth Century America, 1828-1854. Ph.D., University of Iowa, 1985. 453p. UMI# 8611129.

948   Pierce, David C. Jonathan Edwards and the New Sense of Glory. Ph.D., Columbia University, 1965. 171p. UMI# 6507494.

949   Poole, Harry A. The Unsettled Mr. Cotton. Ph.D., University of Illinois at Urbana-Champaign, 1956. 370p. UMI# 18187.

950   Portz, John T. Cotton Mather and Rationalism. Ph.D., Harvard University, 1958.

951   Pratt, Glenn R. Jonathan Edwards as a Preacher of Doctrine. Ph.D., Temple University, 1958.

952   Price, Rebecca R. Jonathan Edwards as a Christian Educator. Ph.D., New York University, 1938.

953   Ransome, Joyce O. Cotton Mather and the Catholic Spirit. Ph.D., University of California-Berkeley, 1966. 338p. UMI# 70-17694.

954   Reed, Billy W. Jonathan Mayhew: A Study in the Rhetoric of Agitation. Ph.D., University of Michigan, 1974. 273p. UMI# 7425305.

955   Roth, David M. Jonathan Trumbull, 1710-1785: Connecticut's Puritan Patriot. Ph.D., Clark University, 1971. 384p. UMI# 7124740.

956   Rudolph, Charles F., Jr. Mark Hopkins and the Log. Ph.D., Yale University, 1953.

957   Sadowy, Chester P. Benjamin Colman (1673-1747) as Literary Artist. Ph.D., University of Pennsylvania, 1974. 262p. UMI# 752773.

958   Shuffelton, Frank C. Light of the Western Churches: The Career of Thomas Hooker, 1586-1647. Ph.D., Stanford University, 1972. 375p. UMI# 7230701.

959   Snyder, Stephen H. The Beechers: A Fabulous American Family. Ph.D., University of Chicago, 1975.

960   Stender, Thomas W. Edward Taylor in Westfield. Ph.D., State University of New York-Buffalo, 1977. 214p. UMI# 7719479.

961   Storer, Clement A.A. Elijah Kellogg: 19th Century New England Orthodox Preacher. Ph.D., Michigan State University, 1969. 237p. UMI# 7015144.

962   Suter, Rufus O., Jr. The Philosophy of Jonathan Edwards. Ph.D., Harvard University, 1932.

963   Swanhart, Harry G. Solomon Stoddard: Puritan Patriarch, a Biography. Ph.D., Boston University, 1961. 398p. UMI# 6103391.

964   Tracy, Patricia J. Jonathan Edwards, Pastor: Minister and Congregation in the Eighteenth-Century Connecticut Valley. Ph.D., University of Massachusetts, 1977. 301p. UMI# 77-30597.

965   Tweet, Roald D. Jonathan Edwards and the Affecting Style. Ph.D., University of Chicago, 1968.

966   Van Dyken, Seymour. Samuel Willard, 1640-1707: Preacher of Orthodoxy in an Era of Change. Th.D., Princeton Theological Seminary, 1963. 462p. UMI# 6308055.

967   Van Halsema, Dick L. Samuel Hopkins (1721-1803), New England Calvinist. Ph.D., Union Theological Seminary, 1956.

968   Waller, Altina L. The Beecher-Tilton Adultery Scandal: Family, Religion, and Politics in Brooklyn, 1865-1875. Ph.D., University of Massachusetts, 1980. 359p. UMI# 8012648.

969   Warren, Alice F. John Cotton: The Father of Boston. Ph.D., University of Wisconsin, 1929.

970   Weber, Donald L. The Image of Jonathan Edwards in American Culture. Ph.D., Columbia University, 1978. 253p. UMI# 7819461.

971   Welles, Judith B. John Cotton, 1584-1652: Churchman and Theologian. Ph.D., University of Edinburgh, 1948. 324p.

972   Wenzke, Annabelle S. Timothy Dwight: The Enlightened Puritan. Ph.D., Pennsylvania State University, 1983. 301p. UMI# 8327571.

973   White, Ruth W. James Marsh, Educator. Ph.D., University of Southern Mississippi, 1963. 260p. UMI# 6404019.

974   Whittaker, Frederick W. Samuel Harris, American Theologian. Ph.D., Yale University, 1950. 256p.

975   Wohl, Harold B. Charles Chauncy and the Age of Enlightenment in New England. Ph.D., Iowa State University, 1956. 216p. UMI# 18565.

976   Wood, Raymond L. Lyman Beecher 1775-1863: A Biographical Study. Ph.D., Yale University, 1961. 359p. UMI# 6609260.

977 Woodworth, Ralph L. The Life and Writings of Charles M. Sheldon (1857-1946), With Special Reference to His Relations With the Press. Ph.D., Southern Illinois University-Carbondale, 1983. 284p. UMI# 8326579.

978 Ziff, Larzer. John Cotton, Congregationalist, Theocrat. Ph.D., University of Chicago, 1956.

Clergy

979 Jacobson, Alf E. The Congregational Clergy in Eighteenth Century New England. Ph.D., Harvard University, 1963.

980 Scholz, Robert F. The Reverend Elders: Faith, Fellowship and Politics in the Ministerial Community of Massachusetts Bay, 1630-1710. Ph.D., University of Minnesota, 1966. 290p. UMI# 68-01180.

981 Youngs, John W.T., Jr. God's Messengers: Religious Leadership in Colonial New England, 1700-1750. Ph.D., University of California-Berkeley, 1970. 514p. UMI# 7115919.

Education

982 Barnard, Virgil J. The Conscience of a College: A Study of Oberlin, 1866-1902. Ph.D., University of Chicago, 1964.

983 Foster, Charles R. Horace Bushnell on Education. Ed.D., Columbia University, 1971. 209p. UMI# 7212803.

984 Harding, Leander S., Jr. Christian Nurture Revisited: A Theological and Psychological Exposition and Development of Horace Bushnell's Work on the Foundations of Christian Child-Rearing. Ph.D., Boston College, 1989. 242p. UMI# 8922283.

985 Olsen, Wesley A. The Philosophy of Jonathan Edwards and Its Significance for Educational Thinking. Ed.D., Rutgers University, 1973. 191p. UMI# 7332229.

986 Ratliff, Ruth E. The Society for the Promotion of Collegiate and Theological Education at the West: A Congregational Education Society. Ph.D., University of Iowa, 1988. 420p. UMI# 8913223.

987 Steward, David S. Horace Bushnell and Contemporary Christian Education: A Study of Revelation and Nurture. Ph.D., Yale University, 1966. 349p. UMI# 6615018.

988 Vanderhoof, Wesley E. New Doctrine and Old Discipline: New

Haven Theology and the Yale Report. Ph.D., State University of New York-Buffalo, 1985. 162p. UMI# 8518781.

989   Wyckoff, D. Campbell. Jonathan Edwards' Contributions to Religious Education. Ph.D., New York University, 1948. 342p. UMI# 73-08840.

Literature

990   Anderson, Wallace E. Mind and Nature in the Early Philosophical Writings of Jonathan Edwards. Ph.D., University of Minnesota, 1961. 239p. UMI# 6104589.

991   Barber, Eddice B. Cotton Mather's Literary Reputation in America. Ph.D., University of Minnesota, 1972. 284p. UMI# 7227723.

992   Bell, Susan C. History and Artistry in Cotton Mather's *Magnalia Christi Americana*. Ph.D., State University of New York-Binghamton, 1981. 298p. UMI# 8116150.

993   Bercovitch, Sacvan. New England Epic: A Literary Study of Cotton Mather's *Magnalia Christi Americana*. Ph.D., Claremont Graduate School, 1965. 422p. UMI# 6603355.

994   Clift, Arlene L. Rhetoric and the Reason-Revelation Relationship in the Writings of Jonathan Edwards. Ph.D., Harvard University, 1969.

995   De Prospo, Richard C. Nature and Spirit in the Writings of Jonathan Edwards. Ph.D., University of Virginia, 1977. 234p. UMI# 7901166.

996   Fender, Stephen A. Edward Taylor and the Sources of American Puritan Wit. Ph.D., Victoria University of Manchester, 1962. 268p.

997   Gatta, John J., Jr. Dogma and Wit in the Poetry of Edward Taylor. Ph.D., Cornell University, 1973. 249p. UMI# 7410829.

998   Gefvert, Constance J. Edward Taylor: An Annotated Bibliography. Ph.D., University of Minnesota, 1971. 159p. UMI# 7205609.

999   Gould, Timothy D. Natural Notions, Uncommon Speech: Strands of Jonathan Edwards' *Enquiry*. Ph.D., Harvard University, 1979.

1000   Hall, Dean G. Edward Taylor: The Evolution of a Poet. Ph.D., Kent State University, 1979. 357p. UMI# 7800344.

1001   Kimnach, Wilson H. The Literary Techniques of Jonathan Edwards. Ph.D., University of Pennsylvania, 1971. 413p. UMI# 7126039.

1002   Knight, Denise D. Cotton Mather's Verse in English. D.A., State
        University of New York-Albany, 1986. 243p. UMI# 8626000.

1003   Kuhn, John F., Jr. Literary Art in the Writings of Jonathan Mayhew.
        Ph.D., University of Notre Dame, 1973. 223p. UMI# 7324318.

1004   Lee, Marc F. A Literary Approach to Selected Writings of Jonathan
        Edwards. Ph.D., University of Wisconsin-Milwaukee, 1973. 185p.
        UMI# 7408976.

1005   McCandlish, George E. Annotations for a New Edition With a
        Definitive Text of Cotton Mather's Magnalia Christi Americana
        (1702), Books I and II. Ph.D., Harvard University, 1963.

1006   Naples, Diane C. The Sensible Order: An Interpretation and Critical
        Edition of Jonathan Edwards' Personal Narrative. Ph.D., University
        of California-Los Angeles, 1973. 258p. UMI# 7328740.

1007   O'Bryan, Daniel W. Law Versus Discipline: An Examination of
        Episcopal and Congregational Modes in Richard Hooker's Of the
        Laws of Ecclesiastical Polity and Thomas Hooker's A Survey of the
        Sum of Church Discipline. Ph.D., University of Washington, 1981.
        341p. UMI# 8121229.

1008   Ogburn, Floyd, Jr. Style as Structure and Meaning: William
        Bradford's Of Plymouth Plantation. Ph.D., University of Cincinnati,
        1978. 199p. UMI# 7904758.

1009   Pfisterer, Karl D. The Prism of Scripture: Studies on History and
        Historicity in the Work of Jonathan Edwards. Ph.D., Columbia
        University, 1973. 388p. UMI# 74-12753.

1010   Post, Constance J. Cotton Mather's Paterna: The Semiotics of an
        American Identity. Ph.D., Columbia University, 1986. 258p. UMI#
        8623588.

1011   Prioli, Carmine A. Emblems, Blind Emblems, and the Visual
        Imagery of Edward Taylor. Ph.D., State University of New
        York-Stony Brook, 1975. 208p. UMI# 7524627.

1012   Reed, Michael D. Edward Taylor: The Poetry of Defiance. Ph.D.,
        University of Oregon, 1974. 252p. UMI# 7503908.

1013   Requa, Kenneth A. Public and Private Voices in the Poetry of Anne
        Bradstreet, Michael Wigglesworth, and Edward Taylor. Ph.D.,
        Indiana University, 1971. 167p. UMI# 7213130.

1014   Rivers, Cheryl. Cotton Mather's Biblia Americana Psalms and the

Nature of Puritan Scholarship. Ph.D., Columbia University, 1977. 459p. UMI# 7714839.

1015   Runyan, Michael G. The Poetry of William Bradford: An Annotated Edition With Essays Introductory to the Poems. Ph.D., University of California-Los Angeles, 1970. 395p. UMI# 7109251.

1016   Russell, Bernie E. Dialectal and Phonetic Features of Edward Taylor's Rhymes: A Brief Study Based Upon a Computer Concordance of His Poems. Ph.D., University of Wisconsin-Madison, 1971. 2432p. UMI# 7109197.

1017   Shepherd, Emma L. The Metaphysical Conceit in the Poetry of Edward Taylor (1644?-1729). Ph.D., University of North Carolina-Chapel Hill, 1960. 218p. UMI# 6004868.

1018   Smith, Roy H. A Study of the Platonic Heritage of Love in the Poetry of Edward Taylor. Ph.D., Bowling Green State University, 1969. 193p. UMI# 7005522.

1019   Smolinski, Reiner. An Authoritative Edition of Cotton Mather's Unpublished Manuscript *Triparadisus*. Ph.D., Pennsylvania State University, 1987. 1097p. UMI# 8807856.

1020   Stanford, Donald E. An Edition of the Complete Poetical Works of Edward Taylor. Ph.D., Stanford University, 1953. 826p. UMI# 6911.

1021   Starkey, Lawrence G. A Descriptive and Analytical Bibliography of the Cambridge, Massachusetts, Press From Its Beginnings to the Publication of Eliot's Indian Bible in 1663. Ph.D., University of Virginia, 1949.

1022   Stein, Stephen J. *Notes on the Apocalypse* by Jonathan Edwards. Ph.D., Yale University, 1971.

1023   Stuart, Robert L. The Table and the Desk: Conversion in the Writings Published by Solomon Stoddard and Jonathan Edwards During Their Northampton Ministries, 1672-1751. Ph.D., Stanford University, 1970. 273p. UMI# 7022207.

1024   Taylor, Douglas H. John Wise and the Development of American Prose Style. Ph.D., University of California-Davis, 1967. 267p. UMI# 6714994.

1025   Wack, Thomas G. The Imagery of Edward Taylor's *Preparatory Meditations*. Ph.D., University of Notre Dame, 1961. 315p. UMI# 6105457.

1026   Wainwright, Jana D. Edward Taylor Studies From 1971-1984: An Analysis and Annotated Bibilography. Ph.D., Texas A&M University, 1985. 126p. UMI# 8528391.

1027   Wiley, Elizabeth. Sources of Imagery in the Poetry of Edward Taylor. Ph.D., University of Pittsburgh, 1962. 246p. UMI# 6205138.

Missions and Missionaries

1028   Andrew, John A., III. Rebuilding the Christian Commonwealth: New England Congregationalists and Foreign Missions, 1800-1830. Ph.D., University of Texas-Austin, 1973. 431p. UMI# 73-25971.

1029   Bryant, Gladys E. American Congregational Missionaries and Social Reform in Meiji Japan (1870-1900). Ph.D., Vanderbilt University, 1971. 435p. UMI# 72-15469.

1030   Johnson, Margery R. The Mayhew Mission to the Indians, 1643-1806. Ph.D., Clark University, 1966. 377p. UMI# 6611757.

Music

1031   Genuchi, Marvin C. The Life and Music of Jacob French (1754-1817), Colonial American Composer. Ph.D., University of Iowa, 1964. 307p. UMI# 6407918.

1032   Hammond, Jeffrey A. Songs From the Garden: Edward Taylor and the Canticles. Ph.D., Kent State University, 1979. 357p. UMI# 8003470.

1033   Taylor, Phyllis J. Non-Keyboard Instrumental Music in the Worship of Certain Congregational Churches in Connecticut From 1636 to 1900. Ph.D., Graduate Theological Union, 1987. 181p. UMI# 8717012.

Newspapers and Periodicals

1034   Housley, Donald D. The *Independent*: A Study in Religious and Social Opinion, 1848-1870. Ph.D., Pennsylvania State University, 1971. 286p. UMI# 71-28698.

Organizational Structure

1035   Alliman, Kirk G. The Incorporation of Massachusetts Congregational Churches, 1692-1833: The Preservation of Religious Autonomy. Ph.D., University of Iowa, 1970. 330p. UMI# 71-05706.

1036   Cohen, Sheldon S. The Connecticut Colony Government and the Polity of the Congregational Churches, 1708-1760. Ph.D., New York University, 1963. 306p. UMI# 64-06455.

1037   Erler, Donald J., Jr. The Political Teaching of John Wise's Second Treatise on Ecclesiastical Government. Ph.D., University of Dallas, 1975. 218p. UMI# 75-17512.

1038   Worthley, Harold F. The Lay Offices of the Particular (Congregational) Churches of Massachusetts, 1620-1755: An Investigation of Practice and Theory. Ph.D., Harvard University, 1970.

Preaching

1039   Alpert, Helle M. Robert Keayne: Notes of Sermons by John Cotton and Proceedings of the First Church of Boston From 23 November 1639 to 1 June 1640. Ph.D., Tufts University, 1974. 426p. UMI# 7428557.

1040   Barlow, Jerry N. A Critical Study of the Homiletics of Joseph Parker. Th.D., New Orleans Baptist Theological Seminary, 1983. 231p. UMI# 8314805.

1041   Batson, Trenton W. Arminianism in New England: A Reading of the Published Sermons of Benjamin Colman, 1673-1747. Ph.D., George Washington University, 1974. 180p. UMI# 7422243.

1042   Boswell, Parley A. "Unspeakable Rich Mercy": Text and Audience in Three Puritan Sermons: John Cotton's *The Covenant of God's Free Grace*, Thomas Hooker's *The Christian's Two Chiefe Lessons*, and Thomas Shepard's *The Saint's Jewel*. Ph.D., Loyola University of Chicago, 1987. 215p. UMI# 8718276.

1043   Burns, Robert E. A Development of Criteria for Effective Preaching From an Analysis of the Preaching of Henry Ward Beecher. S.T.D., Garrett-Evangelical Theological Seminary, 1975. 154p. UMI# 7606629.

1044   Covington, Robert C. A Critical Study of the Preaching of Henry Ward Beecher Based on His Published Sermons. Ph.D., New Orleans Baptist Theological Seminary, 1960.

1045   Darrow, Diane M. Thomas Hooker and the Puritan Art of Preaching. Ph.D., University of California-San Diego, 1968. 231p. UMI# 68-15680.

1046   Dean, Kevin W. A Rhetorical Biography of Jonathan Edwards:

Beyond the Fires of Hell. Ph.D., University of Maryland, 1989. 194p. UMI# 9012451.

1047   Della Vecchia, Phyllis A. Rhetoric, Religion, Politics: A Study of the Sermons of Lyman Beecher. Ph.D., University of Pennsylvania, 1973. 282p. UMI# 73-24133.

1048   Faber, Warren H. A Critical Rhetorical Study of the Effect of Horace Bushnell's Theory of Language Upon His Theory of Homiletics and His Practice of Preaching. Ph.D., Northwestern University, 1962. 244p. UMI# 6301287.

1049   Fain, William M. A Study of the Preaching of Timothy Dwight. Ph.D., New Orleans Baptist Theological Seminary, 1970.

1050   Flynt, William T. Jonathan Edwards and His Preaching. Ph.D., Southern Baptist Theological Seminary, 1954.

1051   Freeman, William G. Homiletical Theory of Cotton Mather. Ph.D., University of Iowa, 1970. 249p. UMI# 7105739.

1052   German, James D. The Preacher and the New Light Revolution in Connecticut: The Pulpit Theology of Benjamin Trumbull, 1760-1800. Ph.D., University of California-Riverside, 1989. 322p. UMI# 9002624.

1053   Grazier, James L. The Preaching of Jonathan Edwards: A Study of His Published Sermons With Special Reference to the Great Awakening. Ph.D., Temple University, 1958.

1054   Hearn, Rosemary. Stylistic Analysis of the Sermons of Jonathan Edwards. Ph.D., Indiana University, 1973. 166p. UMI# 7323009.

1055   Hitchcock, Orville A. A Critical Study of the Oratorical Technique of Jonathan Edwards. Ph.D., University of Iowa, 1937.

1056   Hoffelt, Robert D. Pragmatics on Persuasion and Disciplines of Duty: The Influence of Timothy Dwight in American Preaching. Ph.D., Princeton Theological Seminary, 1983. 411p. UMI# 8320291.

1057   Magee, Robert S. A Critique of the Preaching of William Mackergo Taylor. Ph.D., New Orleans Baptist Theological Seminary, 1962.

1058   Osburg, Barbara J. The Development of Metaphor in the Sermons of Jonathan Edwards: The Individual Reflection of an Historical Progress. Ph.D., Saint Louis University, 1984. 232p. UMI# 8520131.

1059   Register, Milton D. A Critical Analysis of Style in the Preaching of

John Henry Jowett. Th.D., New Orleans Baptist Theological Seminary, 1984. 231p. UMI# 8503932.

1060 Toulouse, Teresa A. The Aesthetic of Persuasion: Plain Style and Audience in John Cotton, Benjamin Colman, and William Ellery Channing. Ph.D., Harvard University, 1980.

1061 Westra, Helen A. Jonathan Edwards' Errand Into the World: The Minister as Christ's Proxy in the Ministerial Sermons. Ph.D., University of Notre Dame, 1982. 213p. UMI# 8225851.

Social Programs

1062 Behan, Warren P. Social Work of the Church of Plymouth Colony, 1620-1691. Ph.D., University of Chicago, 1899. 212p. UMI# 6611152.

1063 Schulz, Louis. Social Applications of the Gospel in Congregational Churches. S.T.D., Temple University, 1942. 164p.

1064 Senior, Robert C. New England Congregationalists and the Anti-Slavery Movement, 1830-1860. Ph.D., Yale University, 1954. 443p. UMI# 6709158.

1065 Voss, Carl H. The Rise of Social Consciousness in the Congregational Churches: 1865-1942. Ph.D., University of Pittsburgh, 1943.

Theology

1066 Albers, Grover. The Heart Divided or John Cotton's Spatial Epistemology of the Knowledge of Christ. Ph.D., St. John's University, 1980.

1067 Alexis, Gerhard T. Calvinism and Mysticism in Jonathan Edwards. Ph.D., University of Minnesota, 1947. 444p.

1068 Baird, Robert D. Religion Is Life: An Inquiry Into the Dominated Motif in the Theology of Horace Bushnell. Ph.D., University of Iowa, 1964. 374p. UMI# 6407904.

1069 Baker, Nelson B. Anthropological Roots of Jonathan Edwards' Doctrine of God. Ph.D., University of Southern California, 1952. 175p.

1070 Ball, John H., III. A Chronicler of the Soul's Windings: Thomas Hooker and His Morphology of Conversion. Ph.D., Westminster Theological Seminary, 1990. 316p. UMI# 9026390.

1071   Barbour, Dennis H. Edward Taylor's Treatment of Hexameral Themes in *Gods Determinations*. Ph.D., Auburn University, 1979. 152p. UMI# 8009575.

1072   Barnett, Das K. The Doctrine of Man in the Theology of Jonathan Edwards (1703-1758). Ph.D., Southern Baptist Theological Seminary, 1943.

1073   Bartlett, Irving G. The Romantic Theology of Horace Bushnell. Ph.D., Brown University, 1952.

1074   Bastaki, Shafikah A.A. A Reconstruction of Jonathan Edwards' Volitional Theory in the Context of Contemporary Action Theory: An Examination of "Freedom of the Will". Ph.D., University of Pittsburgh, 1972. 186p. UMI# 7313189.

1075   Batschelet, Margaret S. Jonathan Edwards' Use of Typology: A Historical and Theological Approach. Ph.D., University of Washington, 1977. 183p. UMI# 77-26796.

1076   Bauer, Charles G. Jonathan Edwards and His Relation to the New England Theology. S.T.D., Temple University, 1912. 30p.

1077   Billings, Mildred K. The Theology of Horace Bushnell Considered in Relation to That of Samuel Taylor Coleridge. Ph.D., University of Chicago, 1960.

1078   Brady, Gertrude V. Basic Principles of the Philosophy of Jonathan Edwards. Ph.D., Fordham University, 1951.

1079   Breed, James L. Sanctification in the Theology of Cotton Mather. Ph.D., Aquinas Institute, 1980. 356p. UMI# 82-13218.

1080   Burman, Ronald S. A Study of the Dynamics of Conversion and Identity in the Life and Works of Jonathan Edwards. Ph.D., University of Minnesota, 1988. 286p. UMI# 8910978.

1081   Carse, James P. The Christology of Jonathan Edwards. Ph.D., Drew University, 1966. 332p. UMI# 6614743.

1082   Cherry, Charles C. The Nature of Faith in the Theology of Jonathan Edwards. Ph.D., Drew University, 1965. 340p. UMI# 6511324.

1083   Colacurcio, Robert E. The Perception of Excellency as the Glory of God in Jonathan Edwards: An Essay Towards the Epistemology of Discernment. Ph.D., Fordham University, 1972. 328p. UMI# 7301470.

1084   Coney, Charles R. Jonathan Edwards and the Northampton Church Controversy: A Crisis of Conscience? Ph.D., University of Texas-Arlington, 1989. 130p. UMI# 9010434.

1085   Cooey-Nichols, Paula M. Nature as Divine Communication in the Works of Jonathan Edwards. Ph.D., Harvard University, 1981.

1086   Crouse, Moses C. A Study of the Doctrine of Conditional Immortality in Nineteenth Century America With Special Reference to the Contributions of Charles F. Hudson and John H. Pettingell. Ph.D., Northwestern University, 1953. 525p. UMI# 06192.

1087   Daub, Oscar C. Ramist Logic and Rhetoric in Edward Taylor's *Preparatory Meditations*. Ph.D., University of Georgia, 1972. 208p. UMI# 7305677.

1088   Davies, Ronald E. Prepare Ye the Way of the Lord: The Missiological Thought and Practice of Jonathan Edwards (1703-1758). Ph.D., Fuller Theological Seminary, 1988. 287p. UMI# 8913951.

1089   Ellzey, Diana S. Edward Taylor's *Christographia*: The Poems and the Sermons. Ph.D., University of Michigan, 1970. 178p. UMI# 7115138.

1090   Emerson, Everett H. Thomas Hooker and the Reformed Theology. Ph.D., Louisiana State University, 1955.

1091   Epperson, William R. The Meditative Structure of Edward Taylor's *Preparatory Meditations*. Ph.D., University of Kansas, 1965. 301p. UMI# 6606020.

1092   Erwin, John S. Like a Thief in the Night: Cotton Mather's Millennialism. Ph.D., Indiana University, 1987. 298p. UMI# 8727464.

1093   Eschenbrenner, Carl F. The Role of the Minister in the Theology of Thomas Hooker. D.Min., Eden Theological Seminary, 1980.

1094   Faust, Clarence H. Jonathan Edwards' View of Human Nature. Ph.D., University of Chicago, 1935.

1095   Feaver, John C. Edwards' Concept of God as Redeemer. Ph.D., Yale University, 1949. 183p.

1096   Fithian, Rosemary. The Influence of the Psalm Tradition on the Meditative Poetry of Edward Taylor. Ph.D., Kent State University, 1979. 291p. UMI# 8001342.

1097   Foard, Lawrence C., Jr. The Copernican Revolution in Theology:

Studies of the Critical and the Romantic Elements in the Theory of Religious Language Proposed by Horace Bushnell. Ph.D., Temple University, 1970. 208p. UMI# 7110566.

1098   Fye, Kenneth P. Jonathan Edwards on Freedom of the Will. Ph.D., Boston University, 1977. 144p. UMI# 7711392.

1099   Gerardi, Donald F. The American Doctor Johnson: Anglican Piety and the Eighteenth-Century Mind. Ph.D., Columbia University, 1973. 435p. UMI# 74-12720.

1100   Gilman, Harvey. From Sin to Song: Image Clusters and Patterns in Edward Taylor's *Preparatory Meditations*. Ph.D., Pennsylvania State University, 1967. 216p. UMI# 6803537.

1101   Goldstein, Steven. The Act of Vision in Edward Taylor's *Preparatory Meditations*. Ph.D., Tufts University, 1972. 186p. UMI# 7318192.

1102   Goodman, Dana R. Edward Taylor's "Brightest Gem": A Religio-Aesthetic Explication of *Gods Determinations*. Ed.D., Ball State University, 1976. 258p. UMI# 7708655.

1103   Grabo, Norman S. Edward Taylor's "Christographia" Sermons: Edited From the Manuscript With a Discussion of Their Relationship to His *Sacramental Mediations*. Ph.D., University of California-Los Angeles, 1958.

1104   Hall, Richard A.S. The Idea of Community in the Thought of Jonathan Edwards: The Neglected Texts From Northampton. Ph.D., University of Toronto, 1984.

1105   Harris, James W. A Study of Nathaniel William Taylor as a Transitional Figure in American Theology. Ph.D., New Orleans Baptist Theological Seminary, 1969.

1106   Hassler, Gregory L. Portrait of a Puritan Self: Increase Mather's Literature of Death. Ph.D., Emory University, 1981. 250p. UMI# 82-11335.

1107   Henderlite, Rachel. The Theological Basis of Horace Bushnell's Christian Nurture. Ph.D., Yale University, 1947. 341p. UMI# 66-08656.

1108   Higgins, John R. Aspects of the Doctrine of the Holy Spirit During the Antinomian Controversy of New England With Special Reference to John Cotton and Anne Hutchinson. Th.D., Westminster Theological Seminary, 1984. 549p. UMI# 8425221.

1109   Holbrook, Clyde A. The Ethics of Jonathan Edwards: A Critical Exposition and Analysis of the Relation of Morality and Religious Conviction in Edwardean Thought. Ph.D., Yale University, 1945. 492p. UMI# 65-12459.

1110   Holtrop, Elton. Edwards' Conception of the Will in the Light of Calvinistic Philosophy. Ph.D., Case Western Reserve University, 1948.

1111   Howell, John E. A Study of the Theological Method of Horace Bushnell and Its Application to His Cardinal Doctrines. Ph.D., Duke University, 1963. 474p. UMI# 64-03298.

1112   Jamieson, John F. Jonathan Edwards and the Renewal of the Stoddardean Controversy. Ph.D., University of Chicago, 1978.

1113   Johnson, Linda K. Apocalyptic Recycling in Cotton Mather and Edward Taylor. Ph.D., University of Minnesota, 1982. 179p. UMI# 8301950.

1114   Jones, Gerald H. George A. Gordon and the New England Theology. Ph.D., Boston University, 1942.

1115   Jones, Janice S. Metaphor and Poetic Structure in the *Preparatory Meditations* by Edward Taylor. Ph.D., Northwestern University, 1973. 231p. UMI# 7407765.

1116   Junkins, Donald A. An Analytical Study of Edward Taylor's *Preparatory Meditations*. Ph.D., Boston University, 1963. 430p. UMI# 6306649.

1117   Kibbey, Ann M. The Language of the Spirit: Typology in John Cotton and William Whitaker. Ph.D., University of Pennsylvania, 1977. 279p. UMI# 7719873.

1118   Kirschenmann, Fred. The Doctrine of Sin in Horace Bushnell and Later Liberals. Ph.D., University of Chicago, 1965.

1119   Knapp, Hugh H. Samuel Hopkins and the New Divinity. Ph.D., University of Wisconsin, 1971. 294p. UMI# 71-28344.

1120   Koelling, Deborah S. The Passover Sermons and Poems: Types and Emblems in Edward Taylor's *Upon the Types of the Old Testament*. Ph.D., University of Nebraska-Lincoln, 1984. 368p. UMI# 8423806.

1121   La Shell, John K. Imaginary Ideas of Christ: A Scottish-American Debate. Ph.D., Westminster Theological Seminary, 1985. 244p. UMI# 8527683.

1122   Leung, Yanwing. "To Dash Out Reasons Brains": A Post-Structuralist Inquiry Into Edward Taylor's *Preparatory Meditations*. Ph.D., Texas A&M University, 1990. 189p. UMI# 9106957.

1123   Lewis, Earl E. The Theology and Politics of Jonathan Mayhew. Ph.D., University of Minnesota, 1966. 295p. UMI# 66-12219.

1124   Lewis, Stephen C. Edward Taylor as a Covenant Theologian. Ph.D., New York University, 1971. 219p. UMI# 72-03093.

1125   Lo, Eddie B. Horace Bushnell's Religious Epistemology in Relation to His Major Christian Doctrines: Historical, Philosophical and Theological Consideration. Ph.D., Claremont Graduate School, 1977. 575p. UMI# 78-14842.

1126   Long, Gary D. The Doctrine of Original Sin in New England Theology: From Jonathan Edwards to Edwards Amasa Park. Ph.D., Dallas Theological Seminary, 1972.

1127   Lovelace, Richard F. Christian Experience in the Theology of Cotton Mather. Th.D., Princeton Theological Seminary, 1968. 541p. UMI# 6902032.

1128   Luisi, Miriam P. The Community of Consent in the Thought of Jonathan Edwards. Ph.D., Fordham University, 1976. 211p. UMI# 7617936.

1129   Lyttle, David J. Jonathan Edwards' Symbolic Structure of Experience. Ph.D., Pennsylvania State University, 1965. 254p. UMI# 6514770.

1130   McCrossin, G. Michael. World Views in Conflict: Evolution, Progress, and Christian Tradition in the Thought of John Fiske, Minot Savage, and Lyman Abbott. Ph.D., University of Chicago, 1971.

1131   McDermott, Gerald R. One Holy and Happy Society: The Public Theology of Jonathan Edwards. Ph.D., University of Iowa, 1989. 343p. UMI# 9009332.

1132   Mead, Sidney E. Nathaniel William Taylor (1786-1858) and the New Haven Theology. Ph.D., University of Chicago, 1941. 369p.

1133   Mignon, Charles W., Jr. The American Puritan and Private Qualities of Edward Taylor, the Poet. Ph.D., University of Connecticut, 1963. 300p. UMI# 64-03547.

1134   Miller, Raymond C. Jonathan Edwards and His Influence Upon Some of the New England Theologians. Ph.D., Temple University, 1945.

1135   Nagy, Paul J. The Doctrine of Experience in the Philosophy of Jonathan Edwards. Ph.D., Fordham University, 1968. 206p. UMI# 6811022.

1136   Pancake, Loral W. Liberal Theology in the Yale Lectures: An Inquiry Into the Extent and Influence of Liberal Theology Upon Christian Preaching as Set Forth in the Lyman Beecher Lectures on Preaching, 1872-1948. Ph.D., Drew University, 1951. 305p. UMI# 8823905.

1137   Parker, William H. The Social Theory of Jonathan Edwards: As Developed in His Works on Revivalism. D.S.S., Syracuse University, 1968. 304p. UMI# 6908641.

1138   Parmer, Phill W. "Like Little Paul in Person, Voice, and Grace": A Comparative Study of Edward Taylor and St. Paul. Ph.D., Louisiana State University, 1981. 273p. UMI# 8126972.

1139   Patterson, J. Daniel. A Critical Edition of Edward Taylor's *Gods Determinations*. Ph.D., Kent State University, 1985. 201p. UMI# 8604188.

1140   Pauw, Amy P. "The Supreme Harmony of All": Jonathan Edwards and the Trinity. Ph.D., Yale University, 1990. 356p. UMI# 9034233.

1141   Peterson, Robert D. The Atonement as Mystical Union With Christ in the Thought of Horace Bushnell. Ph.D., Saint Louis University, 1984. 234p. UMI# 8418684.

1142   Pierce, Howard F. Jonathan Edwards and His Relation to New England Theology. S.T.D., Temple University, 1912. 30p.

1143   Pierpont, Phillip E. "Oh! Angells Stand Agastard at My Song": Edward Taylor's Meditations on Canticles. Ph.D., Southern Illinois University-Carbondale, 1972. 387p. UMI# 7306239.

1144   Rece, Ellis H., Jr. Teleology in the Thought of Horace Bushnell. Ph.D., Emory University, 1971. 326p. UMI# 7122877.

1145   Rhoades, Donald H. Jonathan Edwards: Experimental Theologian. Ph.D., Yale University, 1945. 333p.

1146   Richardson, Herbert W. The Glory of God in the Theology of

Jonathan Edwards: A Study in the Doctrine of the Trinity. Ph.D., Harvard University, 1963.

1147   Rickey, Larry F. History as Divine Dialectical Process in the Works of Horace Bushnell. Ph.D., University of Iowa, 1972. 147p. UMI# 73-00678.

1148   Robbins, Kirk W. The Writings of Horace Bushnell as an Approach to a Theology for Christian Nurture. Ph.D., Drew University, 1938. 376p.

1149   Roberts, Cecil A., Jr. The Apologetic Significance of Jonathan Edwards' Doctrine of Religious Experience. Ph.D., Southwestern Baptist Theological Seminary, 1960.

1150   Rosenmeier, Jesper. The Image of Christ; The Typology of John Cotton. Ph.D., Harvard University, 1966.

1151   Rowe, Karen E. Puritan Typology and Allegory as Metaphor and Conceit in Edward Taylor's *Preparatory Meditations*. Ph.D., Indiana University, 1971. 272p. UMI# 72-06831.

1152   Rowe, Kenneth E. Nestor of Orthodoxy, New England Style: A Study in the Theology of Edwards Amasa Park, 1808-1900. Ph.D., Drew University, 1969. 512p. UMI# 69-18691.

1153   Sairsingh, Krister. Jonathan Edwards and the Idea of Divine Glory: His Foundational Trinitarianism and Its Ecclesial Import. Ph.D., Harvard University, 1986. 314p. UMI# 8620575.

1154   Salter, Darius. Thomas Upham and Nineteenth Century Holiness Theology. Ph.D., Drew University, 1983. 443p. UMI# 8317858.

1155   Scheick, William J. The Will and the Word: The Experience of Conversion in the Poetry of Edward Taylor. Ph.D., University of Illinois at Urbana-Champaign, 1969. 211p. UMI# 7000967.

1156   Shiber, Paul T. "The Conquest of Canaan" as a Youthful Expression of Timothy Dwight's New Divinity and Political Thought. Ph.D., University of Miami, 1972. 185p. UMI# 7231902.

1157   Smith, Burley G. Edward Taylor and the Lord's Supper: The Controversy With Solomon Stoddard. Ph.D., Kent State University, 1975. 208p. UMI# 7614366.

1158   Smith, Claude A. A Sense of the Heart: The Nature of the Soul in the Thought of Jonathan Edwards. Ph.D., Harvard University, 1964.

1159   Smith, David L. Symbolism and Growth: A Study of the Religious Thought of Horace Bushnell. Ph.D., University of Pennsylvania, 1979. 271p. UMI# 79-19515.

1160   Spohn, William C. Religion and Morality in the Thought of Jonathan Edwards. Ph.D., University of Chicago, 1978.

1161   St. John, Raymond A. Biblical Quotation in Edward Taylor's *Preparatory Meditations*. Ph.D., University of North Carolina-Chapel Hill, 1975. 246p. UMI# 7609288.

1162   Stephens, Bruce M. The Doctrine of the Trinity From Jonathan Edwards to Horace Bushnell: A Study in the Eternal Sonship of Christ. Ph.D., Drew University, 1970. 250p. UMI# 70-24591.

1163   Stephenson, Sally A. The Ministerial and Theological Purposes of Jonathan Edwards' Thought: A Study in Source and Content. Ph.D., University of Pennsylvania, 1983. 322p. UMI# 8406723.

1164   Stevens, David M. John Cotton and Thomas Hooker: The Rhetoric of the Holy Spirit. Ph.D., University of California, 1972. 223p. UMI# 7232955.

1165   Storms, Charles S., II. Jonathan Edwards and John Taylor on Human Nature: A Study of the Encounter Between New England Puritanism and the Enlightenment. Ph.D., University of Texas-Dallas, 1985. 466p. UMI# 8506415.

1166   Strader, Ronald E. The Chronological Development of the Spiritual-Aesthetic in the Philosophical-Theology of Jonathan Edwards and Its Relationship to Seventeenth and Eighteenth Century British Philosophy. Ph.D., Claremont Graduate School, 1982. 387p. UMI# 8129373.

1167   Strong, Gregory S. The Substance and Structure of Jonathan Edwards's Ethics in Light of His Metaphysics. Ph.D., Drew University, 1989. 229p. UMI# 9014372.

1168   Swaim, Gary D. Edward Taylor: Toward Union With God; Studies in the *Preparatory Meditations*. Ph.D., University of Redlands, 1971.

1169   Tallon, John W. Flight Into Glory: The Cosmic Imagination of Jonathan Edwards. Ph.D., University of Pennsylvania, 1972. 210p. UMI# 7301458.

1170   Tattrie, George A. Jonathan Edwards' Understanding of the Natural World and Man's Relationship to It. Ph.D., McGill University, 1973.

1171   Thompson, Christa M. Apocalyptic Piety: The Franciscan Spirit and Tradition in Jonathan Edwards' Works. Ph.D., University of Notre Dame, 1982. 218p. UMI# 8225845.

1172   Tomas, Martha M. The Concept of Christian Liberty in the *Christographia* of Edward Taylor. Ph.D., Saint Louis University, 1979. 185p. UMI# 8010767.

1173   Tyner, Wayne C. The Theology of Timothy Dwight in Historical Perspective. Ph.D., University of North Carolina-Chapel Hill, 1971. 278p. UMI# 71-21007.

1174   Van Bibber, James J. The Concepts of Church Membership and Ministry in the Covenantal Theology of Jonathan Edwards. Ph.D., Southwestern Baptist Theological Seminary, 1984. UMI# 0554155.

1175   Watkins, Harold K. The Ecclesiastical Contributions of Increase Mather to Late Seventeenth and Early Eighteenth Century Puritan Thought. Th.D., Pacific School of Religion, 1964. 434p. UMI# 6410517.

1176   Watts, Emily S. Jonathan Edwards and the Cambridge Platonists. Ph.D., University of Illinois at Urbana-Champaign, 1963. 218p. UMI# 6402985.

1177   Widenhouse, Ernest C. The Doctrine of the Atonement in the New England Theology From Jonathan Edwards to Horace Bushnell. Ph.D., Hartford Seminary Foundation, 1931.

1178   Wilcox, William G. New England Covenant Theology: Its English Precursors and Early American Exponents. Ph.D., Duke University, 1959. 372p. UMI# 60-01257.

1179   Williamson, Joseph C. The Excellency of Christ: A Study in the Christology of Jonathan Edwards. Ph.D., Harvard University, 1968.

1180   Willis, Mary S. "United Essential Harmony": The Puritan Perception of Edward Taylor. Ph.D., University of North Carolina-Greensboro, 1979. 263p. UMI# 80-11216.

1181   Wilson, Patricia A. The Theology of Grace in Jonathan Edwards. Ph.D., University of Iowa, 1973. 275p. UMI# 74-16698.

1182   Wisse, Alice S. The Christology of Edward Taylor in *Christographia* With Reference to His Poetry. Ph.D., New York University, 1981. 358p. UMI# 8115585.

1183   Wood, Gary A. The "Festival Frame": The Influence of the Tradition of Right Receiving on the *Preparatory Meditations* of Edward Taylor. Ph.D., University of Pittsburgh, 1972. 275p. UMI# 7302884.

1184   Woolsey, Stephen A. "My Handy Works, are Words, and Wordiness": Edward Taylor and the Life of Language. Ph.D., Drew University, 1988. 392p. UMI# 8817641.

1185   Young, James E. The Expressionistic Theology of Horace Bushnell: A Study of the Approach, Grounding and Form of His Theology. Ph.D., University of Southern California, 1968. 250p. UMI# 6905077.

1186   Youngs, Fred W. The Place of Spiritual Union in the Thought of Jonathan Edwards. Ph.D., Drew University, 1986. 196p. UMI# 8616878.

1187   Zuss, Michael E. Jonathan Edwards in the Context of Early Eighteenth-Century Moral Philosophy. Ph.D., City University of New York, 1986. 290p. UMI# 8629755.

DEIST

1188   Adams, Dickinson W. Jefferson's Politics of Morality: The Purpose and Meaning of His Extracts From the Evangelists. *The Philosophy of Jesus of Nazareth* and *The Life and Morals of Jesus of Nazareth*. Ph.D., Brown University, 1970. 690p. UMI# 75-28838.

1189   Bellesiles, Michael A. Life, Liberty, and Land: Ethan Allen and the Frontier Experience in Revolutionary New England. Ph.D., University of California-Irvine, 1986. 1060p. UMI# 8703941.

1190   Dennis, Donald D. The Deistic Trio: A Study in the Central Religious Beliefs of Ethan Allen, Thomas Paine, and Elihu Palmer. Ph.D., University of Utah, 1979. 303p. UMI# 79-08348.

1191   Gould, William D. The Religious Opinions of Thomas Jefferson. Ph.D., Boston University, 1929.

1192   Grimmelmann, Jan E.L. This World and the Next: Religion, Death, Success, and Love in Jefferson's Virginia. Ph.D., University of Michigan, 1977. 345p. UMI# 78-04714.

1193   Gurley, James L. Thomas Jefferson's Philosophy and Theology: As Related to His Political Principles, Including Separation of Church and State. Ph.D., University of Michigan, 1975. 253p. UMI# 75-20359.

1194   Hail, Francina K. Thomas Paine: An Interpretive Study of the

Treatment of Paine by Biographers, Historians and Critics. Ph.D., University of New Mexico, 1977. 384p. UMI# 7727172.

1195   Healey, Robert M. Jefferson on Religion in Public Education. Ph.D., Yale University, 1959.

1196   King, Arnold K. Thomas Paine in America, 1774-1787. Ph.D., University of Chicago, 1952.

1197   Mercer, Caroline G. The Rhetorical Method of Thomas Paine. Ph.D., University of Chicago, 1949.

1198   Metzgar, Joseph V. Thomas Paine: A Study in Social and Intellectual History. Ph.D., University of New Mexico, 1965. 202p. UMI# 6604447.

1199   Morais, Herbert M. Deism in Eighteenth Century America. Ph.D., Columbia University, 1934.

1200   Schulz, Constance B. The Radical Religious Ideas of Thomas Jefferson and John Adams: A Comparison. Ph.D., University of Cincinnati, 1973. 307p. UMI# 73-24855.

1201   Strickler, Gerald B. An Analysis of the Writings of Thomas Paine With Respect to His Philosophy of Religion. S.T.D., Temple University, 1955.

1202   Williams, Kenneth R. The Ethics of Thomas Jefferson. Ph.D., Boston University, 1962. 247p. UMI# 6205545.

DISCIPLES OF CHRIST

General Studies

1203   Ash, Anthony L. Attitudes Toward the Higher Criticism of the Old Testament Among the Disciples of Christ: 1887-1905. Ph.D., University of Southern California, 1966. 298p. UMI# 66-07063.

1204   Bailey, Fred A. The Status of Women in the Disciples of Christ Movement, 1865-1900. Ph.D., University of Tennessee, 1979. 292p. UMI# 8005363.

1205   Boren, Carter E. The History of the Disciples of Christ in Texas, 1824-1906. Ph.D., University of Chicago, 1953.

1206   Braden, Arthur W. The Background and Self-Definition of the

Disciples of Christ Movement. Ph.D., University of Southern California, 1955.

1207   Eikner, Allen V.D. The Nature of the Church Among the Disciples of Christ. Ph.D., Vanderbilt University, 1962. 400p. UMI# 6203413.

1208   Fife, Robert O. Alexander Campbell and the Christian Church in the Slavery Controversy. Ph.D., Indiana University, 1960. 327p. UMI# 60-06289.

1209   Harrell, David E., Jr. A Social History of the Disciples of Christ to 1866. Ph.D., Vanderbilt University, 1962. 578p. UMI# 6204508.

1210   Hensley, Carl W. The Rhetorical Vision of the Disciples of Christ: A Rhetoric of American Millennialism. Ph.D., University of Minnesota, 1972. 305p. UMI# 7232293.

1211   Holm, James N., Jr. Alexander Campbell's Debate With Robert Owen, April 1829: The Effect of a Rhetorical Event on the Speaker. Ph.D., University of Michigan, 1976. 391p. UMI# 7621799.

1212   Jennings, Walter W. Origin and Early History of the Disciples of Christ, With Special Reference to the Period Between 1809 and 1835. Ph.D., University of Illinois at Urbana-Champaign, 1918. 340p.

1213   Lessner, Richard E. The Imagined Enemy: American Nativism and the Disciples of Christ, 1830-1925. Ph.D., Baylor University, 1981. 415p. UMI# 81-17745.

1214   Lyda, Hap. A History of Black Christian Churches (Disciples of Christ) in the United States Through 1899. Ph.D., Vanderbilt University, 1972. 204p. UMI# 73-14520.

1215   Ollila, John L. The Soul-Politic in Antebellum America: The Political Implication of Alexander Campbell's New Testament Christianity. Ph.D., University of California, 1982. 266p. UMI# 8300611.

1216   Pletcher, Thomas E. Alexander Campbell's Controversy With the Baptists. Ph.D., University of Pittsburgh, 1955. 413p. UMI# 11603.

1217   Smith, Jerry C. The Disciples of Christ and the Expansionist Movement, 1898-1899. D.Div., Vanderbilt University, 1970. 119p. UMI# 71-07892.

1218   Thomas, Cecil K. Alexander Campbell as Translator of the New Testament. Ph.D., Princeton Theological Seminary, 1956.

Biography

1219   Ashby, Leo. Influence of Alexander Campbell Upon the Separation of Disciples and Baptists in Kentucky. Ph.D., University of Kentucky, 1949. 271p.

1220   Gresham, Charles R. Walter Scott Athearn, Pioneer in Religious Education. Ph.D., Southwestern Baptist Theological Seminary, 1959.

1221   Jeter, Joseph R., Jr. Alexander Procter, the Sage of Independence: Incipient Liberalism in the Nineteenth-Century American Pulpit. Ph.D., Claremont Graduate School, 1983. 423p. UMI# 8321054.

1222   Lunger, Harold L. The Political Ethics of Alexander Campbell. Ph.D., Yale University, 1949.

1223   Miethe, Terry L. The Philosophy and Ethics of Alexander Campbell: From the Context of American Religious Thought, 1800-1866. Ph.D., University of Southern California, 1984. UMI# 0555603.

1224   Rushford, Jerry B. Political Disciple: The Relationship Between James A. Garfield and the Disciples of Christ. Ph.D., University of California-Santa Barbara, 1977. 452p. UMI# 78-07029.

1225   Snyder, Lewis L. Alexander Campbell as a Change Agent Within the Stone-Campbell Movement From 1830-1840. Ph.D., Ohio State University, 1987. 411p. UMI# 8717729.

1226   Tucker, William E. James Harvey Garrison (1842-1931) and the Disciples of Christ: An Irenic Editor in an Age of Controversy. Ph.D., Yale University, 1960.

1227   Wasson, Woodrow W. James A. Garfield and Religion: A Study in the Religious Thought and Activity of an American Statesman. Ph.D., University of Chicago, 1948. 226p.

1228   West, Robert F. Alexander Campbell and Natural Religion. Ph.D., Yale University, 1943.

1229   West, William G. Barton W. Stone: His Struggle for Liberty and Christian Unity. Ph.D., Yale University, 1949. 183p.

1230   Williams, David N. The Theology of the Great Revival in the West as Seen Through the Life and Thought of Barton Warren Stone. Ph.D., Vanderbilt University, 1979. 251p. UMI# 7922194.

Clergy

1231   Bennett, Weldon B. The Concept of the Ministry in the Thought of Representative Men of the Disciples of Christ (1804-1906). Ph.D., University of Southern California, 1971. 689p. UMI# 72-11904.

1232   Lemon, Robert L. Alexander Campbell's Doctrine of the Ministry. Th.D., Pacific School of Religion, 1968. 306p. UMI# 68-16963.

1233   Montgomery, Riley B. The Education of Ministers of Disciples of Christ. Ph.D., Yale University, 1929. 266p.

Education

1234   Bennett, Rolla J. History of the Founding of Educational Institutions by the Disciples of Christ in Virginia and West Virginia. Ph.D., University of Pittsburgh, 1932.

1235   Brown, Sterling W. The Changing Function of Disciple Colleges. Ph.D., University of Chicago, 1937.

1236   Ferre, Gustave A. A Concept of Higher Education and Its Relation to the Christian Faith as Evidenced in the Writings of Alexander Campbell. Ph.D., Vanderbilt University, 1958. 329p. UMI# 58-01544.

1237   Lindley, Denton R. The Structure and Function of the Church in the Thought of Alexander Campbell. Ph.D., Yale University, 1947. 371p. UMI# 8014190.

1238   Long, John C. The Disciples of Christ and Negro Education. Ed.D., University of Southern California, 1960. 292p. UMI# 60-02779.

1239   Morrison, John L. Alexander Campbell and Moral Education. Ph.D., Stanford University, 1967. 247p. UMI# 6707951.

1240   Scudder, John R., Jr. A History of Disciple Theories of Religious Education. Ed.D., Duke University, 1961. 272p. UMI# 62-02006.

1241   Sharratt, William B. The Theory of Religious Education of Alexander Campbell and Its Influence Upon the Educational Attitude of the Disciples of Christ. Ph.D., New York University, 1930. 163p. UMI# 72-33738.

1242   Smith, Lawrence T., Jr. The "Amelioration of Society": Alexander Campbell and Educational Reform in Antebellum America. Ph.D., University of Tennessee, 1990. 249p. UMI# 9030739.

1243   Speck, Henry E., Jr. The Educational Contributions of a Religious

Reformer, Alexander Campbell. Ph.D., University of Texas-Austin, 1951.

1244   Tiffin, Gerald C. The Interaction of the Bible College Movement and the Independent Disciples of Christ Denomination. Ph.D., Stanford University, 1968. 228p. UMI# 69-08283.

Missions and Missionaries

1245   Kresel, George F.W. Alexander Campbell's Theology of Missions. Th.D., Boston University, 1961. 419p. UMI# 61-03739.

1246   Webb, Henry E. A History of the Independent Mission Movement of the Disciples of Christ. Ph.D., Southern Baptist Theological Seminary, 1954.

Newspapers and Periodicals

1247   Major, James B. The Role of Periodicals in the Development of the Disciples of Christ, 1850-1910. Ph.D., Vanderbilt University, 1966. 328p. UMI# 66-10992.

Organizational Structure

1248   Bungard, John E. Becoming a Denomination: The Church-Sect Typology and the Stone-Campbell Movement. Ph.D., University of Kansas, 1985. 438p. UMI# 8529071.

Preaching

1249   Berryhill, Carisse M. Sense, Expression, and Purpose: Alexander Campbell's Natural Philosophy of Rhetoric. Ph.D., Florida State University, 1982. 347p. UMI# 8228119.

1250   Casey, Michael W. The Development of Necessary Inference in the Hermeneutics of the Disciples of Christ/Churches of Christ. Ph.D., University of Pittsburgh, 1985. 412p. UMI# 8701998.

1251   Ellis, Carroll B. The Controversial Speaking of Alexander Campbell. Ph.D., Louisiana State University, 1950.

1252   Smith, Bruce L. An Examination of the Concept and Use of Artistic Proofs in Alexander Campbell's Evangelistic Speaking. Ph.D., Ohio University, 1982. 256p. UMI# 8304369.

1253   Taylor, Eunice J. Nourishing Words: Sermon Metaphors in the Religious Experience of Southern Disciples of Christ. Ph.D., University of North Carolina-Chapel Hill, 1984. 389p. UMI# 8425519.

1254   Thurston, Burton B. Alexander Campbell's Principles of Hermeneutics. Ph.D., Harvard University, 1959.

1255   Trimble, John C. The Rhetorical Theory and Practice of John W. McGarvey. Ph.D., Northwestern University, 1966. 273p. UMI# 6614080.

1256   Walker, Granville T. The Place and Function of Preaching in the Thought of Alexander Campbell. Ph.D., Yale University, 1948.

Social Programs

1257   Eminhizer, Earl E. The Abolitionists Among the Disciples of Christ. Th.D., School of Theology-Claremont, 1968. 317p. UMI# 70-19084.

1258   Roos, David C. The Social Thought of Barton Warren Stone and Its Significance Today for the Disciples of Christ in Western Kentucky. D.Div., Vanderbilt University Divinity School, 1973. 232p. UMI# 7323187.

Theology

1259   Bowen, Billy D. Knowledge, the Existence of God, and Faith: John Locke's Influence on Alexander Campbell's Theology. Ph.D., Michigan State University, 1978. 167p. UMI# 7907304.

1260   Creasy, William C. A Study of the Development of the Popular Motives of Health, Wealth, Power, and Success in Practical Theology of the Early Disciples of Christ, as It Appeared in Their Periodicals Through 1850, With Some Consideration of Their Meaning for Today's Preacher. D.Div., Vanderbilt University, 1971. 160p. UMI# 7126141.

1261   Degroot, Alfred T. The Grounds of Divisions Among the Disciples of Christ. Ph.D., University of Chicago, 1940.

1262   Garrison, Winfred E. The Sources of Alexander Campbell's Theology. Ph.D., University of Chicago, 1897.

1263   Phillips, George R. Differences in the Theological and Philosophical Backgrounds of Alexander Campbell and Barton W. Stone and Resulting Differences of Thrust in the Theological Formulations. Ph.D., Vanderbilt University, 1968. 490p. UMI# 6817989.

1264   Richardson, William J. Alexander Campbell's Use of History in His Apologetical Theology. Ph.D., University of Oregon, 1962. 214p. UMI# 6106078.

1265   Shields, James L., Jr. Alexander Campbell: A Synthesis of Faith and Reason (1823-1860). Ph.D., Syracuse University, 1974. 317p. UMI# 76-07941.

1266   Williams, Horace G. Theology of Alexander Campbell. Ph.D., Southwestern Baptist Theological Seminary, 1949. 248p.

DUTCH REFORMED

1267   Balmer, Randall H. Dutch Religion in an English World: Political Upheaval and Ethnic Conflict in the Middle Colonies. Ph.D., Princeton University, 1985. 327p. UMI# 8515861.

1268   Cook, Thomas H. A History of Music at Central College During the Nineteenth Century. D.A., University of Northern Colorado, 1983. 258p. UMI# 8408145.

1269   Luidens, John P. The Americanization of the Dutch Reformed Church. Ph.D., University of Oklahoma, 1969. 442p. UMI# 6910611.

1270   Meeter, Daniel J. The *North American Liturgy*: A Critical Edition of the Liturgy of the Reformed Dutch Church in North America, 1793. Ph.D., Drew University, 1989. 516p. UMI# 8921810.

1271   Rollins, John W. Frederick Theodore Frelinghuysen, 1817-1885: The Politics and Diplomacy of Stewardship. Ph.D., University of Wisconsin-Madison, 1974. 646p. UMI# 7422139.

1272   Smith, George L. Guilders and Godliness: The Dutch Colonial Contribution to American Religious Pluralism. Ph.D., University of Chicago, 1969.

1273   Van Der Merwe, Willem J. The Development of Missionary Attitudes in the Dutch Reformed Church in South Africa. Ph.D., Hartford Seminary Foundation, 1934.

EPISCOPAL

General Studies

1274   Botkin, Samuel L. The Protestant Episcopal Church in Oklahoma, 1835-1941. Ph.D., University of Oklahoma, 1958. 341p. UMI# 58-01951.

1275   Brickley, Charles N. The Episcopal Church in Protestant America, 1800-1860: A Study in Thought and Action. Ph.D., Clark University, 1950. 176p.

1276   Cushman, Joseph D., Jr. The Episcopal Church in Florida: 1821-1892. Ph.D., Florida State University, 1962. 328p. UMI# 63-01805.

1277   Griffen, Clyde. An Urban Church in Ferment: The Episcopal Church in New York City, 1880-1900. Ph.D., Columbia University, 1960. 448p. UMI# 60-05829.

1278   Hayden, John C. Reading, Religion, and Racism: The Mission of the Episcopal Church to Blacks in Virginia, 1865-1877. Ph.D., Howard University, 1972.

1279   Jenkins, Al W. The History of the Episcopal Churchwomen in the Diocese of Tennessee. D.Min., University of the South, 1983.

1280   Laugher, Charles T. The Beginnings of the Library in Colonial America: Dr. Thomas Bray and the Religious Societies, 1695-1795. Ph.D., Case Western Reserve University, 1963.

1281   Lines, Stiles B. Slaves and Churchmen: The Work of the Episcopal Church Among Southern Negroes, 1830-1860. Ph.D., Columbia University, 1960. 323p. UMI# 60-03107.

1282   Malone, Walter K. The Impact of Naturalism and Higher Criticism Upon the Episcopal Church: 1860-1900. Ph.D., Temple University, 1959.

1283   Manross, William W. The Episcopal Church in the United States, 1800-1840: A Study in Church Life. Ph.D., Columbia University, 1939.

1284   McDonald, Patricia M. Early American Church of England and Episcopalian Religious Writings: Their Rhetorical Bases Examined in Selected Texts. Ph.D., Fordham University, 1980. 354p. UMI# 8020072.

1285   Sharber, Patricia F. Social History of Tennessee Episcopalians, 1865-1935, With a Guide to Research in Local Religious History. D.A., Middle Tennessee State University, 1973. 374p. UMI# 7401086.

1286   Taylor, Olive A. The Protestant Episcopal Church and the Negro in Washington, D.C.: A History of the Protestant Episcopal Church and Its Nexus to the Black Population From the Seventeenth-Century Through the Nineteenth-Century. Ph.D., Howard University, 1973. 265p. UMI# 74-16342.

1287   Ulle, Robert F. A History of St. Thomas' African Episcopal Church,

1794-1865. Ph.D., University of Pennsylvania, 1986. 370p. UMI# 8703281.

1288   Witcher, Robert C. The Episcopal Church in Louisiana, 1805-1861. Ph.D., Louisiana State University, 1969. 401p. UMI# 69-17135.

Biography

1289   Acton, Arthur J. The Diary of William Smith, August 26, 1778 to December 31, 1779. Ph.D., University of Michigan, 1970. 535p. UMI# 7104551.

1290   Bothell, Larry L. Cloak and Gown: A Study of Religion and Learning in the Early Career of Samuel Johnson of Connecticut. Ph.D., Princeton University, 1967. 321p. UMI# 6709590.

1291   Byrnes, Don R. The Pre-Revolutionary Career of Provost William Smith 1751-1780. Ph.D., Tulane University, 1969. 280p. UMI# 7006384.

1292   Capossela, Toni-Lee C. Samuel Johnson and Religious Tradition. Ph.D., Brandeis University, 1969. 175p. UMI# 6916306.

1293   Davis, Virgil S. Stephen Elliott: A Southern Bishop in Peace and War. Ph.D., University of Georgia, 1964. 294p. UMI# 64-11699.

1294   Greatwood, Richard N. Charles Todd Quintard (1824-1898): His Role and Significance in the Development of the Protestant Episcopal Church in the Diocese of Tennessee and in the South. Ph.D., Vanderbilt University, 1977. 220p. UMI# 77-19374.

1295   Hance, Kenneth G. The Rhetorical Theory of Phillips Brooks. Ph.D., University of Michigan, 1937.

1296   Hatch, Carl E. The First Heresy Trial of Charles Augustus Briggs: American Higher Criticism in the 1890s. Ph.D., State University of New York-Buffalo, 1964. 153p. UMI# 6501298.

1297   Henry, Stuart C. George Whitefield: A Critical Interpretation. Ph.D., Duke University, 1955.

1298   Holmes, David L., Jr. William Meade and the Church of Virginia, 1789-1829. Ph.D., Princeton University, 1971. 408p. UMI# 71-25943.

1299   Kenney, William H., III. George Whitefield and Colonial Revivalism. The Social Sources of Charismatic Authority 1737-1770. Ph.D., University of Pennsylvania, 1966. 249p. UMI# 67-03080.

1300   King, Charles H. George Whitefield, Revivalist. Ph.D., Cornell University, 1936.

1301   Lambert, Franklin T. Selling Religion in the Consumer Revolution: George Whitefield and the Transatlantic Revivals, 1737-1745. Ph.D., Northwestern University, 1990. 324p. UMI# 9031950.

1302   Noblin, Stuart M. Leonidas Lafayette Polk: A Study in Agrarian Leadership. Ph.D., University of North Carolina-Chapel Hill, 1947.

1303   Noon, Rozanne M. Frederic Dan Huntington, First Bishop of Central New York: His Role in Religion and Reform in the Nineteenth Century. Ph.D., University of California-Berkeley, 1972.

1304   Ott, Thomas G. An Appraisal of the Ministry of Phillips Brooks, 1859-1869. S.T.D., Temple University, 1956. 258p. UMI# 62-02666.

1305   Peters, William R. The Contribution of William Smith, 1727-1803, to the Development of Higher Education in the United States. Ph.D., University of Michigan, 1968. 291p. UMI# 6902368.

1306   Pierce, Roderic H. George Whitefield and His Critics. Ph.D., Princeton University, 1962. 380p. UMI# 6203208.

1307   Pugh, Loren D. Bishop Charles Petit McIlvaine: The Faithful Evangel. Ph.D., Duke University, 1985. 150p. UMI# 8525311.

1308   Rawlinson, John E. William Ingraham Kip: Tradition, Conflict and Transition. Ph.D., Graduate Theological Union, 1982. 520p. UMI# 8219270.

1309   Rila, James S. Charles A. Briggs and the Problem of Religious Authority. Ph.D., University of Iowa, 1965. 243p. UMI# 6506706.

1310   Rogers, Max G. Charles Augustus Briggs: Conservative Heretic. Ph.D., Columbia University, 1964. 541p. UMI# 6507398.

1311   Skardon, Alvin W. William Augustus Muhlenberg: Pioneer Urban Church Leader. Ph.D., University of Chicago, 1961.

1312   Smith, Caroline P. Jacksonian Conservative: The Later Years of William Smith, 1826-1840. Ph.D., Auburn University, 1977. UMI# 7806103.

1313   Stanger, Frank B. The Life and Ministry of the Rev. Joseph Pilmore, D.C. S.T.D., Temple University, 1942.

1314   Steiner, Bruce E. Samuel Seabury and the Forging of the High

Church Tradition: A Study in the Evolution of New England Churchmanship, 1722-1796. Ph.D., University of Virginia, 1962. 1010p. UMI# 62-05950.

1315   Van Horne, John C. "Pious Designs": The American Correspondence of the Associates of Dr. Bray, 1731-1775. Ph.D., University of Virginia, 1979. 978p. UMI# 8002511.

1316   Weiser, John C. A Rhetorical Criticism of Philander Chase, First Bishop of the Episcopal Diocese of Ohio, 1818-1831. Ph.D., Case Western Reserve University, 1962.

1317   Wertz, Richard W. John Henry Hobart, 1775-1830; Pillar of the Episcopal Church. Ph.D., Harvard University, 1967.

Clergy

1318   Donovan, Mary S. Women's Ministries in the Episcopal Church, 1850-1920. Ph.D., Columbia University, 1985. 316p. UMI# 8523154.

1319   Dresbeck, Sandra R. The Episcopalian Clergy in Maryland and Virginia, 1765-1805. Ph.D., University of California-Los Angeles, 1976. 476p. UMI# 77-01622.

Education

1320   Brewer, Clifton H. A History of Religious Education in the Episcopal Church to 1835. Ph.D., Yale University, 1922.

1321   Gegenheimer, Albert F. Provost William Smith and His Group. Ph.D., University of Pennsylvania, 1940.

1322   McGinnis, Robert S., Jr. A Model for Theological Education in Eighteenth Century America: Samuel Johnson, D.D., of King's College. D.Div., Vanderbilt University Divinity School, 1971. 169p. UMI# 71-26146.

1323   PettyJohn, Etta M. Nineteenth Century Protestant Episcopal Schools in Pennsylvania. Ph.D., University of Pennsylvania, 1951. 134p.

1324   Vanderpool, Harold Y. The Andover Conservatives: Apologetics, Biblical Criticism and Theological Change at the Andover Theological Seminary, 1808-1880. Ph.D., Harvard University, 1971.

1325   Yanagihara, Hikaru. Some Educational Attitudes of the Protestant Episcopal Church in America: A History Study of the Attitudes of the Church and Churchmen Toward the Founding and Maintaining of Colleges and Schools Under Their Influence Before 1900. Ph.D.,

Columbia University, 1958. 617p. UMI# 58-02721.

Evangelical

1326   Rankin, Richard E., Jr. Evangelical Awakening and Episcopal Revival: Cultural Change and the Development of Genteel Piety Among North Carolina Episcopalians, 1800-1860. Ph.D., University of North Carolina-Chapel Hill, 1989. 306p. UMI# 9002428.

Missions and Missionaries

1327   Ejofodomi, Luckson E. The Missionary Career of Alexander Crummell in Liberia: 1853 to 1873. Ph.D., Boston University, 1974. 279p. UMI# 74-20383.

1328   Holt, Dean A. Change Strategies Initiated by the Protestant Episcopal Church in Liberia From 1836 to 1950 and Their Differential Effects. Ed.D., Boston University, 1970. 393p. UMI# 70-22489.

1329   Kent, Herbert R. Four Decades of Missionary Enterprise: An Institutional History of the Episcopal Church in the Pacific Northwest, 1851-1889. Ph.D., University of Texas-Austin, 1967. 210p. UMI# 68-04301.

1330   Smith, Garnett R. The Dynamics of Missionary Expansion and Evangelization of the Episcopal Church in the Diocese of Tennessee From 1865 to 1895, Including a Brief Survey of the First Quarter Century of Missionary Work at Tullahoma, Tennessee. D.Min., University of the South, 1982.

Music

1331   Clark, Linda J. Music in Trinity Church, Boston, 1890-1900: A Case-Study in the Relationship Between Worship and Culture. S.M.D., Union Theological Seminary, 1973. 339p. UMI# 73-20062.

1332   Criswell, Paul D. The Episcopal Choir School and Choir of Men and Boys in the United States: Its Anglican Tradition, Its American Past and Present. Ph.D., University of Maryland, 1987. 171p. UMI# 8818382.

1333   Rasmussen, Jane E. Churchmen Concerned: Music in the Episcopal Church 1804-1859. A Study of Church Periodicals and Other Ecclesiastical Writings. Ph.D., University of Minnesota, 1983. 458p. UMI# 8404224.

Organizational Structure

1334   Dator, James A. The Government of the Protestant Episcopal Church in the United States of America: Confederal, Federal or Unitary. Ph.D., American University, 1959. 334p. UMI# 59-03050.

1335   Franklin, Carl M. Organization and Administration in the Protestant Episcopal Church in the United States of America (A Critical Analysis). Ph.D., New York University, 1965. 167p. UMI# 65-09911.

1336   Loveland, Clara O. The Problem of Achieving Agreement on the Form of Government of the Protestant Episcopal Church in the United States of America, 1780-1789. Ph.D., Duke University, 1953.

1337   Ridout, Lionel U. Foundation of the Episcopal Church in the Diocese of California, 1849-1893. Ph.D., University of Southern California, 1953.

Preaching

1338   Carter, Charlotte R. The Homiletic Writings of Dr. Samuel Johnson: Attribution and Dating From Biographical and Religious Sources. Ph.D., Northern Illinois University, 1972. 548p. UMI# 7222781.

1339   Conrad, Flavius L., Jr. The Preaching of George Whitefield, With Special Reference to the American Colonies: A Study of His Published Sermons. S.T.D., Temple University, 1959. 240p. UMI# 66-06754.

1340   McLeod, Norman B. Levels of Relevance in Preaching: A Historical Study of the Communication of the Word to the World by a Witness, With Special Attention to the Principles of Interpretation Used in the Preaching of Phillips Brooks From 1859 to 1892. Th.D., Union Theological Seminary, 1960. 490p. UMI# 60-04355.

1341   Shankle, Nancy W. George Whitefield (1714-1770): A Critical Edition of *The Marks of the New Birth* and *A Sermon on Regeneration* Together With a Descriptive Calendar of His Sermons. Ph.D., Texas A&M University, 1990. 271p. UMI# 9106989.

1342   White, David L. The Preaching of Phillips Brooks. Ph.D., Southern Baptist Theological Seminary, 1949.

Theology

1343   Barker, Frederick T. Holiness, Righteousness, and Life: The Theology of William Porcher DuBose. Ph.D., Drew University, 1985. 375p. UMI# 8515814.

1344   Harm, Rudolph H. Phillips Brooks: A Study of His Understanding
          of the Nature and Development of the Moral and Intellectual Life
          of Man. Ph.D., New York University, 1970. 350p. UMI# 71-13646.

1345   Massa, Mark S. Charles Augustus Briggs and the Crisis of Historical
          Criticism. Th.D., Harvard University, 1987. 286p. UMI# 8719765.

1346   Minyard, Alfred B. The Theology of Phillips Brooks. Ph.D., Boston
          University, 1957. 213p. UMI# 21742.

1347   Mullin, Robert B. Out of Step: High Church Theology and Social
          Thought in Evangelical America, 1800-1865. Ph.D., Yale University,
          1983. 338p. UMI# 8411536.

1348   Prichard, Robert W. Theological Consensus in the Episcopal
          Church, 1801-1873. Ph.D., Emory University, 1983. 322p. UMI#
          8316295.

1349   Temple, Synday A. The Common Sense Theology of Bishop White:
          Selected Essays From the Writings of William White, 1748-1836,
          First Bishop of Pennsylvania and a Patriarch of the American
          Church; With an Introductory Survey of His Theological Position.
          Ph.D., Columbia University, 1947. 169p.

1350   Williams, Theodore M. Humanity and Logos: An Essay in the
          Theology of William Porcher Dubose. Ph.D., Emory University,
          1974. 233p. UMI# 7418396.

1351   Woolverton, John F. William Reed Huntington and Church Unity:
          The Historical and Theological Background of the Chicago-Lambeth
          Quadrilateral. Ph.D., Columbia University, 1963. 462p. UMI#
          64-03134.

EVANGELICAL

General Studies

1352   Bartholomew, Alfred C. An Interpretation of the Evangelical and
          Reformed Church in a Changing American Society. Ph.D., Drew
          University, 1950. 246p. UMI# 8807393.

1353   Broyles, Joseph W. Some Permanent Values in the Evangelical
          Faith: An Effort Toward a Philosophical Basis for Evangelical
          Christianity. Ph.D., Drew University, 1932.

1354   Chun, Randall T. Evangelicalism Divided: An Examination of
          Factors Contributing to Evangelical Political Diversity. Ph.D.,
          University of Minnesota, 1988. 408p. UMI# 8909448.

1355   Colbenson, Pamela E.T. Millennial Thought Among Southern
        Evangelicals, 1830-1885. Ph.D., Georgia State University, 1980. 266p.
        UMI# 8321354.

1356   Ellis, George M. The Evangelical and the Sunday Question,
        1830-1860: Organized Sabbatarianism as an Aspect of the
        Evangelical Movement. Ph.D., Harvard University, 1952. 175p.

1357   Kuykendall, John W. "Southern Enterprize": The Work of National
        Evangelical Societies in the Antebellum South. Ph.D., Princeton
        University, 1975. UMI# 76-16854.

1358   Loomis, Barbara D. Piety and Play: Young Women's Leisure in an
        Era of Evangelical Religion, 1790-1840. Ph.D., University of
        California-Berkeley, 1988. 355p. UMI# 8902188.

1359   Morrison, Michael G. Conceptions of Sin in American Evangelical
        Thought in the Early Nineteenth Century. Ph.D., University of
        Wisconsin-Madison, 1971. 259p. UMI# 7125736.

1360   Ownby, Ted. Evangelicalism and Male Culture: Recreation and
        Religion in the Rural South, 1865-1920. Ph.D., Johns Hopkins
        University, 1986. 387p. UMI# 8707289.

1361   Pocock, Emil. Evangelical Frontier: Dayton, Ohio, 1796-1830. Ph.D.,
        Indiana University, 1984. 189p. UMI# 8417209.

1362   Price, Marian G. A Study of Some of the Effects of
        Nineteenth-Century Revivalism on the Status and Accomplishments
        of Women in the Evangelical Covenant Church of America. Ed.D.,
        Boston University, 1977. 191p. UMI# 77-21672.

1363   Rosenberg, Carroll S. Evangelicalism and the New City: A History
        of the City Mission Movement in New York, 1812-1870. Ph.D.,
        Columbia University, 1968. 475p. UMI# 68-16927.

1364   Scott, Donald M. Watchmen on the Walls of Zion: Evangelicals and
        American Society 1800-1860. Ph.D., University of Wisconsin, 1968.
        502p. UMI# 68-17937.

1365   Seim, James M., Jr. Exploring Our Evangelical Heritage: A Survey
        Course in American Church History. D.Min., Western Conservative
        Baptist Seminary, 1985.

1366   Sparks, Randy J. A Mingled Yarn: Race and Religion in Mississippi,
        1800-1876. Ph.D., Rice University, 1988. 266p. UMI# 8900282.

Art and Architecture

1367   Apostolos-Cappadona, Diane. The Spirit and the Vision: The Influence of Romantic Evangelicalism on Nineteenth-Century American Art. Ph.D., George Washington University, 1988. 648p. UMI# 8815947.

Biography

1368   Crumpacker, Laurie. Esther Burr's Journal 1754-1757: A Document of Evangelical Sisterhood. Ph.D., Boston University, 1978. 444p. UMI# 7808015.

1369   Robert, Dana L. Arthur Tappan Pierson and Forward Movements of Late-Nineteenth-Century Evangelicalism. Ph.D., Yale University, 1984. 457p. UMI# 8514887.

Education

1370   Dominick, Charles A. Ohio's Ante-Bellum Colleges. Ph.D., University of Michigan, 1987. 340p. UMI# 8712099.

1371   Graffam, Alan E. On the Persistence of Denominational Evangelical Higher Education: Case Studies in the History of Geneva College, Roberts Wesleyan College, Nyack College and Houghton College. Ph.D., State University of New York-Buffalo, 1986. 275p. UMI# 8619325.

1372   Hannah, John D. The Social and Intellectual History of the Origins of the Evangelical Theological College. Ph.D., University of Texas-Dallas, 1988. 443p. UMI# 8810432.

1373   Kincheloe, Joe L. The Antebellum Southern Evangelical and State-Supported Colleges: A Comparative Study. Ed.D., University of Tennessee, 1980. 225p. UMI# 8024917.

1374   Lesick, Lawrence T. The Lane Rebels: Evangelicalism and Antislavery in Antebellum America. Ph.D., Vanderbilt University, 1979. 308p. UMI# 79-22176.

1375   McGee, Theron C. Religious Education in Certain Evangelical Colleges: A Study in Status and Tendencies. Ph.D., University of Pennsylvania, 1928. 151p.

1376   Orr, James E. Evangelical Awakenings in Collegiate Communities. Ed.D., University of California-Los Angeles, 1971. 275p. UMI# 7202877.

Literature

1377   Davis, Christian R. The Rhetoric of Nineteenth-Century American Evangelical Autobiography. Ph.D., Pennsylvania State University, 1985. 233p. UMI# 8526009.

Missions and Missionaries

1378   Donahoo, William D. The Missionary Expression of American Evangelical Social Beliefs. Ph.D., Johns Hopkins University, 1977. 288p. UMI# 77-19586.

1379   Frizen, Edwin L., Jr. An Historical Study of the Interdenominational Foreign Mission Association in Relation to Evangelical Unity and Cooperation. D.Miss., Trinity Evangelical Divinity School, 1981.

1380   Larson, Ernest S. The Evangelical Mission Covenant of America: Beginnings. Ph.D., University of Chicago, 1945. 201p.

1381   Lyon, Thomas E. Evangelical Protestant Missionary Activities in Mormon Dominated Areas: 1865-1900. Ph.D., University of Utah, 1962. 289p. UMI# 62-05708.

1382   Warnock, James H. To the Jew First: The Evangelical Mission to Jewish Immigrants, 1885-1915. Ph.D., University of Washington, 1989. 339p. UMI# 9013829.

Organizational Structure

1383   Jordan, Philip D. The Evangelical Alliance for the United States of America: An Evangelical Search for Identity in Ecumenicity During the Nineteenth Century. Ph.D., University of Iowa, 1971. 350p. UMI# 71-22045.

Social Programs

1384   Essig, James D. Break Every Yoke: American Evangelicals Against Slavery, 1770-1808. Ph.D., Yale University, 1978. 249p. UMI# 79-15817.

1385   Lukonic, Joseph L. "Evangelicals in the City": Evangelical Protestant Social Concerns in Early Chicago, 1837-1860. Ph.D., University of Wisconsin-Madison, 1979. 220p. UMI# 79-22819.

1386   MacDonald, Clyde W., Jr. The Massachusetts Peace Society 1815-1828: A Study in Evangelical Reform. Ph.D., University of Maine, 1973. 318p. UMI# 73-19577.

1387   Magnuson, Norris A. Salvation in the Slums: Evangelical Social Welfare Work, 1865-1920. Ph.D., University of Minnesota, 1968. 480p. UMI# 6901548.

1388   Pendleton, Othniel A. The Influence of the Evangelical Churches Upon Humanitarian Reform: A Case Study Giving Particular Attention to Philadelphia, 1790-1840. Ph.D., University of Pennsylvania, 1945. 544p.

1389   Pritchard, Linda K. Religious Change in a Developing Region: The Social Contexts of Evangelicalism in Western New York and the Upper Ohio Valley During the Mid-Nineteenth Century. Ph.D., University of Pittsburgh, 1980. 351p. UMI# 81-12628.

1390   Wright, Albert M. The Development of Institutional Provision for the Care of the Aged in the Evangelical and Reformed Church. Ph.D., University of Pittsburgh, 1956. 381p. UMI# 16528.

Theology

1391   Naumann, William H. Theology and German-American Evangelicalism: The Role of Theology in the Church of the United Brethren in Christ and the Evangelical Association. Ph.D., Yale University, 1966. 506p. UMI# 66-13920.

1392   Schwab, Ralph K. The History of the Doctrine of Christian Perfection in the Evangelical Association. Ph.D., University of Chicago, 1920. 153p.

1393   Wysong, Joan M. The New Evangelical Theology of Henry Drummond (1851-1897): An Historical Analysis. Ph.D., University of Maryland, 1977.

EVANGELISM

General Studies

1394   Armstrong, Daniel W. An Examination of American Evangelism Beginning With the 18th Century in the Light of N.T. Principles of Evangelism. Ph.D., Southern Baptist Theological Seminary, 1955.

1395   Bell, Marion L. Religious Revivalism in Philadelphia: From Finney to Moody. Ph.D., Temple University, 1974. 359p. UMI# 74-28209.

1396   Boles, John B. The Religious Mind of the Old South: The Era of the Great Revival, 1787-1805. Ph.D., University of Virginia, 1969. 400p. UMI# 70-08031.

1397   Braden, Arthur. The Modern Religious Revival and Its After Effects. Ph.D., Syracuse University, 1914.

1398   Bruce, Dickson D., Jr. And They All Sang Hallelujah: Plain-Folk Camp-Meeting Religion, 1800-1845. Ph.D., University of Pennsylvania, 1971. 265p. UMI# 72-06140.

1399   Butler, Jonathan M. Heaven and Hell in American Revivalism, 1870-1920. Ph.D., University of Chicago, 1975.

1400   Cleveland, Catharine C. The Great Revival in the West, 1797-1805. Ph.D., University of Chicago, 1914.

1401   Cole, Charles C., Jr. The Secular Ideas of the Northern Evangelists, 1826-1860. Ph.D., Columbia University, 1951. 430p. UMI# 03329.

1402   Crawford, Michael J. The Invention of the American Revival: The Beginnings of Anglo-American Religious Revivalism, 1690-1750. Ph.D., Boston University, 1978. 409p. UMI# 78-19803.

1403   Dalton, James S. The Kentucky Camp Meeting Revivals of 1797-1805 as Rites of Initiation. Ph.D., University of Chicago, 1973. 211p.

1404   Davenport, Frederick M. Primitive Traits in Religious Revivals: A Study in Mental and Social Evolution. Ph.D., Columbia University, 1905.

1405   Dieter, Melvin E. Revivalism and Holiness. Ph.D., Temple University, 1973. 375p. UMI# 73-18681.

1406   Easton, Barbara L. Women, Religion, and the Family: Revivalism as an Indicator of Social Change in Early New England. Ph.D., University of California-Berkeley, 1975.

1407   Eslinger, Ellen T. The Great Revival in Bourbon County, Kentucky. Ph.D., University of Chicago, 1988.

1408   Hand, George O. Changing Emphases in American Evangelism From Colonial Times to the Present. Ph.D., Southern Baptist Theological Seminary, 1949. 214p.

1409   Hardesty, Nancy A. "Your Daughters Shall Prophesy": Revivalism and Feminism in the Age of Finney. Ph.D., University of Chicago, 1977.

1410   Hendricks, Tyler O. Charles Finney and the Utica Revival of 1826: The Social Effect of a New Religious Paradigm. Ph.D., Vanderbilt

University, 1983. 338p. UMI# 8317337.

1411   Johnson, Curtis D. Islands of Holiness: Rural Religion in Cortland County, New York, 1790-1860. Ph.D., University of Minnesota, 1985. 556p. UMI# 8526480.

1412   Johnson, Paul E. A Shopkeeper's Millenium: Society and Revivals in Rochester, New York, 1815-1837. Ph.D., University of California-Los Angeles, 1975. 304p. UMI# 76-03044.

1413   Long, Ronald W. Religious Revivalism in the Carolinas and Georgia, 1740-1805. Ph.D., University of Georgia, 1968. 257p. UMI# 69-09501.

1414   Lyrene, Edward C., Jr. The Role of Prayer in American Revival Movements, 1740-1860. Ph.D., Southern Baptist Theological Seminary, 1985. 284p. UMI# 8604437.

1415   McLoughlin, William G., Jr. Professional Evangelism: The Social Significance of Religious Revivals Since 1865. Ph.D., Harvard University, 1953.

1416   Opie, John, Jr. Conversion and Revivalism: An Internal History From Jonathan Edwards Through Charles Grandison Finney. Ph.D., University of Chicago, 1964. UMI# 0258094.

1417   Pitzer, Donald E. Professional Revivalism in Nineteenth-Century Ohio. Ph.D., Ohio State University, 1966. 536p.

1418   Prim, Gorrell C., Jr. Born Again in the Trenches: Revivalism in the Confederate Army. Ph.D., Florida State University, 1982. 244p. UMI# 8306171.

1419   Robertson, Darrel M. The Chicago Revival, 1876: A Case Study in the Social Function of a Nineteenth-Century Revival. Ph.D., University of Iowa, 1982. 335p. UMI# 8310083.

1420   Roth, Randolph A. Whence This Strange Fire: Religious and Reform Movements in the Connecticut River Valley of Vermont, 1791-1843. Ph.D., Yale University, 1981. 614p. UMI# 82-10704.

1421   Thompson, William O., Jr. The Public Invitation as a Method of Evangelism: Its Origin and Development. Ph.D., Southwestern Baptist Theological Seminary, 1979.

Biography

1422   Abzug, Robert H. Theodore Dwight Weld: A Biography. Ph.D.,

University of California-Berkeley, 1977. 477p. UMI# 7731265.

1423   Brasher, John L. "Standing Between the Living and the Dead": John Lakin Brasher, Holiness Preacher. Ph.D., Duke University, 1986. 357p. UMI# 8626975.

1424   Carmack, Paul. Theodore Dwight Weld, Reformer. Ph.D., Syracuse University, 1949.

1425   Coffman, Edward F., Jr. Elder T.M. Allen: Pioneer Evangelist, "The Artillery of Heaven." D.Min., Vanderbilt University Divinity School, 1972. 143p. UMI# 72-26070.

1426   Cogdill, James P., Jr. A Major Stream of American Evangelism: The Ministries of R.A. Torrey, J.W. Chapman and W.E. Biederwolf. Ph.D., Southern Baptist Theological Seminary, 1990. 343p. UMI# 9028232.

1427   Findlay, James F., Jr. Dwight L. Moody, Evangelist of the Gilded Age: 1837-1899. Ph.D., Northwestern University, 1961. 393p. UMI# 6105309.

1428   Hamilton, James E. A Comparison of the Moral Theories of Charles Finney and Asa Mahan. Ph.D., State University of New York-Buffalo, 1972. 158p. UMI# 7305117.

1429   Hannah, John D. James Martin Gray, 1851-1935, His Life and Work. Th.D., Dallas Theological Seminary, 1974. UMI# 0286920.

1430   Huber, Robert B. Dwight L. Moody, Salesman of Salvation: A Case Study in Audience Psychology. Ph.D., University of Wisconsin, 1943.

1431   Johnson, James E. The Life of Charles Grandison Finney. Ph.D., Syracuse University, 1959. 445p. UMI# 5906306.

1432   Mattson, John S. Charles Grandison Finney and the Emerging Tradition of New Measure Revivalism. Ph.D., University of North Carolina-Chapel Hill, 1970. 331p. UMI# 71-03581.

1433   McClanahan, James S., Jr. Benjamin B. Warfield: Historian of Doctrine in Defense of Orthodoxy, 1881-1921. Ph.D., Union Theological Seminary in Virginia, 1988. 671p. UMI# 8819786.

1434   McClelland, William L. Church and Ministry in the Life and Thought of Charles G. Finney. Th.D., Princeton Theological Seminary, 1967. 698p. UMI# 68-00260.

1435   Nelson, Daniel W. B. Fay Mills: Revivalist, Social Reformer and

Advocate of Free Religion. D.S.S., Syracuse University, 1964. 312p. UMI# 65-03427.

1436   Quimby, Rollin W. Dwight L. Moody: An Examination of the Historical Conditions and Rhetorical Factors Which Contributed to His Effectiveness as a Speaker. Ph.D., University of Michigan, 1951. 418p. UMI# 02637.

1437   Rosell, Garth M. Charles Grandison Finney and the Rise of the Benevolence Empire. Ph.D., University of Minnesota, 1971. 263p. UMI# 72-14448.

1438   Urbach, Jon L. God and Man in the Life of Louisa Maxwell Holmes Cocke: A Search for Piety and Place in the Old South. Ph.D., Florida State University, 1983. 641p. UMI# 8416730.

1439   Wells, Donald A. D.L. Moody and His Schools: An Historical Analysis of an Educational Ministry. Ph.D., Boston University, 1972. 440p. UMI# 72-25350.

1440   York, Terry W. Charles Hutchinson Gabriel (1856-1932): Composer, Author, and Editor in the Gospel Tradition. D.M.A., New Orleans Baptist Theological Seminary, 1985. 182p. UMI# 8611780.

Education

1441   Bushko, Andrew A. Religious Revivals at American Colleges 1783-1860: An Exploratory Study. Ed.D., Columbia University, 1974. 251p. UMI# 75-06460.

1442   Cornelius, Janet D. God's Schoolmasters: Southern Evangelists to the Slaves, 1830-1860. Ph.D., University of Illinois at Urbana-Champaign, 1977. 326p. UMI# 77-14939.

1443   Talpos, Vasile F. The Importance of Evangelism in Ministerial Training: A Critical Analysis of the Contribution of Selected Nineteenth Century Christian Educators. Ph.D., Southern Baptist Theological Seminary, 1983. 313p. UMI# 8401782.

Ethnic Groups

1444   Maurer, Kenneth R. Nineteenth-Century Revivalistic Trends in the Pennsylvania German Churches. S.T.D., Temple University, 1956.

Music

1445   Downey, James C. The Music of American Revivalism. Ph.D., Tulane University, 1968. 228p. UMI# 6903792.

1446   Ellsworth, Donald P. Music in the Church for Purposes of Evangelism: Historical Antecedents and Contemporary Practices. D.M.A., University of Southern California, 1977.

1447   Hammond, Paul G. Music in Urban Revivalism in the Northern United States, 1800-1835. D.M.A., Southern Baptist Theological Seminary, 1974. 199p. UMI# 74-22660.

1448   Kaatrud, Paul G. Revivalism and the Popular Spiritual Song in Mid-Nineteenth-Century America: 1830-1870. Ph.D., University of Minnesota, 1977. 383p. UMI# 7802682.

1449   Neil, Bobby J. Philip P. Bliss (1838-1876): Gospel Hymn Composer and Compiler. Ed.D., New Orleans Baptist Theological Seminary, 1977. 235p. UMI# 77-21943.

Preaching

1450   Champion, Herman D., Jr. A Rhetorical Analysis of Selected Sermons by Sam Jones During His Emergence as a National Figure, 1872-1885. Ph.D., Louisiana State University, 1980. 300p. UMI# 8110407.

1451   Cheesebro, Roy A. The Preaching of Charles G. Finney. Ph.D., Yale University, 1948. 418p. UMI# 6411868.

1452   Curtis, Richard K. The Pulpit Speaking of Dwight L. Moody. Ph.D., Purdue University, 1954. 458p. UMI# 09861.

1453   Emmel, James R. The Persuasive Techniques of Charles Grandison Finney as a Revivalist and Social Reform Speaker 1820-1860. Ph.D., Pennsylvania State University, 1959. 445p. UMI# 59-05105.

1454   Griffin, Charles J.G. Charles Finney's Prayer: A Dramatistic Interpretation of Charles Grandison Finney's Lectures on Revivals of Religion, 1834-1835. Ph.D., University of Missouri, 1983. 152p. UMI# 8406197.

1455   Ladd, James M. Dwight L. Moody's Use of the Aristotelian Modes of Persuasion. Ph.D., Oklahoma State University, 1960. UMI# 0225570.

1456   Parker, Charles A. A Study of the Preaching at the Ocean Grove, New Jersey, Camp Meeting, 1870-1900. Ph.D., Louisiana State University, 1959. 308p. UMI# 5905524.

1457   White, Eugene E. The Preaching of George Whitefield During the

Great Awakening in America. Ph.D., Louisiana State University, 1947.

Social Programs

1458   Vulgamore, Melvin L. Social Reform in the Theology of Charles Grandison Finney. Ph.D., Boston University, 1963. 274p. UMI# 64-00391.

Theology

1459   Asa, Robert L. The Theology and Methodology of Charles G. Finney as a Prototype for Modern Mass Evangelism. Ph.D., Southern Baptist Theological Seminary, 1983. 392p. UMI# 8405882.

1460   Cafone, James M. The Role of the Holy Spirit in the Theology of Charles Grandison Finney. St.D., Catholic University of America, 1979. 281p. UMI# 7920537.

1461   Gundry, Stanley N. Ruin, Redemption, Regeneration: The Proclamation Theology of Dwight L. Moody, Evangelist. S.T.D., Lutheran School of Theology, 1975. 366p. UMI# 76-11506.

1462   Hollon, David L. Love as Holiness: An Examination of Charles G. Finney's Theology of Sanctification, 1830-1860. Ph.D., Southern Baptist Theological Seminary, 1984. 251p. UMI# 8509888.

1463   Reeve, James H. Holiness and the Holy Spirit in the Thought of Charles G. Finney. Ph.D., Fuller Theological Seminary, 1990. 344p. UMI# 9107408.

FRUITLANDS

1464   Walker, Robert H. Charles Lane and the Fruitlands Utopia. Ph.D., University of Texas-Austin, 1967. 161p. UMI# 67-08171.

FUNDAMENTALISM

1465   Harrington, Carroll E. The Fundamentalist Movement in America, 1870-1920. Ph.D., University of California-Berkeley, 1959.

1466   Rausch, David A. Proto-Fundamentalism's Attitudes Toward Zionism, 1878-1918. Ph.D., Kent State University, 1978. 315p. UMI# 78-12874.

1467   Staggers, Kermit L. Reuben A. Torrey: American Fundamentalist, 1856-1928. Ph.D., Claremont Graduate School, 1986. 338p. UMI# 8607839.

1468   Unger, Walter. "Earnestly Contending for the Faith": The Role of the Niagara Bible Conference in the Emergence of American Fundamentalism, 1875-1900. Ph.D., Simon Fraser University, 1982.

GERMAN REFORMED

1469   Barker, Verlyn L. John W. Nevin: His Place in American Intellectual Thought. Ph.D., Saint Louis University, 1970. 316p. UMI# 71-03248.

1470   Carlough, William L. A Historical Comparison of the Theology of John Williamson Nevin and Contemporary Protestant Sacramentalism. Ph.D., New York University, 1961. 198p. UMI# 61-02546.

1471   Ebbert, Clarence W. The Liturgical Controversy in the German Reformed Church in the United States. Ph.D., Temple University, 1959.

1472   Frantz, John B. Revivalism in the German Reformed Church in America to 1850, With Emphasis on the Eastern Synod. Ph.D., University of Pennsylvania, 1961. 314p. UMI# 61-02031.

1473   Harpster, Donald E. Controversy in the German Reformed Church in Pennsylvania With Emphasis on Nineteenth-Century Philadelphia. Ph.D., Pennsylvania State University, 1976. 222p. UMI# 77-09555.

1474   Kern, Gilbert R., Jr. John Winebrenner: Nineteenth Century Churchman and Reformer. Ph.D., University of Chicago, 1969.

1475   Livingood, F.G. German Reformed Church Education in Pennsylvania During the Eighteenth Century. Ed.D., Harvard University, 1925.

1476   Martin, Roger A. John J. Zubly: Preacher, Planter, and Politician. Ph.D., University of Georgia, 1976. 214p. UMI# 7704142.

1477   Plummer, Kenneth M. The Theology of John Williamson Nevin in the Mercersburg Period, 1840-1852. Ph.D., University of Chicago, 1958.

1478   Ryan, Francis P. John Williamson Nevin: The Concept of Church Authority, 1844-1858. Ph.D., Marquette University, 1968. 375p. UMI# 70-17410.

1479   Ulrich, Reinhard. The School of Prophets: A Study of the Cultural and Theological Patterns in the Establishment and Early Development of the German Reformed Mission House in Wisconsin. Ph.D., Lutheran School of Theology, 1963.

1480   Watts, Franklin P. The Free Synod of the German Reformed Church, 1822-1837. S.T.D., Temple University, 1954.

1481   Ziegler, Howard J. Frederick Augustus Rauch, American Hegelian. Ph.D., Columbia University, 1950. 330p. UMI# 02362.

GLOSSOLALIA

1482   Gonsalvez, Heliodora E. The Theology and Psychology of Glossolalia. Ph.D., Northwestern University, 1978. 166p. UMI# 7907879.

1483   Shumway, Charles W. A Critical History of Glossolalia. Ph.D., Boston University, 1919.

GREAT AWAKENING

General Studies

1484   Bilhartz, Terry D. Urban Religion and the Second Great Awakening: A Religious History of Baltimore, Maryland, 1790-1830. Ph.D., George Washington University, 1979. 442p. UMI# 79-23395.

1485   Blauvelt, Martha T. Society, Religion, and Revivalism: The Second Great Awakening in New Jersey, 1780-1830. Ph.D., Princeton University, 1975. 364p. UMI# 75-23181.

1486   Butler, Alfloyd. The Blacks' Contributions of Elements of African Religion to Christianity in America: A Case Study of the Great Awakening in South Carolina. Ph.D., Northwestern University, 1975. 213p. UMI# 76-12154.

1487   Butler, Jon H. The Christian Experience in the Delaware Valley: The English Churches on the Eve of the Great Awakening. Ph.D., University of Minnesota, 1972. 289p. UMI# 72-20097.

1488   Gaustad, Edwin S. The Great Awakening in New England, 1741-1742. Ph.D., Brown University, 1951.

1489   Gewher, Wesley M. The Great Awakening in Virginia, 1740-1790. Ph.D., University of Chicago, 1922.

1490   Goen, Clarence C. Revivalism and Separatism in New England, 1740-1800: Strict Congregationalists and Separate Baptists in the Great Awakening. Ph.D., Yale University, 1960.

1491   Hogue, William M. The Church of England in the Northern

Colonies and the Great Awakening. Ph.D., Catholic University of America, 1955.

1492   Keller, Charles R. The Second Great Awakening in Connecticut. Ph.D., Yale University, 1934.

1493   Lacey, Barbara E. Women and the Great Awakening in Connecticut. Ph.D., Clark University, 1982. 213p. UMI# 8228821.

1494   Lavengood, Lawrence G. The Great Awakening and New England Society. Ph.D., University of Chicago, 1954.

1495   Lodge, Martin E. The Great Awakening in the Middle Colonies. Ph.D., University of California-Berkeley, 1964. 333p. UMI# 6503027.

1496   Maxson, Charles H. The Great Awakening in the Middle Colonies. Ph.D., University of Chicago, 1915.

1497   McCleave, David H. The Synod of Philadelphia and the Great Awakening. Ph.D., University of Iowa, 1947.

1498   Morgan, David T., Jr. The Great Awakening in the Carolinas and Georgia, 1740-1775. Ph.D., University of North Carolina-Chapel Hill, 1968. 288p. UMI# 6901652.

1499   Orr, J. Edwin. The Millionfold Awakening in America, 1857-1858. Ph.D., Northern Baptist Theological Seminary, 1953.

1500   Parkes, Henry B. New England and the Great Awakening: A Study in the Theory and Practice of New England Calvinism. Ph.D., University of Michigan, 1929.

1501   Peterson, Carl H. The Politics of Revival, 1783-1815. Ph.D., Stanford University, 1974. 489p. UMI# 7420224.

1502   Potash, Paul J. Toward a "New Rural History": Patterns of Community Organization in Three Addison County, Vermont Towns, 1761-1850. Ph.D., University of Chicago, 1986. [Cornwall, Middlebury, Shoreham(VT)].

1503   Reed, Charles R. Image Alteration in a Mass Movement: A Rhetorical Analysis of the Role of the Log College in the Great Awakening. Ph.D., Ohio State University, 1972. 282p. UMI# 73-02103.

1504   Rutter, Robert S. The New Birth: Evangelicalism in the Transatlantic Community During the Great Awakening, 1739-1745. Ph.D., Rutgers University, 1982. 449p. UMI# 82-21701.

1505   Taylor, Thomas T. The Spirit of the Awakening: The Pneumatology of New England's Great Awakening in Historical and Theological Context. Ph.D., University of Illinois at Urbana-Champaign, 1988. 447p. UMI# 8815429.

1506   Thomas, Arthur D., Jr. The Second Great Awakening in Virginia and Slavery Reform, 1785-1837. Th.D., Union Theological Seminary in Virginia, 1981. 783p. UMI# 8202084.

1507   Vos, Howard F. The Great Awakening in Connecticut. Ph.D., Northwestern University, 1967. 373p. UMI# 6715357.

1508   Westerkamp, Marilyn J. Triumph of the Laity: The Migration of Revivalism From Scotland and Ireland to the Middle Colonies, 1625-1760. Ph.D., University of Pennsylvania, 1984. 441p. UMI# 8505144.

Art and Architecture

1509   Horbach, Charles F. The Motifs of the First and Second Great Awakenings, Illustrated by Contemporary American Paintings of Jesus. Ph.D., Temple University, 1972. 281p. UMI# 73-08865.

Biography

1510   Coalter, Milton J., Jr. The Life of Gilbert Tennent: A Case Study of Continental Pietism's Influence on the First Great Awakening in the Middle Colonies. Ph.D., Princeton University, 1982. 433p. UMI# 8209782.

Clergy

1511   Cooper, James F., Jr. A Participatory Theocracy: Church Government in Colonial Massachusetts, 1629-1760. Ph.D., University of Connecticut, 1987. 407p. UMI# 8800210.

1512   Harlan, David C. The Clergy and the Great Awakening in New England. Ph.D., University of California-Irvine, 1979. 257p. UMI# 79-13960.

1513   Kling, David W. Clergy and Society in the Second Great Awakening in Connecticut. Ph.D., University of Chicago, 1985.

1514   Ricard, Laura B. The Evangelical New Light Clergy of Northern New England, 1741-1755: A Typology. Ph.D., University of New Hampshire, 1985. 385p. UMI# 8607462.

1515   Shiels, Richard D. The Connecticut Clergy in the Second Great

Awakening. Ph.D., Boston University, 1976. 466p. UMI# 77-25889.

Education

1516   Havner, Carter S. The Reaction of Yale to the Great Awakening: 1740-1766. Ph.D., University of Texas-Austin, 1977. 291p. UMI# 7807314.

Literature

1517   Lee, William R. A Critical and Historical Survey of Verse Relating to the Great Awakening in New England, 1739-1760. Ph.D., University of Connecticut, 1972. 229p. UMI# 7232150.

Music

1518   Weiss, Joanne G. The Relationship Between the "Great Awakening" and the Transition From Psalmody to Hymnody in the New England Colonies. D.A., Ball State University, 1988. 216p. UMI# 8820744.

Preaching

1519   Enzor, Edwin H., Jr. The Preaching of James M'Gready, Frontier Revivalist. Ph.D., Louisiana State University, 1964. 380p. UMI# 6413253.

1520   Houser, William G. Identifying the Regenerate: The Homiletics of Conversion During the First Great Awakening. Ph.D., University of Notre Dame, 1988. 215. UMI# 8813739.

1521   Stanfield, Vernon L. The Preaching of the Great Awakening and Its Contributions to Political Liberty. Ph.D., Southern Baptist Theological Seminary, 1947.

Theology

1522   Martin, William G., Jr. Theological Concepts in Representative American Dreams During the Second Great Awakening (Circa 1795-1845). Ph.D., University of Wisconsin-Madison, 1971. 362p. UMI# 7200428.

1523   Parry, Mark H. The Theology of the Great Awakening. Th.D., Drew University, 1931.

1524   Valeri, Mark R. Joseph Bellamy: Conversion, Social Ethics, and Politics in the Thought of an Eighteenth-Century Calvinist. Ph.D., Princeton University, 1985. 213p. UMI# 8518647.

GREEK ORTHODOX

1525　Hood, Edmund L. The Greek Church in America. Ph.D., New York University, 1899.

HARMONY SOCIETY

1526　Baldwin, Juliana. The Constitutional History of the New Harmony Experiment. Ph.D., University of Oklahoma, 1937.

1527　Bole, John A. The Harmony Society: A Chapter in German American Culture. Ph.D., University of Pennsylvania, 1903.

1528　Douglas, Paul H. The Material Culture of the Communities of the Harmony Society. Ph.D., George Washington University, 1973. 222p. UMI# 7405113.

1529　Gaglione, Rodger T. Education in Utopia: Curriculum Theory and Design in the New Harmony Communal Settlement. Ed.D., Rutgers University, 1982. 279p. UMI# 8218321.

1530　Mariampolski, Hyman. The Dilemmas of Utopian Communities: A Study of the Owenite Community at New Harmony, Indiana. Ph.D., Purdue University, 1977. 309p. UMI# 7803261.

1531　Miller, Melvin R. Education in the Harmony Society, 1805-1905. Ph.D., University of Pittsburgh, 1972. 349p. UMI# 7313165.

1532　Sluder, Claude K. Music in New Harmony, Indiana, 1825-1865: A Study of the Music and Musical Activities of Robert Owen's Community of Equality (1825-1827) and Its Cultural Afterglow (1827-1865). Ph.D., Indiana University, 1987. 478p. UMI# 8727527.

1533　Wetzel, Richard D. The Music of George Rapp's Harmony Society: 1805-1906. Ph.D., University of Pittsburgh, 1970. 569p. UMI# 7103529.

HOPEDALE

1534　Faulkner, Barbara L. Adin Ballou and the Hopedale Community. Ph.D., Boston University, 1965. 324p. UMI# 6511219.

1535　Gregory, Christopher W. Perpetual Purification and Developing Sense of Self: The Evolving Theology and Person of Adin Ballou. Ph.D., Saint Louis University, 1990. 291p. UMI# 9102904.

1536　Padelford, Philip S. Adin Ballou and the Hopedale Community. Ph.D., Yale University, 1942. 371p.

HUGUENOT

1537   Friedlander, Amy E. Carolina Huguenots: A Study in Cultural Pluralism in the Low Country, 1679-1768. Ph.D., Emory University, 1979. 372p. UMI# 7920609.

1538   Hirsch, Arthur H. The Huguenots in South Carolina. Ph.D., University of Chicago, 1915.

1539   Kamil, Neil D. War, Natural Philosophy, and the Metaphysical Foundations of Artisanal Thought in an American Mid-Atlantic Colony: La Rochelle, New York City, and the Southwestern Huguenot Paradigm, 1517-1730. Ph.D., Johns Hopkins University, 1989. 694p. UMI# 8908118.

JUDAISM

General Studies

1540   Anderson, Elaine S. The Jews of Toledo, 1845-1895. Ph.D., University of Toledo, 1974. 378p. UMI# 75-06486.

1541   Ariel, Yaakov S. American Premillennialism and Its Attitudes Towards the Jewish People, Judaism and Zionism, 1875-1925. Ph.D., University of Chicago, 1986.

1542   Ashkenazi, Elliott. Creoles of Jerusalem: Jewish Businessmen in Louisiana, 1840-1875. Ph.D., George Washington University, 1983. 341p. UMI# 8401315.

1543   Berlin, William S. The Roots of Jewish Political Thought in America. Ph.D., Rutgers University, 1976. 278p. UMI# 76-16386.

1544   Borowitz, Eugene B. The Jewish Religion According to the Liberal-Reform Tradition. Ph.D., Columbia University, 1958.

1545   Braverman, William A. The Ascent of Boston's Jews, 1630-1918. Ph.D., Harvard University, 1990. 460p. UMI# 9021785.

1546   Brickner, Barnett R. The Cincinnati Jewish Community: An Historical Descriptive Study. Ph.D., University of Cincinnati, 1935.

1547   Cohen, Robert. Jewish Demography in the Eighteenth Century: A Study of London, the West Indies, and Early America. Ph.D., Brandeis University, 1976. 245p. UMI# 7625297.

1548   Douglas, Martin I. Chronological Summary of Annotated Cards Toward the History of the Jewish Agricultural Communities in South

Jersey. Ph.D., Jewish Theological Seminary of America, 1960.

1549   Eichhorn, David M. A History of Christian Attempts to Convert the Jews in the United States and Canada. Ph.D., Hebrew Union College, 1949. 288p.

1550   Eisenberg, Ellen M. Jewish Agricultural Colonies in Southern New Jersey: The Processes of Migration, Settlement and Adaptation. Ph.D., University of Pennsylvania, 1990. 377p. UMI# 9010051.

1551   Feibelman, Julian B. A Social and Economic Study of the New Orleans Jewish Community. Ph.D., University of Pennsylvania, 1939.

1552   Feinstein, Marnin. The First Twenty-Five Years of Zionism in the United States, 1882-1906. Ph.D., Columbia University, 1963. 342p. UMI# 6405413.

1553   Fleishaker, Oscar. The Illinois-Iowa Jewish Community of the Banks on the Mississippi River. D.H.L., Yeshiva University, 1957. 450p. UMI# 63-01962.

1554   Freund, Miriam K. Jewish Merchants in Colonial America: Their Achievements and Their Contributions to the Development of America. Ph.D., New York University, 1936. 146p. UMI# 73-17875.

1555   Gastwirt, Harold P. Fraud, Corruption and Holiness: *Kashrut* Supervision in New York City, 1881-1940. Ph.D., Columbia University, 1971. 368p. UMI# 74-08176.

1556   Goldstein, Philip R. Social Aspects of the Jewish Colonies of South Jersey. Ph.D., University of Pennsylvania, 1921. 74p.

1557   Goodman, Avram V. American Overture: Jewish Rights in Colonial Times. Ph.D., University of Texas-Austin, 1949. 265p.

1558   Gordon, Albert I. The Jews of Minneapolis: A Study in Acculturation. Ph.D., University of Minnesota, 1949. 371p.

1559   Gordon, Morton L. The History of the Jewish Farmer in Eastern Connecticut. D.H.L., Yeshiva University, 1974. 244p. UMI# 75-20587.

1560   Grinstein, Hyman B. The Rise of the Jewish Community of New York, 1654-1860. Ph.D., Columbia University, 1944. 645p.

1561   Grossberg, Sidney H. Factors in Historical and Participation Identification of Detroit Area Jews. Ph.D., Wayne State University, 1971. 216p. UMI# 7129741.

1562   Halpert, Max. The Jews of Brownsville, 1880-1925: A Demographic, Economic, Socio-Cultural Study. D.H.L., Yeshiva University, 1958. 348p. UMI# 58-03027.

1563   Harris, Alice K. The Lower Class as a Factor in Reform: New York, the Jews, and the 1890's. Ed.D., Rutgers University, 1968. 363p. UMI# 69-07543.

1564   Heinze, Andrew R. Adapting to Abundance: Eastern European Jews and Urban Consumption in America, 1880-1914. Ph.D., University of California-Berkeley, 1987. 412p. UMI# 8813901.

1565   Herscher, Uri D. Jewish Agricultural Experiments in Late Nineteenth-Century America. D.H.L., Hebrew Union College-Jewish Institute of Religion, 1973.

1566   Hertzberg, Steven. The Jews of Atlanta, 1865-1915. Ph.D., University of Chicago, 1975.

1567   Joseph, Samuel. Jewish Immigration to the United States From 1881 to 1910. Ph.D., Columbia University, 1914. 205p.

1568   Kazis, Israel J. Hasidism: A Study in the Sociology and History of Religion. Ph.D., Harvard University, 1939.

1569   Klatzker, David E. American Christian Travelers to the Holy Land, 1821-1939. Ph.D., Temple University, 1987. 381p. UMI# 8803821.

1570   Korn, Bertram W. American Jewry and the Civil War. Ph.D., Hebrew Union College-Jewish Institute of Religion, 1949.

1571   Kosak, Hadassa. The Rise of the Jewish Working Class, New York, 1881-1905. Ph.D., City University of New York, 1987. 298p. UMI# 8708297.

1572   Kuntz, Leonard I. The Changing Pattern of the Distribution of the Jewish Population of Pittsburgh From Earliest Settlement to 1963. Ph.D., Louisiana State University, 1970. 242p. UMI# 71-06584.

1573   Kuzmack, Linda G. The Emergence of the Jewish Women's Movement in England and the United States, 1881-1933: A Comparative Study. Ph.D., George Washington University, 1986. 623p. UMI# 8615758.

1574   Lamb, Blaine P. Jewish Pioneers in Arizona, 1850-1920. Ph.D., Arizona State University, 1982. 386p. UMI# 82-16446.

1575   Landenberger, Margaret. United States Diplomatic Efforts on Behalf of Moroccan Jews: 1880-1906. Ph.D., St. John's University, 1981. 264p. UMI# 82-01686.

1576   Levinger, Lee J. The Causes of Anti-Semitism in the United States; A Study in Group and Sub-Group. Ph.D., University of Pennsylvania, 1925.

1577   Levinson, Robert E. The Jews in the California Gold Rush. Ph.D., University of Oregon, 1968. 288p. UMI# 69-06642.

1578   Levy, Beryl H. Reform Judaism in America. Ph.D., Columbia University, 1934.

1579   Mazur, Edward H. Minyans for a Prairie City: The Politics of Chicago Jewry, 1850-1940. Ph.D., University of Chicago, 1974. 440p.

1580   Mesinger, Jonathan S. The Jewish Community in Syracuse, 1850-1880: The Growth and Structure of an Urban Ethnic Region. Ph.D., Syracuse University, 1977. 290p. UMI# 78-13323.

1581   Mostov, Stephen G. A "Jerusalem" on the Ohio: The Social and Economic History of Cincinnati's Jewish Community, 1840-1875. Ph.D., Brandeis University, 1981. 309p. UMI# 81-26888.

1582   Nadell, Pamela S. The Journey to America by Steam: The Jews of Eastern Europe in Transition. Ph.D., Ohio State University, 1982. 253p. UMI# 82-22140.

1583   Orentlicher, Edward. The Talmud Torah in America: Its Structure, Philosophy and Decline (1860-1960). Ph.D., Dropsie University, 1962.

1584   Pavin, Michele H. Sports and Leisure of the American Jewish Community, 1848 to 1976. Ph.D., Ohio State University, 1981. 312p. UMI# 82-07242.

1585   Raphael, Marc L. Intra-Jewish Conflict in the United States, 1869-1915. Ph.D., University of California-Los Angeles, 1972. 146p. UMI# 73-01725.

1586   Rischin, Moses. Jewish Life and Labor in New York City, 1870-1914. Ph.D., Harvard University, 1957.

1587   Rockaway, Robert A. From Americanization to Jewish Americanism: The Jews of Detroit, 1850-1914. Ph.D., University of Michigan, 1970. 258p. UMI# 70-21777.

1588   Rogoff, Abraham M. Formative Years of the Jewish Labor

Movement in the United States (1890-1900). Ph.D., Columbia University, 1946. 111p.

1589   Roseman, Kenneth D. The Jewish Population of America, 1850-1860: A Demographic Study of Four Cities. Ph.D., Hebrew Union College, 1972.

1590   Rosenberg, Jacob M. Historical Study of the Elimination of the Religious, Civil, and Political Disabilities of the Jews in the United States From Earliest Days to the Present. Ph.D., New York University, 1914. UMI# 74-01280.

1591   Rosenberg, Stuart E. The Jews of Rochester, New York, 1843-1925. Ph.D., Columbia University, 1953. 202p.

1592   Rubinger, Naphtali J. Albany Jewry of the Nineteenth Century; Historic Roots and Communal Evolution. D.H.L., Yeshiva University, 1970. 600p. UMI# 71-05696.

1593   Seiger, Marvin L. A History of the Yiddish Theatre in New York City to 1892. Ph.D., Indiana University, 1960. 616p. UMI# 60-06324.

1594   Sharfman, Israel H. American "Responsa" as a Source for the History of the Jews of America to 1850. Ph.D., Yeshiva University, 1955. 367p.

1595   Shargel, Baila R. Israel Friedlaender and the Transformation of European Jewish Thought in America. D.H.L., Jewish Theological Seminary of America, 1982. 412p. UMI# 82-16505.

1596   Shuldiner, David P. Of Moses and Marx: Folk Ideology Within the Jewish Labor Movement in the United States. Ph.D., University of California-Los Angeles, 1984. 283p. UMI# 8420245.

1597   Silver, Arthur M. Jews in the Political Life of New York City, 1865-1897. D.H.L., Yeshiva University, 1954. 241p. UMI# 59-01471.

1598   Stern, Malcolm H. Two Studies in the Assimilation of Early American Jewry. Ph.D., Hebrew Union College, 1957.

1599   Tarshish, Allan. The Rise of American Judaism, A History of American Jewish Life From 1848 to 1881. Ph.D., Hebrew Union College, 1949.

1600   Urquhart, Ronald A. The American Reaction to the Dreyfus Affair: A Study of Anti-Semitism in the 1890's. Ph.D., Columbia University, 1972. 279p. UMI# 7512348.

1601   Weissberger, Sidney J. The Rise and Decline of the Yiddish-American Press. Ph.D., Syracuse University, 1972. 674p. UMI# 73-07783.

1602   Winograd, Leonard. The Horse Died at Windber: A History of Johnstown Jewry. Ph.D., Hebrew Union College, 1967.

1603   Yodfat, Aryeh. The Jewish Question in American-Russian Relations (1875-1917). Ph.D., American University, 1963. 245p. UMI# 63-06630.

Biography

1604   Ashton, Dianne C. Rebecca Gratz and the Domestication of American Judaism. Ph.D., Temple University, 1986. 370p. UMI# 8627421.

1605   Bennett, Emanuel. An Evaluation of the Life of Isaac Leeser. Ph.D., Yeshiva University, 1955.

1606   Eckman, Lester S. The Life and Works of Rabbi Israel Meir Kagan-Hafets Hayyim (1838-1933). Ph.D., New York University, 1973. 297p. UMI# 74-01877.

1607   Feierstein, Milton. Isaac Leeser (1806-1868): Founder of Jewish Education in the United States. Ed.D., State University of New York-Buffalo, 1971. 198p. UMI# 71-28036.

1608   Kully, Robert D. Isaac Mayer Wise: His Rhetoric Against Religious Discrimination. Ph.D., University of Illinois at Urbana-Champaign, 1956. 313p. UMI# 19839.

1609   Markovitz, Eugene. Henry Pereira Mendes (1877-1920). D.H.L., Yeshiva University, 1961. 317p. UMI# 6201950.

1610   Nussenbaum, Max S. Champion of Orthodox Judaism: A Biography of the Reverend Sabato Morais, LL.D. D.H.L., Yeshiva University, 1964. 267p. UMI# 64-09395.

1611   Rapport, Joe R. The Lazarus Sisters: A Family Portrait. Ph.D., Washington University, 1988. 249p. UMI# 8907910.

1612   Rosenbloom, Joseph R. "And She Had Compassion": The Life and Times of Rebecca Gratz. Ph.D., Hebrew Union College-Jewish Institute of Religion, 1957.

1613   Rosenstock, Morton. Louis Marshall and the Defense of Jewish

Rights in the United States. Ph.D., Columbia University, 1963. 517p. UMI# 64-02783.

1614   Sarna, Jonathan D. Mordecai M. Noah: Jacksonian Politician and American Jewish Communal Leader: A Biographical Study. Ph.D., Yale University, 1979. 595p. UMI# 79-28093.

1615   Seller, Maxine S. Isaac Leeser, Architect of the American Jewish Community. Ph.D., University of Pennsylvania, 1965. 205p. UMI# 6600297.

1616   Simon, E. Yechiel. Samuel Myer Isaacs: A 19th Century Jewish Minister in New York City. D.H.L., Yeshiva University, 1974. 243p. UMI# 75-09056.

1617   Sussman, Lance J. The Life and Career of Isaac Leeser (1806-1868): A Study of American Judaism in Its Formative Period. Ph.D., Hebrew Union College-Jewish Institute of Religion, 1987. 546p. UMI# 8722618.

1618   Temkin, Sefton D. Isaac Mayer Wise, 1819-1875. Ph.D., Hebrew Union College-Jewish Institute of Religion, 1965.

1619   Wind, James P. The Bible and the University: The Messianic Vision of William Rainey Harper. Ph.D., University of Chicago, 1983. UMI# 0366611.

Education

1620   Dushkin, Alexander M. Jewish Education in New York City. Ph.D., Columbia University, 1918. 559p.

1621   Fierman, Floyd S. Efforts Toward Reform in American Jewish Education Prior to 1881. Ph.D., University of Pittsburgh, 1949.

1622   Fierstien, Robert E. From Foundation to Reorganization: The Jewish Theological Seminary of America, 1886-1902. D.H.L., Jewish Theological Seminary of America, 1986. 200p. UMI# 8611314.

1623   Hertz, Richard C. Religious Education Among American Reformed Jewish Congregations. Ph.D., Northwestern University, 1949. 229p.

1624   Loren, Morris J. Hebrew Higher Educational Institutions in the United States, 1830-1975. Ph.D., Wayne State University, 1976. 199p. UMI# 76-17327.

1625   Newman, Max. Basic Principles of American Reform Judaism and Their Reflection in the Movements Program of Religious Education

From 1848 to Present. Ph.D., Hebrew Union College, 1965.

1626   Rauch, Eduardo L. Jewish Education in the United States, 1840-1920. Ed.D., Harvard University, 1978. 517p. UMI# 78-23684.

1627   Selavan, Ida C. The Columbian Council of Pittsburgh, 1894-1909: A Case Study of Adult Immigrant Education. Ph.D., University of Pittsburgh, 1976. 161p. UMI# 7619928.

1628   Shapiro, Max A. An Historical Analysis and Evaluation of Jewish Religious Textbooks Published in the United States, 1817-1903. Ed.D., University of Cincinnati, 1960. 262p. UMI# 60-06159.

1629   Todes, David U. History of Jewish Education in Philadelphia, 1782-1873. Ph.D., Dropsie University, 1953.

1630   Yapko, Benjamin L. Jewish Elementary Education in the United States: Colonial Period to 1900. Ed.D., American University, 1958. 197p. UMI# 58-03030.

Ethnic Groups

1631   Berman, Myron. The Attitude of American Jewry Towards East European Jewish Immigration, 1881-1914. Ph.D., Columbia University, 1963. 585p. UMI# 64-01545.

1632   Jick, Leon A. Jews in the Synagogue, Americans Everywhere: The German-Jewish Immigration and the Emergence of the American Jewish Pattern, 1820-1870. Ph.D., Columbia University, 1973. 304p. UMI# 74-29601.

1633   Nechushtai, Shai S. Between Hebraism, the Melting Pot and Ethnicity: The American-Hebrew-Language Press, 1871-1914, and the Process of "Americanization" of the Jewish Immigrants. (Hebrew Text). Ph.D., University of California-Los Angeles, 1988. 348p. UMI# 8903657.

1634   Pollack, Herman. The German-Jewish Community: Studies in Aspects of Its Inner-Life (1648-1806). Ph.D., Columbia University, 1958. UMI# 58-02241.

Literature

1635   Demarr, Mary J. In a Strange Land: Contributions to American Literature by Russian and Russian-Jewish Immigrants. Ph.D., University of Illinois at Urbana-Champaign, 1963. 343p. UMI# 6406043.

1636   Gittlen, Arthur J. Political and Social Thought Contained in the Jewish-American Novel (1867-1927). Ph.D., Michigan State University, 1969. 211p. UMI# 69-20862.

1637   Kroloff, Theresa K. The Beginning of American Jewish Fiction. Ph.D., Drew University, 1978. 196p. UMI# 7819265.

1638   Levine, Samuel H. Changing Concepts of Palestine in American Literature to 1867. Ph.D., New York University, 1953. 340p. UMI# 672.

1639   Lichtenstein, Diane M. On Whose Native Ground? Nineteenth-Century Myths of American Womanhood and Jewish Women Writers. Ph.D., University of Pennsylvania, 1985. 377p. UMI# 8515405.

1640   Raphael, Lev. "The Pen and the Pulpit": Isaac Mayer Wise's Fiction in *The Israelite*. Ph.D., Michigan State University, 1986. 230p. UMI# 8707177.

1641   Soviv, Aaron. Attitudes Towards Jewish Life and Education as Reflected in Yiddish and Hebrew Literature in America, 1870-1914. Ph.D., Dropsie University, 1957.

Liturgy

1642   Friedland, Eric L. The Historical and Theological Development of the Non-Orthodox Prayerbooks in the United States. Ph.D., Brandeis University, 1967. 320p. UMI# 67-16549.

Newspapers and Periodicals

1643   Reed, Barbara S. A History and Content Analysis of the Pioneer English-Language American Jewish Periodical Press, 1823-1858. Ph.D., Ohio University, 1987. 426p. UMI# 9033551.

1644   Richman, Harvey A. The Image of America in the European Hebrew Periodicals of the Nineteenth Century (until 1880). Ph.D., University of Texas-Austin, 1971. 257p. UMI# 72-19656.

1645   Weingarten, Irving. The Image of the Jew in the American Periodical Press, 1881-1921. Ph.D., New York University, 1980. 286p. UMI# 8017536.

1646   Wyszkowski, Yehezkel. *The American Hebrew* Views the Jewish Community in the United States, 1879-1884, 1894-1898 and 1903-1908. Ph.D., Yeshiva University, 1979. 720p. UMI# 80-07270.

Preaching

1647   Kaganoff, Nathan M. The Traditional Jewish Sermon in the United States From Its Beginnings to the First World War. Ph.D., American University, 1961. 224p. UMI# 61-03715.

1648   Kahn, Robert I. Liberalism as Reflected in Jewish Preaching in the English Language in the Mid-Nineteenth Century: An Examination of the Jewish Life and Faith (Particularly in the United States) Between 1830 to 1870, as Revealed in the Sermons of That Period. Ph.D., Hebrew Union College-Jewish Institute of Religion, 1951.

Social Programs

1649   Fisher, Terry K. Lending as Philanthrophy: The Philadelphia Jewish Experience, 1847-1954. Ph.D., Bryn Mawr College, 1987. 230p. UMI# 8715259.

1650   Frisch, Ephraim. An Historical Survey of Jewish Philanthropy, From the Earliest Times to the Nineteenth Century. Ph.D., Columbia University, 1924.

1651   Herman, Alan. Institutional Practices in Jewish Hospitals of New York City: 1880-1930. Ph.D., New York University, 1984. 129p. UMI# 8421447.

1652   Kutzik, Alfred J. The Social Basis of American Jewish Philanthropy. Ph.D., Brandeis University, 1967. 1067p. UMI# 68-03406.

1653   Mensch, Jean U. Social Pathology in Urban America: Desertion, Prostitution, Gambling, Drugs and Crime Among Eastern European Jews in New York City Between 1881 and World War I. Ph.D., Columbia University, 1983. 334p. UMI# 8511529.

1654   Polster, Gary E. A Member of the Herd: Growing up in the Cleveland Jewish Orphan Asylum, 1868-1919. Ph.D., Case Western Reserve University, 1984. 352p. UMI# 8425575.

1655   Stein, Herman D. Jewish Social Work in the United States, 1654-1954. D.S.W., Columbia University, 1958. 233p. UMI# 58-02604.

LATTER-DAY SAINTS

General Studies

1656   Abruzzi, William S. Ecological Succession and Mormon Colonization in the Little Colorado River Basin. Ph.D., State University of New

York-Binghamton, 1981. 346p. UMI# 81-13368.

1657 Allen, Edward J. The Second United Order Among the Mormons. Ph.D., Columbia University, 1937.

1658 Arrington, Leonard J. Mormon Economic Policies and Their Implementation on the Western Frontier, 1847-1900. Ph.D., University of North Carolina-Chapel Hill, 1953.

1659 Barlow, Philip L. The Bible in Mormonism. Th.D., Harvard University, 1988. 303p. UMI# 8908497.

1660 Barrus, Roger M. Religion, Regime, and Politics: The Founding and Political Development of Utah. Ph.D., Harvard University, 1984. 392p. UMI# 8419298.

1661 Bassett, Arthur R. Culture and the American Frontier in Mormon Utah, 1850-1896. Ph.D., Syracuse University, 1975. 438p. UMI# 76-07630.

1662 Bennett, Richard E. Mormons at the Missouri: A History of the Latter-Day Saints at Winter Quarters and at Kanesville, 1846-52; A Study in American Overland Trail Migration. Ph.D., Wayne State University, 1984. 536p. UMI# 8414479.

1663 Bishop, Michael G. The Celestial Family: Early Mormon Thought on Life and Death, 1830-1846. Ph.D., Southern Illinois University-Carbondale, 1981. 176p. UMI# 81-22619.

1664 Bouquet, Francis L. The Compilation of the Original Documents Concerning the Nauvoo Illinois Mormon Settlement. S.T.D., Temple University, 1938.

1665 Bringhurst, Newell G. "A Servant of Servants...Cursed as Pertaining to the Priesthood:" Mormon Attitudes Toward Slavery and the Black Man, 1830-1880. Ph.D., University of California-Davis, 1975. 302p. UMI# 76-07829.

1666 Brinley, Eldon D. The Recreational Life of the Mormon People. Ed.D., New York University, 1943. 271p. UMI# 7308447.

1667 Campbell, Eugene E. A History of the Church of Jesus Christ of Latter-Day Saints in California, 1846-1946. Ph.D., University of Southern California, 1952. 175p.

1668 Cannon, M. Hamlin. The "Gathering" of British Mormons to Western America: A Study in Religious Migration. Ph.D., American University, 1951.

1669   Cannon, Mark W. The Mormon Issue in Congress 1872-1882: Drawing on the Experience of Territorial Delegate George Q. Cannon. Ph.D., Harvard University, 1961.

1670   Christian, Lewis C. A Study of the Mormon Westward Migration Between February 1846 and July 1847 With Emphasis on and Evaluation of the Factors That Led to the Mormons' Choice of Salt Lake Valley as the Site of Their Initial Colony. Ph.D., Brigham Young University, 1976. 327p. UMI# 77-04821.

1671   Davies, J. Kenneth. A Study of the Labor Philosophy Developed Within the Church of Jesus Christ of Latter-Day Saints. Ph.D., University of Southern California, 1960. 455p. UMI# 60-00389.

1672   Depillis, Mario S. The Development of Mormon Communitarianism, 1826-1846. Ph.D., Yale University, 1960. 391p. UMI# 72-07736.

1673   Done, G. Byron. The Participation of the Latter-Day Saints in the Community Life of Los Angeles. Ph.D., University of Southern California, 1939.

1674   Dwyer, Robert J. The Gentile Comes to Utah: A Study in Religious and Social Conflict (1862-1890). Ph.D., Catholic University of America, 1941. 239p.

1675   Ericksen, Ephraim E. The Psychological and Ethical Aspects of Mormon Group Life. Ph.D., University of Chicago, 1918. 101p.

1676   Fox, Feramorz Y. The Mormon Land System: A Study of the Settlement and Utilization of Land Under the Direction of the Mormon Church. Ph.D., Northwestern University, 1932.

1677   Francaviglia, Richard V. The Mormon Landscape: Existence, Creation and Perception of a Unique Image in the American West. Ph.D., University of Oregon, 1970. 209p. UMI# 7110722.

1678   Gayler, George R. A Social, Economic, and Political Study of the Mormons in Western Illinois, 1839-1846: A Reevaluation. Ph.D., Indiana University, 1955. 342p. UMI# 14653.

1679   Geddes, Joseph A. The United Order Among the Mormons. Ph.D., Columbia University, 1924. 172p.

1680   Gentry, Leland H. A History of the Latter-Day Saints in Northern Missouri From 1836 to 1839. Ph.D., Brigham Young University, 1965. 776p. UMI# 65-09857.

1681   Godfrey, Kenneth W. Causes of Mormon Non-Mormon Conflict in

Hancock County, Illinois, 1839-1846. Ph.D., Brigham Young University, 1967. 255p. UMI# 67-15572.

1682   Goodliffe, Wilford L. American Frontier Religion: Mormons and Their Dissenters, 1830-1900. Ph.D., University of Idaho, 1976. 295p. UMI# 76-20850.

1683   Hansen, Merrill C. The Role of Rhetoric in the Mormon Suffrage Debate in Idaho, 1880-1906. Ph.D., Stanford University, 1958. 377p. UMI# 58-03607.

1684   Hansen, Warren D. Re-Establishing Community: An Analysis of Joseph Smith's Social Thought in the Context of Philosophical Tradition. Ph.D., Rutgers University, 1980. 730p. UMI# 8105010.

1685   Jackson, Richard H. Myth and Reality: Environmental Perception of the Mormons, 1840-1865, An Historical Geosophy. Ph.D., Clark University, 1970. 348p. UMI# 7114494.

1686   Jennings, Warren A. Zion is Fled: The Expulsion of the Mormons From Jackson County, Missouri. Ph.D., University of Florida, 1962. 364p. UMI# 62-06532.

1687   Keele, Reba L. A Doctrinal Group Counterattacks: An Analysis of the Oral Rhetoric of the Mormons in the Utah War, 1855-1859. Ph.D., Purdue University, 1974. 212p. UMI# 7517224.

1688   Logue, Larry M. Belief and Behavior in a Mormon Town: Nineteenth Century St. George, Utah. Ph.D., University of Pennsylvania, 1984. 286p. UMI# 84-17328.

1689   Louder, Dean R. A Distributional and Diffusionary Analysis of the Mormon Church, 1850-1970. Ph.D., University of Washington, 1972. 297p. UMI# 73-13851.

1690   Luke, Kenneth O. Nauvoo, Illinois, Since the Exodus of the Mormons, 1846-1973. Ph.D., Saint Louis University, 1973. 201p. UMI# 74-24113.

1691   Mangrum, Richard C. Zion's Trial: The Mormon Ecclesiastical Court System in the 19th Century. J.D., Harvard University, 1983.

1692   Melville, James K. The Political Ideas of Brigham Young. Ph.D., University of Utah, 1956. 261p. UMI# 16441.

1693   Neff, Andrew L. The Mormon Migration to Utah. Ph.D., University of California-Berkeley, 1918.

1694   Nelson, Lowry. The Mormon Village: A Study in Social Origins. Ph.D., University of Wisconsin-Madison, 1929.

1695   Olsen, Arden B. The History of Mormon Mercantile Cooperation in Utah. Ph.D., University of California-Berkeley, 1936.

1696   Olsen, Steven L. The Mormon Ideology of Place: Cosmic Symbolism of the City of Zion, 1830-1846. Ph.D., University of Chicago, 1985.

1697   Olson, Vicky B. Family Structure and Dynamics in Early Utah Mormon Families, 1847-1885. Ph.D., Northwestern University, 1975. 219p. UMI# 75-29721.

1698   Parkin, Max H. A History of the Latter-Day Saints in Clay County, Missouri, From 1833-1837. Ph.D., Brigham Young University, 1976. 330p. UMI# 77-04847.

1699   Peterson, Charles S. Settlement on the Little Colorado 1873-1900: A Study of the Processes and Institutions of Mormon Expansion. Ph.D., University of Utah, 1967. 534p. UMI# 67-17089.

1700   Pitman, Leon S. A Survey of Nineteenth-Century Folk Housing in the Mormon Culture Region. Ph.D., Louisiana State University, 1973. 254p. UMI# 73-27863.

1701   Pollock, Gordon D. In Search of Security. The Mormons and the Kingdom of God on Earth 1830-1844. Ph.D., Queen's University-Kingston, 1977.

1702   Porter, Lawrence C. A Study of the Origins of the Church of Jesus Christ of Latter-Day Saints in the States of New York and Pennsylvania, 1816-1831. Ph.D., Brigham Young University, 1971. 400p. UMI# 72-01766.

1703   Raber, Michael S. Religious Polity and Local Production: The Origins of a Mormon Town. Ph.D., Yale University, 1978. 511p. UMI# 79-16476.[Spring City(UT)].

1704   Reeder, Ray M. The Mormon Trail: A History of the Salt Lake to Los Angeles Route to 1869. Ph.D., Brigham Young University, 1966. 442p. UMI# 66-10518.

1705   Ricks, Joel E. Forms and Methods of Early Mormon Settlement in Utah and the Surrounding Region, 1847 to 1877. Ph.D., University of Chicago, 1930.

1706   Rosenvall, Lynn A. Mormon Settlement Patterns: 1830-1900. Ph.D., University of California-Berkeley, 1973. 254p.

1707   Shipps, Jo A.B. The Mormons in Politics: The First Hundred Years. Ph.D., University of Colorado, 1965. 311p. UMI# 66-03281.

1708   Skidmore, Rex A. Mormon Recreation in Theory and Practice: A Study of Social Change. Ph.D., University of Pennsylvania, 1941.

1709   Snow, William J. The Great Basin Before the Coming of the Mormons. Ph.D., University of California-Berkeley, 1923.

1710   Tagg, Melvin S. A History of the Church of Jesus Christ of Latter-Day Saints in Canada, 1830-1963. Ph.D., Brigham Young University, 1963. 312p. UMI# 63-07131.

1711   Thompson, Stephen J. Mormon Economics, 1830 to 1900: The Interaction of Ideas and Environment. Ph.D., University of Illinois at Urbana-Champaign, 1973. 171p.

1712   Valora, Peter J. A Historical Geography of Agriculture in the Upper Snake River Valley, Idaho. Ph.D., University of Colorado-Boulder, 1986. 607p. UMI# 8619007.

1713   Wahlquist, Wayne L. Settlement Processes in the Mormon Core Area, 1847-1890. Ph.D., University of Nebraska-Lincoln, 1974. 347p. UMI# 75-03399.

1714   Wells, Merle W. The Idaho Anti-Mormon Movement, 1872-1908. Ph.D., University of California-Berkeley, 1951.

1715   Wengreen, Arthur D. A History of the Church of Jesus Christ of Latter-Day Saints in Sweden, 1850-1905. Ph.D., Brigham Young University, 1968. 272p. UMI# 69-03530.

1716   Winn, Kenneth H. Exiles in a Land of Liberty: Mormonism's Conflict With American Culture, 1830-1846. Ph.D., Washington University, 1985. 417p. UMI# 8529985.

1717   Wood, Joseph S. The Mormon Settlement in San Bernardino, 1851-1857. Ph.D., University of Utah, 1968. 300p. UMI# 68-11113.

Art and Architecture

1718   Andrew, Laurel B.B. The Nineteenth-Century Temple Architecture of the Latter-Day Saints. Ph.D., University of Michigan, 1973. 387p. UMI# 7403567.

1719   Carter, Thomas R. Building Zion: Folk Architecture in the Mormon Settlements of Utah's Sanpete Valley, 1850-1890. Ph.D., Indiana University, 1984. 367p. UMI# 8425066.

1720   Hamilton, Charles M. The Salt Lake Temple: An Architectural Monograph. Ph.D., Ohio State University, 1979. 228p. UMI# 7915982.

Biography

1721   Andrus, Hyrum L. Joseph Smith, Social Philosopher, Theorist, and Prophet. D.S.S., Syracuse University, 1955. 680p. UMI# 15043.

1722   Brink, T.L. Joseph Smith: A Study in Analytical Psychology. Ph.D., University of Chicago, 1978.

1723   Dunford, Charles K. The Contributions of George A. Smith to the Establishment of the Mormon Society in the Territory of Utah. Ph.D., Brigham Young University, 1970. 297p. UMI# 71-05994.

1724   Flake, Lawrence R. George Q. Cannon: His Missionary Years. D.R.E., Brigham Young University, 1970. 271p. UMI# 71-08840.

1725   Hunter, Milton R. Brigham Young, the Colonizer. Ph.D., University of California-Berkeley, 1936.

1726   Launius, Roger D. And There Came Prophets in the Land Again: The Life of Joseph Smith III, 1832-1914, Mormon Reformer. Ph.D., Louisiana State University, 1982. 487p. UMI# 82-16854.

1727   Madsen, Carol C. A Mormon Woman in Victorian America. Ph.D., University of Utah, 1985. 438p. UMI# 8516347.

1728   Marriott, Laurel D. Lilburn W. Boggs: Interaction With Mormons Following Their Expulsion From Missouri. Ed.D., Brigham Young University, 1979. 115p. UMI# 79-25330.

1729   McBrien, Dean D. The Influence of the Frontier on Joseph Smith. Ph.D., George Washington University, 1929.

1730   McKiernan, F. Mark. The Voice of One Crying in the Wilderness: Sidney Rigdon, Religious Reformer, 1793-1876. Ph.D., University of Kansas, 1968. 308p. UMI# 69-11234.

1731   Mouritsen, Dale C. A Symbol of New Directions: George Franklin Richards and the Mormon Church, 1861-1950. Ph.D., Brigham Young University, 1982. 306p. UMI# 8309551.

1732   Riley, Woodbridge. A Psychological History of Joseph Smith, Jr., the Founder of Mormonism. Ph.D., Yale University, 1902.

1733   Rooker, Nancy B. Mary Ann Burnham Freeze: Utah Evangelist.

Ph.D., University of Utah, 1982. 459p. UMI# 8220784.

1734   Van Orden, Bruce A. George Reynolds: Secretary, Sacrificial Lamb, and Seventy. Ph.D., Brigham Young University, 1986. 386p. UMI# 8627202.

Church and State

1735   Linford, Orma. The Mormons and the Law: The Polygamy Cases. Ph.D., University of Wisconsin-Madison, 1964. 571p. UMI# 6501271.

1736   Lyman, Edward L. The Mormon Quest for Utah Statehood. Ph.D., University of California-Riverside, 1981. 603p. UMI# 81-19574.

1737   Poll, Richard D. The Mormon Question, 1850-1865: A Study in Politics and Public Opinion. Ph.D., University of California-Berkeley, 1949.

1738   Silvey, Lawrence R. Rhetorical Functions and Communicative Roles of Oral Discourse in an Intercultural Conflict Directly Relating to the Issue of Polygamy and the Gaining of Statehood for Utah. Ph.D., University of Utah, 1972. 410p. UMI# 7229248.

Clergy

1739   Pace, Donald G. Community Leadership on the Mormon Frontier: Mormon Bishops and the Political, Economic, and Social Development of Utah Before Statehood. Ph.D., Ohio State University, 1983. 349p. UMI# 8403558.

1740   Talbot, Wilburn D. The Duties and Responsibilities of the Apostles of the Church of Jesus Christ of Latter-Day Saints 1835-1945. Ph.D., Brigham Young University, 1978. 363p. UMI# 79-03623.

Education

1741   Bennion, Milton L. The Origin, Growth, and Extension of the Educational Program of the Mormon Church in Utah. Ph.D., University of California-Berkeley, 1936. 132p.

1742   Coates, Lawrence G. A History of Indian Education by the Mormons, 1830-1900. Ed.D., Ball State University, 1969. 373p. UMI# 70-05259.

1743   Croy, Hazel M. A History of Education in San Bernardino During the Mormon Period. Ph.D., University of California-Los Angeles, 1955. 105p.

1744   Gregerson, Edna J. The Evolution of Dixie College as a Public Institution of Higher Education in Utah From 1871 to 1935. Ed.D., University of Nevada-Las Vegas, 1981. 431p. UMI# 8229756.

1745   Grishman, Lee H. The Influence of Brigham Young on the Development of Education in Early Utah. Ed.D., Columbia University Teachers College, 1983. 182p. UMI# 8403259.

1746   Harris, James R. A Comparison of the Educational Thought of Joseph Smith With That of Certain Contemporary Educators. Ed.D., Brigham Young University, 1965. 204p. UMI# 6512539.

1747   Hartshorn, Leon R. Mormon Education in the Bold Years. Ed.D., Stanford University, 1965. 246p. UMI# 65-12733.

1748   Monnett, John D., Jr. The Mormon Church and Its Private School System in Utah: The Emergence of the Academies 1880-1892. Ph.D., University of Utah, 1984. 238p. UMI# 8421847.

1749   Rich, Wendell O. Certain Basic Concepts in the Educational Philosophy of the Church of Jesus Christ of Latter-Day Saints, 1830-1930. Ph.D., Utah State University, 1954.

1750   Smith, Keith L. A History of the Brigham Young University. The Early Years, 1875-1921. Ph.D., Brigham Young University, 1972. 281p. UMI# 72-23193.

1751   Tickemyer, Garland E. The Philosophy of Joseph Smith and Its Educational Implications. Ph.D., University of Texas-Austin, 1963. 314p. UMI# 6406636.

1752   Ward, Lane D. The Teaching Methods of Joseph Smith. Ed.D., Brigham Young University, 1979. 230p. UMI# 8002149.

Evangelism

1753   Johnson, Paul T. An Analysis of the Spread of the Church of Jesus Christ of Latter-Day Saints From Salt Lake City, Utah, Utilizing a Diffusion Model. Ph.D., University of Iowa, 1966. 498p. UMI# 6607211.

Historiography

1754   Cragun, Leann. Mormons and History: In Control of the Past. Ph.D., University of Hawaii, 1981.

1755   Dobay, Clara M.V. Essays in Mormon Historiography. Ph.D., University of Houston, 1980. 347p. UMI# 81-15454.

1756   Searle, Howard C. Early Mormon Historiography: Writing the History of the Mormons, 1830-1858. Ph.D., University of California-Los Angeles, 1979. 534p. UMI# 80-08527.

Literature

1757   Evans, Edmund E. A Historical Study of the Drama of the Latter Day Saints. Ph.D., University of Southern California, 1941.

1758   Gottfredson, Montchesney R. The Relationship of the Extant Eschatologically-Oriented Work of Joseph Smith to That of Selected Twentieth Century New Testament Scholars. Ph.D., Brigham Young University, 1967. 301p. UMI# 6711537.

1759   Hansen, Harold I. A History and Influence of the Mormon Theatre From 1839-1869. Ph.D., University of Iowa, 1949. 205p.

1760   Haun, Diane. Three Plays: *The Infidels in Spain*, *Spiraling*, and *Brigham's Daughters*. Ph.D., University of Utah, 1978. 440p. UMI# 7824686.

1761   Howe, Susan. Burdens and Illuminations. Ph.D., University of Denver, 1989. 268p. UMI# 8924281.

1762   Petersen, Roger K. Joseph Smith, Prophet-Poet: A Literary Analysis of Writing Commonly Associated With His Name. Ph.D., Brigham Young University, 1981. 215p. UMI# 8206700.

1763   Sherry, Thomas E. Attitudes, Practices, and Positions Toward Joseph Smith's Translation of the Bible: A Historical Analysis of Publications, 1847-1987. Ed.D., Brigham Young University, 1988. 273p. UMI# 8821909.

1764   Stocks, Hugh G. The Book of Mormon in English, 1870-1920: A Publishing History and Analytical Bibliography. Ph.D., University of California-Los Angeles, 1986. 434p. UMI# 8621140.

1765   Whittaker, David J. Early Mormon Pamphleteering. Ph.D., Brigham Young University, 1982. 494p. UMI# 82-19181.

Missions and Missionaries

1766   Britsch, Ralph L. Early Latter-Day Saint Missions to South and East Asia. Ph.D., Claremont Graduate School, 1968. 392p. UMI# 68-10498.

1767   Ellsworth, Samuel G. A History of Mormon Missions in the United

States and Canada, 1830-1860. Ph.D., University of California-Berkeley, 1951.

1768   Hardy, Blaine C. The Mormon Colonies of Northern Mexico: A History, 1885-1912. Ph.D., Wayne State University, 1963. 205p. UMI# 68-06639.

1769   Haslam, Gerald M. The Norwegian Experience With Mormonism, 1842-1920. Ph.D., Brigham Young University, 1981. 486p. UMI# 81-26346.

1770   Mulder, William. Mormons From Scandinavia, 1850-1905. The Story of a Religious Migration. Ph.D., Harvard University, 1955. 930p.

1771   Parry, Keith W.J. To Raise These People up: An Examination of a Mormon Mission to an Indian Community as an Agent of Social Change. Ph.D., University of Rochester, 1972. 269p. UMI# 7228785.

Music

1772   Laycock, Harold R. A History of Music in the Academies of the Latter-Day Saints Church, 1876-1926. D.M.A., University of Southern California, 1961. 521p. UMI# 61-03821.

1773   Macare, Helen H. The Singing Saints: A Study of the Mormon Hymnal, 1835-1950. Ph.D., University of California-Los Angeles, 1961.

1774   Weight, Newell B. An Historical Study of the Origin and Character of Indigenous Hymn Tunes of the Latter-Day Saints. D.M.A., University of Southern California, 1961. 465p. UMI# 61-06310.

1775   Wheelwright, David S. The Role of Hymnody in the Development of the Latter-Day Saint Movement. Ph.D., University of Maryland, 1944. 490p.

Newspapers and Periodicals

1776   Greenwell, James R. The Mormon-Anti-Mormon Conflict in Early Utah as Reflected in the Local Newspapers 1850-1869. Ph.D., University of Utah, 1963.

1777   McLaws, Monte B. Early Mormon Journalism and the *Desert News*, 1830-1898. Ph.D., University of Missouri-Columbia, 1971. 315p. UMI# 71-22924.

Organizational Structure

1778   Cooper, Rex E. The Promises Made to the Fathers: A Diachronic Analysis of Mormon Covenant Organization With Reference to Puritan Federal Theology. Ph.D., University of Chicago, 1985.

1779   Esplin, Ronald K. The Emergence of Brigham Young and the Twelve to Mormon Leadership, 1830-1841. Ph.D., Brigham Young University, 1981. 530p. UMI# 81-17136.

1780   Hansen, Asael T. The Role of Auxiliary Organizations in the Mormon System of Social Control. Ph.D., University of Wisconsin-Madison, 1931.

1781   Larche, Douglas W. The Mantle of the Prophet: A Rhetorical Analysis of the Quest for Mormon Post-Martyrdom Leadership 1846-1860. Ph.D., Indiana University, 1977. 353p. UMI# 77-22601.

1782   Lloyd, Wesley P. The Rise and Development of Lay Leadership in the Latter-Day Saint Movement. Ph.D., University of Chicago, 1937.

1783   Quinn, Dennis M. The Mormon Hierarchy, 1832-1932: An American Elite. Ph.D., Yale University, 1976. 335p. UMI# 76-30227.

Preaching

1784   Higdon, Barbara J.M. The Role of Preaching in the Early Latter-Day Saint Church, 1830-1846. Ph.D., University of Missouri-Columbia, 1961. 363p. UMI# 61-06059.

1785   Jarvis, Joseph B. Preaching in the General Conferences of the Mormon Church, 1870-1900. Ph.D., Northwestern University, 1958. 625p. UMI# 58-05758.

1786   Myers, Chester J. A Critical Analysis and Appraisal of the Work of Brigham Young as a Public Speaker. Ph.D., University of Southern California, 1940.

1787   Smith, Calvin N. A Critical Analysis of the Public Speaking of Joseph Smith, First President of the Church of Jesus Christ of Latter-Day Saints. Ph.D., Purdue University, 1965. 245p. UMI# 66-05304.

Theology

1788   Durham, Reed C., Jr. A History of Joseph Smith's Revision of the Bible. Ph.D., Brigham Young University, 1965. 322p. UMI# 6513028.

1789   Furr, Carl J. The Religious Philosophy of Brigham Young. Ph.D., University of Chicago, 1938.

1790   Hansen, Klaus J. The Kingdom of God in Mormon Thought and Practice, 1830-1896. Ph.D., Wayne State University, 1963. 363p. UMI# 68-06636.

1791   Hill, Marvin S. The Role of Christian Primitivism in the Origin and Development of the Mormon Kingdom, 1830-1844. Ph.D., University of Chicago, 1968.

1792   Millet, Robert L. The Development of the Concept of Zion in Mormon Theology. Ph.D., Florida State University, 1983. 303p. UMI# 8317379.

1793   Persons, William R. An Analysis of Changes in the Interpretation and Utilization of Revelation in the Church of Jesus Christ of Latter Day Saints, 1830-1918. Ph.D., Iliff School of Theology, 1964.

1794   Taylor, Eldon R. The Principles of Election and Predestination in the Teachings of Paul and in the Church of Jesus Christ of Latter-Day Saints. Ph.D., Brigham Young University, 1967. 216p. UMI# 67-17223.

1795   Underwood, Grant R. The Millenarian World of Early Mormonism. Ph.D., University of California-Los Angeles, 1988. 438p. UMI# 8907568.

1796   Warner, Edward A. Mormon Theodemocracy: Theocratic and Democratic Elements in Early Latter-Day Saint Ideology, 1827-1846. Ph.D., University of Iowa, 1973. 463p. UMI# 73-30998.

LUTHERAN

General Studies

1797   Bachmann, C. Charles. The Development of Lutheran Pastoral Care in America. Ph.D., Boston University, 1949. 239p.

1798   Bachmann, Ernest T. The Rise of Missouri Lutheranism. Ph.D., University of Chicago, 1947. 381p.

1799   Gustafson, David A. The Americanization of the Lutheran Church: The Mid-Nineteenth Century Controversy Between Confessional Lutherans and Proponents of an Americanized Lutheranism. Ph.D., Union Institute, 1990. 283p. UMI# 9033586.

1800   Heathcote, Charles W. The Lutheran Church and the Civil War.

Ph.D., George Washington University, 1918. 154p.

1801 Kreider, Harry J. Lutheranism in Colonial New York. Ph.D., Columbia University, 1942. 158p.

1802 Kuenning, Paul P. American Lutheran Pietism, Activist and Abolitionist. Ph.D., Marquette University, 1985. 655p. UMI# 8526786.

1803 Lenski, Gerhard E. Marriage in the Lutheran Church: An Historical Study. Ph.D., American University, 1936.

1804 Lindquist, Maude L. Efforts Toward Lutheran Union in the United States to 1860. Ph.D., University of Minnesota, 1949. 125p.

1805 Monseth, Francis W. Millennialism in American Lutheranism in Light of Augsburg Confession, Article XVII. Th.D., Concordia Seminary, 1986.

1806 Nichol, Todd W. The American Lutheran Church: An Historical Study of Its Confession of Faith According to Its Constituting Documents. Th.D., Graduate Theological Union, 1988. 596p. UMI# 8816916.

1807 Seagle, Gladys I. The Rappist Revolt Against Lutheranism, 1804-1904. Ph.D., New York University, 1963. 241p. UMI# 63-06678.

Biography

1808 Ander, Oscar F. The Career and Influence of T.N. Hasselquist, a Swedish-American Clergyman, Journalist, and Educator. Ph.D., University of Illinois at Urbana-Champaign, 1931. 260p.

1809 Baur, Richard H. Paul Henkel, Pioneer Lutheran Missionary. Ph.D., University of Iowa, 1968. 211p. UMI# 68-16782.

1810 Bost, Raymond M. The Reverend John Bachman and the Development of Southern Lutheranism. Ph.D., Yale University, 1963. 560p. UMI# 65-09085.

1811 Briere, Melvin A. A Study of the Life and Teachings of Samuel Simon Schmucker and a Comparison of His Teachings With the Beliefs of the Members of First Lutheran Church of Red Wing, Minnesota. D.Min., Luther Northwestern Theological Seminary, 1980.

1812 Eggold, Henry J. Walther, the Preacher. Ph.D., Concordia Seminary, 1962.

1813   Fry, Charles G. Matthias Loy, Patriarch of Ohio Lutheranism, 1828-1915. Ph.D., Ohio State University, 1965. 503p. UMI# 66-06256.

1814   Greenholt, Homer R. A Study of Wilhelm Loehe, His Colonies and the Lutheran Indian Missions in the Saginaw Valley of Michigan. Ph.D., University of Chicago, 1937.

1815   Haney, James L., Jr. The Religious Heritage and Education of Samuel Simon Schmucker: A Study in the Rise of "American Lutheranism." Ph.D., Yale University, 1968. 519p. UMI# 68-11188.

1816   Nelson, Harvey L. A Critical Study of Henry Melchior Muhlenberg's Means of Maintaining His Lutheranism. Ph.D., Drew University, 1980. 431p. UMI# 8104827.

1817   Riforgiato, Leonard R. Missionary of Moderation: Henry Melchior Muhlenberg and the Lutheran Church in English America. Ph.D., Pennsylvania State University, 1971. 276p. UMI# 72-19368.

1818   Toms, Deella V. The Intellectual and Literary Background of Francis Daniel Pastorius. Ph.D., Northwestern University, 1953. 281p. UMI# 6251.

1819   Weaver, John D. Franz Daniel Pastorius (1651-c.1720): Early Life in Germany With Glimpses of His Removal to Pennsylvania. Ph.D., University of California-Davis, 1985. 497p. UMI# 8607618.

1820   Winters, Roy L. John Caspar Stoever, Junior, (1707-1779), in the Colonial Lutheran Church of Pennsylvania. Ph.D., Hartford Seminary Foundation, 1932.

Church and State

1821   Barby, Curtiss B. The Interaction of Church and State for the Lutheran Church Missouri Synod. Ph.D., Saint Louis University, 1972. 100p. UMI# 72-23895.

Clergy

1822   Glatfelter, Charles H. The Colonial Pennsylvania German Lutheran and Reformed Clergyman. Ph.D., Johns Hopkins University, 1952.

1823   Huber, Donald L. The Controversy Over Pulpit and Altar Fellowship in the General Council of the Evangelical Lutheran Church, 1866-1889. Ph.D., Duke University, 1971. 311p. UMI# 72-10885.

Education

1824   Beck, Walter H. Lutheran Elementary Schools in the United States: A History of Synodical Educational Policies and Administration From 1818 to the Present. Ph.D., Temple University, 1937.

1825   Bosse, Richard C. Origins of Lutheran Higher Education in Ohio. Ph.D., Ohio State University, 1969. 434p. UMI# 70-06729.

1826   Damm, John S. The Growth and Decline of Lutheran Parochial Schools in the United States, 1638-1962. Ed.D., Columbia University, 1963. 371p. UMI# 64-01469.

1827   Freitag, Alfred J. A History of Concordia Teachers College, 1864-1964. Ed.D., University of Southern California, 1965. 561p. UMI# 65-08909.

1828   Heisey, Paul H. The Lutheran Graded Series of Sunday School Materials: An Historical, Critical, and Constructive Study. Ph.D., Northwestern University, 1924. 226p.

1829   Maurer, Charles L. Early Lutheran Education in Pennsylvania. Ed.D., Temple University, 1931. 294p.

1830   Nolde, Otto F. The Department of Christian Education in the Theological Seminary: A Type Study of the Lutheran Theological Seminary at Philadelphia, Pennsylvania. Ph.D., University of Pennsylvania, 1929. 167p.

1831   Northwick, Byron. The Development of the Missouri Synod: The Role of Education in the Preservation and Promotion of Lutheran Orthodoxy, 1839-1872. Ph.D., Kansas State University, 1987. 122p. UMI# 8715231.

1832   Schmidt, Wayne E. Wisconsin Synod Lutheran Parochial Schools: An Overview of the Years 1850-1890. Ph.D., University of Wisconsin, 1968. 380p. UMI# 68-09123.

1833   Schnackenberg, Walter C. The Development of Norwegian Lutheran Schools in the Pacific Northwest, 1890-1920. Ph.D., Washington State University, 1950. 117p.

1834   Stach, John F. A History of Lutheran Schools of the Missouri Synod in Michigan, 1845-1940. Ph.D., University of Michigan, 1943.

1835   Thurau, Robert H. A Study of the Lutheran Sunday School in America to 1865. Ph.D., University of Pittsburgh, 1946. 399p.

1836   Zeddies, Leslie R. Music Education Principles and Practices in the Elementary Schools of the Lutheran Church-Missouri Synod. Ph.D., Northwestern University, 1959. 186p. UMI# 5904856.

Ethnic Groups

1837   Anders, John O. The Origin and History of Swedish Religious Organizations in Minnesota. Ph.D., University of Minnesota, 1930.

1838   Belgum, Gerhard L. The Old Norwegian Synod in America, 1853-1890. Ph.D., Yale University, 1957. 466p. UMI# 67-14561.

1839   Crouse, Russel J. History of the Lutheran Salzburgers in Georgia. S.T.D., Temple University, 1954.

1840   Eklund, Emmet E. Acculturation in the Swedish Lutheran Congregations of the Boston Area: 1867-1930. Ph.D., Boston University, 1964. 339p. UMI# 64-11625.

1841   Fevold, Eugene L. The History of Norwegian-American Lutheranism, 1870-1890. Ph.D., University of Chicago, 1951.

1842   Kimmerle, Marjorie M. Norwegian Surnames of the Koshkonong and Springdale Congregations in Dane County, Wisconsin. Ph.D., University of Wisconsin, 1938.

1843   Lagerquist, L. DeAne. That It May Be Done Also Among Us: Norwegian-American Lutheran Women. Ph.D., University of Chicago, 1986.

1844   Legreid, Ann M. The Exodus, Transplanting and Religious Reorganization of a Group of Norwegian Lutheran Immigrants in Western Wisconsin, c. 1836-1900. Ph.D., University of Wisconsin-Madison, 1985. 525p. UMI# 8516770.

1845   Mauelshagen, Carl. The Effect of German Immigration Upon the Lutheran Church in America, 1820-1870. Ph.D., University of Minnesota, 1935.

1846   Nelson, E. Clifford. The Union Movement Among Norwegian-American Lutherans From 1880 to 1917. Ph.D., Yale University, 1952. 681p. UMI# 67-04124.

1847   Nyholm, Paul C.E. The Americanization of the Danish Lutheran Churches in America. Ph.D., University of Chicago, 1952. 222p.

1848   Raun, James J. The Danish Lutherans in America. Ph.D., University of Chicago, 1930.

1849   Weng, Armin G. The Language Problem in the Lutheran Church in Pennsylvania, Particularly in Philadelphia, 1724-1820. Ph.D., Yale University, 1928.

1850   Wolf, Richard C. The Americanization of the German Lutherans, 1683 to 1829. Ph.D., Yale University, 1947. 594p. UMI# 72-05042.

Literature

1851   Williamson, Mary A.L. The History of the Henkel Press and Impact on Children's Literature. Ed.D., University of Virginia, 1977. 417p. UMI# 7901144.

Liturgy

1852   Scheidt, David L. Linguistic Transition in the Muhlenberg Tradition of American Lutheranism. S.T.D., Temple University, 1963. 248p. UMI# 63-07512.

Missions and Missionaries

1853   Larsen, Herman A. The Growth of Foreign Mission Interest and Support in the Evangelical Lutheran Church to 1890. Ph.D., Yale University, 1947.

1854   Syrdal, Rolf A. American Lutheran Mission Work in China. Ph.D., Drew University, 1942. 553p. UMI# 8823915.

Music

1855   Cartford, Gerhard M. Music in the Norwegian Lutheran Church: A Study of Its Development in Norway and Its Transfer to America, 1825-1917. Ph.D., University of Minnesota, 1961. 409p. UMI# 62-01768.

1856   Lehmann, Arnold O. The Music of the Lutheran Church, Synodical Conference, Chiefly the Areas of Missouri, Illinois, Wisconsin and Neighboring States, 1839-1941. Ph.D., Case Western Reserve University, 1967. 442p. UMI# 67-08841.

1857   Smith, Carlton Y. Early Lutheran Hymnody in America From the Colonial Period to the Year 1850. Ph.D., University of Southern California, 1958.

1858   Wolf, Edward C. Lutheran Church Music in America During the Eighteenth and Early Nineteenth Centuries. Ph.D., University of Illinois at Urbana-Champaign, 1960. 473p. UMI# 61-00218.

Newspapers and Periodicals

1859   Gimmestad, Victor E. A History of the *Evangelical Review*. Ph.D., University of Wisconsin, 1951. 184p.

Organizational Structure

1860   Ferm, Vergilius T.A. The *Definite Synodical Platform*: Controversy in the History of the American Lutheran Church. Ph.D., Yale University, 1925.

1861   Forster, Walter O. Settlement of the Saxon Lutherans in Missouri, 1839-1847: A Study in the Origins of the Missouri Synod. Ph.D., Washington University, 1942. 371p.

1862   Fortenbaugh, Robert. The Development of the Synodical Polity of the Lutheran Church in America, to 1829. Ph.D., University of Pennsylvania, 1926. 48p.

1863   Good, William A. A History of the General Council of the Evangelical Lutheran Church in North America. Ph.D., Yale University, 1967. 326p. UMI# 68-04870.

1864   Greising, Jack H. The Status of Confessional Conservatism: Background and Issues in the Lutheran Church-Missouri Synod. Ph.D., Saint Louis University, 1972. 245p. UMI# 72-23943.

1865   Heintzen, Erich H. Wilhelm Loehe and the Missouri Synod, 1841-1853. Ph.D., University of Illinois at Urbana-Champaign, 1964. 276p. UMI# 6408389.

1866   Ottersberg, Gerhard S. The Evangelical Lutheran Synod of Iowa and Other States, 1854-1904. Ph.D., University of Nebraska, 1949. 125p.

1867   Tietjan, John H. The Principles of Church Union Espoused in the 19th Century Attempts to Unite the Lutheran Church in America. Ph.D., Union Theological Seminary, 1959.

Social Programs

1868   Anderson, Hugh G. A Social History of Lutheranism in the Southeastern States 1860-1886. Ph.D., University of Pennsylvania, 1962. 365p. UMI# 63-04138.

Theology

1869   Haug, Hans R. The Predestination Controversy in the Lutheran

Church in North America. Ph.D., Temple University, 1968. 977p. UMI# 68-14135.

1870   Koenning, Alton R. Henkel Press: A Force for Conservative Lutheran Theology in Pre-Civil War, Southeastern America. Ph.D., Duke University, 1972. 266p. UMI# 73-08085.

1871   McDaniel, Michael C.D. Evolution in American Lutheran Thought, 1860-1925: A Historical Account and a Theological Reflection. Ph.D., University of Chicago, 1978.

MENNONITE

General Studies

1872   Buchheit, Robert H. Mennonite *Plautdietsch* A Phonological and Morphological Description of a Settlement Dialect in York and Hamilton Counties, Nebraska. Ph.D., University of Nebraska-Lincoln, 1978. 267p. UMI# 79-06221.

1873   Cronk, Sandra L. Gelassenheit: The Rites of the Redemptive Process in Old Order Amish and Old Order Mennonite Communities. Ph.D., University of Chicago, 1977.

1874   Gingerich, Melvin. The Mennonites in Iowa. Ph.D., University of Iowa, 1938. 78p.

1875   Harder, Leland D. The Quest for Equilibrium in an Established Sect: A Study of Social Change in the General Conference Mennonite Church. Ph.D., Northwestern University, 1962. 385p. UMI# 63-01296.

1876   Heatwole, Charles A. Religion in the Creation and Preservation of Sectarian Culture Areas: A Mennonite Example. Ph.D., Michigan State University, 1974. 227p. UMI# 75-07181.[Rockingham County(VA)].

1877   Hiebert, Clarence R. The Holdeman People: A Study of the Church of God in Christ, Mennonite, 1858-1969. Ph.D., Case Western Reserve University, 1971. 642p. UMI# 72-00046.

1878   Hostetler, Beulah S. Franconia Mennonite Conference and American Protestant Movements, 1840-1940. Ph.D., University of Pennsylvania, 1977. 329p. UMI# 77-19862.

1879   Janzen, Cornelius C. A Social Study of the Mennonite Settlement in the Counties of Marion, McPherson, Harvey, Reno, and Butler, Kansas. Ph.D., University of Chicago, 1926.

1880   Juhnke, James C. The Political Acculturation of the Kansas Mennonites, 1870-1940. Ph.D., Indiana University, 1968. 299p. UMI# 68-15445.

1881   Longhofer, Jeffrey L. Land, Household, and Community: A Study of the Alexanderwohl Mennonites. Ph.D., University of Kansas, 1986. 249p. UMI# 8711245.

1882   Nyce, James M. Convention, Power and the Self in German Mennonite Magic. Ph.D., Brown University, 1987. 194p. UMI# 8715542.

1883   Sawatsky, Rodney J. History and Ideology: American Mennonite Identity: Definition Through History. Ph.D., Princeton University, 1977. 350p. UMI# 77-21474.

1884   Smith, Henry. The Mennonites in Pennsylvania. Ph.D., University of Chicago, 1907.

1885   Stoltzfus, Grant M. Mennonites of the Ohio and Western Conference: From the Colonial Period in Pennsylvania to 1968. Ph.D., Southwestern Baptist Theological Seminary, 1969.

1886   Weber, Harry F. History of the Mennonites of Illinois. Ph.D., Hartford Seminary Foundation, 1926.

Biography

1887   Dean, William W. John F. Funk and the Mennonite Awakening. Ph.D., University of Iowa, 1965. 299p. UMI# 65-11611.

Education

1888   Brubaker, Jacob L. A History of the Mennonite Elementary School Movement. Ed.D., University of Virginia, 1966. 351p. UMI# 6615214.

1889   Harder, Menno S. The Origin, Philosophy, and Development of Education Among the Mennonites. Ph.D., University of Southern California, 1949.

1890   Hartzler, John E. Education Among the Mennonites of America. Ph.D., Hartford Seminary Foundation, 1924.

1891   Lederach, Paul M. History of Religious Education in the Mennonite Church. Ph.D., Southwestern Baptist Theological Seminary, 1949. 258p.

Ethnic Groups

1892   Loewen, Royden K. Family, Church and Market: A History of a Mennonite Community Transplanted From Russia to Canada and the United States, 1850-1930. Ph.D., University of Manitoba, 1990.

1893   Schelbert, L. Swiss Migration to America: The Swiss Mennonites. Ph.D., Columbia University, 1966. 335p. UMI# 67-00807.

Evangelism

1894   Dickey, Dale F. The Tent Evangelism Movement of the Mennonite Church: A Dramatistic Analysis. Ph.D., Bowling Green State University, 1980. 163p. UMI# 8106885.

Missions and Missionaries

1895   Adrian, Marlin W. Mennonites, Missionaries, and Native Americans: Religious Paradigms and Cultural Encounters. Ph.D., University of Virginia, 1989. 234p. UMI# 9014570.[Arizona, Montana].

1896   Kaufman, Edmund G. The Development of the Missionary Interest Among the Mennonites of America. Ph.D., University of Chicago, 1928.

1897   Peters, Gergard W. The Growth of Foreign Missions in the Mennonite Brethren Church. Ph.D., Hartford Seminary Foundation, 1947. 456p.

1898   Toews, Jacob J. The History of Mennonite Brethren Missions in Latin America. Ph.D., Dallas Theological Seminary, 1972.

Music

1899   Jost, Walter J. The Hymn Tune Tradition of the General Conference Mennonite Church. D.M.A., University of Southern California, 1966. 318p. UMI# 66-08792.

1900   Wohlgemuth, Paul W. Mennonite Hymnals Published in the English Language. Ph.D., University of Southern California, 1958.

1901   Yoder, Paul M. Nineteenth Century Sacred Music of the Mennonite Church in the United States. Ph.D., Florida State University, 1961. 188p. UMI# 61-03653.

Organizational Structure

1902   Pannabecker, Samuel F. The Development of the General

Conference of the Mennonite Church of North America in the American Environment. Ph.D., Yale University, 1944.

Preaching

1903   Umble, Roy H. Mennonite Preaching, 1864-1944. Ph.D., Northwestern University, 1949.

1904   Waltner, James H. The Authentication Preaching in the Anabaptist-Mennonite Tradition. Ph.D., School of Theology-Claremont, 1972.

Social Programs

1905   Burkholder, John L. The Problem of Social Responsibility From the Perspective of the Mennonite Church. Ph.D., Princeton Theological Seminary, 1958. 172p.

METHODIST

General Studies

1906   Andrews, Doris E. Popular Religion and the Revolution in the Middle Atlantic Ports: The Rise of the Methodists, 1770-1800. Ph.D., University of Pennsylvania, 1986. 370p. UMI# 8623969.

1907   Arends, Robert L. Early American Methodism and the Church of England. Ph.D., Yale University, 1948.

1908   Armour, Robert A. The Opposition to the Methodist Church in Eighteenth-Century Virginia. Ph.D., University of Georgia, 1968. 163p. UMI# 60-03438.

1909   Baker, George C., Jr. An Introduction to the History of Early New England Methodism, 1789-1839. Ph.D., Columbia University, 1941.

1910   Blankenship, Paul F. History of Negotiations for Union Between Methodists and Non-Methodists in the United States. Ph.D., Northwestern University, 1965. 372p. UMI# 65-12051.

1911   Boase, Paul H. The Methodist Circuit Rider on the Ohio Frontier. Ph.D., University of Wisconsin, 1953.

1912   Boigegrain, Walter J. A History of the Methodist Church in the Eagle-- Colorado River Valley in Colorado From 1880 to 1906. Ph.D., Iliff School of Theology, 1962.

1913   Coleman, Robert E. Factors in the Expansion of the Methodist

Episcopal Church From 1784 to 1812. Ph.D., University of Iowa, 1954. 554p. UMI# 10201.

1914   Collier, Karen Y. An Examination of Varied Aspects of Race and Episcopacy in American Methodism, 1844-1939. Ph.D., Duke University, 1984. 224p. UMI# 8423939.

1915   Evans, Paul O. The Ideology of Inequality: Asbury, Methodism, and Slavery. Ph.D., State University of New Jersey, 1981. 487p. UMI# 8122066.

1916   Farish, Hunter D. A Social History of Southern Methodism, 1865-1900. Ph.D., Harvard University, 1936.

1917   Harvey, Marvin E. The Wesleyan Movement and the American Revolution. Ph.D., University of Washington, 1962. 409p. UMI# 6303118.

1918   Hildebrand, Carroll D. Borden P. Bowne's Teaching Concerning the Speculative Significance of Freedom. Ph.D., Boston University, 1929.

1919   Jervey, Edward D. The History of Methodism in Southern California and Arizona, 1850-1939. Ph.D., Boston University, 1958. 287p. UMI# 58-03102.

1920   Jones, Donald G. The Moral, Social, and Political Ideas of the Methodist Episcopal Church From the Closing Years of the Civil War Through Reconstruction, 1864-1876. Ph.D., Drew University, 1969. 408p. UMI# 69-18625.

1921   Jordan, Marjorie W. Mississippi Methodists and the Division of the Church Over Slavery. Ph.D., University of Southern California, 1972. 287p. UMI# 72-26558.

1922   Kilgore, Charles F. The James O'Kelly Schism in the Methodist Episcopal Church. Ph.D., Emory University, 1961. 158p. UMI# 62-00031.

1923   Lee, Umphrey. The Historical Backgrounds of Early Methodist Enthusiasm. Ph.D., Columbia University, 1931. 170p.

1924   Lenhart, Thomas E. Methodist Piety in an Industrializing Society: Chicago, 1865-1914. Ph.D., Northwestern University, 1981. 350p. UMI# 81-24941.

1925   Linn, Theodore C. Religion and Nationalism: American Methodism and the New Nation in the Early National Period 1766-1844. Ph.D., Drew University, 1971. 311p. UMI# 71-29412.

1926   Lowe, Clarice P. The Division of the Methodist Episcopal Church, 1844: An Example of Failure in Rhetorical Strategy. Ph.D., University of Wisconsin, 1970. 283p. UMI# 71-05651.

1927   MacKenzie, Kenneth M. American Methodism and Imperialism (1865-1900). Ph.D., New York University, 1957. 284p. UMI# 59-06680.

1928   Martin, B. Joseph. History of the Attitudes of the Methodist Church in the United States of America Toward Recreation. Ph.D., University of Southern California, 1945. 114p.

1929   May, James W. From Revival Movement to Denomination: A Reexamination of the Beginnings of American Methodism. Ph.D., Columbia University, 1962. 378p. UMI# 65-07379.

1930   McNairn, Norman A. The American Contribution to Early Methodism in Canada, 1790-1840. Ph.D., Iliff School of Theology, 1969.

1931   Morrow, Ralph E. The Methodist Episcopal Church, the South, and Reconstruction, 1865-1880. Ph.D., Indiana University, 1954. 361p. UMI# 07535.

1932   Ott, Philip W. The Mind of Early American Methodism: 1800-1844. Ph.D., University of Pennsylvania, 1968. 239p. UMI# 69-05653.

1933   Peters, Robert N. From Sect to Church: A Study in the Permutation of Methodism on the Oregon Frontier. Ph.D., University of Washington, 1973. 405p. UMI# 73-22590.

1934   Pool, Frank K. The Southern Negro in the Methodist Episcopal Church. Ph.D., Duke University, 1939.

1935   Powell, Webster H. A Discussion of Henri Bergson's Metaphysical Views According to the Philosophy of Borden P. Bowne. Ph.D., Boston University, 1915.

1936   Purifoy, Lewis M., Jr. The Methodist Episcopal Church, South, and Slavery, 1844-1865. Ph.D., University of North Carolina-Chapel Hill, 1965. 240p. UMI# 66-04728.

1937   Reeves, Howard N., Jr. Methodism in Chester County Pennsylvania, 1772-1900. Ph.D., Temple University, 1956.

1938   Reinhard, James A. Personal and Sociological Factors in the Formation of the Free Methodist Church, 1852-1860. Ph.D., University of Iowa, 1971. 259p. UMI# 71-30482.

1939   Ricker, Roy C., III. The Transition of the Concept of Discipline in Early American Methodism. D.Min., Southern Methodist University, 1978.

1940   Roberts, Millard G. The Methodist Book Concerning the West, 1800-1870. Ph.D., University of Chicago, 1947. 440p.

1941   Sanders, Paul S. An Appraisal of John Wesley's Sacramentalism in the Evolution of Early American Methodism. Th.D., Union Theological Seminary, 1954. 617p. UMI# 67-12529.

1942   Schneider, A. Gregory. Perfecting the Family of God: Religious Community and Family Values in Early American Methodism. Ph.D., University of Chicago, 1981.

1943   Soderwall, Lorin H. The Rhetoric of the Methodist Camp Meeting Movement: 1800-1850. Ph.D., University of Southern California, 1971. 398p. UMI# 72-06110.

1944   Sweet, William W. The Methodist Episcopal Church and the Civil War. Ph.D., University of Pennsylvania, 1912. 228p.

1945   Walker, Clarence E. A Rock in a Weary Land: A History of the African Methodist Church During the Civil War and Reconstruction. Ph.D., University of California-Berkeley, 1976.

1946   Watson, David L. The Origins and Significance of the Early Methodist Class Meeting. Ph.D., Duke University, 1978. 484p. UMI# 79-05376.

1947   Whitner, Robert L. The Methodist Episcopal Church and Grant's Peace Policy: A Study of the Methodist Agencies, 1870-1882. Ph.D., University of Minnesota, 1959. 298p. UMI# 59-03770.

Biography

1948   Agnew, Theodore L., Jr. Peter Cartwright and His Times: The First Fifty Years, 1785-1835. Ph.D., Harvard University, 1954.

1949   Brown, Joanne E.C. Jennie Fowler Willing (1834-1916): Methodist Churchwoman and Reformer. Ph.D., Boston University, 1983. 406p. UMI# 8309753.

1950   Culver, Mearl P. The Contribution of Bishop John H. Vincent to the Development of Religious Education. Ph.D., Yale University, 1926.

1951   Cummings, Melbourne S. The Rhetoric of Bishop Henry McNeal Turner, Leading Advocate in the African Emigration Movement,

1866-1907. Ph.D., University of California-Los Angeles, 1972. 282p. UMI# 7301691.

1952   Davies, Daniel M. The Missionary Thought and Activity of Henry Gerhard Appenzeller. Ph.D., Drew University, 1986.

1953   Decker, Robert J. Jason Lee, Missionary to Oregon. A Reevaluation. Ph.D., Indiana University, 1961. 329p. UMI# 61-04432.

1954   Douglass, Donald D. Psychological Aspects of the Pastoral Ministry of Francis Asbury. Ph.D., Boston University, 1957. 218p. UMI# 21545.

1955   Fletcher, Thomas R. Gilbert Haven: Jeremiad Abolitionist Preacher. Ph.D., University of Oregon, 1982. 321p. UMI# 8301777.

1956   Franquiz, Jose A. Borden Parker Bowne's Treatment of the Problem of Change and Identity. Ph.D., Boston University, 1940.

1957   Giles, Philip L. Workingman and Theologian: Edward Henry Rogers (1824-1909) and the Impact of Evangelicalism on the Making of the American Working Class. Ph.D., University of Rochester, 1990. 287p. UMI# 9111492.

1958   Gilligan, Adrian. Freedom and Self-Realization in the Thought of Borden Parker Bowne. Ph.D., Catholic University of America, 1980. 244p. UMI# 8012215.

1959   Gravely, William B. Gilbert Haven, Racial Equalitarian. A Study of His Career in Racial Reform, 1850-1880. Ph.D., Duke University, 1969. 372p. UMI# 7002153.

1960   Herrmann, Richard E. Nathan Bangs: Apologist for American Methodism. Ph.D., Emory University, 1973. 236p. UMI# 73-19763.

1961   Hunter, Howard E. William Fairfield Warren: Methodist Theologian. Ph.D., Boston University, 1957. 355p. UMI# 21547.

1962   Johnson, Michael D. The History and Theology of Joseph Pilmore. Ph.D., Northwestern University, 1976. 250p. UMI# 7710041.

1963   Killian, Charles D. Bishop Daniel A. Payne: Black Spokesman for Reform. Ph.D., Indiana University, 1971. 220p. UMI# 71-21281.

1964   Kirby, James E., Jr. The Ecclesiastical and Social Thought of Matthew Simpson. Ph.D., Drew University, 1963. 372p. UMI# 6307380.

1965   Lane, Leroy L. John F. Nessly: The Rhetoric of His Ministry and Message. Ph.D., University of Oregon, 1972. 205p. UMI# 7228157.

1966   Mack, Henry W. Borden Parker Bowne as an Educational Philosopher. Ph.D., New York University, 1931. 246p. UMI# 7233624.

1967   Mann, Harold W. The Life and Times of Atticus Greene Haygood. Ph.D., Duke University, 1962. 444p. UMI# 6303600.

1968   Markle, David H. Wilbur Fisk, Pioneer Methodist Educator. Ph.D., Yale University, 1935.

1969   Mauck, Donald M. Glory for the Land: A Drama of Three Acts Based on the Early Career of Francis Asbury. Ph.D., Boston University, 1957. 297p. UMI# 21548.

1970   Minnix, Kathleen M. God's Comedian: The Life and Career of Evangelist Sam Jones. Ph.D., Georgia State University, 1986. 567p. UMI# 8612005.

1971   Raser, Harold E. The Way of Holiness: Phoebe Palmer and Perfectionistic Revivalism in Nineteenth-Century American Religion. Ph.D., Pennsylvania State University, 1987. 373p. UMI# 8714868.

1972   Scherer, Lester B. Ezekiel Cooper, 1763-1847: An Early American Methodist Leader. Ph.D., Northwestern University, 1965. 249p. UMI# 65-12164.

1973   Shipps, Howard F. The Forgotten Apostle of Methodism: Being an Evaluation of the Life and Work of the Reverend Benjamin Abbott. S.T.D., Temple University, 1955.

1974   Simpson, Robert D. Freeborn Garrettson, American Methodist Pioneer. Ph.D., Drew University, 1954.

1975   Smith, Marion L. Atticus Greene Haygood: Christian Educator. Ph.D., Yale University, 1929.

1976   Smith, Warren T. Thomas Coke and Early American Methodism. Ph.D., Boston University, 1953.

1977   Stewart, Sonja M. John Heyl Vincent: His Theory and Practice of Protestant Religious Education From 1855-1920. Ph.D., University of Notre Dame, 1977. 222p. UMI# 77-19153.

1978   Stokes, Arthur P. Daniel Alexander Payne: Churchman and Educator. Ph.D., Ohio State University, 1973. 262p. UMI# 74-11057.

1979   Thacker, Joseph A., Jr. James B. Finley: A Biography. Ph.D., University of Kentucky, 1967. 371p. UMI# 6915495.

1980   Trimmer, Edward A. John Heyl Vincent: An Evangelist for Education. Ed.D., Columbia University Teachers College, 1986. 195p. UMI# 8611703.

1981   White, Charles E. The Beauty of Holiness: Phoebe Palmer as Theologian, Revivalist, Feminist, and Humanitarian. Ph.D., Boston University, 1986. 510p. UMI# 8609264.

1982   Williamson, Douglas J. The Ecclesiastical Career of Wilbur Fisk: Methodist Educator, Theologian, Reformer, Controversialist. Ph.D., Boston University, 1988. 296p. UMI# 8810232.

Clergy

1983   Dougherty, Mary A.T. The Methodist Deaconess, 1885-1918: A Study in Religious Feminism. Ph.D., University of California-Davis, 1979.

1984   Eversole, John A. Ordination in American Methodism. Ph.D., Iliff School of Theology, 1963.

1985   King, Luther W. An Historical Study of Ministerial Authority in American Methodism: 1760 to 1940. Ph.D., Columbia University, 1981. 266p. UMI# 8307594.

1986   Lynn, James D. The Concept of the Ministry in the Methodist Episcopal Church, 1784-1844. Ph.D., Princeton Theological Seminary, 1973. 310p. UMI# 73-28007.

1987   Noren, Carol M. A Study of Wesley's Doctrine of Christian Perfection in the Theology and Method of Nineteenth Century Swedish Methodist Preachers in Northern Illinois, With Particular Emphasis on the Writings of Nels O. Westergreen. Ph.D., Princeton Theological Seminary, 1986. 405p. UMI# 8616951.

1988   Patterson, Louis D. The Ministerial Mind of American Methodism: The Courses of Study for the Ministry of the Methodist Episcopal Church, the Methodist Episcopal Church, South, and the Methodist Protestant Church: 1880-1920. Ph.D., Drew University, 1984. 413p. UMI# 8416257.

Education

1989   Alderson, Willis B. A History of Methodist Higher Education in

Arkansas, 1836-1933. Ed.D., University of Arkansas, 1971. 439p. UMI# 71-19528.

1990   Allan, Henry C., Jr. History of the Non-Residential Degree Program at Illinois Wesleyan University, 1873-1910: A Study of a Pioneer External Degree Program in the United States. Ph.D., University of Chicago, 1984.

1991   Bartlett, Willard W. A Historical Study of Otterbein College at Westerville in the State of Ohio. Ph.D., Ohio State University, 1934.

1992   Becker, James M. Was Randolph-Macon Different? Revivalism, Sectionalism, and the Academic Tradition: The Methodist Mission in Higher Education, 1830-1880. Ph.D., University of North Carolina-Chapel Hill, 1980. 436p. UMI# 81-14788.

1993   Buell, Harold E. The Development of Higher Education Under the Methodist Episcopal Church in the Pittsburgh Area. Ph.D., University of Pittsburgh, 1950. 117p.

1994   Bullock, Henry M. A History of Emory College, 1834-1915. Ph.D., Yale University, 1932.

1995   Chaffin, Nora C. Trinity College, 1839-1892: The Beginnings of Duke University. Ph.D., Duke University, 1943.

1996   Clary, George E., Jr. The Founding of Paine College: A Unique Venture in Inter-Racial Cooperation in the New South, 1882-1903. Ed.D., University of Georgia, 1965. 152p. UMI# 65-10286.

1997   Dannelly, Clarence M. The Development of Collegiate Education in the Methodist Episcopal Church, South, 1846-1902. Ph.D., Yale University, 1933. 454p. UMI# 72-22304.

1998   Duvall, Sylvaus M. The Methodist Episcopal Church and Education up to 1869. Ph.D., Columbia University, 1928. 127p.

1999   Griffin, Paul R. Black Founders of Reconstruction Era Methodist Colleges: Daniel A. Payne, Joseph C. Price, and Isaac Lane, 1863-1890. Ph.D., Emory University, 1983. 300p. UMI# 8316279.

2000   High, Juanita J. Black Colleges as Social Intervention: The Development of Higher Education Within the African Methodist Episcopal Church. Ed.D., Rutgers University, 1978. 251p. UMI# 78-10230.

2001   Holsclaw, David F. The Demise of Disciplined Christian Fellowship: The Methodist Class Meeting in Nineteenth-Century America.

Ph.D., University of California-Davis, 1979. 327p. UMI# 80-09501.

2002   Howard, Ivan C. Controversies in Methodism Over Methods of Education of Ministers up to 1856. Ph.D., University of Iowa, 1965. 332p. UMI# 65-6692.

2003   Johnson, Henry M. The Methodist Episcopal Church and the Education of Southern Negroes, 1862-1900. Ph.D., Yale University, 1939. 620p. UMI# 71-01771.

2004   Johnson, Terrell E. A History of Methodist Education and Its Influence on American Public Education. Ph.D., Southern Illinois University-Carbondale, 1989. 260p. UMI# 9012573.

2005   Jordahl, Donald C. Greenville College: The Antecedents; A History of Almira College. Ph.D., Southern Illinois University-Carbondale, 1974. 259p. UMI# 75-00122.

2006   Otte, Louis E. The Educational Policy of the Methodist Episcopal Church in Ohio During the Nineteenth Century. Ph.D., Ohio State University, 1946. 213p.

2007   Reamey, George S. A History of Religious Education in the Methodist Episcopal Church, South, 1870-1908. Ph.D., Yale University, 1932.

2008   Renn, William A. The Theological School of Drew University. D.Min., Drew University, 1981. 130p. UMI# 8119848.

2009   Salen, George P. Methodist Schools in the North West Indiana Conference From 1852 to 1892. Ed.D., Indiana University, 1953. 259p. UMI# 06123.

2010   Smith, David L. Developing a Curriculum on the History of the Wesleyan Church Since 1843. D.Min., Drew University, 1978. 213p. UMI# 7910224.

2011   Smith, Willard G. The History of Church-Controlled Colleges in the Wesleyan Methodist Church. Ph.D., New York University, 1951. 433p. UMI# 73-08779.

2012   Taylor, Charles W. History of the (Higher) Educational Movement of the Wesleyan Methodist Church of America. Ph.D., Indiana University, 1959. 361p. UMI# 59-04043.

2013   Taylor, Prince A., Jr. A History of Gammon Theological Seminary. Ed.D., New York University, 1948. 169p. UMI# 01155.

2014   Thomas, Lavens M., Jr. A History of Religious Education in the Methodist Episcopal Church, South, to 1870. Ph.D., Yale University, 1927.

2015   Tingle, Larry O. The Wesleyan Class Meeting: Its History and Adaptability for the Twentieth-Century Church. D.Min., Wesley Theological Seminary, 1984.

2016   Wardle, Addie G. History of the Sunday School Movement in the Methodist Episcopal Church. Ph.D., University of Chicago, 1915. 232p.

2017   Wright, Donald G. The Employment of the Wesleyan Class Meeting Model as a Means of Evangelistic Outreach and Assimilation. D.Min., Emory University, 1985.

Ethnic Groups

2018   Lakeberg, Arvid P. A History of Swedish Methodism in America. Ph.D., Drew University, 1937.

2019   Lawson, Evald B. The Origin of Swedish Religious Organizations in the United States With Special Reference to Olof Gustaf Hedstrom and the Early Structure of Swedish Methodism. Ph.D., New York Theological Seminary, 1937.

2020   Van Dussen, Dean G. The American Methodist Response to Irish Catholic Immigration, 1830-1870. D.Min., Colgate Rochester Divinity School/Bexley Hall/Crozer Theological Seminary, 1986.

2021   Whyman, Henry C. The Conflict and Adjustments of Two Religious Cultures: The Swedish and the American. Ph.D., New York University, 1937. 259p. UMI# 73-03486.

Evangelism

2022   Brown, Kenneth O. Leadership in the National Holiness Association With Special Reference to Eschatology, 1867-1919. Ph.D., Drew University, 1988. 327p. UMI# 8906802.

2023   Johnson, Charles A. The Frontier Camp Meeting: Methodist Harvest Time, 1800-1840. Ph.D., Northwestern University, 1951.

2024   Nickerson, Michael G. Sermons, Systems, and Strategies: The Geographic Strategies of the Methodist Episcopal Church in Its Expansion Into New York State, 1788-1810. Ph.D., Syracuse University, 1988. 423p. UMI# 8914585.

Literature

2025   Byrne, Donald E. Methodist Itinerant Folklore of the Nineteenth Century With Particular Reference to Autobiography and Biography. Ph.D., Duke University, 1972. 425p. UMI# 72-23228.

2026   Tenney, Mary A. Early Methodist Autobiography (1739-1791): A Study in the Literature of the Inner Life. Ph.D., University of Wisconsin, 1940. 199p.

Liturgy

2027   Grabner, John D. A Commentary on the Rites of An Ordinal, The United Methodist Church. Ph.D., University of Notre Dame, 1983. 504p. UMI# 8318689.

2028   Hohenstein, Charles R. The Revisions of the Rites of Baptism in the Methodist Episcopal Church, 1784-1939. Ph.D., University of Notre Dame, 1990. 331p. UMI# 9024235.

2029   Wade, William N. A History of Public Worship in the Methodist Episcopal Church and Methodist Episcopal Church, South, From 1784 to 1905. Ph.D., University of Notre Dame, 1981. 418p. UMI# 81-18594.

Missions and Missionaries

2030   Creel, Margaret W. Antebellum Religion Among the Gullahs; A Study of Slave Conversion and Religious Culture in the South Carolina Sea Islands. Ph.D., University of California-Davis, 1980. 324p. UMI# 8111983.

2031   Myers, Sara J. Southern Methodist Women Leaders and Church Missions, 1878-1910. Ph.D., Emory University, 1990. 216p. UMI# 9106731.

2032   Najarian, Nishan J. A Symbolic Interactionist Approach to the Religious Stranger Concept: Protestant Missionaries in China, 1845-1900. Ph.D., Drew University, 1982. 548p. UMI# 8302198.

Music

2033   Baldridge, Terry L. Evolving Tastes in Hymntunes of the Methodist Episcopal Church in the Nineteenth Century. Ph.D., University of Kansas, 1982. 494p. UMI# 8301665.

2034   Crawford, Benjamin F. Changing Conceptions and Motivations of Religion as Revealed in One Hundred Years of Methodist

Hymnology, 1836-1935. Ph.D., University of Pittsburgh, 1937.

2035   Hill, Double E. A Study of Tastes in American Church Music as Reflected in the Music of the Methodist Episcopal Church to 1900. Ph.D., University of Illinois at Urbana-Champaign, 1962. 900p. UMI# 63-03270.

2036   Kindley, Carolyn E. Miriam's Timbrel: A Reflection of the Music of Wesleyan Methodism in America: 1843-1899. D.A., Ball State University, 1985. 342p. UMI# 8605933.

2037   Rice, William C. A Century of Methodist Music: 1850-1950. Ph.D., University of Iowa, 1953. 478p. UMI# 05492.

Organizational Structure

2038   Barton, Jesse H., Jr. The Definition of the Episcopal Office in American Methodism. Ph.D., Drew University, 1960. 243p. UMI# 60-05302.

2039   Brannan, Emora T. The Presiding Elder Question: Its Critical Nature in American Methodism, 1820-1824, and Its Impact Upon Ecclesiastical Institutions. Ph.D., Duke University, 1974. 370p. UMI# 75-02361.

2040   Caldwell, John M. The Methodist Organization of the United States, 1784-1844: An Historical Geography of the Methodist Episcopal Church From Its Formation to Its Division. Ph.D., University of Oklahoma, 1982. 229p. UMI# 8306739.

2041   Goodloe, Robert W. The Office of Bishop in the Methodist Church. Ph.D., University of Chicago, 1929.

2042   Price, Fred W. The Role of the Presiding Elder in the Growth of the Methodist Episcopal Church, 1784-1832. Ph.D., Drew University, 1987. 349p. UMI# 8716917.

2043   Spellmann, Norman W. The General Superintendency in American Methodism, 1784-1870. Ph.D., Yale University, 1961. 387p. UMI# 72-09859.

2044   Tucker, Robert L. The Separation of the Methodists From the Church of England. Ph.D., Columbia University, 1918. 184p.

2045   Worley, Harry W. The Central Conference of the Methodist Episcopal Church. Ph.D., Yale University, 1938.

Preaching

2046   Clark, Robert D. The Pulpit and Platform Career and the Rhetorical Theory of Bishop Matthew Simpson. Ph.D., University of Southern California, 1946. 275p.

2047   Davis, Douglas W., Jr. A Rhetorical Study of the Early Preaching of Edward Eggleston. Ph.D., Indiana University, 1971. 210p. UMI# 7206767.

2048   Hickey, Timothy R. Methodist Preaching at the Time of the Formation and Development of the Detroit Annual Conference of the Methodist Church, 1856-1869. Ph.D., University of Michigan, 1969. 196p. UMI# 70-04102.

2049   Lloyd, Mark B. A Rhetorical Analysis of the Preaching of Bishop Francis Asbury. Ph.D., Michigan State University, 1965. 444p. UMI# 68-04173.

2050   Vaughn, Damon V. A Critical Study of the Preaching of Samuel Porter Jones. Ph.D., New Orleans Baptist Theological Seminary, 1962.

Social Programs

2051   Barnhart, Kenneth E. The Evolution of Social Consciousness in Methodism. Ph.D., University of Chicago, 1924.

2052   Brown, Forrest R. The Development of the Social Creed of the Methodist Church. Ph.D., Boston University, 1942.

2053   Crummey, David C. Factors in the Rise of Methodist Hospitals and Homes. Ph.D., University of Chicago, 1964.

2054   Huber, Milton J., Jr. A History of the Methodist Federation for Social Action. Ph.D., Boston University, 1949. 373p.

2055   Mathews, Donald G. Antislavery, Piety, and Institutionalism: The Slavery Controversies in the Methodist Episcopal Church, 1780 to 1844. Ph.D., Duke University, 1962. 406p. UMI# 64-13179.

2056   North, Eric M. Early Methodist Philanthropy. Ph.D., Columbia University, 1914. 181p.

2057   Norwood, John N. The Slavery Schism in the Methodist Episcopal Church: A Study of Slavery and Ecclesiastical Politics. Ph.D., Cornell University, 1915.

2058   Powell, Milton B. The Abolitionist Controversy in the Methodist Episcopal Church, 1840-1864. Ph.D., University of Iowa, 1963. 247p. UMI# 64-03415.

2059   Swaney, Charles B. Episcopal Methodism and Slavery, With Sidelights on Ecclesiastical Politics. Ph.D., Northwestern University, 1927. 356p.

2060   Williams, Thomas L. The Methodist Mission to the Slaves. Ph.D., Yale University, 1943.

2061   Wills, David W. Aspects of Social Thought in the African Methodist Episcopal Church, 1884-1910. Ph.D., Harvard University, 1975.

Theology

2062   Barnhardt, William H. The Influence of Borden Park Bowne Upon Theological Thought in the Methodist Episcopal Church. Ph.D., University of Chicago, 1928.

2063   Beeson, John F. The Americanization of John Wesley's Theology Prior to 1884. D.Min., Colgate Rochester Divinity School/Bexley Hall/Crozer Theological Seminary, 1985.

2064   Carter, Ronald L. An Examination of the Logic of Borden Parker Bowne's Response to the Problem of Good and Evil. Ph.D., Boston University, 1985. 348p. UMI# 8525212.

2065   Chiles, Robert E. Theological Transition in American Methodism. Ph.D., Columbia University, 1964. 337p. UMI# 64-09866.

2066   Clark, Robert B. The History of the Doctrine of Christian Perfection in the Methodist Church up to 1845. Ph.D., Temple University, 1946.

2067   Felton, Gayle C. Evolving Baptismal Theology and Practice in American Methodism From the Days of John Wesley to the End of the Nineteenth Century. Ph.D., Duke University, 1987. 290p. UMI# 8810874.

2068   Harrison, Samuel J. A History of Methodist Theology. Th.D., Boston University, 1931.

2069   Lang, Edward M., Jr. The Theology of Francis Asbury. Ph.D., Northwestern University, 1972. 316p. UMI# 7232488.

2070   Mills, Ernest L. A Comparison of the Main Points in the Epistemological Theories of Borden Parker Bowne and Henri Bergson. Ph.D., Boston University, 1914.

2071   Peters, John L., Jr. The Development of the Wesleyan Doctrine of Christian Perfection in American Methodism in the Nineteenth Century. Ph.D., Yale University, 1950. 256p.

2072   Puls, Mary S. The Personalistic Theism of Borden Parker Bowne. Ph.D., Marquette University, 1965. 325p. UMI# 6703635.

2073   Ransdell, Edward T. Pragmatic Elements in the Epistemology of Borden P. Bowne. Ph.D., Boston University, 1932.

2074   Scott, Leland, II. Methodist Theology in America in the Nineteenth Century. Ph.D., Yale University, 1955.

2075   Trotter, Frederick T. The Christian Theology of Borden Parker Bowne. Ph.D., Boston University, 1958. 297p. UMI# 5803126.

MILLENARIANISM

2076   Beam, Christopher M. Millennialism in American Thought, 1740-1840. Ph.D., University of Illinois at Urbana-Champaign, 1976. 374p. UMI# 7616090.

2077   Bloch, Ruth H. Visionary Republic: Millennial Themes in American Ideology, 1756-1800. Ph.D., University of California-Berkeley, 1980. 559p. UMI# 8112969.

2078   Eichler, Margrit. Charismatic and Ideological Leadership in Secular and Religious Millenarian Movements: A Sociological Study. Ph.D., Duke University, 1972. 239p. UMI# 7223230.

2079   Gray, Harry B. The Eschatology of the Millennial Cults. Th.D., Dallas Theological Seminary, 1956.

2080   Hales, John R. Time's Last Offspring: Millennialism in America From John Cotton to James Fenimore Cooper. Ph.D., State University of New York-Binghamton, 1985. 364p. UMI# 8506867.

2081   Ludwigson, Carl R. The Apocalyptic Interpretation of History of American Premillennial Groups. Ph.D., University of Iowa, 1945. 352p.

2082   MacSorley, Ray H. Millennialism in Eighteenth Century America. Ph.D., University of Maryland, 1983. 419p. UMI# 8419522.

2083   Pickering, Ernest D. The Premillennial Concept of the Kingdom of God. Th.D., Dallas Theological Seminary, 1957.

2084   Thomas, Nathan G. The Second Coming in the Third New England.

The Millennial Impulse in Michigan, 1830-1860. Ph.D., Michigan State University, 1967. 199p. UMI# 6714554.

2085   Weber, Timothy P. Living in the Shadow of the Second Coming: American Premillennialism, 1875-1925. Ph.D., University of Chicago, 1976.

2086   Whalen, Robert K. Millenarianism and Millennialism in America, 1790-1880. Ph.D., State University of New York-Stony Brook, 1972. 339p. UMI# 7216969.

2087   Wilt, Paul C. Pre-Millennialism in America, 1865-1918, With Special Reference to Attitudes Toward Social Reform. Ph.D., American University, 1970. 279p. UMI# 7023267.

MORAVIAN

General Studies

2088   Davis, Emilie-Louise. Salem, North Carolina: A Study of a Moravian Community in the South, 1766-1816. Ph.D., Howard University, 1988.

2089   Gollin, Gillian L. Communal Pietism and the Secular Drift: A Comparative Study of Social Change in the Moravian Communities of Bethlehem, Pennsylvania and Herrnhut Saxony, in the Eighteenth and Early Nineteenth Centuries. Ph.D., Columbia University, 1965. 634p. UMI# 69-00549.

2090   Hudson, Jean S. Emmaus, Pennsylvania; Conflict and Stability in an Eighteenth-Century Moravian Community. Ph.D., Lehigh University, 1977. 214p. UMI# 87-00837.

2091   Patterson, Jo E. Church Control and Family Structure in a Moravian Community of North Carolina: 1753-1857. Ph.D., University of North Carolina-Greensboro, 1981. 144p. UMI# 81-18781.

2092   Sawyer, Edwin A. The Religious Experience of the Colonial American Moravians. Ph.D., Columbia University, 1956. 323p. UMI# 17079.

2093   Sessler, Jacob J. Communal Pietism Among Early American Moravians. Ph.D., Columbia University, 1933. 265p.

2094   Smaby, Beverly P. From Communal Pilgrims to Family Householders: The Moravians in Bethlehem, Pennsylvania, 1742-1844. Ph.D., University of Pennsylvania, 1986. 349p. UMI# 8624027.

2095   Thorp, Daniel B. Moravian Colonization of Wachovia, 1753-1772: The Maintenance of Community in Late Colonial North Carolina. Ph.D., Johns Hopkins University, 1982. 448p. UMI# 82-13436.

2096   Williams, Margaret C. An Interpretation of the Philosophy of the Wachovia Moravians, 1753-1822: How Their Way of Life Related to the Evolution of Industrial Arts. Ed.D., North Carolina State University-Raleigh, 1979. 107p. UMI# 8020517.

2097   Wright, Barbara D. Pilgrim in Bethlehem: A Study of the Influence of American Moravian Pietism on the Identity Formation of a Nineteenth Century Adolescent Woman. Ph.D., Drew University, 1989. 161p. UMI# 9014374.

Art and Architecture

2098   Murtagh, William J. Moravian Architecture and City Planning: A Study of Eighteenth Century Moravian Settlements in the American Colonies With Particular Emphasis on Bethlehem, Pennsylvania. Ph.D., University of Pennsylvania, 1963. 461p. UMI# 6307072.

Biography

2099   Mueller, Paul E. David Zeisberger's Official Diary, Fairfield, 1791-1795. Ph.D., Columbia University, 1956. 314p. UMI# 17070.

Education

2100   Haller, Mabel. Early Moravian Education in Pennsylvania. Ph.D., University of Pennsylvania, 1951.

2101   Handler, Bonnie S. The Schooling of "Unmarried Sisters": Linden Hall and the Moravian Educational Tradition, 1863-1940. Ed.D., Pennsylvania State University, 1980. 329p. UMI# 81-07575.

Literature

2102   Pirscenok, Anna. Czech Literature in the Moravian Archives in Bethlehem, Pennsylvania. Ph.D., University of Pennsylvania, 1956. 168p. UMI# 17263.

Liturgy

2103   Kortz, Edwin W. The Liturgical Development of the American Moravian Church. S.T.D., Temple University, 1955.

Missions and Missionaries

2104   Radloff, Ralph M. Moravian Mission Methods Among the Indians of Ohio. Ph.D., University of Iowa, 1973. 205p. UMI# 7416680.

Music

2105   Birney, Allan D. Four Unpublished Anthems by David Moritz Michael, Moravian Composer (1751-1827), Edited and Provided With a Biographical Sketch. Ph.D., Juilliard School, 1971.

2106   Duncan, Timothy P. The Role of the Organ in Moravian Sacred Music Between 1740-1840. D.M.A., University of North Carolina-Greensboro, 1989. 162p. UMI# 9020149.

2107   Falconer, Joan O. Bishop Johannes Herbst (1735-1812), An American-Moravian Musician, Collector, and Composer. Ph.D., Columbia University, 1969. 564p. UMI# 72-15571.

2108   Hoople, Donald G. Moravian Music Education and the American Moravian Music Tradition. Ed.D., Columbia University Teachers College, 1976. 230p. UMI# 77-06715.

2109   McCorkle, Donald M. Moravian Music in Salem: A German-American Heritage. Ph.D., Indiana University, 1958. 432p. UMI# 59-00333.

2110   Poole, Franklin P. The Moravian Musical Heritage: Johann Christian Geisler's Music in America. Ph.D., George Peabody College for Teachers, 1971. 359p. UMI# 71-26217.

2111   Roberts, Dale A. The Sacred Vocal Music of David Moritz Michael: An American Moravian Composer. D.M.A., University of Kentucky, 1978. 508p. UMI# 79-18113.

Organizational Structure

2112   Dimock, Alice B. Organization Study of Moravian Churches in the New York City Metropolitan Area. Ph.D., Columbia University, 1969. 391p. UMI# 70-06958.

2113   Surratt, Jerry L. From Theocracy to Voluntary Church and Secularized Community: A Study of the Moravians in Salem, North Carolina, 1772-1860. Ph.D., Emory University, 1968. 375p. UMI# 68-15763.

MYSTICISM

2114 Pelfrey, Charles J. Elements of Mysticism in the Writings of John Burroughs and John Muir. Ph.D., University of Kentucky, 1958. 237p. UMI# 6307405.

2115 Stoeffler, F. Ernest. Mysticism in the German Devotional Literature of Colonial Pennsylvania. Ph.D., Temple University, 1948.

2116 Wincell, Wallace. The Mystical Experience of Thomas Lake Harris: The Seer as a Creator of His Own Visionary World. Ph.D., Hartford Seminary Foundation, 1976. 330p. UMI# 7710454.

2117 Wright, Eugene P. A Descriptive Catalogue of the Joanna Southcott Collection at the University of Texas. Ph.D., University of Texas-Austin, 1966. 144p. UMI# 6915893.

NATIVE AMERICAN

General Studies

2118 Bruchman, Robert C. Native American Revitalized Prophecy: A Process of Enculturation. Ph.D., Arizona State University, 1978. 281p. UMI# 7820681.

2119 Dowd, Gregory E. Paths of Resistance: American Indian Religion and the Quest for Unity, 1745-1815. Ph.D., Princeton University, 1986. 786p. UMI# 8629429.

2120 Frisch, Jack A. Revitalization, Nativism, and Tribalism Among the St. Regis Mohawks. Ph.D., Indiana University, 1970. 217p. UMI# 7026921.

2121 Gelo, Daniel J. Comanche Belief and Ritual. Ph.D., Rutgers University, 1986. 293p. UMI# 8620033.

2122 Grim, John A. The Shaman: An Interpretation of This Religious Fraternity Based on Ethnographic Data From the Siberian Tribes and the Woodland Ojibway of North America. Ph.D., Fordham University, 1980. 264p. UMI# 8012786.

2123 Hendren, Samuel R. Government and Religion of the Virginia Indians. Ph.D., Johns Hopkins University, 1895.

2124 Irvin, Michael T. My Grandfathers Built the House: The Tlingit Potlatch as a System of Religious Belief. Ph.D., State University of New York-Stony Brook, 1985. 287p. UMI# 8518368.

2125   Irwin, T. Lee. The Bridge of Dreams: Myth, Dreams and Visions in Native North America. Ph.D., Indiana University, 1989. 491p. UMI# 9020688.

2126   Kan, Sergei. "Wrap Your Father's Brother in Kind Words": An Analysis of the Nineteenth-Century Tlingit Mortuary and Memorial Rituals. Ph.D., University of Chicago, 1982.

2127   Kelly, Thomas M.L. Medicine Men, Shamans, and Psychotherapists: An Exploration Into the Origin of Wisdom and Healing in the West. Ed.D., East Texas State University, 1979. 120p. UMI# 7918457.

2128   Kracht, Benjamin R. Kiowa Religion: An Ethnohistorical Analysis of Ritual Symbolism, 1832-1987. Ph.D., Southern Methodist University, 1989. 1122p. UMI# 9004377.

2129   Labarre, Weston. The Peyote Cult. Ph.D., Yale University, 1937.

2130   March, Kathleen D. Uncommon Civility: The Narragansett Indians and Roger Williams. Ph.D., University of Iowa, 1985. 334p. UMI# 8611112.

2131   Martin, Joel W. Cultural Hermeneutics on the Frontier: Colonialism and the Muscogulge Millenarian Revolt of 1813. Ph.D., Duke University, 1988. 428p. UMI# 8825721.

2132   Mathes, Valerie S. Friends of the California Mission Indians: Helen Hunt Jackson and Her Legacy. Ph.D., Arizona State University, 1988. 408p. UMI# 8907719.

2133   McPherson, Robert S. The Northern Navajo Frontier, 1860-1900: Expansion Through Adversity. Ph.D., Brigham Young University, 1987. 239p. UMI# 8709218.

2134   Morgan, George R. Man, Plant, and Religion: Peyote Trade on the Mustang Plains of Texas. Ph.D., University of Colorado-Boulder, 1976. 158p. UMI# 7623637.

2135   Morrison, Dane A. "A Praying People": The Transition From Remnant to Convert Among the Indians of Massachusetts Bay Colony. Ph.D., Tufts University, 1983. 352p. UMI# 8316859.

2136   Nash, Philleo. The Place of Religious Revivalism in the Formation of the Intercultural Community on Klamath Reservation. Ph.D., University of Chicago, 1938.

2137   Packer, Rhonda. Sorcerers, Medicine-Men, and Curing Doctors: A Study of Myth and Symbol in North American Shamanism. Ph.D.,

University of California-Los Angeles, 1983. 272p. UMI# 8407969.

2138   Ricketts, Mac L. The Structure and Religious Significance of the Trickster-Transformer-Culture Hero in the Mythology of the North American Indians. Ph.D., University of Chicago, 1965.

2139   Roediger, Virginia M. Ceremonial Costumes of the Pueblo Indians: Their Evolution, Fabrication, and Significance in the Prayer-Drama. Ph.D., Yale University, 1937.

2140   Taylor, Maxwell F., Jr. The Influence of Religion on White Attitudes Toward Indians in the Early Settlement of Virginia. Ph.D., Emory University, 1970. 280p. UMI# 7115606.

2141   Thomas, Trudy C. Crisis and Creativity: Visual Symbolism of the Ghost Dance Tradition. Ph.D., Columbia University, 1988. 310p. UMI# 9102463.

2142   Voegelin, Erminie W. Shawnee Mortuary Customs. Ph.D., Yale University, 1939.

Biography

2143   Luebke, Barbara F. Elias Boudinot, Cherokee Editor: The Father of American Indian Journalism. Ph.D., University of Missouri-Columbia, 1981. 403p. UMI# 8205400.

Education

2144   Abbott, Devon I. History of the Cherokee Female Seminary: 1851-1910. Ph.D., Texas Christian University, 1989. 254p. UMI# 8919932.

Evangelism

2145   Forbes, Bruce D. Evangelization and Acculturation Among the Santee Dakota Indians, 1834-1864. Ph.D., Princeton Theological Seminary, 1977. 364p. UMI# 7721192.

Liturgy

2146   Berube, David M. The Lakotan Ghost Dance of 1890: A Historiocritical Performance Analysis. Ph.D., New York University, 1990. 357p. UMI# 9102501.

2147   Brito, Silvester J. The Development and Change of the Peyote Ceremony Through Time and Space. Ph.D., Indiana University, 1975. 313p. UMI# 7602792.

2148   Dugan, Kathleen M. The Vision Quest of the Plains Indians: Its Spiritual Significance. Ph.D., Fordham University, 1977. 306p. UMI# 7714891.

Missions and Missionaries

2149   Conard, Arlyn M. The Christianization of Indians in Colonial Virginia. Th.D., Union Theological Seminary in Virginia, 1979. 572p. UMI# 79-21994.

2150   Devens, Carol A. Separate Confrontations: Indian Women and Christian Missions, 1630-1900. Ph.D., Rutgers University, 1986. 245p. UMI# 8704060.

2151   Edwards, Martha L. Government Patronage of Indian Missions. Ph.D., University of Wisconsin, 1916.

2152   Harrod, Howard L. Mission Among the Blackfeet: An Evaluation of Protestant and Catholic Missions Among the Blackfeet Indians. Ph.D., Yale University, 1965. 339p. UMI# 65-15052.

Music

2153   Whitinger, Julius E. Hymnody of the Early American Indian Missions. Ph.D., Catholic University of America, 1971. 344p. UMI# 71-25237.

Theology

2154   Schwarz, O. Douglas. Plains Indian Theology: As Expressed in Myth and Ritual, and in the Ethics of the Culture. Ph.D., Fordham University, 1981. 288p. UMI# 8111316.

ONEIDA COMMUNITY

2155   Bowden, James H. The Religious Significance of the Oneida Experiment. Ph.D., University of Minnesota, 1970. 243p. UMI# 71-08128.

2156   Fogarty, Robert S. The Oneida Community, 1848-1880: A Study in Conservative Christian Utopianism. Ph.D., University of Denver, 1968. 355p. UMI# 69-07008.

2157   Haight, Norman W. Faith and Freedom in Christian Utopia: An Analysis of the Thought of John Humphrey Noyes and the Oneida Community. Ph.D., Syracuse University, 1972. 210p. UMI# 73-07726.

2158   Klass, Dennis E. John Humphrey Noyes and the Oneida

Community: A Psychohistorical Study. Ph.D., University of Chicago, 1974.

2159   Kopp, Michael J. Spiritual Odyssey of John Noyes. Ph.D., University of Minnesota, 1971. 157p. UMI# 7128253.

2160   Thomas, Robert D., Jr. The Development of a Utopian Mind: A Psychoanalytic Study of John Humphrey Noyes, 1828-1869. Ph.D., State University of New York-Stony Brook, 1973. 333p. UMI# 7408942.

PENTECOSTAL

2161   Bowers, James P. A Wesleyan-Pentecostal Vision of the Christian Life With Pedagogical Implications for Christian Education. Ed.D., Southern Baptist Theological Seminary, 1990. 287p. UMI# 9107132.

2162   Francis, Russel E. Pentecost: 1858. A Study in Religious Revivalism. Ph.D., University of Pennsylvania, 1948.

PIETISM

2163   Eisenach, George. Pietism and the Russian Germans in the United States. Ph.D., University of Chicago, 1945. 159p.

2164   Schrag, Felix J. Pietism in Colonial America. Ph.D., University of Chicago, 1945. 177p.

PRAGMATISM

2165   Bergin, James M. "Experience" in William James as a Starting Point for Theology. Ph.D., Marquette University, 1985. 269p. UMI# 8525671.

2166   Bixler, Julius S. Some Aspects of the Religious Philosophy of William James. Ph.D., Yale University, 1924.

2167   Chiles, Richard P. William James: A Damaged Self Journeys Toward Reparation. Ph.D., Northwestern University, 1990. 392p. UMI# 9114531.

2168   Croce, Paul J. The Education of William James: Religion, Science, and the Possibilities for Belief Without Certainty in the Early Intellectual Development of William James. Ph.D., Brown University, 1987. 550p. UMI# 8715478.

2169   Dooley, Patrick K. "Humanism" in the Philosophy of William James. Ph.D., University of Notre Dame, 1969. 281p. UMI# 7007887.

2170   Duncan, Franklin D. The Contribution of William James to the Psychology of Religion. Th.D., Southern Baptist Theological Seminary, 1974. 227p. UMI# 74-22658.

2171   George, Samuel S. The Influence of Pragmatism Upon American Religion. S.T.D., Temple University, 1939. 322p.

2172   Graham, George P. William James and the Affirmation of God. Ph.D., New York University, 1988. 328p. UMI# 8910632.

2173   Haines, Wesley N. The Function of the Factor of God in the Philosophy of William James. Ph.D., Harvard University, 1949.

2174   Huyke, Hector J. Pragmatism and Faith in William James and Miguel de Unamuno. Ph.D., Columbia University, 1987. 351p. UMI# 8724038.

2175   Kessler, Gary E. Experience, Language, and Religion: A Study in the Significance of William James for the Analysis of Religious Discourse. Ph.D., Columbia University, 1970. 223p. UMI# 7106202.

2176   Kuo, Catherine C. William James as an Exemplar for the Study of Religion: *The Varieties of Religious Experience*. Ed.D., Columbia University Teachers College, 1982. 176p. UMI# 82-23145.

2177   Leslie, Charles W. The Religious Philosophy of William James. Ph.D., Harvard University, 1945.

2178   MacMillan, Donald. William James' Philosophy of Religion, With Specific Reference to His Philosophy of Mind. Ph.D., University of Toronto, 1963.

2179   Ramsey, Bennett H. An Apparition of Difference: The Religious Vision of William James. Ph.D., Union Theological Seminary, 1985. 317p. UMI# 8518795.

2180   Reilly, William F., Jr. The Pragmatism of William James as a Religious Philosophy. Ph.D., Fordham University, 1961. 326p. UMI# 6201039.

2181   Snowden, Barnard F. The Religious Experience and Its Interpretation in the Philosophies of William James and Josiah Royce. Ph.D., Tulane University, 1989. 343p. UMI# 9023206.

2182   Strug, Cordell T. William James and the Gods: A Peek at the Conceptual Underbelly of the *Varieties of Religious Experience*. Ph.D, Purdue University, 1973. 218p. UMI# 7328147.

2183   Turner, Charles C. The Meaning of God in the Philosophy of William James. Ph.D., Tulane University, 1977. 362p. UMI# 7807667.

PRESBYTERIAN

General Studies

2184   Barrus, Ben M. A Study of the Factors Involved in the Origin of the Cumberland Presbyterian Church: 1800-1813. Ph.D., Vanderbilt University, 1964. 390p. UMI# 64-10546.

2185   Bass, Thomas N. The Nature of Schism: A Comparative Analysis of Three Schisms in American Presbyterianism. D.Min, Eden Theological Seminary, 1975.

2186   Baughn, Milton L. Social Views Reflected in Official Publications of the Cumberland Presbyterian Church, 1875-1900. Ph.D., Vanderbilt University, 1954. 278p. UMI# 09931.

2187   Bender, Norman J. The Crusade of the Blue Banner: Rocky Mountain Presbyterianism, 1870-1900. Ph.D., University of Colorado, 1971. 500p. UMI# 72-03625.

2188   Bigelow, Ernest N. Presbyterian Church Discipline in Ohio, 1865-1965. Ph.D., Case Western Reserve University, 1967. 427p. UMI# 67-08835.

2189   Binnington, Alfred F. The Glasgow Colonial Society and Its Work in the Development of the Presbyterian Church in British North America, 1825-1840. Th.D., Victoria University, 1960.

2190   Blanks, William D. Ideal and Practice: A Study of the Conception of the Christian Life Prevailing in the Presbyterian Churches of the South During the Nineteenth-Century. Th.D., Union Theological Seminary in Virginia, 1960. 332p. UMI# 7425388.

2191   Boston, Walter M., Jr. A Study of Presbyterianism in Colonial New England. Ph.D., Michigan State University, 1972. 242p. UMI# 73-12679.

2192   Bozeman, Theodore D. Baconianism and the Bible: The Baconian Ideal in Ante-Bellum American Presbyterian Thought. Ph.D., Duke University, 1974. 377p. UMI# 75-02360.

2193   Brown, James H. Presbyterian Beginnings in Ohio. Ph.D., University of Pittsburgh, 1952. 278p.

2194   Brown, Katherine L. The Role of Presbyterian Dissent in Colonial and Revolutionary Virginia, 1740-1785. Ph.D., Johns Hopkins University, 1969. 437p. UMI# 69-13488.

2195   Carson, David M. A History of the Reformed Presbyterian Church in America to 1871. Ph.D., University of Pennsylvania, 1964. 281p. UMI# 64-10358.

2196   Davies, George K. A History of the Presbyterian Church in Utah. Ph.D., University of Pittsburgh, 1943.

2197   Davis, Dennis R. Presbyterian Attitudes Toward Science and the Coming of Darwinism in America, 1859 to 1929. Ph.D., University of Illinois at Urbana-Champaign, 1980. 444p. UMI# 81-08478.

2198   Davis, James T. The Relations Between the Northern and Southern Presbyterian Churches, 1861-1888. Ph.D., Vanderbilt University, 1949. 248p.

2199   Deschamps, Margaret B. The Presbyterian Church in the South Atlantic States, 1801-1861. Ph.D., Emory University, 1952. 241p. UMI# 58-05132.

2200   Ellis, George E. Nation, Creed and Unity: The Significance of the Subscription Controversy for the Development of Colonial Presbyterianism. Ph.D., Temple University, 1984. 783p. UMI# 8410190.

2201   Hale, Ann W. God's Disciplined Society: Presbyterian Concepts of Education, Revivalism and Slavery in the Pre-Civil War South. Ph.D., University of California-Berkeley, 1984.

2202   Hare, John C. The Presbyterian Church in Pittsburgh: 1837-1870. Ph.D., University of Pittsburgh, 1951.

2203   Hix, Clarence E., Jr. The Conflict Between Presbyterianism and Free-Thought in the South, 1776-1838. Ph.D., University of Chicago, 1937.

2204   Hood, Fred J. Presbyterianism and the New American Nation, 1783-1826: A Case Study of Religion and National Life. Ph.D., Princeton University, 1968. 380p. UMI# 6914445.

2205   Kirk, Cooper C. A History of the Southern Presbyterian Church in Florida: 1821-1891. Ph.D., Florida State University, 1966. 344p. UMI# 67-06471.

2206   McClurkin, Paul T. Presbyterianism in Colonial New England.

Ph.D., Hartford Seminary Foundation, 1939.

2207　McCort, Elizabeth E. Changes in Theory and Practice of Confirmation in the (United) Presbyterian Church in the United States of America, 1789-1958. Th.D., Union Theological Seminary, 1967. 375p. UMI# 67-08818.

2208　McKinney, William W. The Early History of the Presbyterian Church in Pittsburgh. Ph.D., University of Pittsburgh, 1936.

2209　Melton, Julius W., Jr. The Reshaping of Presbyterian Worship by Nineteenth Century America. Ph.D., Princeton University, 1966. 327p. UMI# 66-07175.

2210　Miller, Page P. The Evolving Role of Women in the Presbyterian Church in the Early Nineteenth Century. Ph.D., University of Maryland, 1979. 351p. UMI# 79-26503.

2211　Monroe, Haskell M., Jr. The Presbyterian Church in the Confederacy. Ph.D., Rice University, 1961.

2212　Murray, Andrew E. A History of Presbyterianism in Colorado. Ph.D., Princeton Theological Seminary, 1947. 278p.

2213　Paschal, George H., Jr. The History of the USA Presbyterian Church in Texas and Louisiana, 1868-1920. Ph.D., Louisiana State University, 1967. 443p. UMI# 67-17340.

2214　Pope, Earl A. New England Calvinism and the Disruption of the Presbyterian Church. Ph.D., Brown University, 1962. 444p. UMI# 63-01048.

2215　Rudolph, Lavere C. A Study of the Presbyterians in Indiana to 1850. Ph.D., Yale University, 1958. 172p.

2216　Shiffler, Harrold C. The Opposition of the Presbyterian Church in the United States of America to the Theatre in America, 1750-1891. Ph.D., University of Iowa, 1953. 511p. UMI# 4990.

2217　Smoot, John M. Presbyterianism in Revolutionary Pennsylvania: Constitutionalism and Freedom. Ph.D., St. Mary's Seminary and University, 1982. 192p. UMI# 8205357.

2218　Sung, Kee H. Doctrine of the Second Coming in the Writings of Albert B. Simpson. Ph.D., Drew University, 1990. 226p. UMI# 9032133.

2219　Vander Velde, Lewis G. The Presbyterian Churches and the Federal

Union, 1861-1869. Ph.D., Harvard University, 1931.

2220 Waller, Wilson L. Cumberland Presbyterian Evangelicalism Before and After Default in Ecumenical Union in 1906. Ph.D., Vanderbilt University Divinity School, 1971. 291p. UMI# 71-26142.

Biography

2221 Alley, Robert S. The Reverend Mr. Samuel Davies: A Study in Religion and Politics, 1747-1759. Ph.D., Princeton University, 1962. 208p. UMI# 63-02393.

2222 Bailey, Alvin K. The Strategy of Sheldon Jackson in Opening the West for National Missions, 1860-1880. Ph.D., Yale University, 1948. 502p. UMI# 66-05587.

2223 Behannon, Woodrow. Benjamin B. Warfield's Concept of Religious Authority. Ph.D., Southwestern Baptist Theological Seminary, 1964.

2224 Berg, Kenneth P. Charles A. Hodge, Controversialist. Ph.D., University of Iowa, 1952.

2225 Bost, George H. Samuel Davies, Colonial Revivalist and Champion of Religious Toleration. Ph.D., University of Chicago, 1942.

2226 Bowdle, Donald N. Evangelism and Ecumenism in Nineteenth-Century America: A Study in the Life and Literature of Samuel Irenaeus Prime, 1812-1885. Th.D., Union Theological Seminary in Virginia, 1970. 347p. UMI# 74-28290.

2227 Brink, Frederick W. The Contribution of Gilbert Tennent to American Christianity and the American Nation. S.T.D., Temple University, 1942. 205p. UMI# 66-06755.

2228 Buxbaum, Melvin. Benjamin Franklin and the Zealous Presbyterians. Ph.D., University of Chicago, 1968.

2229 Carlson, Alden L. The Life and Educational Contributions of John Holt Rice. Ph.D., University of Virginia, 1954. 296p. UMI# 09637.

2230 Chapman, Clayton H. The Life and Influence of Reverend Benjamin Colman, D.D. (1673-1747). Ph.D., Boston University, 1948. 322p.

2231 Chrisope, Terry A. The Bible and Historical Scholarship in the Early Life and Thought of J. Gresham Machen, 1881-1915. Ph.D., Kansas State University, 1988. 311p. UMI# 8901139.

2232 Churchman, Charles J. Samuel Davies: Representative

Eighteenth-Century Poet. Ph.D., University of Tennessee, 1973. 285p. UMI# 7319999.

2233   Davis, Edward B. Albert Barnes, 1798-1870: An Exponent of New School Presbyterianism. Th.D., Princeton Theological Seminary, 1961. 561p. UMI# 61-05442.

2234   Eubank, Wayne C. Benjamin Morgan Palmer, a Southern Divine. Ph.D., Louisiana State University, 1943.

2235   Ferry, Henry J. Francis James Grimke: Portrait of a Black Puritan. Ph.D., Yale University, 1970. 386p. UMI# 7116235.

2236   Gill, John G. The Issues Involved in the Death of the Rev. Elijah P. Lovejoy, Alton, 1837. Ph.D., Harvard University, 1947.

2237   Gustafson, Robert K. A Study of the Life of James Woodrow Emphasizing His Theological and Scientific Views as They Relate to the Evolution Controversy. Ph.D., Union Theological Seminary in Virginia, 1964. 777p. UMI# 83-00756.

2238   Guthrie, Dwight R. John McMillan, the Apostle of Presbyterianism in the West. Ph.D., University of Pittsburgh, 1949.

2239   Hardman, Keith J. Jonathan Dickinson and the Course of American Presbyterianism, 1717-1747. Ph.D., University of Pennsylvania, 1971. 378p. UMI# 72-06162.

2240   Hart, Darryl G. "Doctor Fundamentalis": An Intellectual Biography of J. Gresham Machen, 1881-1937. Ph.D., Johns Hopkins University, 1988. 427p. UMI# 8819061.

2241   Hickey, Doralyn J. Benjamin Morgan Palmer, Churchman of the Old South. Ph.D., Duke University, 1962. 324p. UMI# 63-03592.

2242   Hinckley, Theodore C., Jr. The Alaska Labors of Sheldon Jackson, 1877-1890. Ph.D., Indiana University, 1961. 290p. UMI# 6104445.

2243   Jenkins, Ronald B. The Life and Sermons of Henry Smith. Ph.D., University of North Carolina-Chapel Hill, 1977. UMI# 7702056.

2244   Jeschke, Channing R. The Briggs Case: The Focus of a Study in Nineteenth Century Presbyterian History. Ph.D., University of Chicago, 1967.

2245   Jones, Charles T., Jr. George Champlin Sibley, the Prairie Puritan (1782-1863). Ph.D., University of Missouri-Columbia, 1969. 354p. UMI# 69-16083.

2246   Lamb, Wallace E. George Washington Gale, Theologian and Educator. Ph.D., Syracuse University, 1949.

2247   Lane, Belden C. Democracy and the Ruling Eldership: Samuel Miller's Response to Tensions Between Clerical Power and Lay Activity in Early Nineteenth-Century America. Ph.D., Princeton Theological Seminary, 1976. 451p. UMI# 7624279.

2248   Lewis, Frank B. Robert Lewis Dabney: Southern Presbyterian Apologist. Ph.D., Duke University, 1946.

2249   Loring, Eduard N. Charles C. Jones: Missionary to Plantation Slaves 1831-1847. Ph.D., Vanderbilt University, 1976. 396p. UMI# 76-22353.[Liberty County(GA)].

2250   Matthews, Merrill, Jr. Robert Lewis Dabney and Conservative Thought in the Nineteenth Century South: A Study in the History of Ideas. Ph.D., University of Texas-Dallas, 1989. 405p. UMI# 9012624.

2251   Mayse, Edgar C. Robert Jefferson Breckinridge: American Presbyterian Controversialist. Th.D., Union Theological Seminary in Virginia, 1974. 780p. UMI# 74-25478.

2252   McCarthy, Rockne M. The Presbyterian Church Crosses the Mississippi: The Life and Ministry of Salmon Giddings. Ph.D., Saint Louis University, 1971. 216p. UMI# 72-05303.

2253   Milkman, Howard L., Jr. Thomas Dewitt Talmage: An Evangelical Nineteenth Century Voice on Technology, Urbanization, and Labor-Management Conflicts. Ph.D., New York University, 1979. 426p. UMI# 80-10297.

2254   Monsma, John W., Jr. Thomas Dewitt Talmage: Orthodox Spokesman on the Gilded Age. Ph.D., Indiana University, 1966. 288p. UMI# 6703696.

2255   Mulder, John M. The Gospel of Order: Woodrow Wilson and the Development of His Religious, Political, and Educational Thought, 1856-1910. Ph.D., Princeton University, 1974. 440p. UMI# 74-17480.

2256   Munger, Bernard V. William Greenough Thayer Shedd: Reformed Traditionalist, 1820-1894. Ph.D., Duke University, 1957.

2257   Overy, David H. Robert Lewis Dabney: Apostle of the Old South. Ph.D., University of Wisconsin, 1967. 338p.

2258   Pranger, Gary K. Philip Schaff (1819-1893): Portrait of an Immigrant

Theologian. Ph.D., University of Illinois-Chicago, 1987. 427p. UMI# 8726098.

2259   Rich, George E. John Witherspoon: His Scottish Intellectual Background. D.S.S., Syracuse University, 1964. 212p. UMI# 65-03433.

2260   Ruthven, Jon M. On the Cessation of the Charismata: The Protestant Polemic of Benjamin B. Warfield. Ph.D., Marquette University, 1989. 392p. UMI# 9014061.

2261   Samworth, Herbert L. Those Astonishing Wonders of His Grace: Jonathan Dickinson and the Great Awakening. Th.D., Westminster Theological Seminary, 1988. 375p. UMI# 8813324.

2262   Swanson, Michael R.H. Robert Baird and the Evangelical Crusade in America, 1820-1860. Ph.D., Case Western Reserve University, 1971. 340p. UMI# 7200113.

2263   Thomas, Reid S. Thomas Dewitt Talmage in Perspective. Ph.D., Emory University, 1974. 205p. UMI# 7423674.

2264   Ware, James H., Jr. The Modern Protestant Quest for the Essence of Christianity Focused in William Adams Brown. Ph.D., Duke University, 1964. 398p. UMI# 6411505.

2265   Willey, Larry G. The Reverend John Rankin: Early Ohio Antislavery Leader. Ph.D., University of Iowa, 1976. 329p. UMI# 7626350.

2266   Witte, Wayne W. John Witherspoon: An Exposition and Interpretation of His Theological Views as the Motivation of His Ecclesiastical, Educational, and Political Career in Scotland and America. Th.D., Princeton Theological Seminary, 1954. 351p. UMI# 74-07914.

Church and State

2267   McAlpin, William B. Presbyterians and the Relation of Church and State: An Interpretation of the Pronouncements Made in the Meetings of the General Assemblies of the Presbyterian Church in the U.S.A. as Recorded in *The Journal of the General Assembly, 1789-1953*. Ph.D., University of Pittsburgh, 1954. 199p. UMI# 07993.

Clergy

2268   Foushee, Richard E. The Reciprocal Influences Between Clergy and Laity on Social Issues: An Historical Investigation of Missouri's Presbyterian Clergy in Marion County on the Subject of Abolition:

1835-1845. Ph.D., Saint Louis University, 1969. 158p. UMI# 70-20385.

2269   Kramer, Leonard J. The Political Ethics of the American Presbyterian Clergy in the Eighteenth Century. Ph.D., Yale University, 1942.

2270   See, Ruth D. The Protestant Doctrine of Vocation in the Presbyterian Thought of Nineteenth-Century America. Ph.D., New York University, 1953. 264p. UMI# 05426.

2271   Watkin, Robert N., Jr. The Forming of the Southern Presbyterian Minister: From Calvin to the American Civil War. Ph.D., Vanderbilt University, 1969. 517p. UMI# 69-13476.

2272   Wingo, Barbara C.G. Politics, Society, and Religion: The Presbyterian Clergy of Pennsylvania, New Jersey, and New York, and the Formation of the Nation, 1775-1808. Ph.D., Tulane University, 1976. 458p. UMI# 76-21430.

Education

2273   Bartley, David D. John Witherspoon and the Right of Resistance. Ph.D., Ball State University, 1989. 378p. UMI# 9018457.

2274   Basham, Robert H. A History of Cane Hill College in Arkansas. Ed.D., University of Arkansas, 1969. 408p. UMI# 70-00373.

2275   Brittain, Raymond F. The History of the Associate, Associate Reformed, and United Presbyterian Theological Seminaries in the United States. Ph.D., University of Pittsburgh, 1946. 399p.

2276   Bryan, Alison R. The Westminster Foundation: Its History, Program, and Goal, Particularly as Represented in Five University Centers. D.T.S., Temple University, 1954.

2277   Calhoun, David B. The Last Command: Princeton Theological Seminary and Missions (1812-1862). Ph.D., Princeton Theological Seminary, 1983. 546p. UMI# 8320287.

2278   Carson, Paul E. The Synodical Colleges of the United Presbyterian Church of North America. Ph.D., University of Pittsburgh, 1942.

2279   Debolt, Thomas H. Presbyterian Educational Institutions in Virginia: 1740-1785. Ph.D., George Peabody College for Teachers of Vanderbilt University, 1976. 267p. UMI# 76-21623.

2280   Decker, Rodger W. Founding St. Andrews Presbyterian College: A

Case Study of Presbyterian Higher Education in North Carolina. Ed.D., Columbia University, 1968. 133p. UMI# 69-08069.

2281   Doncaster, William T., Jr. Thaddeus Dod and the Pioneer Educational Efforts of the Presbyterian Church in Southwestern Pennsylvania. Ph.D., University of Pittsburgh, 1953. 323p.

2282   Dressler, Arthur J. Secondary Education Under the Auspices of the Presbyterian Church, U.S.A., 1846-1870. Ph.D., Hartford Seminary Foundation, 1930.

2283   Evans, Henry B. A History of Higher Education in the Cumberland Presbyterian Church. Ph.D., George Peabody College for Teachers, 1939.

2284   Geiger, C. Harve. The Program of Higher Education of the Presbyterian Church in the United States of America: An Historical Analysis of Its Growth in the United States. Ph.D., Columbia University Teachers College, 1940. 238p.

2285   George, Arthur A. The History of Johnson C. Smith University, 1867 to the Present. Ed.D., New York University, 1954. 352p. UMI# 10661.

2286   Haden, Eric G. The Shorter Catechism in the Religious Education of the Presbyterian Church in the United States. Ph.D., Yale University, 1939.

2287   Hoyle, Hughes B., Jr. The Early History of Queens College to 1872. Ph.D., University of North Carolina, 1963. 319p. UMI# 64-09415.

2288   Hunter, Margaret A. Education in Pennsylvania by the Presbyterian Church of United States of America, 1726-1837. Ph.D., Temple University, 1937.

2289   Kelly, Carl R. The History of Religious Instruction in United Presbyterian Colleges. Ph.D., University of Pittsburgh, 1953. 323p.

2290   Kepner, Charles W. The Contributions Early Presbyterian Leaders Made in the Development of the Educational Institutions in Western Pennsylvania Prior to 1850. Ph.D., University of Pittsburgh, 1942. 249p.

2291   Lesesne, Joab M., Jr. A Hundred Years of Erskine College, 1839-1939. Ph.D., University of South Carolina, 1967. 318p. UMI# 68-03932.

2292   Mahler, Henry R. A History of Union Theological Seminary in

Virginia, 1807-1865. Th.D., Union Theological Seminary, 1951.

2293   McKaig, Charles D. The Educational Philosophy of A.B. Simpson, Founder of the Christian and Missionary Alliance. Ph.D., New York University, 1948. 256p. UMI# 73-08681.

2294   Proctor, Sandra B. The Role of the Presbyterian Church U.S.A. in the Development of Education for Black Americans in the South: 1865-1958. Ed.D., Rutgers University, 1989. 241p. UMI# 9008011.

2295   Robinson, W.C. Columbia Theological Seminary and the Southern Presbyterian Church. Th.D., Harvard University, 1928.

2296   Scovel, Raleigh D. Orthodoxy at Princeton: A Social and Intellectual History of Princeton Theological Seminary, 1812-1860. Ph.D., University of California-Berkeley, 1970. 358p. UMI# 71-09920.

2297   Shereshewsky, Murray S. Academy Keeping and the Great Awakening: The Presbyterian Academies, College of New Jersey, and Revivalism, 1727-1768. Ph.D., New York University, 1980. 304p. UMI# 81-10685.

2298   Sherrill, Lewis J. Presbyterian Parochial Schools 1846-1870. Ph.D., Yale University, 1929. 261p.

2299   Taylor, Marion A. The Old Testament in the Old Princeton School. Ph.D., Yale University, 1988. 584p. UMI# 9009429.

2300   Trowbridge, John E. Presbyterian Interest in Elementary Education in New Jersey, 1816-1866. Ed.D., Rutgers University, 1957. 503p. UMI# 23290.

Ethnic Groups

2301   Fox, Harry C. German Presbyterianism in the Upper Mississippi Valley. Ph.D., University of Iowa, 1942. 146p.

Evangelism

2302   Walzer, William C. Charles Grandison Finney and the Presbyterian Revivals of Central and Western New York. Ph.D., University of Chicago, 1945. 254p.

Historiography

2303   Meyer, John C. Philip Schaff's Concept of Organic Historiography as Related to the Development of Doctrine: A Catholic Appraisal. Ph.D., Catholic University of America, 1968. 315p. UMI# 6909171.

2304 Shriver, George H., Jr. Philip Schaff's Concept of Organic Historiography Interpreted in Relation to the Realization of an Evangelical Catholicism Within the Christian Community. Ph.D., Duke University, 1961. 362p. UMI# 61-02929.

Literature

2305 Susskind, Jacob L. A Critical Edition of the Scientific Sections of Samuel Miller's *A Brief Retrospect of the Eighteenth Century*. Ph.D., George Peabody College for Teachers of Vanderbilt University, 1969. 686p. UMI# 7007645.

Liturgy

2306 Hall, Stanley R. The American Presbyterian *Directory for Worship*: History of a Liturgical Strategy. Ph.D., University of Notre Dame, 1990. 600p. UMI# 9022954.

2307 Holper, James F. Presbyteral Office and Ordination in American Presbyterianism: A Liturgical-Historical Study. Ph.D., University of Notre Dame, 1988. 609p. UMI# 8815174.

2308 Schmidt, Leigh E. Scottish Communions and American Revivals: Evangelical Ritual, Sacramental Piety, and Popular Festivity From the Reformation Through the Mid-Nineteenth-Century. Ph.D., Princeton University, 1987. 364p. UMI# 8714917.

Missions and Missionaries

2309 Banker, Mark T. They Made Haste Slowly: Presbyterian Mission Schools and Southwestern Pluralism, 1870-1920. Ph.D., University of New Mexico, 1987. 458p. UMI# 8808132.

2310 Coleman, Michael C. Presbyterian Missionaries and Their Attitudes to the American Indians, 1837-1893. Ph.D., University of Pennsylvania, 1977. 319p. UMI# 77-30187.

2311 Faust, Harold S. The Presbyterian Mission to the American Indian During the Period of Indian Removal (1838-1893). S.T.D., Temple University, 1943.

2312 Foreman, Kenneth J., Jr. The Debate on the Administration of Missions Led by James Henley Thornwell in the Presbyterian Church, 1839-1861. Ph.D., Princeton Theological Seminary, 1977. 769p. UMI# 77-21193.

2313 Hodgson, Eva N. The Presbyterian Mission to Liberia, 1832-1900. Ph.D., Columbia University, 1980. UMI# 8222405.

2314   Webster, John C.B. The Christian Community and Change in North India: A History of the Punjab and North India Missions of the Presbyterian Church in the USA, 1834-1914. Ph.D., University of Pennsylvania, 1971. 501p. UMI# 71-26106.

2315   Weir, John B. Presbyterian Church and Mission Cooperation Studied Historically. Ph.D., University of Chicago, 1934.

2316   Yohn, Susan M. Religion, Pluralism, and the Limits of Progressive Reform: Presbyterian Women Home Missionaries in New Mexico, 1870-1930. Ph.D., New York University, 1987. 307p. UMI# 8801587.

Music

2317   Martin, Raymond J. The Transition From Psalmody to Hymnody in Southern Presbyterianism, 1753-1901. S.M.D., Union Theological Seminary, 1963. 173p. UMI# 63-07852.

2318   Rightmyer, James R. A Documentary History of the Music Program of Second Presbyterian Church, Louisville, Kentucky: 1830-1980. D.M.A., Southern Baptist Theological Seminary, 1980. 190p. UMI# 81-08425.

Organizational Structure

2319   Anderson, Philip J. Presbyterianism and the Gathered Churches in Old and New England, 1640-1662: The Struggle for Church Government in Theory and Practice. D.Phil., University of Oxford, 1979. 324p.

2320   Newland, Guy. A Case Study of the New Providence Presbyterian Church, Presbytery of Transylvania-Union, Synod of the Mid-South, Salvisa, Kentucky, Organized in 1784. Ph.D., Louisville Presbyterian Theological Seminary, 1974.

2321   Olmstead, Clifton E. A History of the Presbytery of Washington City. Ph.D., Princeton Theological Seminary, 1951.

2322   Reifsnyder, Richard W. The Reorganizational Impulse in American Protestantism: The Presbyterian Church (U.S.A.) as a Case Study, 1788-1983. Ph.D., Princeton Theological Seminary, 1984. 512p. UMI# 8418189.

2323   Schlenther, Boyd S. The Presbytery as Organ of Church Life and Government in American Presbyterianism From 1706 to 1788. Ph.D., University of Edinburgh, 1965. 412p.

2324   Wade, William J. The Origins and Establishment of the Presbyterian

Church in the United States. Ph.D., University of North Carolina-Chapel Hill, 1959. 516p. UMI# 5906451.

Preaching

2325   Arlington, Larry D. Moses A. Williams: A Rhetoric of Preaching and Praying. Ph.D., University of Oregon, 1973. 306p. UMI# 7320190.

2326   Baker, Harold S. A Rhetorical Study of the Preaching of John McMillan From 1820 to 1830. Ph.D., Louisiana State University, 1967. 210p. UMI# 6708767.

2327   Bos, William H. A Study of the Preaching of Henry Van Dyke. Ph.D., University of Michigan, 1955. 377p. UMI# 11250.

2328   Ehret, Thomas K. Four Sermons of Henry Smith: A Critical Edition. Ph.D., University of Illinois at Urbana-Champaign, 1968. 275p. UMI# 6812110.

2329   Larson, Barbara A. A Rhetorical Study of the Preaching of the Reverend Samuel Davies in the Colony of Virginia From 1747-1759. Ph.D., University of Minnesota, 1969. 347p. UMI# 69-20080.

2330   Paul, Wilson B. John Witherspoon's Theory and Practice of Public Speaking. Ph.D., University of Iowa, 1941.

2331   Prichard, Samuel V.O., Jr. Theodore Ledyard Cuyler's Theory and Practice of Preaching. Ph.D., Pennsylvania State University, 1972. 327p. UMI# 7320117.

2332   Smith, Alvin D. A Study and Appraisal of the Evangelistic Preaching of J. Wilbur Chapman, D.D., 1859-1918; Being an Investigation of the Preaching Ideals, Messages, and Methods of Early Twentieth-Century Urban Evangelism. S.T.D., Temple University, 1954.

2333   Stuart, John W., III. The Rev. John Brown of Virginia (1728-1803): His Life and Selected Sermons. Ph.D., University of Massachusetts, 1988. 251p. UMI# 8822855.

2334   Swabb, Luke J., Jr. The Rhetorical Theory of Reverend Joseph Ruggles Wilson, Doctor of Divinity. Ph.D., Ohio State University, 1971. 307p. UMI# 72-15308.

Social Programs

2335   Hirrel, Leo P. The Ideology of Antebellum Reform Within the New

School Calvinist Community. Ph.D., University of Virginia, 1989. 432p. UMI# 8922424.

2336   Howard, Victor B. The Anti-Slavery Movement in the Presbyterian Church, 1835-1861. Ph.D., Ohio State University, 1961. 380p. UMI# 62-00778.

2337   Miller, Guy H. A Contracting Community: American Presbyterians, Social Conflict, and Higher Education 1730-1820. Ph.D., University of Michigan, 1970. 562p. UMI# 71-15239.

2338   Taylor, Hubert V. Slavery and the Deliberations of the Presbyterian General Assembly, 1833-1838. Ph.D., Northwestern University, 1964. 286p. UMI# 6503316.

Theology

2339   Clyde, Walter R., Jr. The Development of American Presbyterian Theology, 1705-1823. Ph.D., Hartford Seminary Foundation, 1939.

2340   Fechner, Roger J. The Moral Philosophy of John Witherspoon and the Scottish-American Enlightenment. Ph.D., University of Iowa, 1974. 298p. UMI# 7513747.

2341   Garber, Paul L. The Religious Thought of James Henley Thornwell. Ph.D., Duke University, 1939.

2342   Garth, David K. The Influence of Scottish Common Sense Philosophy on the Theology of James Henley Thornwell and Robert Lewis Dabney. Th.D., Union Theological Seminary in Virginia, 1979. 214p. UMI# 7921995.

2343   Goliber, Thomas J. Philip Schaff (1819-1893): A Study in Conservative Biblical Criticism. Ph.D., Kent State University, 1976. 282p. UMI# 7618228.

2344   Graham, Stephen R. "Cosmos in the Chaos": A Study of Philip Schaff's Interpretation of Nineteenth Century American Religion. Ph.D., University of Chicago, 1989.

2345   Harper, Miles D., Jr. Gilbert Tennent: Theologian of the "New Light". Ph.D., Duke University, 1958. 477p. UMI# 5803395.

2346   Hoyt, William R., II. The Religious Thought of Gardiner Spring With Particular Reference to His Doctrine of Sin and Salvation. Ph.D., Duke University, 1962. 528p. UMI# 6300872.

2347   Jones, Charles A., III. Charles Hodge, the Keeper of Orthodoxy: the

Method, Purpose and Meaning of His Apologetic. Ph.D., Drew University, 1989. 317p. UMI# 9014367.

2348   Jones, David C. The Doctrine of the Church in American Presbyterian Theology in the Mid-Nineteenth Century. Ph.D., Concordia Seminary, 1970.

2349   Kelley, Delores G. A Rhetorical Analysis of an 1884-1888 Controversy in American Religious Thought: Response Within the Presbyterian Church in the United States to Evolutionism. Ph.D., University of Maryland, 1977. 108p. UMI# 77-28742.

2350   Kraus, Clyde N. The Principle of Authority in the Theology of B.B. Warfield, William Adams Brown, and Gerald Birney Smith. Ph.D., Duke University, 1961. 315p. UMI# 6201995.

2351   Markarian, John J. The Calvinistic Concept of the Biblical Revelation in the Theology of B.B. Warfield. Ph.D., Drew University, 1963. 269p. UMI# 6307377.

2352   Marsden, George M. The New School Presbyterian Mind: A Study of Theology in Mid-Nineteenth Century America. Ph.D., Yale University, 1966. 347p. UMI# 66-04913.

2353   McGraw, Gerald E. The Doctrine of Sanctification in the Published Writings of Albert Benjamin Simpson. Ph.D., New York University, 1986. 732p. UMI# 8625635.

2354   Morrow, Hubert W. The Background and Development of Cumberland Presbyterian Theology. Ph.D., Vanderbilt University, 1965. 427p. UMI# 65-10479.

2355   Nelson, John O. The Rise of the Princeton Theology: A Genetic Study of American Presbyterianism Until 1850. Ph.D., Yale University, 1935. 381p. UMI# 64-11382.

2356   Penzel, Klaus. Church History and the Ecumenical Quest. A Study of the German Background and Thought of Philip Schaff. Th.D., Union Theological Seminary, 1962. 377p. UMI# 6204003.

2357   Plaster, David R. The Theological Method of the Early Princetonians. Th.D., Dallas Theological Seminary, 1989. 257p. UMI# 9020892.

2358   Sawyer, M. James, Jr. Charles Augustus Briggs and Tensions in Late Nineteenth Century American Theology. Th.D., Dallas Theological Seminary, 1987. 313p. UMI# 8729708.

2359   Scott, Jack A. A Critical Edition of John Witherspoon's *Lectures on Moral Philosophy*. Ph.D., Claremont Graduate School, 1970. 357p. UMI# 7113733.

2360   Stewart, John W. The Tethered Theology: Biblical Criticism, Common Sense Philosophy, and the Princeton Theologians, 1812-1860. Ph.D., University of Michigan, 1990. 334p. UMI# 9023645.

2361   Van Bemmelen, Peter M. Issues in Biblical Inspiration: Sanday and Warfield. Th.D., Andrews University, 1987. 432p. UMI# 8725231.

2362   Vance, John L. The Ecclesiology of James Henley Thornwell: An Old South Presbyterian Theologian. Ph.D., Drew University, 1990. 438p. UMI# 9112371.

PROTESTANT

General Studies

2363   Abell, Aaron I. The Impact of the City on American Protestantism, 1850-1900. Ph.D., Harvard University, 1938.

2364   Anderson, Richard J. The Urban Revivalists, 1880-1910. Ph.D., University of Chicago, 1974. 344p.

2365   Bass, Archer B. The Need and Progress of Interdenominational Cooperation in American Protestantism. Ph.D., Southern Baptist Theological Seminary, 1927.

2366   Bendroth, Margaret L. The Social Dimensions of "Women's Sphere": The Rise of Women's Organizations in Late Nineteenth-Century Protestantism. Ph.D., Johns Hopkins University, 1985. 203p. UMI# 8510399.

2367   Bode, Frederick A. Southern White Protestantism and the Crisis of the New South: North Carolina, 1894-1903. Ph.D., Yale University, 1953. 425p. UMI# 70-02697.

2368   Boorman, John A. A Comparative Study of the Theory of Human Nature as Expressed by Jonathan Edwards, Horace Bushnell and William Adams Brown, Representative American Protestant Thinkers of the Past Three Centuries. Ph.D., Columbia University, 1954. 222p. UMI# 8608.

2369   Chapman, Stuart W. The Protestant Campaign for the Union: A Study of the Re-Actions of Several Evangelical Denominations to the Civil War. Ph.D., Yale University, 1939.

2370   Cobb, Jimmy G. A Study of White Protestants' Attitudes Toward Negroes in Charleston, South Carolina, 1790-1845. Ph.D., Baylor University, 1976. 123p. UMI# 77-03066.

2371   Crowther, Edward R. Southern Protestants, Slavery and Secession: A Study in Religious Ideology, 1830-1861. Ph.D., Auburn University, 1986. 403p. UMI# 8618609.

2372   Daniel, Wilborn H. The Protestant Church in the Confederate States of America. Ph.D., Duke University, 1957.

2373   Engelder, Conrad J. The Churches and Slavery. A Study of the Attitudes Toward Slavery of the Major Protestant Denominations. Ph.D., University of Michigan, 1964. 329p. UMI# 64-12589.

2374   Fogde, Myron J. Protestantism in Frontier Montana, 1860-1925. Ph.D., University of Chicago, 1964.

2375   Fones-Wolf, Kenneth A. Trade Union Gospel: Protestantism and Labor in Philadelphia, 1865-1915. Ph.D., Temple University, 1985. 475p. UMI# 8611847.

2376   Graebner, Norman B. Protestants and Dissenters: An Examination of the Seventeenth-Century Eatonist and New England Antinomian Controversies in Reformation Perspective. Ph.D., Duke University, 1984. 268p. UMI# 8516846.

2377   Hanley, Mark Y. Beyond a Christian Commonwealth: The Protestant Quarrel With the American Republic, 1830-1860. Ph.D., Purdue University, 1989. 277p. UMI# 9018837.

2378   Hill, Patricia R. One Unbroken Household: The Definition and Embodiment of a Rhetoric of Mission Among Protestant Women in America, 1870-1917. Ph.D., Harvard University, 1981.

2379   Holter, Don W. Beginnings of Protestantism in Trans-Missouri. Ph.D., University of Chicago, 1934.

2380   Houf, Walter R. The Protestant Church in the Rural Midwestern Community, 1820-1870. Ph.D., University of Missouri-Columbia, 1967. 350p. UMI# 68-00306.

2381   Hudson, Richard L. The Challenge of Dissent: Religious Conditions in New Hampshire in the Early Nineteenth Century. Ph.D., Syracuse University, 1970. 220p. UMI# 71-18487.

2382   Jones, Daniel P. From Radical Yeomen to Evangelical Farmers: The Transformation of Northwestern Rhode Island, 1780-1850. Ph.D.,

Brown University, 1987. 485p. UMI# 8715513.

2383   Keller, Robert H., Jr. The Protestant Churches and Grant's Peace
        Policy: A Study in Church Relations, 1869-1882. Ph.D., University
        of Chicago, 1967.

2384   Kennedy, Charles J. The Congregationalists and the Presbyterians
        on the Wisconsin Frontier. Ph.D., University of Wisconsin, 1940.
        114p.

2385   King, John O., III. The Ascetic Self: Mental Pathology and the
        Protestant Ethic in America, 1870-1914. Ph.D., University of
        Wisconsin-Madison, 1976. 578p. UMI# 77-03406.

2386   Lawless, Richard M. To Do Right to God and Man: Northern
        Protestants and the Kansas Struggle, 1854-1859. Th.D., Graduate
        Theological Union, 1974. 291p. UMI# 74-29533.

2387   Lazerow, Jama. A Good Time Coming: Religion and the Emergence
        of Labor Activism in Antebellum New England. Ph.D., Brandeis
        University, 1983. 483p. UMI# 8310610.

2388   Ledbetter, Robert E., Jr. The Planting and Growth of the Protestant
        Denominations in Texas Prior to 1850. Ph.D., University of Chicago,
        1951.

2389   Leonard, Richard D. The Presbyterian and Congregational
        Convention of Wisconsin, 1840-1850. Ph.D., University of Chicago,
        1939.

2390   Lewis, L. David. The Efficient Crusade: Lay Protestantism in
        Chicago, 1874-1925. Ph.D., University of Chicago, 1979.

2391   Malefyt, Calvin S.D. The Changing Concept of Pneumatology in
        New England Trinitarianism, 1635-1755. Ph.D., Harvard University,
        1966.

2392   May, Henry F., Jr. Protestant Churches and Industrial Society,
        1865-1895. Ph.D., Harvard University, 1948.

2393   McIlwaine, Henry R. The Struggle of Protestant Dissenters for
        Religious Toleration in Virginia. Ph.D., Johns Hopkins University,
        1893.

2394   McTighe, Michael J. Embattled Establishment: Protestants and
        Power in Cleveland, 1836-60. Ph.D., University of Chicago, 1983.

2395   Miller, Dale, Jr. Protestantism and Politics in Rhode Island,

1636-1657. Ph.D., University of Chicago, 1955.

2396   Million, Elmer G. A Study of Protestantism in the Kentucky Blue Grass, 1865-1940. Ph.D., University of Chicago, 1951.

2397   Miyakawa, Tetsuo S. American Frontier and Protestantism: A Study of Protestantism, Voluntarism, and Ethos of American Frontier Society. Ph.D., Columbia University, 1951. 590p. UMI# 03110.

2398   Moore, Roberta J. The Beginning and Development of Protestant Journalism in the United States, 1743-1850. Ed.D., Syracuse University, 1968. 477p. UMI# 69-07761.

2399   Moorhead, James H. American Apocalypse: Northern Protestant Interpretations of National Purpose, 1860-1869. Ph.D., Yale University, 1975. 356p. UMI# 75-27027.

2400   Newman, Harvey K. The Vision of Order: White Protestant Christianity in Atlanta, 1865-1906. Ph.D., Emory University, 1977. 208p. UMI# 77-19322.

2401   Patterson, Charles W. Social Perspectives of Protestant Journals During the Depression of 1893-1897. Ph.D., Columbia University, 1970. 325p. UMI# 70-18843.

2402   Payne, Rodger M. "When the Times of Refreshing Shall Come": Interpreting American Protestant Narratives of Conversion, 1630-1830. Ph.D., University of Virginia, 1989. 314p. UMI# 8922427.

2403   Pope, Jesse C. The Restoration Ideal in American Religious Thought. Ph.D., Florida State University, 1990. 365p. UMI# 9103111.

2404   Raimo, John W. Spiritual Harvest: The Anglo-American Revival in Boston, Massachusetts, and Bristol, England, 1739-1742. Ph.D., University of Wisconsin-Madison, 1974. 287p. UMI# 7419575.

2405   Richards, Katharine L. How Christmas Came to the Sunday-Schools: The Observance of Christmas in the Protestant Church Schools of the United States, An Historical Study. Ph.D., Columbia University, 1934.

2406   Roberts, Windsor H. The Reaction of American Protestant Churches to the Darwinian Philosophy, 1860-1900. Ph.D., University of Chicago, 1936.

2407   Sernett, Milton C. Black Religion and American Evangelicalism: White Protestants, Plantation Missions, and the Independent Negro

Church, 1787-1865. Ph.D., University of Delaware, 1972. 416p. UMI# 72-32017.

2408   Sharp, Frank A. The Development of Protestant Co-Operation in Allegheny County, Pennsylvania. Ph.D., University of Pittsburgh, 1948.

2409   Singleton, Gregory H. Religion in the City of the Angels: American Protestant Culture and Urbanization, Los Angeles, 1850-1930. Ph.D., University of California-Los Angeles, 1976. 441p. UMI# 77-08535.

2410   Smith, John A. National Christianity: The Search for Unity Among American Protestants, 1880-1920. Ph.D., Johns Hopkins University, 1971. 743p. UMI# 72-16924.

2411   Smith, R. Drew. A Question of Authority: Protestants in Virginia and the Carolinas and the Tension Between Religion and Politics, 1835-1861. Ph.D., Yale University, 1990. 209p. UMI# 9035370.

2412   Swanson, Richard A. American Protestantism and Play 1865-1915. Ph.D., Ohio State University, 1967. 230p. UMI# 67-16340.

2413   Turner, Elizabeth H. Women's Culture and Community: Religion and Reform in Galveston, 1880-1920. Ph.D., Rice University, 1990. 504p. UMI# 9111029.

2414   Voorhees, David W. "In Behalf of the True Protestants Religion": The Glorious Revolution in New York. Ph.D., New York University, 1988. 526p. UMI# 8825068.[Jacob Leisler].

2415   Walker, Randi J. Protestantism in the Sangre de Cristos: Factors in the Growth and Decline of the Hispanic Protestant Churches in Northern New Mexico and Southern Colorado, 1850-1920. Ph.D., Claremont Graduate School, 1983. 341p. UMI# 8309651.

2416   Walsh, Joseph H. Protestant Response to Materialism in American Life, 1865-1900. Ed.D., Columbia University, 1974. 316p. UMI# 74-15991.

2417   Ward, Donal. Religious Enthusiasm in Vermont, 1761-1847. Ph.D., University of Notre Dame, 1980. 339p. UMI# 80-21373.

2418   Wauzzinski, Robert A. God and Mammon: The Interrelationship of Protestant Evangelicalism and the Industrial Revolution in America, 1820-1914. Ph.D., University of Pittsburgh, 1985. 369p. UMI# 8519463.

2419   Wheelock, Lewis F. Urban Protestant Reactions to the Chicago

Haymarket Affair, 1886-1893. Ph.D., Iowa State University, 1957.

2420   Wiederaenders, Arthur G. The American Frontier as a Factor in Protestant Denominationalism in the United States. Ph.D., University of Texas-Austin, 1942. 371p.

Art and Architecture

2421   Newman, Richard K., Jr. Yankee Gothic: Medieval Architectural Forms in the Protestant Church Building of Nineteenth Century New England. Ph.D., Yale University, 1949. 394p.

2422   Pyne, Kathleen A. Immanence, Transcendence, and Impressionism in Late Nineteenth-Century American Painting. Ph.D., University of Michigan, 1988. 522p. UMI# 8812968.

Biography

2423   Brockmann, Henry C. Frank Hugh Foster: A Chapter in the American Protestant Quest for Authority in Theology. Ph.D., Union Theological Seminary, 1967. 337p. UMI# 67-08816.

2424   McGaha, Ruth K. The Journals of S. Elizabeth Dusenbury, 1852-1857; Portrait of a Teacher's Development. Ph.D., Iowa State University, 1990. 607p. UMI# 9035099.

2425   Miller, Frank L.C., IV. Fathers and Sons: The Binghams and American Reform, 1790-1970. Ph.D., Johns Hopkins University, 1980. 351p. UMI# 8106627.

2426   Pointer, Steven R. The Perils of History: The Meteoric Career of Joseph Cook (1838-1901). Ph.D., Duke University, 1981. 234p. UMI# 8212973.

2427   Tibbetts, Joel W. Women Who Were Called: A Study of the Contributions to American Christianity of Ann Lee, Jemima Wilkinson, Mary Baker Eddy, and Aimee Semple McPherson. Ph.D., Vanderbilt University, 1976. 491p. UMI# 76-22371.

Clergy

2428   Baird, Ernest C. The Professional Socialization of the Negro American Protestant Clergy: A Theoretical Study. Ph.D., Princeton Theological Seminary, 1968.

2429   Smylie, John E. Protestant Clergymen and America's World Role, 1865-1900: A Study of Christianity, Nationality, and International

Relations. Th.D., Princeton Theological Seminary, 1959. 630p. UMI# 71-23406.

Education

2430   Anderson, Mary R. Protestant Mission Schools for Girls in South China (1827 to the Japanese Invasion). Ph.D., Columbia University, 1943. 365p.

2431   Bassett, T. Robert. Integration of Religion and Education in Protestant Secondary Schools of the United States. Ph.D., Temple University, 1950. 117p.

2432   Beaty, Earl R. A Comparison of Bible College Curricula Among Five Religious Groups Through Three Eras. Ed.D., University of Missouri-Saint Louis, 1986. 304p. UMI# 8609077.

2433   Boylan, Anne M. "The Nursery of the Church": Evangelical Protestant Sunday Schools, 1820-1880. Ph.D., University of Wisconsin-Madison, 1973. 366p. UMI# 73-20981.

2434   Crandall, Robert A. The Sunday School as an Instructional Agency for Religious Instruction in American Protestantism, 1872-1922. Ph.D., University of Notre Dame, 1977. 235p. UMI# 77-19144.

2435   Dunbar, Willis F. The Influence of Protestant Denominations on Higher Education in Michigan, 1817-1900. Ph.D., University of Michigan, 1939.

2436   Freese, Doris A. The Role of the Sunday School Conventions in the Preparation of Protestant Sunday School Teachers, 1832-1903. Ph.D., Loyola University of Chicago, 1979. 251p. UMI# 79-21786.

2437   Gleason, Daniel M. A Study of the Christian School Movement. Ed.D., University of North Dakota, 1980. 183p. UMI# 8110238.

2438   Hardt, Erna P.H. Christian Education in New Jersey: A History of Protestant Cooperative Religious Education in the State, Its Origin, Development and Relationship to Other Movements of the Times. Ph.D., New York University, 1951. 483p. UMI# 02764.

2439   Kansfield, Norman J. "Study the Most Approved Authors": The Role of the Seminary Library in Nineteenth-Century American Protestant Ministerial Education. Ph.D., University of Chicago, 1981.

2440   McCloy, Frank D. The Founding of Protestant Theological Seminaries in the United States, 1784-1840. Ph.D., Harvard University, 1960.

2441   Patterson, Joseph N. A Study of the History of the Contribution of the American Missionary Association to the Higher Education of the Negro With Special Reference to Five Selected Colleges Founded by the Association, 1865-1900. Ed.D., Cornell University, 1956. 346p. UMI# 20423.

2442   Perry, Lloyd M. Trends and Emphases in the Philosophy, Materials, and Methodology of American Protestant Homiletical Education as Established by a Study of Selected Trade and Textbooks Published Between 1834 and 1954. Ph.D., Northwestern University, 1961. 570p. UMI# 62-00869.

2443   Ringenberg, William C. The Protestant College on the Michigan Frontier. Ph.D., Michigan State University, 1970. 219p. UMI# 70-20522.

2444   Schultz, Joseph R. A History of Protestant Christian Day Schools in the United States. Ph.D., Southwestern Baptist Theological Seminary, 1954.

2445   Seymour, Jack L. From Sunday School to Church School: Continuities in Protestant Church Education in the United States, 1860-1929. Ph.D., George Peabody College for Teachers of Vanderbilt University, 1982. 259p. UMI# 8227096.

2446   Shewmaker, William O. The Training of the Protestant Ministry of the United States of America Before the Establishment of Theological Seminaries. Ph.D., Hartford Seminary Foundation, 1914.

2447   Sparkman, Grady T. The Influence of Two Theological Concepts: "The Image of God in Man" and "Fallen Man" on the Thought of Selected American Protestant Religious Education Theorists. Ed.D., University of Kansas, 1980. 222p. UMI# 8111800.[Horace Bushnell, George A. Coe, Timothy Dwight, Jonathan Edwards].

2448   Tappan, Richard E. The Dominance of Men in the Domain of Women: The History of Four Protestant Church Training Schools 1880-1918. Ed.D., Temple University, 1979. 351p. UMI# 79-24082.

2449   Warford, Malcolm L. Piety, Politics, and Pedagogy: An Evangelical Protestant Tradition in Higher Education at Lane, Oberlin, and Berea, 1834-1904. Ed.D., Columbia University, 1973. 231p. UMI# 74-09654.

2450   Webber, Martin I. A History of Lay Nonprofessional Leadership Education in the Protestant Churches of the United States. Ph.D., Northwestern University, 1936.

2451   Wentz, Richard E. The Role of Evangelical Protestantism in the Formative Years of the Pennsylvania State University. Ph.D., George Washington University, 1971. 185p. UMI# 71-19633.

2452   Winkleman, Gerald G. Polemics, Prayers, and Professionalism: The American Protestant Theological Seminaries From 1784 to 1920. Ph.D., State University of New York-Buffalo, 1975. 412p. UMI# 76-09132.

Ethnic Groups

2453   Umbeck, Sharvy G. The Social Adaptations of a Selected Group of the German-Background Protestant Churches in Chicago. Ph.D., University of Chicago, 1941. 248p.

Evangelical

2454   Maffly-Kipp, Laurie F. The Cause of the West: Protestant Home Missions in California, 1848-1870. Ph.D., Yale University, 1990. 482p. UMI# 9034214.

2455   Widder, Keith R. Together as Family: Metis Children's Response to Evangelical Protestants at the Mackinaw Mission, 1823-1837. Ph.D., Michigan State University, 1989. 317p. UMI# 8916535.

Evangelism

2456   Brandt, Leroy C. Socio-Geographical Influences on the Techniques of Evangelism Amongst Protestants in the United States. Ph.D., New York University, 1938.

2457   Hanck, Gerold L. American Revivalism and the Convert Role: A Study in the Sociology of Religion. Ph.D., University of Pennsylvania, 1977. 289p. UMI# 77-19855.

2458   Ogden-Malouf, Susan M. American Revivalism and Temperance Drama: Evangelical Protestant Ritual and Theatre in Rochester, New York, 1830-1845. Ph.D., Northwestern University, 1981. 366p. UMI# 8124967.

Literature

2459   Verduin, Kathleen. Religious and Sexual Love in American Protestant Literature: Puritan Patterns in Hawthorne and John Updike. Ph.D., Indiana University, 1980. 420p. UMI# 8020042.

Missions and Missionaries

2460   Antakly, Waheeb G. American Protestant Educational Missions: Their Influence on Syria and Arab Nationalism, 1820-1923. Ph.D., American University, 1976. 161p. UMI# 76-19776.

2461   Banner, Lois W. The Protestant Crusade: Religious Missions, Benevolence, and Reform in the United States, 1790-1840. Ph.D., Columbia University, 1970. 409p. UMI# 73-08931.

2462   Barnett, Suzanne W. Practical Evangelism: Protestant Missions and the Introduction of Western Civilization Into China, 1820-1850. Ph.D., Harvard University, 1973.

2463   Berkhofer, Robert F., Jr. Protestant Missionaries to the American Indians, 1787-1862. Ph.D., Cornell University, 1960. 544p. UMI# 61-02441.

2464   Cocks, James R., III. The Selfish Savage: Protestant Missionaries and Nez Perce and Cayuse Indians, 1835-1847. Ph.D., University of Michigan, 1975. 260p. UMI# 76-09370.

2465   Copeland, Edwin L. The Crisis of Protestant Missions to Japan, 1889-1900. Ph.D., Yale University, 1949. 398p. UMI# 65-06546.

2466   Diffendal, Anne E. The Society for the Propagation of the Gospel in Foreign Parts and the Assimilation of Foreign Protestants in British North America. Ph.D., University of Nebraska-Lincoln, 1974. 160p. UMI# 75-03419.

2467   Goertz, Peter S. A History of the Development of the Chinese Indigenous Christian Church Under the American Board in Fukien Province. Ph.D., Yale University, 1933.

2468   Gossett, Edward F. The American Protestant Missionary Endeavor in North Africa From Its Origins to 1939. Ph.D., University of California-Los Angeles, 1961.

2469   Graham, Gael N. Gender, Culture, and Christianity: American Protestant Mission Schools in China, 1880-1930. Ph.D., University of Michigan, 1990. 484p. UMI# 9034428.

2470   Gregg, Alice H. China and Educational Autonomy; The Changing Role of the Protestant Educational Missionary in China, 1807-1937. Ph.D., Columbia University, 1947.

2471   Haines, Joseph H. A History of Protestant Missions in Malaya During the Nineteenth Century 1815-1881. Th.D., Princeton Theological Seminary, 1962. 386p. UMI# 62-05849.

2472   Harr, Wilber C. The Negro as an American Protestant Missionary in Africa. Ph.D., University of Chicago, 1945. 214p.

2473   Lane, Ortha M. An Analysis of the Treatment of Protestant Foreign Missions in American Magazines Since 1810. Ph.D., University of Iowa, 1935.

2474   Paik, Lark-June G. The History of Protestant Missions in Korea, 1832-1910. Ph.D., Yale University, 1927. 491p. UMI# 6912579.

2475   Pan, Chia-Yao. The Chinese Response to the Early Protestant Missions at the Chinese Treaty-Ports (1842-1852): A Study of the Missionary Work of the American Board of Commissioners for Foreign Missions in Canton and Amoy Between 1842 and 1852. Th.D., Lutheran School of Theology, 1987. 189p. UMI# 8722130.

2476   Pathak, Sushil M. American Protestant Missionaries in India: A Study of Their Activities and Influence 1813-1910. Ph.D., University of Hawaii, 1964. 389p. UMI# 64-11915.

2477   Phillips, Clifton J. Protestant America and the Pagan World: The First Half Century of the American Board of Commissioners for Foreign Missions, 1810-1860. Ph.D., Harvard University, 1954.

2478   Rubinstein, Murray A. Zion's Corner: Origins of the American Protestant Missionary Movement in China, 1827-1839. Ph.D., New York University, 1976. 497p. UMI# 77-05462.

2479   Stevens, Michael E. The Ideas and Attitudes of Protestant Missionaries to the North American Indians, 1643-1776. Ph.D., University of Wisconsin-Madison, 1978. 385p. UMI# 78-11743.

2480   Taylor, Alan R. The American Protestant Mission and the Awakening of Modern Syria, 1820-1870. Ph.D., Georgetown University, 1958.

2481   Teruya, Yoshihiko. Bernard J. Bettelheim and Okinawa: A Study of the First Protestant Missionary to the Island Kingdom, 1846-1854. Ph.D., University of Colorado, 1969. 419p. UMI# 70-16526.

2482   Udy, James S. Attitudes Within the Protestant Churches of the Occident Toward the Propagation of Christianity in the Orient: An Historical Survey up to 1914. Ph.D., Boston University, 1952. 222p.

2483   Voninski, Paul. Reciprocal Change: The Case of American Protestant Missionaries to China. Ph.D., Syracuse University, 1975. 203p. UMI# 76-18571.

2484   Warner, Michael J. Protestant Missionary Work With the Navajo Indians From 1846 to 1912. Ph.D., University of New Mexico, 1977.

2485   Willis, Mary B. The History of American Protestant Missions in India. Ph.D., University of Wisconsin, 1932.

2486   Wright, Irvin L. Piety, Politics, and Profit: American Indian Missions in the Colonial Colleges. Ed.D., Montana State University, 1985. 215p. UMI# 8607966.

2487   Yamamoto, Masaya. Image-Makers of Japan: A Case Study in the Impact of the American Protestant Foreign Missionary Movement, 1859-1905. Ph.D., Ohio State University, 1967. 406p. UMI# 67-16349.

Music

2488   Cantwell, Richard E. The Relationship Between Numerical Growth and Selected Theological Concepts as Reflected in the Texts of the Music Used in the General Conferences of the Methodist Church and the Church of the Nazarene Between 1784 and 1985: A Statistical Study. D.M.A., University of Missouri-Kansas City, 1990. 355p. UMI# 9026053.

2489   McCarroll, Jesse C. Black Influence on Southern White Protestant Church Music During Slavery. Ed.D., Columbia University, 1972. 176p. UMI# 74-02126.

2490   Pope, Mary B. We Shall Meet on That Beautiful Shore: Hymns of Death in the New South, 1865-1900. Ph.D., Emory University, 1985. 212p. UMI# 8516584.

2491   Stoughton, Marion W. The Influence of the Kirchenlied of the Reformation on Protestant Hymnody in England and America. Ph.D., Northwestern University, 1935.

Newspapers and Periodicals

2492   Burlingham, Katharine L. "The Necessity of Sound Doctrine": A Study of Calvinism and Its Opponents as Seen in American Religious Periodicals, 1800-1815. Ph.D., University of Oregon, 1965. 386p. UMI# 65-12208.

2493   Stone, William J., Jr. A Historical Survey of Leading Texas Denominational Newspapers: 1846-1861. Ph.D., University of Texas-Austin, 1974. 135p. UMI# 74-24941.

Preaching

2494   Brownlow, Paul C. The Northern Protestant Pulpit on Reconstruction: 1865-1877. Ph.D., Purdue University, 1970. 302p. UMI# 71-02566.

2495   Button, Carl L. The Rhetoric of Immediacy: Baptist and Methodist Preaching on the Trans-Appalachian Frontier. Ph.D., University of California-Los Angeles, 1972. 351p. UMI# 72-20427.

2496   Grosjean, Paul E. The Concept of American Nationhood: Theological Interpretation as Reflected by the Northern Mainline Protestant Preachers in the Late Civil War Period. Ph.D., Drew University, 1977. 264p. UMI# 7808001.

2497   Stewart, Charles J. A Rhetorical Study of the Reaction of the Protestant Pulpit in the North to Lincoln's Assassination. Ph.D., University of Illinois at Urbana-Champaign, 1963. 203p. UMI# 64-02975.

Social Programs

2498   Baghdadi, Mania K. Protestants, Poverty and Urban Growth: A Study of the Organization of Charity in Boston and New York, 1820-1865. Ph.D., Brown University, 1975. 364p. UMI# 76-15607.

2499   Bonkowsky, Elizabeth L. The Church and the City: Protestant Concern for Urban Problems, 1800-1840. Ph.D., Boston University, 1973. 251p. UMI# 73-23463.

2500   Hopkins, Charles H. The Rise of Social Christianity in American Protestantism 1865-1912. Ph.D., Yale University, 1937. 1124p. UMI# 76-11786.

2501   Jaros, James A. The Gospel of Americanization: The Influence of the Protestant Economy of Salvation in Defining the Ideal Immigrant Experience. Ph.D., Case Western Reserve University, 1973. 297p. UMI# 74-02531.

2502   Keller, Ralph A. Northern Protestant Churches and the Fugitive Slave Law of 1850. Ph.D., University of Wisconsin, 1969. 432p. UMI# 70-03577.

2503   McBride, Esther B. Protestant Contributions to American Social Work, 1870-1912. Ph.D., Tulane University, 1972. 599p. UMI# 72-24414.

2504   Peterson, Walter F. Social Aspects of Protestantism in the Midwest,

1870-1910. Ph.D., University of Iowa, 1951. 82p.

2505   Titus, Mathew P. A Study of Protestant Charities in Chicago: History, Development, and Philosophy. Ph.D., University of Chicago, 1939.

2506   Van Dusen, Albert P. The Socialization of the Protestant Churches. Ph.D., Clark University, 1919.

2507   Woo, Wesley S. Protestant Work Among the Chinese in the San Francisco Bay Area, 1850-1920. Ph.D., Graduate Theological Union, 1984. 365p. UMI# 8418058.

Theology

2508   Behney, John B. Conservatism and Liberalism in the Theology of Late Nineteenth Century American Protestantism: A Comparative Study of the Basic Doctrines of Typical Representatives. Ph.D., Yale University, 1941. 523p. UMI# 8809493.

2509   Berger, Howard D. Theological Considerations of Beauty: An Examination of the Aesthetic Thought That Emerged From the American Protestant Theological Community in the Nineteenth Century. Ph.D., University of Washington, 1982. 281p. UMI# 82-18200.

2510   Mullen, Bradford A. The Centrality of Jesus Christ for American Protestant Liberalism, 1884-1934. Ph.D., Boston University, 1990. 404p. UMI# 9105311.

2511   Roberts, Jon H. The Impact of Darwinism on American Protestant Theology, 1859-1890. Ph.D., Harvard University, 1980.

2512   Trechock, Mark A. Orthodoxy for a Critical Period: Five Case Studies in American Protestant Theology Circa 1870. Th.D., Iliff School of Theology, 1987. 222p. UMI# 8728416.[George P. Fisher, Octavius B. Frothingham, Charles P. Krauth, W.G.T. Shedd, Ellen G. White].

2513   Tredway, John T. Eucharistic Theology in American Protestantism 1820-1860. Ph.D., Northwestern University, 1964. 331p. UMI# 65-03318.

PURITAN

General Studies

2514   Armitage, Frank G. Reconsideration of Puritan Recreation in

Massachusetts. Ph.D., Clark University, 1927.

2515   Beasley, James R. The Success of the Cambridge Platform: Interchurch Communion in Early Massachusetts. Ph.D., Tufts University, 1980. 274p. UMI# 8019283.

2516   Bradley, Michael R. The Puritans of Virginia: Their Influence on the Religious Life of the Old Dominion, 1607-1659. Ph.D., Vanderbilt University, 1971. 220p. UMI# 7203206.

2517   Breen, Timothy H. The Character of the Good Ruler: A Study of Puritan Political Ideas in New England, 1630-1730. Ph.D., Yale University, 1968. 431p. UMI# 69-08322.

2518   Bremer, Francis J. Puritan Crisis: New England and the English Civil Wars, 1630-1670. Ph.D., Columbia University, 1972. 388p. UMI# 75-25653.

2519   Bryan, George C. Concepts of Leadership in American Political Thought: The Puritan Period. Ph.D., Harvard University, 1950. 227p.

2520   Calder, Isabel M. The Jurisdiction of New Haven, A Seventeenth Century Puritan Colony. Ph.D., Yale University, 1929.

2521   Carroll, Peter N. Puritanism and the Wilderness: The Intellectual Significance of the New England Frontier: 1629-1675. Ph.D., Northwestern University, 1968. 249p. UMI# 69-01810.

2522   Clark, Michael P. The Crucified Phrase: Puritan Semiology and Its Development in Colonial America. Ph.D., University of California-Irvine, 1977. 245p. UMI# 78-02424.

2523   Cobbledick, Melville R. The Status of Women in Puritan New England, 1630-1660: A Demographic Study. Ph.D., Yale University, 1936. 334p. UMI# 7110074.

2524   Coffman, Ralph J., Jr. Gardens in the Wilderness: Stuart Puritan Reforms and the Diversity of New England Puritanism, 1604-1650. Ph.D., Harvard University, 1976.

2525   Cohen, Charles L. The Heart and the Book: Faith, the Bible, and the Psychology of Puritan Religious Experience. Ph.D., University of California-Berkeley, 1982.

2526   Colman, George T. Certain Movements in England and America Which Influenced the Transition From the Ideals of Personal Righteousness of the Seventeenth Century to the Modern Ideals of Social Service. Ph.D., University of Chicago, 1914. 107p.

2527   Creelan, Paul G. Puritanism and the Rise of American Psychology. Ph.D., University of Chicago, 1978.

2528   Cross, Wilford O. The Role and Status of the Unregenerate in the Massachusetts Bay Colony, 1629-1729. Ph.D., Columbia University, 1957. 505p. UMI# 23072.

2529   Davis, Thomas M. The Traditions of Puritan Typology. Ph.D., University of Missouri-Columbia, 1968. 422p. UMI# 69-03373.

2530   Dawson, Jan C. Changing Conceptions of Puritanism in America, 1830-1910. Ph.D., University of Washington, 1976. 373p. UMI# 76-25397.

2531   Earley, Lawrence S. Endangered Innocent, Arrogant Queen: Images of New England Controversies Over Puritan Persecution, 1630-1730. Ph.D., University of North Carolina-Chapel Hill, 1975. 302p. UMI# 76-09237.

2532   Foster, Stephen. The Puritan Social Ethic: Class and Calling in the First Hundred Years of Settlement in New England. Ph.D., Yale University, 1966. 431p. UMI# 66-14981.

2533   Geddes, Gordon E. Welcome Joy: Death in Puritan New England, 1630-1730. Ph.D., University of California-Riverside, 1976. 380p. UMI# 77-11771.

2534   Gueguen, John A., Jr. Political Order and Religious Liberty: A Puritan Controversy. Ph.D., University of Chicago, 1970.

2535   Hammer, Dean C. Puritanism in the Making of a Nation. Ph.D., University of California-Berkeley, 1989. 346p. UMI# 9028854.

2536   Hogan, Charles J. Puritans and Meadows: The Interplay of English Culture and the American Environment in the Massachusetts Bay Colony, 1630-1660. Ph.D., University of California-Berkeley, 1986. 398p. UMI# 8624789.

2537   Holbrook, Thomas A. The Elaborated Labyrinth: The American Habit of Typology. Ph.D., University of Maryland, 1984. 464p. UMI# 8506536.

2538   Hornberger, Theodore R. American Puritanism and the Rise of the Scientific Mind. Ph.D., University of Michigan, 1934.

2539   Huber, Richard M. The Idea of Success in America, 1865-1929. A History of the Puritan Ethic. Ph.D., Yale University, 1953. 318p.

2540   Hughes, Paul L. The Puritan Concept of Empire. Ph.D., University of Iowa, 1951. 345p.

2541   Jeske, Jeffrey M. The Origins and Development of the Puritan Idea of Nature. Ph.D., Kent State University, 1978. 268p. UMI# 79-04803.

2542   Johnsen, Leigh D. Toward Pluralism: Society and Religion in Middleborough, Massachusetts, 1741-1807. Ph.D., University of California-Riverside, 1984. 305p. UMI# 9034608.

2543   Judson, Allan B. Some Characteristics of the Bay Colony Founders' Early Thinking About Their Dealings With the Physical Environment in New England. Ph.D., Harvard University, 1976.

2544   Karlsen, Carol F. The Devil in the Shape of a Woman: The Witch in Seventeenth-Century New England. Ph.D., Yale University, 1980. 429p. UMI# 8109795.

2545   Knight, Janice L. A Garden Enclosed: The Tradition of Heart Piety in Puritan New England. Ph.D., Harvard University, 1988. 562p. UMI# 8908984.

2546   Lewis, Mary J. A Sweet Sacrifice: Civil War in New England. Ph.D., State University of New York-Binghamton, 1986. 407p. UMI# 8608717.

2547   Lichtenthal, Jack. Eschatology and the Political Life: An Analysis of Seventeenth Century Origins in Puritan New England. Ph.D., New School for Social Research, 1970. 245p. UMI# 71-10623.

2548   Lockridge, Kenneth A. Dedham 1636-1736. The Anatomy of a Puritan Utopia. Ph.D., Princeton University, 1965. 378p. UMI# 66-04595.

2549   Lowance, Mason I., Jr. Images and Shadows of Divine Things: Puritan Typology in New England From 1660 to 1750. Ph.D., Emory University, 1967. 249p. UMI# 6804482.

2550   Lucas, Paul R. Valley of Discord: The Struggle for Power in the Puritan Churches of the Connecticut Valley, 1636-1720. Ph.D., University of Minnesota, 1970. 375p. UMI# 70-20214.

2551   McGee, James S. The Rhetoric of Suffering in New England, 1630-1670: An Inquiry in Fundamental Anglican-Puritan Differences. Ph.D., Yale University, 1971. 370p. UMI# 7217139.

2552   Menning, Viiu. Mystery and Idea: An Examination of Anglican and

Puritan Styles. Ph.D., Harvard University, 1974.

2553   Minor, Dennis E. The Evolution of Puritanism Into the Mass Culture of Early Nineteenth-Century America. Ph.D., Texas A&M University, 1973. 176p. UMI# 74-13090.

2554   Mooney, Michael E. Millennialism and Antichrist in New England, 1630-1760. Ph.D., Syracuse University, 1982. 437p. UMI# 8229003.

2555   North, Gary K. The Concept of Property in Puritan New England, 1630-1720. Ph.D., University of California-Riverside, 1972. 478p. UMI# 74-09240.

2556   Parrella, Michael J. The Battle for Control: A Study of the Controversy Over Political Control in the Massachusetts Bay Colony During the Early Years of Settlement. Ph.D., New York University, 1982. 284p. UMI# 8307693.

2557   Perluck, Herbert A. Puritan Expression and the Decline of Piety. Ph.D., Brown University, 1955. 238p. UMI# 13182.

2558   Perzel, Edward S. The First Generation of Settlement in Colonial Ipswich, Massachusetts, 1633-1660. Ph.D., Rutgers University, 1967. 417p. UMI# 6714745.

2559   Pettit, Norman. The Image of the Heart in Early Puritanism: The Emergence in England and America of the Concept of Preparation for Grace. Ph.D., Yale University, 1963.

2560   Puglisi, Michael J. The Legacies of King Philip's War in the Massachusetts Bay Colony. Ph.D., College of William and Mary, 1987. 349p. UMI# 8717074.

2561   Randall, Daniel R. The Puritan Colony at Annapolis, Maryland. Ph.D., Johns Hopkins University, 1887.

2562   Richards, Phillip M. The New Divinity: Puritanism as Ideology in the Eighteenth Century. Ph.D., University of Chicago, 1987.

2563   Rindler, Edward P. The Migration From the New Haven Colony to Newark, East New Jersey: A Study of Puritan Values and Behavior, 1630-1720. Ph.D., University of Pennsylvania, 1977. 467p. UMI# 7806636.

2564   Rosenberg, Gary L. Family and Society in the Early Seventeenth Century Massachusetts Bay Area. Ph.D., State University of New York-Buffalo, 1980. 283p. UMI# 8016241.

2565   Saxton, Martha P. Being Good: Moral Standards for Puritan Women, Boston: 1630-1730. Ph.D., Columbia University, 1989. 335p. UMI# 9005929.

2566   Schmeltekopf, Donald D. Puritan Thought and the Formation of the Early American Political Tradition, 1630-1787. Ph.D., Drew University, 1975. 342p. UMI# 75-24218.

2567   Schneiderman, Howard G. The Antinomian Founding of Rhode Island and the Spirit of Factionalism. Ph.D., University of Pennsylvania, 1978. 225p. UMI# 7816354.

2568   Searl, Stanford J., Jr. The Symbolic Imagination of American Puritanism: Metaphors for the Invisible World. Ph.D., Syracuse University, 1970. 214p. UMI# 71-18507.

2569   Shute, Michael N. Earthquakes and Early American Imagination: "Decline and Renewal in Eighteenth-Century Puritan Culture." Ph.D., University of California-Berkeley, 1977. 255p. UMI# 77-31538.

2570   Stannard, David E. The Puritan Way of Death: A Study in Religion, Culture and Social Change. Ph.D., Yale University, 1975. 315p. UMI# 75-27110.

2571   Straub, Carl B. Providential Ecology: Puritan Envisagement of Their Wilderness Environment. Ph.D., Harvard University, 1971.

2572   Terris, Walter F. The Right to Speak: Massachusetts, 1628-1685. Ph.D., Northwestern University, 1962. 364p. UMI# 6303451.

2573   Todd, Margo F. Christian Humanism and the Puritan Social Order. Ph.D., Washington University, 1981. 420p. UMI# 8201763.

2574   Tucker, Edward B. The Founders Remembered: The Anglicization of the Puritan Tradition in New England, 1690-1760. Ph.D., Brown University, 1979. 242p. UMI# 80-07080.

2575   Twomey, Rosemary K. From Pure Church to Pure Nation: Massachusetts Bay, 1630-1692. Ph.D., University of Rochester, 1971. 299p. UMI# 72-00777.

2576   Ulrich, Laurel T. Good Wives: A Study in Role Definition in Northern New England, 1650-1750. Ph.D., University of New Hampshire, 1980. 548p. UMI# 8027802.

2577   Van Til, L. John. Liberty of Conscience: The History of a Puritan Idea. Ph.D., Michigan State University, 1971. 257p. UMI# 71-31329.

2578   Vaughan, Alden T. New England Puritans and the American Indian, 1620-1675. Ph.D., Columbia University, 1964. 489p. UMI# 67-10393.

2579   Wagner, Hans-Peter. Puritan Attitudes Towards Recreation in Seventeenth-Century New England, With Particular Consideration of Physical Recreation. Dr.Phil., Universitat des Saarlandes, 1978. 359p.

2580   Walsh, James P. The Pure Church: In Eighteenth Century Connecticut. Ph.D., Columbia University, 1967. 293p. UMI# 67-14104.

2581   Wells, Michael V. Sex and the Law in Colonial New England. Ph.D., Ohio State University, 1974. 207p. UMI# 753222.

2582   Wexler, Laura J. The Puritan in the Photograph. Ph.D., Columbia University, 1986. 227p. UMI# 8703107.

2583   Williams, David R. Wilderness Lost: New England in the Jaws of an Angry God. Ph.D., Brown University, 1982. 415p. UMI# 8228351.

2584   Williams, Ray S. The American National Covenant: 1730-1800. Ph.D., Florida State University, 1965. 166p. UMI# 6605461.

2585   Woolley, Bruce C. Reverend Thomas Shepard's Cambridge Church Members 1636-1649: A Socio-Economic Analysis. Ph.D., University of Rochester, 1973. 227p. UMI# 7325867.

2586   Zabierek, HenryC. Puritans and Americans: An Inquiry Into the Nature of English Settlement in New England. D.A., Carnegie-Mellon University, 1971. 436p. UMI# 72-08076.

2587   Zakai, Avihu. Exile and Kingdom: Reformation, Separation, and the Millennial Quest in the Formation of Massachusetts and Its Relationship With England,1628-1660. Ph.D., Johns Hopkins University, 1983. 620p. UMI# 8302696.

Art and Architecture

2588   Haims, Lynn M. The American Puritan Aesthetic: Iconography in Seventeenth-Century Poetry and Tombstone Art. Ph.D., New York University, 1981. 227p. UMI# 81-15550.

2589   Ludwig, Allan I. Carved Stone-Markers in New England, 1650-1815. Ph.D., Yale University, 1964. 428p.

Biography

2590   Blackmon, Joab L, Jr. Judge Samuel Sewall, 1652-1730: A Biography. Ph.D., University of Washington, 1964. 335p. UMI# 6411157.

2591   Boyd, Richard B. Three Generations of Puritan Spiritual Autobiography: Problems of Self-Definition in a Time of Declension. Ph.D., University of California-San Diego, 1985. 189p. UMI# 8510904.[Anne Bradstreet, Thomas Shepard, Edward Taylor].

2592   Burg, Barry R. Richard Mather (1596-1669): The Life and Work of a Puritan Cleric in New England. Ph.D., University of Colorado, 1967. 459p. UMI# 68-10612.

2593   Finberg, Stanley P. Thomas Goodwin, Puritan Pastor and Independent Divine. Ph.D., University of Chicago, 1974.

2594   Harvey, Shirley W. Nathaniel Ward: His Life and Work, Together With an Edited Text of His *Simple Cobler*. Ph.D., Boston University, 1936. 450p.

2595   Hasler, Richard A. Thomas Shepard: Pastor-Evangelist (1605-1649). A Study in the New England Puritan Ministry. Ph.D., Hartford Seminary Foundation, 1964. 344p. UMI# 6502674.

2596   Kaledin, Arthur D. The Mind of John Leverett. Ph.D., Harvard University, 1965. 331p.

2597   Kennedy, Rick A. Thy Patriarchs' Desire: Thomas and William Brattle in Puritan Massachusetts. Ph.D., University of California-Santa Barbara, 1987. 353p. UMI# 8727837.

2598   Marquit, Doris G. Thomas Shepard: The Formation of a Puritan Identity. Ph.D., University of Minnesota, 1978. 372p. UMI# 78-13430.

2599   Polf, William A. Puritan Gentlemen: The Dudleys of Massachusetts, 1576-1686. Ph.D., Syracuse University, 1973. 328p. UMI# 74-17613.

2600   Stearns, Raymond P. Hugh Peter: A Biography. Ph.D., Harvard University, 1934. 809p.

2601   Van De Wetering, John E. Thomas Prince: Puritan Polemicist. Ph.D., University of Washington, 1959. 416p. UMI# 59-02212.

2602   Wilbur, Raymond B. Diary of the Damned: A Study in Theocentric Anxiety in Pre-Awakening New England. Ph.D., University of New

Hampshire, 1981. 393p. UMI# 8228016.

Church and State

2603   Allen, David G. In English Ways: The Movement of Societies and the Transferal of English Local Law and Custom to Massachusetts Bay, 1600-1690. Ph.D., University of Wisconsin-Madison, 1974. 608p. UMI# 7505917.

2604   Loubser, Johannes J. Puritanism and Religious Liberty: Change in the Normative Order in Massachusetts, 1630-1850. Ph.D., Harvard University, 1964.

2605   Sehr, Timothy J. Colony and Commonwealth: Massachusetts Bay, 1649-1660. Ph.D., Indiana University, 1977. 321p. UMI# 7730321.

2606   Stifler, Susan M.R. Church and State in Massachusetts, 1691-1740. Ph.D., University of Illinois at Urbana-Champaign, 1914. 208p.

Clergy

2607   Carden, Mark A. The Ministry and the Word: The Clergy, the Bible, and Biblical Themes in Five Massachusetts Towns, 1630-1700. Ph.D., University of California-Irvine, 1977. 335p. UMI# 78-05041.[Boston, Cambridge, Dedham, Dorchester, Roxbury(MA)].

2608   Hall, David D. The Faithful Shepherd: The Puritan Ministry in Old and New England, 1570-1660. Ph.D., Yale University, 1964.

2609   Signett, Roland D. The Image of Christ and Symbolism of Atonement Among the Puritan Clergy: Theology, Personality and the Social Order, 1600-1745. Ph.D., University of Washington, 1974. 226p. UMI# 75-04048.

2610   Van De Wetering, Maxine S. The New England Clergy and the Development of Scientific Professionalism. Ph.D., University of Washington, 1970. 237p. UMI# 71-08557.

Education

2611   Cunningham, Homer F. The Effect of the Decline of the Puritan Oligarchy Upon the Schools of Massachusetts Between 1664 and 1758. Ph.D., New York University, 1954. 350p. UMI# 10625.

2612   Davis, Leroy A. A Comparative Investigation of Certain Similarities of Educational Concern Between New England Puritanism and the Proposals for National Systems of Education in the

Eighteenth-Century. Ph.D., Ohio University, 1973. 341p. UMI# 73-25739.

2613   Hoffmann, John M. Commonwealth College: The Governance of Harvard in the Puritan Period. Ph.D., Harvard University, 1972.

2614   Johnson, Daniel T. Puritan Power in Illinois Higher Education Prior to 1870. Ph.D., University of Wisconsin-Madison, 1974. 234p. UMI# 74-30109.

2615   Murphy, Geraldine J. Massachusetts Bay Colony: The Role of Government in Education. Ph.D., Radcliffe College, 1960.

2616   Potter, Robert A. Church, Converts, and Children: Implications for Christian Education in the Doctrine of the Church Held by Seventeenth Century New England Puritans as Particularly Exemplified in John Norton's *The Answer*. Ed.R.D., Hartford Seminary Foundation, 1968. 262p. UMI# 6911585.

2617   Rolph, Rebecca S. Emmanuel College, Cambridge, and the Puritan Movements of Old and New England. Ph.D., University of Southern California, 1979.

Historiography

2618   Arch, Stephen C. Mastering History: Puritan Historians in Colonial America. Ph.D., University of Virginia, 1989. 387p. UMI# 9002811.

2619   Halbert, Cecelia L. The Art of the Lords Remembrancers: A Study of New England Puritan Histories. Ph.D., University of California, 1968. 217p. UMI# 69-00850.

2620   Hart, Sidney. The American Sense of Mission, 1738-1810: Puritan Historical Myths in Post-Revolutionary New England. Ph.D., Clark University, 1973. 440p. UMI# 73-22629.

2621   Howard, Alan B. The Web in the Loom: An Introduction to the Puritan Historians of New England. Ph.D., Stanford University, 1968. 443p. UMI# 69-00232.

2622   Rushing, Stanley B. The Recovery of New England Puritanism: A Historiographical Investigation. Ph.D., New Orleans Baptist Theological Seminary, 1971. 215p.

2623   White, Paula K. Hawthorne's Use of the Puritan Theory of History. Ph.D., Columbia University, 1975. 371p. UMI# 77-27877.

Literature

2624   Bell, Michael D. Hawthorne and the Romantic Treatment of Puritanism: Seventeenth-Century New England in American Fiction, 1820-1850. Ph.D., Harvard University, 1969.

2625   Bernhard, Virginia P. *Essays to Do Good*: A Puritan Gospel of Wealth, 1690-1740. Ph.D., Rice University, 1971. 166p. UMI# 71-26258.

2626   Brooks, Charles B. Puritanism in New England Fiction, 1820-1870. Ph.D., Princeton University, 1943. 247p. UMI# 02921.

2627   Burstein, Frances B. The Picture of New England Puritanism Presented in the Fiction of Henry James. Ph.D., Boston University, 1964. 601p. UMI# 64-11659.

2628   Bush, Sargent, Jr. The Relevance of Puritanism to Major Themes in Hawthorne's Fiction. Ph.D., University of Iowa, 1967. 283p. UMI# 67-16783.

2629   Caldwell, Patricia L. A Literary Study of Puritan Testimonies of Religious Experience From the 1630's to the 1660's Including a Critical Edition of Thomas Shepard's Manuscript, *The Confessions of Diverse Propounded to Be Received and Were Entertayned as Members*. From the First Church of Cambridge, Massachusetts, 1637-1645. Ph.D., Harvard University, 1979.

2630   Cardwell, Patricia B. Death and the Child: An Historical Analysis of Selected Puritan Works of Children's Literature With Implications for Modern Education. Ph.D., Catholic University of America, 1982. 431p. UMI# 82-21473.

2631   Colacurcio, Michael J., Jr. The Progress of Piety: Hawthorne's Critique of the Puritan Spirit. Ph.D., University of Illinois at Urbana-Champaign, 1963. 316p. UMI# 64-06038.

2632   Craig, Raymond A. The Stamp of the Word: The Poetics of Biblical Allusion in American Puritan Poetry. Ph.D., University of California-Davis, 1989. 179p. UMI# 9009236.

2633   Daly, Robert J. God's Altar: A Study of Puritan Poetry. Ph.D., Cornell University, 1972. 285p. UMI# 73-06642.

2634   Elliot, Emory B., Jr. Generations in Crisis: The Imaginative Power of Puritan Writing, 1660-1700. Ph.D., University of Illinois at Urbana-Champaign, 1972. 258p. UMI# 73-09922.

2635   Fitzgibbons, Kathleen C. A History of the Evolution of the Didactic Literature for Puritan Children in America From 1656-1856. Ed.D., University of Massachusetts, 1987. 106p. UMI# 8727046.

2636   Gallagher, Edward J. A Critical Study of Edward Johnson's *Wonder-Working Providence of Sions Savior in New England*. Ph.D., University of Notre Dame, 1970. 222p. UMI# 7105535.

2637   Garcia-Rouphail, Maria. Anne Bradstreet, Her Poetry, and the Politics of Exclusion: A Study of the Developing Sense of Poetic Purpose. Ph.D., Ohio State University, 1982. 220p. UMI# 8300250.

2638   Hubbard, Claude. English and American Puritan Autobiographies in the Seventeenth-Century. Ph.D., University of Chicago, 1978.

2639   Israel, Calvin. American Puritan Literary Theory: 1620-1660. Ph.D., University of California-Davis, 1970. 264p. UMI# 71-15538.

2640   Johnston, Eleanor I. Puritan Poetics: The Development of Literal Metaphor From John Bunyan to Nathaniel Hawthorne. Ph.D., University of Manitoba, 1985.

2641   Johnston, Thomas E., Jr. American Puritan Poetic Voices: Essays on Anne Bradstreet, Edward Taylor, Roger Williams, and Philip Pain. Ph.D., Ohio University, 1968. 167p. UMI# 6905095.

2642   Lockyer, Timothy J. Religion and Good Literature: Puritan Devotional Poetry. Ph.D., Pennsylvania State University, 1977. 280p. UMI# 78-08387.

2643   McCartney, Lisa M. Form and Voice in Selected American Puritan Spiritual Autobiographies. Ph.D., University of Notre Dame, 1982. 169p. UMI# 82-25827.

2644   McCune, Marjorie W. The Danforths: Puritan Poets. Ph.D., Pennsylvania State University, 1968. 338p. UMI# 69-09786.

2645   Mullin, Joan A. The Transformation: The Puritan Past and Language in Hawthorne's Novels. Ph.D., Loyola University of Chicago, 1988. 257p. UMI# 8805556.

2646   O'Donnell, James P. Thomas Shepard's *The Sincere Convert*: A Critical Edition. Ph.D., University of South Carolina, 1980. 503p. UMI# 8102781.

2647   Olsson, Karl A. Theology and Rhetoric in the Writings of Thomas Shepard. Ph.D., University of Chicago, 1949. 144p.

2648   Perry, Dennis R. Autobiographical Structures in Seventeenth-Century Puritan Histories. Ph.D., University of Wisconsin-Madison, 1986. 245p. UMI# 8614390.

2649   Quartermain, Peter A. Nathaniel Hawthorne and Puritanism: A Study of Puritan Influences on Nineteenth-Century New England Literature. Ph.D., University of Nottingham, 1959. 396p.

2650   Rowlette, Edith J.H. The Works of Anne Bradstreet. Ph.D., Boston University, 1964. 594p. UMI# 6411645.

2651   Scheer, Thomas F. "The Spectacles of God's Word": Spiritual Vision and Salvation in Seventeenth and Eighteenth Century Puritan History and Allegory. Ph.D., University of Notre Dame, 1972. 216p. UMI# 72-26820.

2652   Schweitzer, Ivy T. Literature as Sacrament: The Evolution of Puritan Sacramentalism and Its Influence on Puritan and Emersonian Aesthetics. Ph.D., Brandeis University, 1983. 404p. UMI# 8318245.

2653   Scott, Sarah M. A Thematic Study of the Writings of Puritan Women From the Time of the Original Settlers to 1770. Ph.D., Southern Illinois University-Carbondale, 1981. 240p. UMI# 81-22666.

2654   Stone, Alan N. Nature's Fountain: Samuel Sewall's Gathering of a Pragmatic Literary Heritage During New England's Second Generation. Ph.D., Syracuse University, 1976. 263p. UMI# 7724412.

2655   Thickstun, Margaret O. Fictions of the Feminine: Puritan Doctrine and the Representation of Women. Ph.D., Cornell University, 1984. 181p. UMI# 8427218.

2656   Trimpey, John E. The Poetry of Four American Puritans: Edward Johnson, Peter Bulkeley II, Nicholas Noyes, and John Danforth. Ph.D., Ohio University, 1968. 327p. UMI# 69-05108.

2657   Watters, David H. "With Bodilie Eyes": Eschatological Themes in the Literature and Funerary Art of Early New England. Ph.D., Brown University, 1979. 343p. UMI# 8007084.

2658   Whelan, Timothy D. "Mirror of Her Age": The Place of Human and Divine Knowledge in the Poetry and Prose of Anne Bradstreet. Ph.D., University of Maryland, 1989. 220p. UMI# 8924251.

2659   White, Anne S. The Poetry of Anne Bradstreet. Ph.D., University of California-Los Angeles, 1962. 285p.

2660   Zilboorg, Caroline C. The Speaking Self in American Puritan
          Literature: A Study in Genre and Rhetorical Continuities. Ph.D.,
          University of Wisconsin-Madison, 1976. 345p. UMI# 76-20146.

Liturgy

2661   Hambrick-Stowe, Charles E. The Practice of Piety: Puritan
          Devotional Disciplines in Seventeenth Century New England. Ph.D.,
          Boston University, 1980. 547p. UMI# 80-13282.

2662   Stallings, Louise R. The Unpolished Altar: The Place of the *Bay
          Psalm Book* in American Culture. Ph.D., Texas A&M University,
          1977. 310p. UMI# 7806837.

2663   Turner, Maxine T. A History of the *Bay Psalm Book*. Ph.D., Auburn
          University, 1971. 124p. UMI# 7120212.

Missions and Missionaries

2664   Salisbury, Neal E. Conquest of the "Savage": Puritans, Puritan
          Missionaries, and Indians, 1620-1680. Ph.D., University of
          California-Los Angeles, 1972. 302p. UMI# 7218141.

Newspapers and Periodicals

2665   Jackson, Elizabeth. Reaction Against Puritanism in American
          Periodicals of the Eighteenth Century. Ph.D., Harvard University,
          1916. 257p.

Organizational Structure

2666   Moran, Gerald F. The Puritan Saint: Religious Experience, Church
          Membership, and Piety in Connecticut, 1636-1776. Ph.D., Rutgers
          University, 1974. 470p. UMI# 74-27637.

Preaching

2667   Benton, Robert M. The American Puritan Sermon Before 1700.
          Ph.D., University of Colorado, 1967. 304p. UMI# 68-10607.

2668   Engebretsen, Terry O. Pillars of the House: Puritan Funeral
          Sermons Through the *Magnalia Christi Americana*. Ph.D.,
          Washington State University, 1982. 293p. UMI# 8215136.[Cotton
          Mather, Edward Taylor, Samuel Willard].

2669   Erklauer, William H. The Dynamic Forms of Puritan Discourse: The
          Rhetorical Practice of Six New England Puritans. Ph.D., University
          of Massachusetts, 1983. 328p. UMI# 8310281.[William Bradford,

Anne Bradstreet, John Cotton, Edward Johnson, Cotton Mather, Edward Taylor].

2670   Harris, Billy L. The New England Fast Sermon, 1639-1763. Ph.D., Florida State University, 1968. 205p. UMI# 68-16373.

2671   Henson, Robert E. Sorry After a Godly Manner: A Study of the Puritan Funeral Elegy in New England, 1625-1722. Ph.D., University of California-Los Angeles, 1957.

2672   Levy, Babette M. Preaching in the First Half Century of New England History. Ph.D., Columbia University, 1946.

2673   Ricketson, William F., Jr. A Puritan Approach to Manifest Destiny: Case Studies From Artillery Election Sermons. Ph.D., University of Georgia, 1965. 158p. UMI# 6602497.

2674   Roen, William H. Prophets and Angels: A Study of the Self-Presentation of Selected American Puritan Preachers. Ph.D., Catholic University of America, 1987. 166p. UMI# 8713910.

2675   Strother, Bonnie L. The Imagery in the Sermons of Thomas Shepard. Ph.D., University of Tennessee, 1968. 348p. UMI# 6815432.

2676   Trefz, Edward K. A Study of Satan, With Particular Emphasis Upon His Role in the Preaching of Certain New England Puritans. Ph.D., Union Theological Seminary, 1953.

2677   Van Hof, Charles L. The Theory of Sermon Rhetoric in Puritan New England: Its Origins and Expression. Ph.D., Loyola University of Chicago, 1979. 500p. UMI# 79-21805.

Social Programs

2678   Botond-Blazek, Joseph B. Puritans and Sex. An Inquiry Into the Legal Enforcement of Sexual Morality in 17th Century Massachusetts. Ph.D., University of California-Los Angeles, 1962.

2679   Schmitt, Dale J. The Response to Social Problems in Seventeenth-Century Connecticut. Ph.D., University of Kansas, 1970. 313p. UMI# 7113358.

Theology

2680   Battis, Emery J. Troublers in Israel: The Antinomian Controversy in the Massachusetts Bay Colony, 1636-1638. Ph.D., Columbia University, 1958. 610p. UMI# 58-02610.

2681   Beebe, David L. The Seals of the Covenant: The Doctrine and Place of the Sacraments and Censures in the New England Puritan Theology Underlying the Cambridge Platform of 1648. Th.D., Pacific School of Religion, 1966. 338p. UMI# 6610153.

2682   Dejong, Peter Y. The Covenant Idea in New England Theology. Ph.D., Hartford Seminary Foundation, 1942.

2683   Fulcher, John R. Puritan Piety in Early New England: A Study in Spiritual Regeneration From the Antinomian Controversy to the Cambridge Synod of 1648 in the Massachusetts Bay Colony. Ph.D., Princeton University, 1963. 354p. UMI# 6401326.

2684   Gilsdorf, Aletha J.B. The Puritan Apocalypse: New England Eschatology in the Seventeenth Century. Ph.D., Yale University, 1965. 238p. UMI# 65-09673.

2685   Haroutunian, Joseph. Piety Versus Moralism: The Passing of the New England Theology. Ph.D., Columbia University, 1932. 329p.

2686   Holifield, Elmer B. The Covenant Sealed: The Development of Puritan Sacramental Theology in Old and New England 1570-1720. Ph.D., Yale University, 1970. 450p. UMI# 7116250.

2687   Humphrey, Richard A. The Concept of Conversion in the Theology of Thomas Shepard (1605-1649). Ph.D., Drew University, 1967. 263p. UMI# 6714376.

2688   Jones, James W., III. The Beginnings of American Theology: John Cotton, Thomas Hooker, Thomas Shepard and Peter Bulkeley. Ph.D., Brown University, 1970. 352p. UMI# 71-13877.

2689   Lang, Amy S. The Antinomian Strain in American Culture. Ph.D., Columbia University, 1980. 221p. UMI# 80-17080.

2690   Lowrie, Ernest B. A Complete Body of Puritan Divinity: An Exposition of Samuel Willard's Systematic Theology. Ph.D., Yale University, 1971. 270p. UMI# 71-28911.

2691   McCoy, Michael R. In Defense of the Covenant: The Sacramental Debates of Eighteenth Century New England. Ph.D., Emory University, 1986. 288p. UMI# 8626526.

2692   Miller, Perry. The Establishment of Orthodoxy in Massachusetts. Ph.D., University of Chicago, 1931. 405p.

2693   Morgans, John I. The National and International Aspects of Puritan Eschatology, 1640-1660: A Comparative Study. Ph.D., Hartford

Seminary Foundation, 1970. 357p. UMI# 7111447.

2694   Murphy, Susan. In Remembrance of Me: Sacramental Theology and Practice in Colonial New England. Ph.D., University of Washington, 1978. 271p. UMI# 78-20752.

2695   Rumsey, Peter L. Acts of God: The Rhetoric of Providence in New England, 1620-1730. Ph.D., Columbia University, 1984. 319p. UMI# 8473024.

2696   Selement, George J. The Means to Grace: A Study of Conversion in Early New England. Ph.D., University of New Hampshire, 1974. 401p. UMI# 7717203.

2697   Smith, Lewis. Changing Conceptions of God in Colonial New England. Ph.D., University of Iowa, 1953. 290p. UMI# 04992.

2698   Stoever, William K.B. The Covenant of Works in Puritan Theology: The Antinomian Crisis in New England. Ph.D., Yale University, 1970. 278p. UMI# 71-16858.

REFORMED CHURCH IN AMERICA

2699   David, S. Immanuel. God's Messengers: Reformed Church in America Missionaries in South India, 1839-1938. Th.D., Lutheran School of Theology, 1984. 231p.

2700   Nettinga, James Z. Social and Economic Influences on the Reformed Church in Manhattan Since 1865. Ph.D., Union Theological Seminary, 1946. UMI# 01-58835.

2701   Ryder, Stephen W. A Historical-Educational Study of the Japan Mission of the Reformed Church in America. Ph.D., Columbia University, 1935.

2702   Taylor, Paul V. A Philosophy of Values in Education Revealed in the Work of Religious Education Conducted by the Reformed Church in the United States in China. Ph.D., Hartford Seminary Foundation, 1929.

2703   Van Dyk, Gerard. A Study of the History and Development of the Sunday School in the Reformed Church in America: An Examination of the Influences of Secular Educational Developments on Religious Education From 1870-1910. Ed.D., Rutgers University, 1979. 284p. UMI# 80-11434.

2704   Van Dyke, Albert H. A History of Youth Work in the Reformed

Church in America. Ed.D., New York University, 1957. 211p. UMI# 22749.

2705   Weber, William A. Theological Education in the Reformed Church in America. Ph.D., Yale University, 1934.

2706   Yoder, Donald H. Church Union Efforts of the Reformed Church in the United States to 1934. Ph.D., University of Chicago, 1948. 310p.

RESTORATION MOVEMENT

2707   Bergeson, Ronald S. The Plea for Christian Unity: Enthymeme and Metaphor in the Rhetoric of the Restoration Movement, 1800-1830. Ph.D., University of Oregon, 1978. 336p. UMI# 7912557.

2708   Bever, Ronald D. An Analysis of Speaking in the American Restoration Movement, 1820-1849. Ph.D., Northwestern University, 1968. 260p. UMI# 6906893.

2709   Castleberry, Ottis L. A Study of the Nature and Sources of the Effectiveness of the Preaching of Benjamin Franklin in the Restoration Movement in America, 1840-1878. Ph.D., Pennsylvania State University, 1957. 608p. UMI# 20953.

2710   Foster, Douglas A. The Struggle for Unity During the Period of Division of the Restoration Movement: 1875-1900. Ph.D., Vanderbilt University, 1987. 429p. UMI# 8714429.

2711   Humble, Bill J. The Missionary Society Controversy in the Restoration Movement (1823-1875). Ph.D., University of Iowa, 1964. 355p. UMI# 65-00471.

2712   Johnson, Kenneth M. The Doctrine of Universal Salvation and the Restorationist Controversy in Early Nineteenth-Century New England. Ph.D., University of Ottawa, 1977.

2713   McMillon, Lynn A. The Quest for the Apostolic Church: A Study of Scottish Origins of American Restorationism. Ph.D., Baylor University, 1972. 217p. UMI# 73-07322.

2714   Moorhouse, William M. The Restoration Movement: The Rhetoric of Jacksonian Restorationism in a Frontier Religion. Ph.D., Indiana University, 1968. 284p. UMI# 68-15452.

2715   Randall, Max W. Revival and the Restoration Movement. D.Miss., Fuller Theological Seminary, 1979.

2716   Walker, David E., Jr. The Rhetoric of the Restoration Movement: The Period of Inception: 1800-1832. Ph.D., University of Florida, 1969. 385p. UMI# 7020621.

RUSSIAN ORTHODOX

2717   Barkey, Paul E. The Russian Orthodox Church in Its Mission to the Aleuts. D.Miss., Fuller Theological Seminary, 1988. 215p. UMI# 8827520.

2718   Kovach, Michael G. The Russian Orthodox Church in Russian America. Ph.D., University of Pittsburgh, 1957. 297p. UMI# 22851.

SALVATION ARMY

2719   Bosch, Allan W. The Salvation Army in Chicago, 1885-1914. Ph.D., University of Chicago, 1965.

2720   Murdoch, Norman H. The Salvation Army: An Anglo-American Revivalist Social Mission. Ph.D., University of Cincinnati, 1985. 559p. UMI# 8526540.

SCHWENKFELDERS

2721   Dollin, Norman. The Schwenkfelders in Eighteenth Century America. Ph.D., Columbia University, 1971. 209p. UMI# 7201298.

2722   Seipt, Allen A. Schwenkfelder Hymnology and the Sources of the First Schwenkfelder Hymn Book Printed in America. Ph.D., University of Pennsylvania, 1906.

SHAKER

General Studies

2723   Borges, Richard C. The Canterbury Shakers: A Demographic Study. Ph.D., University of New Hampshire, 1988. 249p. UMI# 8907437.

2724   Butts, Carl F. The Shakers: A Case Study in Social Variation. Ph.D., Yale University, 1942.

2725   Chase, Daryl. The Early Shakers: An Experiment in Religious Communism. Ph.D., University of Chicago, 1937.

2726   Goodall, David J. New Light on the Border: New England Squatter Settlements in New York During the American Revolution. Ph.D., State University of New York-Albany, 1984. 394p. UMI# 8414332.

2727   Graham, Judith. The Shaker Children's Order. Ph.D., Iowa State University, 1989. 184p. UMI# 9003521.

2728   Ham, Francis G. Shakerism in the Old West. Ph.D., University of Kentucky, 1962. 334p. UMI# 72-02939.

2729   Procter-Smith, Marjorie. Women in Shaker Community and Worship: A Feminist Theological Analysis of the Uses of Religious Symbolism. Ph.D., University of Notre Dame, 1983. 240p. UMI# 8316727.

2730   Promey, Sally M. Spiritual Spectacles: Shaker Gift Images in Religious Context. Ph.D., University of Chicago, 1988.

2731   Taylor, Michael B. Developments in Early Shaker Ethical Thought. Ph.D., Harvard University, 1976.

2732   Youngerman, Suzanne. "Shaking is No Foolish Play": An Anthropological Perspective on the American Shakers: Person, Time, Space, and Dance Ritual. Ph.D., Columbia University, 1983. 276p. UMI# 8406574.

Art and Architecture

2733   Anderson, Philip J. The Simple Builders: The Shakers, Their Villages and Architecture. Ph.D., Saint Louis University, 1969. 367p. UMI# 70-01840.

Biography

2734   Sasson, Sarah D. The Shaker Personal Narrative: Studies in a Nineteenth-Century Autobiographical Tradition. Ph.D., University of North Carolina-Chapel Hill, 1980. 352p. UMI# 8114860.

2735   Setta, Susan M. Woman of the Apocalypse: The Reincorporation of the Feminine Through the Second Coming of Christ in Ann Lee. Ph.D., Pennsylvania State University, 1979. 239p. UMI# 7922345.

Education

2736   Taylor, Frank G. An Analysis of Shaker Education: The Life and Death of an Alternative Educational System, 1774-1950. Ph.D., University of Connecticut, 1976. 332p. UMI# 76-19003.

Literature

2737   Gooden, Rosemary D. The Language of Devotion: Gospel Affection and Gospel Union in the Writings of Shaker Sisters. Ph.D.,

University of Michigan, 1987. 201p. UMI# 8720272.

2738   McAdams, Ruth A. The Shakers in American Fiction. Ph.D., Texas Christian University, 1985. 215p. UMI# 8517258.

Music

2739   Christenson, Donald E. Music of the Shakers From Union Village, Ohio: A Repertory Study and Tune Index of the Manuscripts Originating in the 1840's. Ph.D., Ohio State University, 1988. 621p. UMI# 8812237.

2740   Cook, Harold. Shaker Music. A Manifestation of American Folk Culture. Ph.D., Case Western Reserve University, 1947. 339p.

2741   Smith, Harold V. Oliver C. Hampton and Other Shaker Teacher-Musicians of Ohio and Kentucky. D.A., Ball State University, 1981. 255p. UMI# 8201910.

Organizational Structure

2742   Mihok, Marsha. Women in the Authority Structure of Shakerism: A Study of Social Conflict and Social Change. Ph.D., Drew University, 1989. 331p. UMI# 9014369.

Theology

2743   Deignan, Kathleen P. The Eschatology of Shaker Christianity. Ph.D., Fordham University, 1986. 291p. UMI# 8615730.

2744   Morgan, John H. Communitarian Communism as a Religious Experience: Exemplified in the Development of the Shaker Theology. Ph.D., Hartford Seminary Foundation, 1972. 291p. UMI# 7315935.

SOCIETY OF FRIENDS

General Studies

2745   Applegarth, Albert C. The Holy Experiment: Or the Society of Friends in Pennsylvania, 1682-1776. Ph.D., Johns Hopkins University, 1887.

2746   Bauman, Richard. For the Reputation of Truth: Quaker Political Behavior in Pennsylvania, 1750-1800. Ph.D., University of Pennsylvania, 1968. 334p. UMI# 6905607.

2747   Beeth, Howard. Outside Agitators in Southern History: The Society of Friends, 1656-1800. Ph.D., University of Houston, 1984. 570p. UMI# 8428106.

2748   Benjamin, Philip S. The Philadelphia Quakers in the Industrial Age, 1865-1920. Ph.D., Columbia University, 1967. 436p. UMI# 70-18784.

2749   Brown, E. Leonard. Quaker Migration to "Miami Country," 1798-1861. Ph.D., Michigan State University, 1974. 162p. UMI# 7507128.[Miami(OH)].

2750   Brown, Marley R., III. "Among Weighty Friends": The Archaeology and Social History of the Jacob Mott Family, Portsmouth, Rhode Island, 1640-1800. Ph.D., Brown University, 1987. 352p. UMI# 8715462.

2751   Brutz, Judith L. Development of Pacifism in Quakers. Ph.D., Iowa State University, 1988. 210p. UMI# 8825905.

2752   Buys, John W. Quakers in Indiana in the Nineteenth-Century. Ph.D., University of Florida, 1973. 338p. UMI# 74-10029.

2753   Chu, Jonathan M. Madmen and Friends: Quakers and the Puritan Adjustment to Religious Heterodoxy in Massachusetts Bay During the Seventeenth Century. Ph.D., University of Washington, 1978.

2754   Damiano, Kathryn A. On Earth as It Is in Heaven: Eighteenth-Century Quakerism as Realized Eschatology. Ph.D., Union for Experimenting Colleges and Universities, 1988. 259p. UMI# 8913771.

2755   Davidson, Robert L.D. War Comes to Penn's Province: A Study of the Events Leading to the Failure of the Holy Experiment With Special Attention to Pennsylvania's Participation in the Early Colonial Wars. Ed.D., Temple University, 1947.

2756   Dowless, Donald V. The Quakers of Colonial North Carolina, 1672-1789. Ph.D., Baylor University, 1989. 315p. UMI# 8919926.

2757   Ferguson, Leroy C. The Quakers in American Politics. Ph.D., Ohio State University, 1948.

2758   Frost, Jerry W. The Quaker Family in Colonial America: A Social History of the Society of Friends. Ph.D., University of Wisconsin, 1968. 533p. UMI# 68-17894.

2759   Gadt, Jeanette C. Women and Protestant Culture: The Quaker Dissent From Puritanism. Ph.D., University of California-Los Angeles, 1974. 347p. UMI# 74-20269.

2760   Goldsmith, Myron D. William Hobson and the Founding of Quakerism in the Pacific Northwest. Ph.D., Boston University, 1962. 339p. UMI# 62-05542.

2761   Gragg, Larry D. Migration in Early America: The Virginia Quaker Experience. Ph.D., University of Missouri-Columbia, 1978. 190p. UMI# 79-06877.

2762   Griffith, Lee E. Line and Berry and Inlaid Furniture: A Regional Craft Tradition in Pennsylvania, 1682-1790. Ph.D., University of Pennsylvania, 1988. 278p. UMI# 8824743.

2763   Grundy, Martha P. "In the World But Not of It": Quaker Faith and the Dominant Culture, Middletown Meeting, Bucks County, Pennsylvania, 1750-1850. Ph.D., Case Western Reserve University, 1990. 343p. UMI# 9035282.

2764   Hagglund, Carol. Disowned Without Just Cause: Quakers in Rochester, Massachusetts, During the Eighteenth Century. Ph.D., University of Massachusetts, 1980. 344p. UMI# 80-12607.

2765   Hamm, Thomas D. The Transformation of American Quakerism, 1800-1910. Ph.D., Indiana University, 1985. 407p. UMI# 8516638.

2766   Henley, David E. The Society of Friends and Creative Peace. Making a Study in Social Values. Ph.D., University of Southern California, 1935.

2767   Hershberger, Guy F. Quaker Pacifism and the Provincial Government of Pennsylvania, 1682-1756. Ph.D., University of Iowa, 1936.

2768   Hickey, Damon D. The Quakers in the New South, 1865-1920. Ph.D., University of South Carolina, 1989. 248p. UMI# 9005117.

2769   Hilty, Hiram H. North Carolina Quakers and Slavery. Ph.D., Duke University, 1969. 381p. UMI# 69-16757.

2770   Holtzclaw, Louis R. Newport, Indiana: A Study of Quaker Ante-Bellum Reform. Ed.D., Ball State University, 1975. 163p. UMI# 76-16468.

2771   Jones, Louis T. The Quakers of Iowa. Ph.D., University of Iowa, 1913. 354p.

2772   Kerr, Russell N. The Trans-Allegheny Movement of the Society of Friends. Ph.D., Lutheran School of Theology, 1963.

2773   Kobrin, David R. The Saving Remnant: Intellectual Sources of Change and Decline in Colonial Quakerism, 1690-1810. Ph.D., University of Pennsylvania, 1968. 350p. UMI# 69-05637.

2774   Le Shana, David C. Friends in California: A Study of the Effect of Nineteenth Century Revivalism Upon Western Quakerism. Ph.D., University of Southern California, 1967. 326p. UMI# 68-01196.

2775   Magee, John B., Jr. Sri Ramakrishna and John Woolman: A Study in the Sociology of Sanctity. Ph.D., Harvard University, 1950.

2776   Marietta, Jack D. Ecclesiastical Discipline in the Society of Friends, 1682-1776. Ed.D., Stanford University, 1968. 221p. UMI# 69-08223.

2777   McCormick, Jo A. The Quakers of Colonial South Carolina 1670-1807. Ph.D., University of South Carolina, 1984. 226p. UMI# 8419065.

2778   McGinty, Claudius L. Quakerism: Its Rise, Content, and Tendencies. Ph.D., Southern Baptist Theological Seminary, 1913.

2779   Meinke, Robert J. The Sociology of Inner-Worldly Mysticism: Freedom, Power and Authority in the Society of Friends. Ph.D., New School for Social Research, 1983. 196p. UMI# 8329137.

2780   Mekeel, Arthur J. The Society of Friends and the American Revolution. Ph.D., Harvard University, 1940. 166p.

2781   Meyerson, Joel D. A Quaker Commonwealth: Society and the Public Order in Pennsylvania, 1681-1765. Ph.D., Harvard University, 1971.

2782   Nelson, Jacquelyn S. The Society of Friends in Indiana During the Civil War. Ph.D., Ball State University, 1984. 343p. UMI# 8410457.

2783   Norton, James H. Quakers West of the Alleghenies and in Ohio to 1861. Ph.D., Case Western Reserve University, 1965. 370p. UMI# 66-05205.

2784   Radbill, Kenneth A. Socioeconomic Background of Nonpacifist Quakers During the American Revolution. Ph.D., University of Arizona, 1971. 149p. UMI# 71-28659.

2785   Reuben, Odell R. Peace Against Justice: A Nineteenth-Century Dilemma of Quaker Conscience. Ph.D., Duke University, 1970.

2786   Rothenberg, Diane B. Friends like These: An Ethnohistorical Analysis of the Interaction Between Allegany Senecas and Quakers,

1798-1823. Ph.D., City University of New York, 1976. 275p. UMI# 76-11970.

2787   Sheeran, Michael J. Friendly Persuasion: Voteless Decisions in the Religious Society of Friends. Ph.D., Princeton University, 1977. 250p. UMI# 78-00273.

2788   Tolles, Frederick B. The Quaker Merchants of Colonial Philadelphia, 1682-1763: A Study in Social and Cultural History. Ph.D., Harvard University, 1947. 210p.

2789   Wahl, Albert J. Congregational or Progressive Friends in the Pre-Civil-War Reform Movement. Ph.D., Temple University, 1951.

2790   Wells, Robert V. A Demographic Analysis of Some Middle Colony Quaker Families of the Eighteenth Century. Ph.D., Princeton University, 1969. 169p. UMI# 70-14249.

2791   White, Steven J. Early American Quakers and the Transatlantic Community, 1700-1756. Ph.D., University of Illinois at Urbana-Champaign, 1990. 313p. UMI# 9114459.

2792   Wood, Richard E. Evangelical Quakers in the Mississippi Valley, 1854-1894. Ph.D., University of Minnesota, 1985. 314p. UMI# 8519304.

2793   Worrall, Arthur J. New England Quakerism, 1656-1830. Ph.D., Indiana University, 1969. 247p. UMI# 69-18699.

2794   Yogg, Michael R. The Best Place for Health and Wealth: A Demographic and Economic Analysis of the Quakers of Pre-Industrial Bucks County, Pennsylvania. Ph.D., Harvard University, 1978.

Art and Architecture

2795   Lee-Whitman, Leanna. Silks and Simplicity: A Study of Quaker Dress as Depicted in Portraits, 1718-1855. Ph.D., University of Pennsylvania, 1987. 340p. UMI# 8714076.

Biography

2796   Allen, Jay T. The Guide for Ethics in the Thought of William Penn. Ph.D., Syracuse University, 1967. 476p. UMI# 6805442.

2797   Altman, Walter F. John Woolman's Reading. Ph.D., Florida State University, 1957. 297p. UMI# 23971.

2798   Amoroso, Kenneth S. Gerrard Winstanley: Secular Marxist or Religious Mystic. Ph.D., University of Toronto, 1976.

2799   Beatty, Edward C.O. The Social Philosophy of William Penn. Ph.D., University of Chicago, 1936.

2800   Bittle, William G. James Nayler: A Study in Seventeenth-Century Quakerism. Ph.D., Kent State University, 1975. 406p. UMI# 76-04912.

2801   Boroughs, Philip L. John Woolman (1720-1772): Spirituality and Social Transformation in Colonial America. Ph.D., Graduate Theological Union, 1989. 356p. UMI# 8924366.

2802   Brookes, George S. The Life and Letters of Anthony Benezet. Ph.D., Hartford Seminary Foundation, 1933.

2803   Camp, Hilliard D. William Penn and the Doctrine of Salvation. Ph.D., Case Western Reserve University, 1966. 372p. UMI# 6704630.

2804   Davison, Robert A. Isaac Hicks, Capitalist and Quaker, 1787-1820. Ph.D., New York University, 1956.

2805   Good, Donald G. Elisha Bates: American Quaker Evangelical in the Early Nineteenth Century. Ph.D., University of Iowa, 1967. 376p. UMI# 67-16793.

2806   Hopkins, Jon J. A Rhetorical Analysis of the Oratory of William Penn. Ph.D., Pennsylvania State University, 1961. 327p. UMI# 6102373.

2807   Hornick, Nancy S. Anthony Benezet: Eighteenth-Century Social Critic, Educator and Abolitionist. Ph.D., University of Maryland, 1974.

2808   Lashley, Leonard C. Anthony Benezet and His Anti-Slavery Activities. Ph.D., Fordham University, 1939.

2809   Lerner, Gerda. Abolitionists From South Carolina: A Life of Sarah and Angelina Grimke. Ph.D., Columbia University, 1966. 579p. UMI# 6915566.

2810   Livesay, Edith K. John Woolman: Persona and Person. Ph.D., University of Delaware, 1976. 319p. UMI# 7624248.

2811   Maples, Mary. A Cause to Plead: The Political Thought and Career of William Penn From 1660 to 1701. Ph.D., Bryn Mawr College, 1959. 263p. UMI# 5906990.

2812   Nelson, Russell S., Jr. Backcountry Pennsylvania (1709 to 1774): The Ideals of William Penn in Practice. Ph.D., University of Wisconsin-Madison, 1968. 370p. UMI# 6816012.

2813   Romanek, Carl L. John Reynell, Quaker Merchant of Colonial Philadelphia. Ph.D., Pennsylvania State University, 1969. 223p. UMI# 70-07244.

2814   Stewart, Roberta J. "Being a Child in the Father's House": The Life of Faith in the Published Works of Hannah Whitall Smith. Ph.D., Drew University, 1990. 247p. UMI# 9032132.

2815   Thayer, Theodore G. Israel Pemberton, King of the Quakers. Ph.D., University of Pennsylvania, 1941. 421p.

Education

2816   Babbidge, Homer D., Jr. Swarthmore College in the 19th Century: A Quaker Experience in Education. Ph.D., Yale University, 1953.

2817   Bickley, William P. Education as Reformation: An Examination of Orthodox Quakers' Formation of the Haverford School Association and Founding of Haverford School, 1815-1840. Ed.D., Harvard University, 1983. 314p.

2818   Dobbert, Marion L. The Friends at Clear Creek: Education and Change, 1830-1930. Ph.D., University of Wisconsin, 1973. UMI# 73-28323.

2819   Dunlap, William C. Quaker Education in Baltimore and Virginia. Yearly Meetings Based on the Manuscript Sources. Ph.D., University of Pennsylvania, 1933.

2820   Klain, Zora. Quaker Contributions to Education in North Carolina. Ph.D., University of Pennsylvania, 1924. 351p.

2821   Mendenhall, Raymond E. Quaker Contributions to American Education. Ph.D., New York University, 1925. 272p. UMI# 72-33647.

2822   Moore, George H. A History of the Curriculum and Instruction of William Penn College, 1873-1954. Ph.D., University of Iowa, 1954. 232p. UMI# 10231.

2823   Woody, Thomas. Early Quaker Education in Pennsylvania. Ph.D., Columbia University, 1918. 287p.

Ethnic Groups

2824   Carter, Max L. Quaker Relations With Midwestern Indians to 1833. Ph.D., Temple University, 1989. 290p. UMI# 8920223.

2825   Levy, Barry J. The Light in the Valley: The Chester and Welsh Tract Quaker Communities and the Delaware Valley, 1681-1750. Ph.D., University of Pennsylvania, 1976. 279p. UMI# 77-00855.

Evangelism

2826   Farr, Wendell G. The Background of the Revival Movement in Indiana Yearly Meeting of the Religious Society of Friends. Ph.D., Hartford Seminary Foundation, 1933.

Literature

2827   Bitterman, Mary G.F. The Early Quaker Literature of Defense. Ph.D., Bryn Mawr College, 1971.

2828   Heller, Michael A. Soft Persuasion: A Rhetorical Analysis of John Woolman's Essays and *Journal*. Ph.D., Arizona State University, 1989. 284p. UMI# 8919608.

2829   Hoy, Joan M. The Publication and Distribution of Books Among New England Quakers, 1775-1836. Ph.D., Boston University, 1989. 366p. UMI# 8917619.

2830   Levenduski, Cristine M. Elizabeth Ashbridge's *Remarkable Experiences*: Creating the Self in a Quaker Personal Narrative. Ph.D., University of Minnesota, 1989. 234p. UMI# 9003005.

Music

2831   Linder, John M. William Evander Penn: His Contribution to Church Music. D.M.A., Southwestern Baptist Theological Seminary, 1985. UMI# 0556707.

Social Programs

2832   Abend, Rosemary. Constant Samaritans: Quaker Philanthropy in Philadelphia, 1680-1799. Ph.D., University of California-Los Angeles, 1988. 282p. UMI# 8813362.

2833   Cromwell, Paul F. The "Holy Experiment": An Examination of the Influence of the Society of Friends Upon the Development and Evolution of American Correctional Philosophy. Ph.D., Florida State University, 1986. 211p. UMI# 8612198.

2834   Drake, Thomas E. Northern Quakers and Slavery. Ph.D., Yale University, 1933.

2835   Foster, Richard J. Quaker Concern in Race Relations Then and Now. Ph.D., Fuller Theological Seminary, 1970.

2836   Gladfelter, Valerie G. Caring and Control: The Social Psychology of an Authoritative Group, The Burlington (NJ) Friends Meeting, 1678-1720. D.S.W., University of Pennsylvania, 1983. 172p. UMI# 8322502.

2837   James, Sydney V., Jr. The Benevolence of American Friends Before 1810: Christian Charity, Justice and Humanitarianism, Interpreted and Practiced by the Society of the People Called Quakers. Ph.D., Harvard University, 1958.

2838   Jones, Lester M. Quakers in Action: Recent Humanitarian and Reform Activities of the American Quakers. Ph.D., University of Wisconsin, 1927. 226p.

2839   Milner, Clyde A., II. With Good Intentions: Quaker Work and Indian Survival; The Nebraska Case, 1869-1882. Ph.D., Yale University, 1979. 492p. UMI# 7926661.

2840   Popiden, John R. Christians and Punishment by the State: Ethical Reflection on the Contribution of Some Pennsylvania Quakers. Ph.D., University of Notre Dame, 1980. 196p. UMI# 80-28470.

2841   Qualls, Youra T. Friend and Freedman: The Work of the Association of Friends of Philadelphia and Its Vicinity for the Relief and Education of Freedmen During the Civil War and Reconstruction, 1862-1872. Ph.D., Radcliffe College, 1956.

2842   Soderlund, Jean R. Conscience, Interest, and Power: The Development of Quaker Opposition to Slavery in the Delaware Valley, 1688-1780. Ph.D., Temple University, 1982. 407p. UMI# 82-10558.

Theology

2843   Barrus, Paul W. Emerson and Quakerism. Ph.D., University of Iowa, 1950. 199p.

2844   Endy, Melvin B., Jr. William Penn and Early Quakerism: A Theological Study. Ph.D., Yale University, 1969. UMI# 70-02727.

SPIRITUALISM

2845   Bednarowski, Mary F. Nineteenth-Century American Spiritualism: An Attempt at a Scientific Religion. Ph.D., University of Minnesota, 1973. 198p. UMI# 7325581.

2846   Braude, Ann D. Spiritualism, Reform and Woman's Rights in Nineteenth Century America. Ph.D., Yale University, 1987. 372p. UMI# 9019007.

2847   Brown, Burton G., Jr. Spiritualism in Nineteenth-Century America. Ph.D., Boston University, 1973. 366p. UMI# 7314130.

2848   Delp, Robert W. The Harmonial Philosopher, Andrew Jackson Davis, and the Foundation of Modern American Spiritualism. Ph.D., George Washington University, 1965.

2849   Fuller, Robert C. The American Mesmerists, 1835-1900. Ph.D., University of Chicago, 1978.

2850   Isaacs, Ernest J. A History of Nineteenth-Century American Spiritualism as a Religious and Social Movement. Ph.D., University of Wisconsin-Madison, 1975. 397p. UMI# 75-20774.

2851   O'Sullivan, Michael A. A Harmony of Worlds: Spiritualism and the Quest for Community in Nineteenth-Century America. Ph.D., University of Southern California, 1981.

2852   Rakow, Mary M. Melinda Rankin and Magdalen Hayden: Evangelical and Catholic Forms of Nineteenth Century Christian Spirituality. Ph.D., Boston College, 1982. 645p. UMI# 8215662.

SWEDENBORG

2853   Block, Marguerite B. The New Church in the New World: A Study of Swedenborgianism in America. Ph.D., Columbia University, 1932. 462p.

2854   Calathello, Robert L. The Basic Philosophy of Emanuel Swedenborg, With Implications for Western Education. Ed.D., University of Southern California, 1966. 210p. UMI# 66-08777.

2855   Silver, Richard K. The Spiritual Kingdom in America: The Influence of Emanuel Swedenborg on American Society and Culture: 1815-1860. Ph.D., Stanford University, 1983. 350p. UMI# 8329776.

2856   Swank, Scott T. The Unfettered Conscience: A Study of Sectarianism, Spiritualism, and Social Reform in the New Jerusalem

Church, 1840-1870. Ph.D., University of Pennsylvania, 1970. 525p. UMI# 7025740.

THEOSOPHY

2857   Linville, William R. Helena Petrovna Blavatsky, Theosophy, and American Thought. Ph.D., University of Hawaii, 1983.

2858   Mody, Cawas M. The Political Thought of Mrs. Annie Besant: The English Years (1847-1893). Ph.D., University of Kansas, 1973. 496p. UMI# 7330847.

TRACTARIAN

2859   Mussina, Malcolm V. The Background and Origins of the American Religious Tract Movement. Ph.D., Drew University, 1936.

2860   Neufeldt, Harvey G. The American Tract Society, 1825-1865: An Examination of Its Religious, Economic, Social, and Political Ideas. Ph.D., Michigan State University, 1971. 566p. UMI# 72-08750.

2861   Slocum, Stephen E., Jr. The American Tract Society: 1825-1975. An Evangelical Effort to Influence the Religious and Moral Life of the United States. Ph.D., New York University, 1975. 273p. UMI# 76-12598.

2862   Wosh, Peter J. Bibles, Benevolence, and Emerging Bureaucracy: The Persistence of the American Bible Society, 1816-1890. Ph.D., New York University, 1988. 411p. UMI# 8910616.

TRANSCENDENTALISM

General Studies

2863   Albrecht, Robert C. The New England Transcendentalists' Response to the Civil War. Ph.D., University of Minnesota, 1962. 223p. UMI# 64-04079.

2864   Cannom, Charles W. The Influences Determining Emerson's Conception of Jesus. Ph.D., University of Iowa, 1937.

2865   Charvat, Charles C. Emerson and Catholicism. Ph.D., University of Iowa, 1940. 304p.

2866   Christy, Edward A. The Orient in American Transcendentalism: A Study of Emerson, Thoreau, and Alcott. Ph.D., Columbia University, 1932.

2867   Downs, Lenthiel H. Emerson and Dr. Channing. Ph.D., University of Iowa, 1940.

2868   Edrich, Mary W. Emerson's Apostasy. Ph.D., University of Wisconsin-Madison, 1965. 373p. UMI# 6506201.

2869   Erickson, John H. Emerson and the Transcendentalists: Their Attitudes Toward Puritanism. Ph.D., University of Chicago, 1973. 237p.

2870   Gawronski, Donald V. Transcendentalism: An Ideological Basis for Manifest Destiny. Ph.D., Saint Louis University, 1964. 235p. UMI# 64-13444.

2871   Goddard, Harold C. Studies in New England Transcendentalism. Ph.D., Columbia University, 1908. 217p.

2872   Goudie, Andrea K. Precursors of Humanistic, Existential, and Social Cognitive Approaches in American Psychology: The Contributions of Emerson and Thoreau. Ph.D., Texas Tech University, 1990. 266p. UMI# 9104823.

2873   Gray, Henry D. Emerson: A Statement of New England Transcendentalism as Expressed in the Philosophy of Its Chief Exponent. Ph.D., Columbia University, 1905. 110p.

2874   Grusin, Richard A. Interpretation and the Institution of the Self in New England Transcendentalism. Ph.D., University of California-Berkeley, 1983. 286p. UMI# 8328894.

2875   Gura, Philip F. The Philosophy of Language: The Dialogue in Transcendentalist Circles, 1820-54. Ph.D., Harvard University, 1977.

2876   Headington, Charles E. Americans in the Wilderness: A Study of Their Encounters With Otherness From the Initial Contact Through Henry David Thoreau. Ph.D., University of Chicago, 1985.

2877   Hotson, Clarence P. Emerson and Swedenborg. Ph.D., Harvard University, 1929.

2878   Huggard, William A. Emerson and the Problem of War and Peace. Ph.D., University of Iowa, 1938.

2879   Hutchison, William R. The Transcendentalists as Church Reformers. Ph.D., Yale University, 1956.

2880   Irvin, William J. The Idea of Power and the Experience of the

Sublime: Emerson's Transcendental Method. Ph.D., Harvard University, 1976.

2881   Johnson, Denis G. "Nature's" Nurture: Emerson and the Age of the Child. Ph.D., Rutgers University, 1978. 189p. UMI# 7901273.

2882   Jones, William C. The New England Transcendentalists and the Mexican War. Ph.D., University of Minnesota, 1970. 120p. UMI# 71-18756.

2883   Kim, Heisook. Transcendental Arguments, Objectivity, and the Nature of Philosophical Inquiry. Ph.D., University of Chicago, 1987.

2884   Lawton, John H. A Rhetorical Analysis of Representative Ceremonial Addresses of Ralph Waldo Emerson. Ph.D., University of Iowa, 1957. 350p. UMI# 23762.

2885   Lindner, Carl M. Ralph Waldo Emerson: The Conceptualization of Experience. Ph.D., University of Wisconsin-Madison, 1970. 205p. UMI# 7011843.

2886   Lyons, Eleanor J. The Parti-Colored Wheel: A Study of Emerson's Thought. Ph.D., University of Virginia, 1967. 233p. UMI# 6803114.

2887   Marrs, Suzanne. Ralph Waldo Emerson and the Eighteenth-Century English Moralists. Ph.D., University of Oklahoma, 1973. 188p. UMI# 7406972.

2888   McLennan, William G.L. Transcendentalism, 1832-1862. Ph.D., University of Toronto, 1973. [Bronson Alcott, Ralph Waldo Emerson, Margaret Fuller, Theodore Parker, Henry David Thoreau, Walt Whitman].

2889   Meese, Elizabeth A. Transcendental Vision: A History of the Doctrine of Correspondence and Its Role in American Transcendentalism. Ph.D., Wayne State University, 1972. 322p. UMI# 73-12568.

2890   Midy, Godefroy. Ralph Waldo Emerson's Philosophy of the Person. Ph.D., Fordham University, 1971. 207p. UMI# 7126981.

2891   Obuchowski, Peter A., Jr. The Relationship of Emerson's Interest in Science to His Thought. Ph.D., University of Michigan, 1969. 285p. UMI# 7004158.

2892   Paul, Sherman. The Angle of Vision and the Arc of the Circle: "Correspondence" in Emerson's Transcendental Vision. Ph.D., Harvard University, 1950.

2893   Porter, Lawrence C. New England Transcendentalism: A Self-Portrait. Ed.D., University of Michigan, 1964. 255p. UMI# 65-05363.

2894   Rao, Adapa R. Emerson's Attitude Toward Humanitarian Reform. Ph.D., University of Wisconsin-Madison, 1964. 214p. UMI# 6410296.

2895   Rein, Irving J. The New England Transcendentalists: Rhetoric of Paradox. Ph.D., University of Pittsburgh, 1966. 201p. UMI# 6703041.

2896   Santas, Constantine. Emerson's Theory of the Hero. Ph.D., Northwestern University, 1971. 226p. UMI# 7130941.

2897   Schamberger, John E. Emerson's Concept of the "Moral Sense": A Study of Its Sources and Its Importance to His Intellectual Development. Ph.D., University of Pennsylvania, 1969. 200p. UMI# 7016207.

2898   Shukla, Kamal K. Emerson and Hindu Thought. Ph.D., Wayne State University, 1973. 283p. UMI# 7411156.

2899   Silver, Mildred. Emerson and the Idea of Progress. Ph.D., University of Iowa, 1939.

2900   Thurin, Erik I. Love and Friendship: Emerson and the Platonic Tradition. Ph.D., University of Minnesota, 1970. 483p. UMI# 7027198.

2901   Turpie, Mary C. The Growth of Emerson's Thought. Ph.D., University of Minnesota, 1944.

2902   Vance, William S. Carlyle and the American Transcendentalists. Ph.D., University of Chicago, 1941. 445p.

2903   Versluis, Arthur J. Ex Oriente Lux: American Transcendentalism and the Orient. Ph.D., University of Michigan, 1990. 352p. UMI# 9034535.

2904   Wicke, Myron F. Emerson's Mysticism. Ph.D., Case Western Reserve University, 1941.

2905   Wilson, John B. Activities of the New England Transcendentalists in the Dissemination of Culture. Ph.D., University of North Carolina-Chapel Hill, 1941. 425p.

2906   Wood, Barry A. Order and Method in Emerson. Ph.D., Stanford University, 1974. 419p. UMI# 7506942.

2907   Wortman, Marc J. The Idea of Natural History in Cultural Criticism: Emerson's Uses of Goethe. Ph.D., Princeton University, 1987. 375p. UMI# 8709209.

Biography

2908   Abbott, John P. Emerson and the Conduct of Life: The Early Years. Ph.D., University of Iowa, 1940.

2909   Bennett, Fordyce R. Bronson Alcott: The Transcendental Reformer as Educator. Ph.D., University of Illinois at Urbana-Champaign, 1976. 440p. UMI# 7624042.

2910   Bilbo, Q.M. Elizabeth Palmer Peabody, Transcendentalist. Ph.D., New York University, 1932. UMI# 7320687.

2911   Buell, Lawrence I. Emerson: From Preacher to Poet. Ph.D., Cornell University, 1966. 196p. UMI# 6701450.

2912   Cummins, Roger W. The Second Eden: Charles Lane and American Transcendentalism. Ph.D., University of Minnesota, 1967. 307p. UMI# 68-01640.

2913   Fertig, Walter L. John Sullivan Dwight, Transcendentalist and Literary Amateur of Music. Ph.D., University of Maryland, 1953. 345p.

2914   George, Roger A. The Transcendental Traveler. Ph.D., University of Washington, 1986. 290p. UMI# 8706561.[Henry David Thoreau].

2915   Gougeon, Leonard G. The Forgotten God: A Study of Ralph Waldo Emerson as Man and Myth. Ph.D., University of Massachusetts, 1974. 181p. UMI# 74-25895.

2916   Heath, William G., Jr. Cyrus Bartol, Transcendentalist: An Early Critic of Emerson. Ph.D., University of Minnesota, 1970. 206p. UMI# 7108260.

2917   Hoffman, Richard E. Ralph Waldo Emerson: His Reasons for Leaving the Ministry. Ph.D., Bowling Green State University, 1989. 229p. UMI# 9011620.

2918   Hourihan, Paul. The Inner Dynamics of the Emerson-Thoreau Relationship. Ph.D., Boston University, 1967. 393p. UMI# 6713301.

2919   Hudspeth, Robert N. The Casual Transcendentalist Ellery Channing. Ph.D., Syracuse University, 1967. 215p. UMI# 6807063.

2920   Hutch, Richard A. The Self and the Phenomenal World: A Structural Biographical Study of the Early Life of Ralph Waldo Emerson From 1803 to 1838. Ph.D., University of Chicago, 1974.

2921   Jeswine, Miriam A. Henry David Thoreau: Apprentice to the Hindu Sages. Ph.D., University of Oregon, 1971. 241p. UMI# 7200939.

2922   Jordan, Thornton F. Dependence and Initiative: The Psychological Framework in Emerson's Life and Works. Ph.D., Indiana University, 1977. 307p. UMI# 7722659.

2923   Keller, Michael R. Henry David Thoreau: Mystic. Ed.D., Ball State University, 1977. 334p. UMI# 7715316.

2924   Kenney, Stephen A.O. Home Grown: The Native American Spirituality of Henry David Thoreau. Ph.D., State University of New York-Buffalo, 1989. 260p. UMI# 9013066.

2925   Kopp, Charles C. The Mysticism of Henry David Thoreau. Ph.D., Pennsylvania State University, 1963. 449p. UMI# 6405372.

2926   Lockwood, Francis C. Emerson as a Philosopher. Ph.D., Northwestern University, 1896.

2927   Miller, Frederick D. Christopher Pearse Cranch: Transcendentalist. Ph.D., University of Virginia, 1942. 177p.

2928   Morgan, Bradford A. Thoreau's Maine Woods: Transcendental Traveler in a Primordial Landscape. Ph.D., University of Denver, 1978. 332p. UMI# 7910676.

2929   Packer, Barbara L. Emerson's Apocalypse of Mind. Ph.D., Yale University, 1973. 212p. UMI# 7411623.

2930   Paulits, F. Joseph. Emerson's Concept of Good and Evil. Ph.D., University of Pittsburgh, 1955. 338p. UMI# 11602.

2931   Paulson, Arthur B. The Transparent Eyeball: Identity and Young Man Emerson, a Psychoanalytic Study. Ph.D., State University of New York-Buffalo, 1974. 225p. UMI# 7507784.

2932   Rice, Fredrica D. Emerson's Debt to Natural Science During His Early Life and Work. Ph.D., University of Washington, 1984. 224p. UMI# 8412414.

2933   Tranquilla, Ronald E. Henry David Thoreau and the New England Transcendentalists. Ph.D., University of Pittsburgh, 1973. 173p. UMI# 74-18414.

2934   Welch, Althea R. The Way and the Life: Bronson Alcott's Private Revelation. Ph.D., University of Dallas, 1976. 328p. UMI# 8008390.

2935   Wells, Ronald V. Three Christian Transcendentalists: James Marsh, Caleb Sprague Henry, Frederic Henry Hedge. Ph.D., Columbia University, 1944.

Church and State

2936   Flanagan, John T. Emerson and the State. Ph.D., University of Minnesota, 1935.

Education

2937   Foy, Rena L.W. The Philosophy of Ralph Waldo Emerson and Its Educational Implications. Ph.D., University of Texas-Austin, 1962. 380p. UMI# 6204838.

2938   Kennedy, Steele M. Emerson's *The American Scholar*, and the Other Harvard Phi Beta Kappa Operations. Ph.D., New York University, 1956. 750p. UMI# 17653.

2939   Olson, Wayne C. Emerson, Thoreau and Fuller: Transcendentalist Insights for Education. Ed.D., Columbia University Teachers College, 1980. 192p. UMI# 80-22142.

Ethnic Groups

2940   Groth, John H.C. German Backgrounds of American Transcendentalism: Prolegomena to the Study of Influence. Ph.D., University of Washington, 1941. 617p.

2941   Vogel, Stanley M. The Influence of German Culture on the New England Transcendentalists From 1810 to 1840. Ph.D., Yale University, 1949.

Historiography

2942   Adams, John M. The Philosophical Historian: Emerson's Theory of History. Ph.D., University of Kansas, 1960. 192p. UMI# 6100265.

2943   Lerner, Saul. The Concepts of History, Progress and Perfectibility in Nineteenth Century American Transcendentalist Thought. Ph.D., University of Kansas, 1966. 405p. UMI# 68-05105.

Literature

2944   Albanese, Catherine L. Charon and the River: The Changing

Religious Symbols of Six American Transcendentalists. Ph.D., University of Chicago, 1972. 333p. [Amos B. Alcott, Ralph Waldo Emerson, Theodore Parker, Henry David Thoreau].

2945   Amacher, Richard E. The Literary Reputation of Ralph Waldo Emerson, 1882-1945. Ph.D., University of Pittsburgh, 1947.

2946   Arnold, Rebecca L. Toward Heaven Still: Henry Thoreau's Last Natural History Essays. Ph.D., University of Missouri-Columbia, 1989. 188p. UMI# 8925269.

2947   Baker, Robert H. The Unsettled Wilderness: Aspects of Existential Phenomenology in the Works of Henry David Thoreau. Ph.D., University of Texas-Austin, 1979. 215p. UMI# 7928259.

2948   Barber, Patricia G. Ralph Waldo Emerson's Antislavery Notebook, *Wo Liberty*. Ph.D., University of Massachusetts, 1975. 258p. UMI# 7527567.

2949   Baumgartner, Alexander M. Associationism and Emerson's Prose Style, 1819-1841. Ph.D., University of Pennsylvania, 1971. 213p. UMI# 7217324.

2950   Berke, Richard D. The Transcendental Economics of Thoreau's *Walden*. Ph.D., Columbia University, 1980. 215p. UMI# 8023477.

2951   Blansett, Barbara R. Melville and Emersonian Transcendentalism. Ph.D., University of Texas-Austin, 1963. 210p. UMI# 64-00042.

2952   Bogart, Herbert. Ralph Waldo Emerson: Self and Society, 1850-1870. Ph.D., New York University, 1963. 433p. UMI# 6410052.

2953   Bowden, Larry R. Emerson's *Illusions*: The Essay and the Idea in Transcendental Perspective. Ph.D., Drew University, 1979. UMI# 80-12339.

2954   Brickett, Elsie F. Studies in the Poets and Poetry of New England Transcendentalism. Ph.D., Yale University, 1937.

2955   Burns, John R. Thoreau's Use of the Bible. Ph.D., University of Notre Dame, 1966. 242p. UMI# 67-06092.

2956   Burress, Lee A., Jr. The Relationship of Christian Theology to the Idea Content of Emerson's Poetry. Ph.D., Boston University, 1955. 930p.

2957   Cadava, Eduardo L. Nature's Politics: Emerson and the Institution of American Letters. Ph.D., University of California-Irvine, 1988. 275p. UMI# 8820674.

2958   Carson, Barbara H. Orpheus in New England: Alcott, Emerson, and Thoreau. Ph.D., Johns Hopkins University, 1968. 223p. UMI# 6816401.

2959   Dennis, Carl E. The Poetry of Mind and Nature: A Study of the Idea of Nature in American Transcendental Poetry. Ph.D., University of California-Berkeley, 1966. 360p. UMI# 66-15381.

2960   Duncan, Jeffrey L. Power and Form: The Theme of Dualism in Emerson's Work. Ph.D., University of Virginia, 1965. 260p. UMI# 6603149.

2961   Dunn, Elizabeth S. "A Deranged Balance": Emerson's Creator in the Finite. Ph.D., University of North Carolina-Chapel Hill, 1985. 196p. UMI# 8527273.

2962   Fink, Steven S. Prophet in the Marketplace: Thoreau's Early Development as a Professional Writer. Ph.D., University of Washington, 1981. 477p. UMI# 8126101.

2963   Francis, Elamanamadathil V. Emerson and the Hindu Scriptures. Ph.D., Howard University, 1970. 251p. UMI# 7214019.

2964   Furbush, Elisabeth B. The Epistemic Transformation: Emerson and Freedom in Light of *Advaita* Vedanta. Ph.D., Syracuse University, 1988. 407p. UMI# 8907873.

2965   Gervich, Don S. The Writer and the Mystic: Henry David Thoreau. Ed.D., Boston University, 1979. 346p. UMI# 7923862.

2966   Gilbert, Armida J. Emerson and the English Romantic Poets. Ph.D., University of South Carolina, 1989. 394p. UMI# 9017124.

2967   Grice, Stephen E. Death in the Writings of Henry David Thoreau. Ph.D., University of Utah, 1984. 305p. UMI# 8406432.

2968   Hall, Gary R. Emerson and the Bible: Transcendentalism as Scriptural Interpretation and Revision. Ph.D., University of California-Los Angeles, 1989. 408p. UMI# 8919917.

2969   Hansen, Arlen J. Emerson's Poetry of Thought. Ph.D., University of Iowa, 1969. 194p. UMI# 7004367.

2970   Harding, Brian R. "Transcendental Symbolism" in the Works of

Emerson, Thoreau, and Whitman. Ph.D., Brown University, 1971. 333p. UMI# 72-12045.

2971 Hellal, Farida. Emerson's Knowledge and Use of Islamic Literature. Ph.D., University of Houston, 1971. 413p. UMI# 7216944.

2972 Hill, David W. Emerson's Search for the Universal Symbol. Ph.D., Indiana University, 1971. 165p. UMI# 7129576.

2973 Hodder, Alan D. Emerson's Rhetoric of Revelation: Nature, the Reader, and the Apocalypse Within. Ph.D., Harvard University, 1986. 234p. UMI# 8620569.

2974 Hopkins, Vivian C. The Aesthetic Theory of Ralph Waldo Emerson. Ph.D., University of Michigan, 1944.

2975 Ihrig, Mary A. Emerson's Transcendental Vocabulary: An Expositional Analysis and Concordance to Seven Word-Clusters in His Prose. Ph.D., University of North Carolina-Chapel Hill, 1973. 795p. UMI# 7326188.

2976 Jordan, Leah E. The Fundamentals of Emerson's Literary Criticism. Ph.D., University of Pennsylvania, 1945.

2977 Kane, T. Paul. The Stairway of Surprise: Form and Power in Emerson's Poetry. Ph.D., Yale University, 1990. 454p. UMI# 9101272.

2978 Kloeckner, Alfred J. The Moral Sentiment: A Study of Emerson's Moral Terminology. Ph.D., Indiana University, 1956. 231p. UMI# 19465.

2979 Kurtz, Kenneth. The Sources and Development of Emerson's *Representative Men*. Ph.D., Yale University, 1947. 447p. UMI# 6610954.

2980 Lawrence, Robert W. Essays on Epistemology in American Transcendentalism. Ph.D., University of Nebraska-Lincoln, 1990. 101p. UMI# 9030134.[Ralph Waldo Emerson, Margaret Fuller, Theodore Parker].

2981 Lee, Leon H., Sr. The Historical and Literary Context of Henry David Thoreau's *Civil Disobedience*. D.A., Middle Tennessee State University, 1990. 196p. UMI# 9026933.

2982 Long, Larry R. *Walden* and the Bible: A Study in Influence and Composition. Ph.D., Ohio State University, 1976. 176p. UMI# 7710564.

2983   Mauldin, Jane E. *On That Shaded Day*: Ralph Waldo Emerson's Response to Suffering. D.Min., Meadville/Lombard Theological School, 1981.

2984   Maulsby, David L. The Contribution of Emerson to Literature. Ph.D., University of Chicago, 1909.

2985   McInerney, Peter F. Edenist Literary Statesmanship and *The Writings of Henry Thoreau*. Ph.D., Johns Hopkins University, 1977. 272p. UMI# 77-19598.

2986   Metzger, Charles R. The Transcendental Esthetics in America: Essays on Emerson, Greenough, Thoreau, and Whitman. Ph.D., University of Washington, 1954. 408p. UMI# 08357.

2987   Miller, Lee W. Emerson and the New Testament. Ph.D., Louisiana State University, 1953. 345p.

2988   Mott, Wesley T. Emerson and Thoreau as Heirs to the Tradition of New England Puritanism. Ph.D., Boston University, 1975. 251p. UMI# 75-12259.

2989   Neal, Valerie S. Transcendental Optics: Science, Vision, and Imagination in the Works of Emerson and Thoreau. Ph.D., University of Minnesota, 1979. 143p. UMI# 7918376.

2990   Osborne, Clifford H. Emerson's Reading. Ph.D., Indiana University, 1936.

2991   Page, Lane V. Emerson's "Agony" Towards a Reinterpretation of Transcendentalism. Ph.D., Saint Louis University, 1975. 212p. UMI# 76-22578.

2992   Porte, Joel M. Emerson and Thoreau: Transcendentalists in Conflict. Ph.D., Harvard University, 1962.

2993   Roberts, James R. Seventeenth Century Contributions to Emerson's Thought. Ph.D., University of Washington, 1940.

2994   Robinson, David M. The Context and Development of Emerson's Philosophy of Human Culture. Ph.D., University of Wisconsin-Madison, 1976. 272p. UMI# 7628934.

2995   Rogers, Jane E. The Transcendental Quest in Emerson and Melville. Ph.D., University of Pittsburgh, 1973. 189p. UMI# 7418413.

2996   Ronda, Bruce A. The Transcendental Child: Images and Concepts of the Child in American Transcendentalism. Ph.D., Yale University, 1975. 415p. UMI# 76-13750.

2997   Rosa, Alfred F. A Study of Transcendentalism in Salem With Special Reference to Nathaniel Hawthorne. Ph.D., University of Massachusetts, 1971. 226p. UMI# 71-23642.

2998   Srinath, Closepet N. Aspects of Transcendentalist Literary Criticism: An Anthology. Ph.D., University of Utah, 1974. 157p. UMI# 75-12511.

2999   Stuart, John A. Emerson's Nature: Its Relation to Coleridge's Transcendental Idealism. Ph.D., Northwestern University, 1946. 292p.

3000   Sturm, Rita L. The Dialectic Imagery in Emerson's *The Conduct of Life*. Ph.D., University of New Mexico, 1976. 229p. UMI# 7716121.

3001   Summerlin, Charles T. The Possible Oracle: Three Transcendentalist Poets. Ph.D., Yale University, 1973. 151p. UMI# 73-29485.[Ralph Waldo Emerson, Very Jones, Henry David Thoreau].

3002   Tan, Hongbo. Emerson, Thoreau, and the Four Books: Transcendentalism and the Neo-Confucian Classics in Historical Context. Ph.D., Washington State University, 1989. 350p. UMI# 9016019.

3003   Taylor, John F. A Search for Eden: Thoreau's Heroic Quest. Ph.D., University of Maryland, 1971. 137p. UMI# 72-01652.

3004   Turner, Robert C. Emersonian France: The Influence of French Culture and French Literature Upon Emerson Before 1850. Ph.D., Yale University, 1935.

3005   Waters, Laura O. Hymns of the Pearl: Gnostic Impulses in Emerson and Melville. Ph.D., State University of New York-Binghamton, 1990. 283p. UMI# 9028131.

3006   Whitaker, Rosemary. *A Week on the Concord and Merrimack Rivers*: An Experiment in the Communication of Transcendental Experience. Ph.D., University of Oklahoma, 1970. 164p. UMI# 70-14437.

3007   Widdicombe, Richard T. Continuity and Change: The Influence of Transcendentalism on Nineteenth-Century American Literature. Ph.D., University of California-Irvine, 1984. 438p. UMI# 8427823.

3008   Williams, Paul O. The Transcendental Movement in American

Poetry. Ph.D., University of Pennsylvania, 1962. 504p. UMI# 62-04353.

3009 Wynkoop, William M. Three Children of the Universe: Emerson's View of Shakespeare, Bacon, and Milton. Ph.D., Columbia University, 1962. 247p. UMI# 6301533.

3010 Zwirn, Gail S. Ralph Waldo Emerson as Mystic: A Study of His "Double-Consciousness." Ph.D., University of Pittsburgh, 1981. 175p. UMI# 8213123.

Music

3011 Kavanaugh, James V. Music and American Transcendentalism: A Study of Transcendental Pythagoreanism in the Works of Henry David Thoreau, Nathaniel Hawthorne and Charles Ives. Ph.D., Yale University, 1978. 270p. UMI# 78-19501.

3012 Rider, Daniel E. The Musical Thought and Activities of the New England Transcendentalists. Ph.D., University of Minnesota, 1964. 341p. UMI# 6515319.

Newspapers and Periodicals

3013 Gohdes, Clarence L.F. The Periodicals of American Transcendentalism. Ph.D., Columbia University, 1931. 264p.

3014 Green, Judith A. Religion, Life, and Literature in the *Western Messenger*. Ph.D., University of Wisconsin-Madison, 1981. 657p. UMI# 8120306.

3015 Habich, Robert D. The History and Achievement of the *Western Messenger*, 1835-1841. Ph.D., Pennsylvania State University, 1982. 365p. UMI# 8228894.

3016 Mueller, Roger C. The Orient in American Transcendental Periodicals (1835-1886). Ph.D., University of Minnesota, 1968. 240p. UMI# 69-01525.

3017 Reuben, Paul P. Dynamics of New England Transcendentalism in Benjamin Orange Flower's *Arena* (1889-1909). Ph.D., Bowling Green State University, 1970. 138p. UMI# 71-06765.

Preaching

3018 Tester, Sue K. Ralph Waldo Emerson's Sermons: A Critical Introduction. Ph.D., Boston University, 1978. 344p. UMI# 7819835.

3019 Wider, Sarah A. The "Building of Discourse" in Emerson's Sermons. Ph.D., Cornell University, 1986. 307p. UMI# 8628415.

Social Programs

3020 Coleman, William E., Jr. The Role of Prophet in the Abolition Rhetoric of the Reverend Theodore Parker, 1845-1860. Ph.D., Ohio State University, 1974. 194p. UMI# 7503032.

3021 Erlich, Michael G. Selected Anti-Slavery Speeches of Henry David Thoreau, 1848-1859: A Rhetorical Analysis. Ph.D., Ohio State University, 1970. 341p. UMI# 7107446.

3022 Glick, Wendell. Thoreau and Radical Abolitionism: A Study of the Native Background of Thoreau's Social Philosophy. Ph.D., Northwestern University, 1950.

3023 Rose, Anne C. Transcendentalism as a Social Movement, 1830-1850. Ph.D., Yale University, 1979. 417p. UMI# 80-11545.

3024 Straube, Arvid. Transcendentalism and the New Age: The Inseparability of Spiritual Growth and Social Action. D.Min., Meadville/Lombard Theological School, 1979.

Theology

3025 Barnett, Peter H. Retreat From Idealism: Emersonian Themes in American Religious Philosophy. Ph.D., Columbia University, 1970. 282p. UMI# 7117464.

3026 Clendenning, John L. Emerson's Response to Skepticism. Ph.D., University of Iowa, 1962. 222p. UMI# 6202382.

3027 Detweiler, Robert. Emerson's Concept of God. Ph.D., University of Florida, 1962. 349p. UMI# 68-12959.

3028 Gelpi, Donald L. Emerson's Philosophy of Religious Experience. Ph.D., Fordham University, 1970. 778p. UMI# 7108715.

3029 Gordon-McCutchan, Robert C. Fate Into Freedom: Emerson's Philosophy of Spiritual Process. Ph.D., Princeton University, 1980. 331p. UMI# 8101539.

3030 Ireland, Robert E. The Concept of Providence in the Thought of William Ellery Channing, Ralph Waldo Emerson, Theodore Parker, and Orestes A. Brownson: A Study in Mid-Nineteenth-Century American Intellectual History. Ph.D., University of Maine, 1972. 241p. UMI# 7313073.

3031   Keating, Annlouise. Beyond the Fall: Emerson's Redemptive Epistemology. Ph.D., University of Illinois-Chicago, 1990. 304p. UMI# 9104468.

3032   Le, Van-Diem. Puritan Idealism and the Transcendental Movement. Ph.D., University of Minnesota, 1960. 205p. UMI# 60-05161.

3033   Lee, Roland F. Emerson and Christian Existentialism. Ph.D., Ohio State University, 1952. 320p. UMI# 5800790.

3034   Moran, Virginia A. This Guiding Identity: The Evolution of Ralph Waldo Emerson's Ontology. Ph.D., New York University, 1978. 189p. UMI# 7824255.

3035   Smith, John S. The Philosophical Naturism of Henry David Thoreau With Special Reference to Its Epistemological Presuppositions and Theological Implications. Ph.D., Drew University, 1948. 360p.

3036   Tenzis, Louis. Ralph Waldo Emerson's Approach to God. Ph.D., Loyola University of Chicago, 1970.

3037   Williams, Wallace E. Emerson and the Moral Law. Ph.D., University of California-Berkeley, 1963. 614p. UMI# 6402155.

UNITARIAN

General Studies

3038   Bartlett, Laile E. Unitarian Fellowships: A Case Study in Liberal Religious Development. Ph.D., University of California-Berkeley, 1966. 613p. UMI# 6708517.

3039   Basden, James. A Study in the Rise of Early American Unitarianism. Ph.D., Southwestern Baptist Theological Seminary, 1956.

3040   Chable, Eugene R. A Study of the Interpretation of the New Testament in New England Unitarianism. Ph.D., Columbia University, 1955. 386p. UMI# 15623.

3041   Cory, Earl W., Jr. The Unitarians and Universalists of the Southeastern United States During the Nineteenth Century. Ph.D., University of Georgia, 1970. 148p. UMI# 71-13038.

3042   Denton, Charles R. American Unitarians, 1830-1865: A Study of Religious Opinion on War, Slavery, and the Union. Ph.D., Michigan State University, 1969. 205p. UMI# 70-09520.

3043   Geffen, Elizabeth M. Philadelphia Unitarianism (1796-1861). Ph.D.,

University of Philadelphia, 1958. 405p. UMI# 58-01842.

3044   Gysan, William H. Early American Unitarianism and Philosophy: A Study of the Philosophical Antecedents and the Philosophical Issues of Early American Unitarianism (Circa 1750-1860). Ph.D., Harvard University, 1950. 256p.

3045   Howe, Daniel W. The Unitarian Conscience: Harvard Moral Philosophy and the Second Great Awakening (1805-1861). Ph.D., University of California-Berkeley, 1966. 487p. UMI# 71-00872.

3046   Johnson, Jane M. "Through Change and Through Storm": A Study of Federalist-Unitarian Thought, 1800-1860. Ph.D., Radcliffe College, 1958.

3047   McGeehon, Carl W. The Controversial Writings of William Ellery Channing. Ph.D., University of Iowa, 1940.

3048   Small, Lawrence F. Unitarianism Down East: The Movement in Maine to 1900 With Its Colonial New England Background. Ph.D., Harvard University, 1955.

3049   Stange, Douglas C. Patterns of Antislavery Among American Unitarians, 1831-1860. Ph.D., Harvard University, 1974.

3050   Sykes, Richard E. Massachusetts Unitarianism and Social Change: A Religious Social System in Transition, 1780-1870. Ph.D., University of Minnesota, 1966. 404p. UMI# 68-01604.

Biography

3051   Ahlstrom, Sydney E. Francis Ellingwood Abbot: His Education and Active Career. Ph.D., Harvard University, 1952.

3052   Bolster, Arthur S., Jr. The Life of James Freeman Clarke. Ph.D., Harvard University, 1954.

3053   Brown, Arthur W. Always Young for Liberty: A Critical Biography of Dr. William Ellery Channing. Ph.D., Syracuse University, 1950.

3054   Callaghan, William J. The Philosophy of Francis Ellingwood Abbot. Ph.D., Columbia University, 1958. 329p. UMI# 5803215.

3055   Carley, Peter K. The Early Life and Thought of Frederick Henry Hedge, 1805-1850. Ph.D., Syracuse University, 1973. 345p. UMI# 7408237.

3056   Cassara, Ernest. Hosea Ballou, Preacher of Universal Salvation.

Ph.D., Boston University, 1957. 387p. UMI# 21544.

3057   Colville, Derek K. James Freeman Clarke: A Practical Transcendentalist and His Writings. Ph.D., Washington University, 1953. 265p. UMI# 08244.

3058   Dekay, Sam H. An American Humanist: The Religious Thought of Francis Ellingwood Abbot. Ph.D., Union Theological Seminary, 1978. 283p. UMI# 77-24084.

3059   Delbanco, Andrew H. William Ellery Channing: An Essay on the Liberal Spirit in America. Ph.D., Harvard University, 1980.

3060   Edgell, David P. William Ellery Channing: A Chapter in American Intellectual History. Ph.D., Brown University, 1950.

3061   Martin, John H. Theodore Parker. Ph.D., University of Chicago, 1953.

3062   Sexton, John E. Charles W. Eliot, Unitarian Exponent of the Doctrine of Tolerance in Religion. Ph.D., Fordham University, 1978. 347p. UMI# 78-14902.

3063   Thomas, John W. James Freeman Clarke: Apostle of German Culture to America. Ph.D., Pennsylvania State University, 1942. 186p. UMI# 514.

3064   Weeks, Louis B., III. Theodore Parker: The Minister as Revolutionary. Ph.D., Duke University, 1970. 269p. UMI# 71-10435.

3065   Yacovone, Donald. Samuel Joseph May, Antebellum Religion and Reform: Dilemmas of the Liberal Persuasion. Ph.D., Claremont Graduate School, 1984. 579p. UMI# 8416468.

Clergy

3066   Collison, Gary L. A Critical Edition of the Correspondence of Theodore Parker and Convers Francis, 1836-1859. Ph.D., Pennsylvania State University, 1979. 596p. UMI# 8007222.

3067   Katz, Seymour. The Unitarian Ministers of Boston, 1790-1860. Ph.D., Harvard University, 1961.

Education

3068   Barnette, Helen P. Implications of Horace Mann's Educational Philosophy and Praxis in Relation to "Secular Humanism" in Public

Schools. Ed.D., Southern Baptist Theological Seminary, 1987. 233p. UMI# 8805800.

3069   Culver, Raymond B. Horace Mann's Relation to the Teaching of Religion in the Massachusetts Public Schools. Ph.D., Yale University, 1924.

Literature

3070   Kroeger, Frederick P. The Unitarian Novels of William Ware. Ph.D., University of Michigan, 1967. 209p. UMI# 6807649.

Music

3071   Knight, Harold A. The Life and Musical Activities of Henry Kemble Oliver (1800-1885). Ph.D., University of Iowa, 1988. 476p. UMI# 8913194.

Organizational Structure

3072   Adamek, Michael B. The Provisional Unit of Freedom: The Formation of the Unitarian Denomination as an Attempt to Institutionalize Pure Religion in the United States: 1825-1925. D.Min., Meadville/Lombard Theological School, 1987.

Preaching

3073   Hochmuth, Marie K. William Ellery Channing, D.D.: A Study in Public Address. Ph.D., University of Wisconsin-Madison, 1946.

3074   McCall, Roy C. The Public Speaking Principles and Practice of Theodore Parker. Ph.D., University of Iowa, 1937.

Social Programs

3075   Scheck, John F. Transplanting a Tradition: Thomas Lamb Eliot and the Unitarian Conscience in the Pacific Northwest, 1865-1905. Ph.D., University of Oregon, 1969. 390p. UMI# 70-09470.

Theology

3076   Dirks, John E. The Critical Theology of Theodore Parker. Ph.D., Columbia University, 1948. 173p.

3077   Duran, Juan B. The Theological Anthropology of Leonard Woods. Ph.D., Drew University, 1983. 431p. UMI# 8317850.

3078   Hayes, Paul. The Comprehensive Theology of James Freeman

Clarke. Ph.D., Pacific School of Religion, 1960.

3079   Rivers, Fred M. Francis Ellingwood Abbot: Free Religionist and Cosmic Philosopher. Ph.D., University of Maryland, 1970. 241p. UMI# 71-10488.

UNIVERSALIST

3080   Chestnut, Paul I. The Universalist Movement in America, 1770-1803. Ph.D., Duke University, 1974. 285p. UMI# 74-13470.

3081   French, Roderick S. The Trials of Abner Kneeland: A Study in the Rejection of Democratic Secular Humanism. Ph.D., George Washington University, 1971. 382p. UMI# 7208998.

3082   Sweeny, Joseph R. Elhanan Winchester and the Universal Baptists. Ph.D., University of Pennsylvania, 1969. 293p. UMI# 70-07858.

UTOPIANISM

General Studies

3083   Aiken, John R. Utopianism and the Emergence of the Colonial Legal Profession: New York 1664-1710. A Test Case. Ph.D., University of Rochester, 1967. 313p. UMI# 67-08943.

3084   Bronner, Edwin B. Pennsylvania: 1681 to 1701: Utopian Failure, Practical Success. Ph.D., University of Pennsylvania, 1952. 247p.

3085   Bundy, James F. Fall From Grace: Religion and the Communal Ideal in Two Suburban Villages, 1870-1917. Ph.D., University of Chicago, 1979. [Evanston, Oak Park(IL)].

3086   Burt, Donald C. Utopia and the Agrarian Tradition in America 1865-1900. Ph.D., University of New Mexico, 1973. 272p. UMI# 74-11785.

3087   Chmielewski, Wendy E. Search for Community: Feminism and the Utopian Tradition, 1830-1915. Ph.D., State University of New York-Binghamton, 1988. 419p. UMI# 8926256.

3088   Fellman, Michael D. The Unbounded Frame: Freedom and Community in Nineteenth Century American Utopianism. Ph.D., Northwestern University, 1969. 324p. UMI# 70-00050.

3089   Guarneri, Carl J. Utopian Socialism and American Ideas: The Origins and Doctrine of American Fourierism, 1832-1848. Ph.D., Johns Hopkins University, 1979. 428p. UMI# 79-24614.

3090   Kern, Louis J. Love, Labor, and Self-Control: Sex-Roles and Sexuality in Three Nineteenth-Century American Utopian Communities. Ph.D., Rutgers University, 1977. 536p. UMI# 78-05092.

3091   Kesten, Seymour R. The Utopian Episodes: A Humanistic Study of Nineteenth-Century American Experiments in Social Reorganization. Ph.D., Syracuse University, 1983. 601p. UMI# 8326600.[Icaria(IL), New Harmony(IN), Brook Farm(MA)].

3092   Keyes, Jane G. Institutionalized Charisma in Nineteenth-Century Utopias. Ph.D., Southern Illinois University-Carbondale, 1976. 211p. UMI# 76-28751.[Amana Church Society(IA), New Harmony(IN), Oneida Community(NY), Shakers].

3093   Kitch, Sally L. A Body of Her Own: Female Celibacy in Three Nineteenth-Century American Utopian Communities. Ph.D., Emory University, 1984. 319p. UMI# 8504957.

3094   Kolmerten, Carol A. Unconscious Sexual Stereotyping in Utopian Thought: A Study of the American Owenite Communities, 1825 to 1829. Ph.D., Purdue University, 1978. 219p. UMI# 79-14917.

3095   Lipscomb, Winifred L. Status and Structure of the Family in Idealistic Communities: A Study of Selected Utopias, Literary, Religious and Secular. Ph.D., University of North Carolina-Chapel Hill, 1948.

3096   Mandelker, Ira L. Religion, Society and Utopia in Nineteenth-Century America. Ph.D., New School for Social Research, 1982. 315p. UMI# 8222998.

3097   Muncy, Raymond L. Sex and Marriage in Nineteenth Century Utopian Communities in America. Ph.D., University of Mississippi, 1971. 430p. UMI# 71-25693.

3098   Roemer, Kenneth M. America as Utopia (1888-1900): New Visions, Old Dreams. Ph.D., University of Pennsylvania, 1971. 512p. UMI# 72-06221.

3099   Sobel, May L. An Experiment in Perfectionism: The Religious Life of the Putney and Oneida Communities. Ph.D., Boston University, 1968. 280p. UMI# 68-18087.

3100   Thrift, Ronald E. Two Paths to Utopia: An Investigation of Robert Owen in New Lanark and Brigham Young in Salt Lake City. Ph.D., University of New Mexico, 1976. 278p. UMI# 76-25684.

3101   Weeks, Vickie D.P. Late Nineteenth Century Kansas Utopian Communities: The Value of Hostility in Commitment Development. Ph.D., Kansas State University, 1980. 112p. UMI# 8111834.

Art and Architecture

3102   Dostoglu, Neslihan T. Architectural Deterministic Thinking in the Development of Urban Utopias, 1848-1947. Ph.D., University of Pennsylvania, 1986. 230p. UMI# 8614783.

Biography

3103   Blankenship, William R. The Perfectionism of John Humphrey Noyes in Relation to Its Social Background. Ph.D., University of Washington, 1935.

Literature

3104   Carlock, Nancy E. An Analysis of Utopian Concepts in Selected Nineteenth Century Fiction. Ph.D., Occidental College, 1964.

3105   Cary, Francine C. Shaping the Future in the Gilded Age: A Study of Utopian Thought, 1888-1900. Ph.D., University of Wisconsin-Madison, 1975. 499p. UMI# 75-18584.

3106   Clapper, Thomas H. American Conservative Utopias. Ph.D., University of Oklahoma, 1983. 358p. UMI# 8314761.

3107   Curzon, Gordon A. Paradise Sought: A Study of the Religious Motivation in Representative British and American Literary Utopias, 1850-1950. Ph.D., University of California-Riverside, 1969. 314p. UMI# 7006347.

3108   Dowst, Kenneth I. The Rhetoric of Utopian Fiction. Ph.D., University of Pittsburgh, 1979. 184p. UMI# 80-04857.[Edward Bellamy, Aldous Huxley].

3109   Egbert, Nelson N. Problems of Form and Content in Six Utopian Responses to Edward Bellamy's *Looking Backward: 2000-1887*. Ph.D., State University of New York-Albany, 1979. 175p. UMI# 79-27482.

3110   Ekstrom, William F. The Social Idealism of William Morris and of William Dean Howells, A Study of Four Utopian Novels. Ph.D., University of Illinois at Urbana-Champaign, 1947. 315p.

3111   Kateb, George A. Anti-Utopianism. Ph.D., Columbia University, 1960. 318p. UMI# 6003091.

3112   Keeler, Clinton C. The Grass Roots of Utopia: A Study of the Literature of the Agrarian Revolt in America, 1880-1902. Ph.D., University of Minnesota, 1954. 292p. UMI# 08123.

3113   Kopp, James J. Curing the Ills of Society: Medicine and the Public's Health in American Utopian Fiction, 1888-1914. Ph.D., George Washington University, 1990. 325p. UMI# 9027596.

3114   Majkut, Paul T. From Daydream to Nightmare: Utopian Fiction in the Late Nineteenth and Early Twentieth Centuries. Ph.D., Indiana University of Pennsylvania, 1986. 278p. UMI# 8712935.

3115   McCord, Sue G. The Utopian Consciousness in Edward Bellamy's Short Fiction. Ph.D., University of South Florida, 1979. 242p. UMI# 80-09800.

3116   McFarland, Jo A.Y. A Dialogic Analysis of American Utopian Novels by Women, 1888-1900. Ph.D., University of Utah, 1988. 360p. UMI# 8825892.

3117   Myers, Anne C. The Novels of Charles Brockden Brown: A Rejection of Utopia. Ph.D., Arizona State University, 1981. 275p. UMI# 81-17177.

3118   Nydahl, Joel M. Utopia Americana: Early American Utopian Fiction, 1790-1864. Ph.D., University of Michigan, 1974. 277p. UMI# 75-10251.

3119   Papson, Stephen D. A Qualitative Analysis of Western Literary Utopias: A Study of the Relationship of Utopian Ideas to Their Socio-Historical Location. Ph.D., University of Kentucky, 1976. 272p. UMI# 7705699.

3120   Parrington, Vernon L., Jr. The Utopian Novel in America. Ph.D., Brown University, 1943. 287p.

3121   Quissell, Barbara C. The Sentimental and Utopian Novels of Nineteenth-Century America: Romance and Social Issues. Ph.D., University of Utah, 1973. 318p. UMI# 73-23112.

3122   Ransom, Ellene. Utopus Discovers America, or Critical Realism in the American Utopian Novel, 1798-1900. Ph.D., Vanderbilt University, 1947. 107p.

3123   Rooney, Charles J., Jr. Utopian Literature as a Reflection of Social Forces in America, 1865-1917. Ph.D., George Washington University, 1968. 296p. UMI# 68-11765.

3124   Sataty, Nechama. Utopian Visions and Their Critics: Press Reactions to American Utopias in the Ante-Bellum Era. Ph.D., University of Pennsylvania, 1986. 749p. UMI# 8624024.

3125   Senescu, Betty C. The Utopia Within: Some Psychological Aspects of Edward Bellamy's Early Writing. Ph.D., University of New Mexico, 1977. 213p. UMI# 77-27157.

3126   Shurter, Robert L. The Utopian Novel in America, 1865-1900. Ph.D., Case Western Reserve University, 1936.

3127   Simmons, James R. Politics and Vision in the American Utopian Novel. Ph.D., Indiana University, 1983. 191p. UMI# 8317112.

3128   Stupple, Alexander J. Utopian Humanism in American Fiction, 1888-1900. Ph.D., Northwestern University, 1971. 252p. UMI# 71-30962.

3129   Suksang, Duangrudi. Social Relationships in Nineteenth Century Utopias by Women. Ph.D., University of Iowa, 1988. 340p. UMI# 8903973.

3130   Sweetland, James H. American Utopian Fiction, 1798-1926. Ph.D., University of Notre Dame, 1976. 269p. UMI# 76-19990.

3131   Thiem, Jon E. The Artist in the Ideal State: A Study of the Troubled Relations Between the Arts and Society in Utopian Fiction. Ph.D., Indiana University, 1975. 277p. UMI# 76-02902.

3132   Tuttle, Robert B. Society, Politics, and the Utopian Imagination: The Literary Utopia in America, 1865-1900. Ph.D., Rutgers University, 1982. 533p. UMI# 8221717.

3133   Ziemba, Margaret M. Contrasting Social Theories of Utopia: An Analysis of *Looking Backward* and *Walden Two*. Ph.D., American University, 1977. 47p. UMI# 77-18658.

YMCA AND YWCA

3134   Bouseman, John. The Pulled-Away College: A Study of Separation of Colleges From the Young Men's Christian Association. Ph.D., University of Chicago, 1970.

3135   MacLeod, David I. Good Boys Made Better: The Boy Scouts of America, Boys' Brigades, and YMCA Boys' Work, 1880-1920. Ph.D., University of Wisconsin-Madison, 1973. 511p. UMI# 7320265.

3136   Mjagkij, Nina. History of the Black YMCA in America, 1853-1946.

Ph.D., University of Cincinnati, 1990. 311p. UMI# 9108753.

3137   Morgan, William H. Student Religion During Fifty Years: Programs and Policies of the Intercollegiate Y.M.C.A. Ph.D., Columbia University, 1935.

3138   Sims, Mary S. The Natural History of a Social Institution: The Young Women's Christian Association. Ph.D., New York University, 1936. 241p. UMI# 73-03420.

3139   Wilson, Grace H. The Religious and Educational Philosophy of the Young Women's Christian Association. Ph.D., Columbia University, 1933. 156p.

3140   Wu, Chih-Kang. The Influence of the YMCA on the Development of Physical Education in China. Ph.D., University of Michigan, 1957. 218p. UMI# 58-01019.

PART TWO

TOPICAL STUDIES

AMERICAN RELIGION, GENERAL STUDIES

3141   Beales, Ross W., Jr. Cares for the Rising Generation: Youth and
        Religion in Colonial New England. Ph.D., University of
        California-Davis, 1971. 260p. UMI# 72-09875.

3142   Berman, Milton. John Fiske and the Evolution of American
        Religion, 1842-1902. Ph.D., Harvard University, 1959.

3143   Bigham, Darrel E. American Christian Thinkers and the Function
        of War 1861-1920. Ph.D., University of Kansas, 1970. 447p. UMI#
        71-13275.

3144   Charney, Linda A. Religious Conversion: A Longitudinal Study.
        Ph.D., University of Utah, 1986. 238p. UMI# 8609624.

3145   Clebsch, William A. Baptism of Blood: A Study of Christian
        Contributions to the Interpretation of the Civil War in American
        History. Th.D., Union Theological Seminary, 1957.

3146   Clemmer, Robert R. Enlightenment Church History in the United
        States, 1800-1850. Ph.D., University of Pennsylvania, 1961. 332p.
        UMI# 61-02024.

3147   Crocker, Richard R. Belief and Unbelief: A Pragmatic Pastoral
        Perspective. Ph.D., Vanderbilt University, 1988. 288p. UMI#
        8910844.

3148   Dorough, Charles D. Religion in the Old South: A Pattern of
        Behavior and Thought. Ph.D., University of Texas-Austin, 1947.

3149   Dunn, Elizabeth E. "The Power of a Wise Imagination": Case
        Studies in Value Conflict in Early Eighteenth Century America.

Ph.D., University of Illinois at Urbana-Champaign, 1990. 298p. UMI# 9114229.

3150   Farnham, Wallace D. Religion as an Influence in Life and Thought: Jackson County, Oregon, 1860-1890. Ph.D., University of Oregon, 1955.

3151   Finke, Roger K. The Churching of America: 1850-1980. Ph.D., University of Washington, 1984. 232p. UMI# 8412387.

3152   Fleming, Sandford. Children in the Life and Thought of the New England Churches, 1620-1847. Ph.D., Yale University, 1929.

3153   Foster, William L. Between Two Worlds: The Origins of Shaker Celibacy, Oneida Community Complex Marriage, and Mormon Polygamy. Ph.D., University of Chicago, 1976.

3154   Franch, Michael S. Congregation and Community in Baltimore, 1840-1860. Ph.D., University of Maryland, 1984. 422p. UMI# 8512188.

3155   Gardella, Peter L. Innocent Ecstasy: How Christianity Gave America an Ethic of Sexual Pleasure, 1830-1930. Ph.D., Yale University, 1983. 250p. UMI# 8621234.

3156   Godbeer, Richard. The Devil's Dominion: Magic and Religion in Early New England. Ph.D., Brandeis University, 1989. 347p. UMI# 8922187.

3157   Gorrell, Donald K. American Churches and American Territorial Expansion. Ph.D., Case Western Reserve University, 1960.

3158   Grayson, John T. Frederick Douglass' Intellectual Development: His Concepts of God, Man, and Nature in the Light of American and European Influences. Ph.D., Columbia University, 1981. 179p. UMI# 82-22396.

3159   Hatch, Roger D. The Issue of Race and the Writing of the History of Christianity in America. Ph.D., University of Chicago, 1974.

3160   Heckman, Oliver S. Northern Church Penetration of the South, 1860-1880. Ph.D., Duke University, 1939.

3161   Henry, James O. History of the United States Christian Commission. Ph.D., University of Maryland, 1959. 338p. UMI# 60-02272.

3162   Hess, Bartlett. Religion and Popularism at the Opening of the

Nineteenth Century. Popularism vs. Reaction. Ph.D., University of Kansas, 1934.

3163   Hodson, Dean R. The Origin of Non-Mormon Settlements in Utah: 1847-1896. Ph.D., Michigan State University, 1971. 153p. UMI# 7131227.

3164   Jacobsen, Douglas G. "An Unprov'd Experiment": Religious Pluralism in Colonial New Jersey. Ph.D., University of Chicago, 1983.

3165   Keating, Jerome F. Personal Identity in Jonathan Edwards, Ralph Waldo Emerson, and Alfred North Whitehead. Ph.D., Syracuse University, 1972. 163p. UMI# 7309539.

3166   Kremer, Michael N. Church Support in the United States. Ph.D., Catholic University in America, 1930.

3167   Kwilecki, Susan E. Through the Needle's Eye: Religion in the Lives of Wealthy Colonial Americans. Ph.D., Stanford University, 1982. 259p. UMI# 8301240.

3168   Marini, Stephen A. New England Folk Religions, 1770-1815: The Sectarian Impulse in Revolutionary Society. Ph.D., Harvard University, 1976.

3169   Mattice, Alice L. The Quest for the Mysterious East: Max Mueller, Blavatsky, Gandhi. Ph.D., Harvard University, 1975.

3170   McDannell, Mary C. The Home as Sacred Space in American Protestant and Catholic Popular Thought 1840 to 1900. Ph.D., Temple University, 1984. 296p. UMI# 8419775.

3171   Medhurst, Martin J. "God Bless the President": The Rhetoric of Inaugural Prayer. Ph.D., Pennsylvania State University, 1980. 670p. UMI# 81-05770.

3172   Morgan, Edmund S. Religion and the Family in Seventeenth-Century New England. Ph.D., Harvard University, 1942. 312p.

3173   Naveh, Eyal J. The Martyr Image in American Political Culture. Ph.D., University of California-Berkeley, 1986. 290p. UMI# 8624875.[Abraham Lincoln].

3174   Nielsen, Alan W. Salmi Morse's *Passion*, 1879-1884: The History and Consequences of a Theatrical Obsession. Ph.D., City University of New York, 1989. 467p. UMI# 9000055.

3175   Nordquist, Philip A. The Ecology of Religious Denominational Preference in the United States: 1850. Ph.D., University of Washington, 1964. 294p. UMI# 65-01894.

3176   Pauley, William E., Jr. Religion and the American Revolution in the South: 1760-1781. Ph.D., Emory University, 1974. 272p. UMI# 74-23669.

3177   Peacock, John H., Jr. The Breach of Such a Covenant: Individualism and American Community, 1630-1981. Ph.D., Columbia University, 1980. 139p. UMI# 8307620.

3178   Persons, Stow S. The Free Religious Movements in America, 1867-1893. Ph.D., Yale University, 1940. 114p.

3179   Pestana, Carla G. Sectarianism in Colonial Massachusetts. Ph.D., University of California-Los Angeles, 1987. 456p. UMI# 8719937.

3180   Pitt, Arthur S. Franklin and Religious Sectarianism. Ph.D., Yale University, 1939.

3181   Pointer, Richard W. Seedbed of American Pluralism: The Impact of Religious Diversity in New York, 1750-1800. Ph.D., Johns Hopkins University, 1982. 357p. UMI# 8205127.

3182   Rabinowitz, Richard I. Soul, Character, and Personality: The Transformation of Personal Religious Experience in New England, 1790-1860. Ph.D., Harvard University, 1977.

3183   Ramsbottom, Mary M. Religious Society and the Family in Charlestown, Massachusetts, 1630-1740. Ph.D., Yale University, 1987. 292p. UMI# 8729132.

3184   Reilly, Mary P. Francis Parkman and the Spiritual Factors at Work in New France. Ph.D., Saint Louis University, 1942. 381p. UMI# 610.

3185   Reilly, Timothy F. Religious Leaders and Social Criticism in New Orleans, 1800-1861. Ph.D., University of Missouri-Columbia, 1972. 353p. UMI# 73-07076.

3186   Richardson, Paul D. Some Social Influences in the Development of Major Religious Denominations in Kentucky. Ph.D., University of Kentucky, 1956. 171p. UMI# 6100306.

3187   Romero, Sidney J., Jr. Religion in the Rebel Ranks. Ph.D., Louisiana State University, 1953.

3188   Rowe, Henry K. Rise and Development of Religious Denominations in New England. Ph.D., Boston University, 1905.

3189   Salstrand, George A.E. The Story of Stewardship in the United States of America. Ph.D., Northern Baptist Theological Seminary, 1953.

3190   Schattenmann, Johannes. The Correlation of Religion and Economics in the History of the United States, 1720-1880. Th.D., Union Theological Seminary, 1929.

3191   Schuldiner, Michael J. The Doctrine of Spiritual Growth and Church Polity in Early America. Ph.D., Kent State University, 1979. 254p. UMI# 79-22727.

3192   Schuyler, David P. Public Landscapes and American Urban Culture 1800-1870: Rural Cemeteries, City Parks, and Suburbs. Ph.D., Columbia University, 1979. 313p. UMI# 8009699.

3193   Schwartz, Sally. "A Mixed Multitude": Religion and Ethnicity in Colonial Pennsylvania. Ph.D., Harvard University, 1981.

3194   Scott, Barbara J. Faith and Chaos: The Quest for Meaning in the Writings of Jonathan Edwards and William James. Ph.D., Syracuse University, 1979. 147p. UMI# 80-13412.

3195   Scott, William B. Every Man Under His Own Vine and Fig Tree: American Conceptions of Property From the Puritans to Henry George. Ph.D., University of Wisconsin-Madison, 1973. 248p. UMI# 74-10268.

3196   Seager, Richard H. The World's Parliament of Religions, Chicago, Illinois, 1893: America's Religious Coming of Age. Ph.D., Harvard University, 1987. 300p. UMI# 8711542.

3197   Searcy, Herbert L. Parochial Libraries in the American Colonies. Ph.D., University of Illinois at Urbana-Champaign, 1963. 234p. UMI# 6406146.

3198   Seymour, J.A. The Development of New England Thought. S.T.D., Temple University, 1912.

3199   Shattuck, Gardiner H., Jr. A Shield and Hiding Place: The Religious Life of the Civil War Armies. Ph.D., Harvard University, 1985. 269p. UMI# 8520287.

3200   Shea, John J. Toward a Process Understanding in Religious

Experience: William James and Eugene Gendlin. Ph.D., University of Ottawa, 1980.

3201   Shepard, John W., Jr. The American Tradition of Freedom: An Historical Analysis and Christian Evaluation. Ph.D., Southern Baptist Theological Seminary, 1956.

3202   Shipton, Clifford K. New England in Social Transition, 1680-1740: An Historical Introduction to Volume Four of Sibley's *Harvard Graduates*; Biographical Sketches of Harvard Graduates of the Classes of 1690-1700 (Alumni Harvardienses). Ph.D., Harvard University, 1933. 394p.

3203   Smith, Cortland V. Church Organization as an Agency of Social Control: Church Discipline in North Carolina, 1800-1860. Ph.D., University of North Carolina-Chapel Hill, 1967. 361p. UMI# 68-02235.

3204   Smith, George D. Religion and the Development of American Culture: Western Pennsylvania, 1760-1820. Ph.D., Harvard University, 1976.

3205   Smith, Jesse G. A History of Christian Denominations in the Republic of Texas. Ph.D., University of Texas-Austin, 1951.

3206   Snydacker, Daniel. Traders in Exile: Quakers and Jews of New York and Newport in the New World Economy, 1650-1776. Ph.D., Johns Hopkins University, 1982. 466p. UMI# 82-19581.

3207   Snyder, Howard A. Pietism, Moravianism, and Methodism as Renewal Movements: A Comparative and Thematic Study. Ph.D., University of Notre Dame, 1983. 329p. UMI# 8316733.

3208   Starbuck, Edwin D. Some Aspects of Religious Growth. Ph.D., Clark University, 1897.

3209   Stephens, Alonzo T. An Account of the Attempts at Establishing a Religious Hegemony in Colonial North Carolina, 1663-1773. Ph.D., University of Pittsburgh, 1955. 299p. UMI# 15118.

3210   Terman, William J., Jr. The American Revolution and the Baptist and Presbyterian Clergy of Virginia: A Study of Dissenter Opinion and Action. Ph.D., Michigan State University, 1974. 439p. UMI# 74-27492.

3211   Weeks, Stephen B. The Religious Development of the Province North Carolina. Ph.D., Johns Hopkins University, 1891.

3212   White, Kermit E. Abraham Lincoln and Christianity. Ph.D., Boston University, 1954.

3213   Wight, Willard E. Churches in the Confederacy. Ph.D., Emory University, 1958. 242p. UMI# 58-05190.

3214   Wilson, Charles R. Baptized in Blood: Southern Religion and the Cult of the Lost Cause, 1865-1920. Ph.D., University of Texas-Austin, 1977. 493p. UMI# 77-29117.

3215   Young, Ralph F. Good News From New England: The Influence of the New England Way of Church Polity on Old England, 1635-1660. Ph.D., Michigan State University, 1971. 204p. UMI# 71-31339.

ART AND ARCHITECTURE

3216   Baldwin, David. Puritan Aristocrat in the Age of Emerson: A Study of Samuel Gray Ward. Ph.D., University of Pennsylvania, 1961. 332p. UMI# 6103483.

3217   Bjelajac, David V. Washington Allston's Unfinished Masterpiece *Belshazzar's Feast* (1817-1843): Millennial Desire and Social Conservatism in the New American Israel. Ph.D., University of North Carolina-Chapel Hill, 1984. 384p. UMI# 8425454.

3218   Burnham, Patricia M. The Religious Paintings of John Trumbull: An Anglo-American Experiment. Ph.D., Boston University, 1984. 477p. UMI# 8416873.

3219   Corcoran, Mary A. A Study of Parallels Between Ecclesiastical and Theatre Architecture. Ph.D., Tufts University, 1970. 326p.

3220   Sechrist, Gail L. Church Buildings Enter the Urban Age: A Louisiana Example of the Church in Settlement Geography (1885-1930). Ph.D., Louisiana State University, 1986. 269p. UMI# 8629197.

3221   Wedell, Roger W. Images and Visions: Art and Religion in America, 1700-1975. Ph.D., Graduate Theological Union, 1982. 218p. UMI# 82-19507.

3222   Zimmerman, Philip D. Ecclesiastical Architecture in the Reformed Tradition in Rockingham County, New Hampshire, 1790-1860. Ph.D., Boston University, 1985. 501p. UMI# 8418796.

BIBLICAL STUDIES

3223   Brown, Jerry W. Conflict and Criticism, Biblical Studies in New

England, 1800-1860. Ph.D., Princeton University, 1964. 254p. UMI# 65-02117.

3224   Brown, Jesse H. The Contribution of William Robertson Smith to Old Testament Scholarship, With Special Emphasis on Higher Criticism. Ph.D., Duke University, 1964. 340p. UMI# 65-02787.

3225   Campbell, Jerry D. Biblical Criticism in America 1858-1892: The Emergence of the Historical Critic. Ph.D., University of Denver, 1982. 378p. UMI# 8315894.

3226   Cheek, John L. The Translation of the Greek New Testament in America: A Phase of the History of American Criticism and Interpretation. Ph.D., University of Chicago, 1939.

3227   Farace, Charles. The History of Old Testament Higher Criticism in the United States. Ph.D., University of Chicago, 1940. 122p.

3228   Klaiss, Donald S. The History of the Interpretation and Criticism of the New Testament in America, 1620-1900. Ph.D., University of Chicago, 1935.

CHURCH AND STATE

3229   Anderson, Richard V. Religion and the Public School of Colorado. An Historical Analysis, 1851-1963. Ed.D., University of Colorado, 1965. 383p. UMI# 66-03217.

3230   Baldwin, Alice M. The Influence of the New England Clergy Upon the Constitutional Doctrines of the American Revolution. Ph.D., University of Chicago, 1926.

3231   Bates, George E., Jr. The Emergence of a Modern Mind in Colonial America, 1700-1760. Ph.D., University of Illinois at Urbana-Champaign, 1970. 236p. UMI# 7114672.

3232   Bauer, Monica T. An Open Question: The Attempt to Evolve a Consistent Philosophy of the Separation of Church and State in America, 1787-1987. Ph.D., University of Nebraska-Lincoln, 1989. 141p. UMI# 8925226.

3233   Beliekowsky, Sadie. The Church, the State and Education in Virginia. Ph.D., University of Pennsylvania, 1929.

3234   Bennett, William L. Factors in the Struggle for Religious Liberty in North Carolina, 1663-1776. Ph.D., New Orleans Baptist Theological Seminary, 1965.

3235   Beth, Loren P. Church and State in American Political Theory. Ph.D., University of Chicago, 1950. 298p.

3236   Bodo, John R. Pattern for an American Theocracy, 1812-1848. Ph.D., Princeton Theological Seminary, 1952. 175p.

3237   Bowser, Anita O. The Meaning of Religion in the Constitution. Ph.D., University of Notre Dame, 1976. 329p. UMI# 76-20647.

3238   Branson, Roy E. Theories of Religious Pluralism and the American Founding Fathers. Ph.D., Harvard University, 1968.

3239   Brinsfield, John W., Jr. The Separation of Church and State in Colonial South Carolina During the American Revolution. Ph.D., Emory University, 1973. 328p. UMI# 74-00440.

3240   Buckley, Thomas E. Church and State in Virginia, 1776-1787. Ph.D., University of California-Santa Barbara, 1973. 300p. UMI# 74-27705.

3241   Cartwright, Marguerite. Legislation Against Discrimination in Employment in New York State: A Study of the Historical Antecedents, From 1609 to 1945, of Attempts to Direct and Influence Change Through Legislation as It Relates to Racial and Religious Discrimination in Employment. Ed.D., New York University, 1948. 399p. UMI# 981.

3242   Chatfield, John H. "Already We Are a Fallen Country": The Politics and Ideology of Connecticut Federalism, 1797-1812. Ph.D., Columbia University, 1988. 337p. UMI# 8827548.

3243   Chesebrough, David B. The Call to Battle: The Stances of Parker, Finney, Beecher, and Brooks on the Great Issues Surrounding the Civil War and a Comparison of Those Stances With Other Clergy in the Nation. D.A., Illinois State University, 1988. 328p. UMI# 8818708.

3244   Cody, Edward J. Church and State in the Middle Colonies, 1689-1763. Ph.D., Lehigh University, 1970. 256p. UMI# 71-10502.

3245   Coleman, George S. The Religious Background of the Federal Constitution. Ph.D., Harvard University, 1933.

3246   Conry, Thomas P. Church and State in Ohio. Ph.D., Saint Louis University, 1950. 227p.

3247   Cox, James L. The Role of the Establishment of Religion Clause as It Relates to the Church's Activity. Ph.D., Vanderbilt University, 1965. 553p. UMI# 6510466.

3248   Curley, Michael J. Church and State in the Spanish Floridas (1783-1822). Ph.D., Catholic University of America, 1939.

3249   Curry, Thomas J. The First Freedoms: The Development of the Concepts of Freedom of Religion and Establishment of Religion in America From the Early Settlements to the Passage of the First Amendment to the Constitution. Ph.D., Claremont Graduate School, 1983. 898p. UMI# 8321047.

3250   Davis, Edwin V. Christian Understandings of the Legislator and His Responsibility in Puritan Massachusetts Bay (1630-1700) and Quaker Pennsylvania (1680-1750). Ph.D., Drew University, 1970. 382p. UMI# 70-24583.

3251   Dettmering, Karl. Church, Civil Court, and Church Union in the United States. Ph.D., Hartford Seminary Foundation 1929.

3252   Donovan, Thomas F. The Status of the Church in American Civil Law and Canon Law. Ph.D., Catholic University of America, 1967.

3253   Dozier, Robert R. Ministerial Efforts to Combat Revolutionary Propaganda, 1789-1793. Ph.D., University of California-Berkeley, 1969. 237p. UMI# 70-06092.

3254   Drachler, Norman. The Influence of Sectarianism, Non-Sectarianism, and Secularism Upon the Public Schools of Detroit and the University of Michigan, 1837-1900. Ph.D., University of Michigan, 1948. 174p. UMI# 02398.

3255   Drakeman, Donald L. The Past as Prologue: Making Sense of the Establishment Clause. Ph.D., Princeton University, 1988.

3256   Ehle, Carl F., Jr. Prolegomena to Christian Zionism in America: The Views of Increase Mather and William E. Blackstone Concerning the Doctrine of the Restoration of Israel. Ph.D., New York University, 1977. 394p. UMI# 78-08520.

3257   Ekman, Richard H. Northern Religion and the Civil War. Ph.D., Harvard University, 1972.

3258   Elder, Fred K. Freedom in South Carolina as Shown by Church-State Relationships in Higher Education in South Carolina. Ph.D., University of North Carolina-Chapel Hill, 1940. 239p.

3259   Emrick, Howard C. The Role of the Church in the Development of Education in Pennsylvania, 1638 to 1834. Ph.D., University of Pittsburgh, 1959. 369p. UMI# 59-04445.

3260   Engh, Michael E. Frontier Religion in an Era of Transition: Los Angeles, 1848-1885. Ph.D., University of Wisconsin-Madison, 1987. 511p. UMI# 8800708.

3261   Faber, Eli. The Evil That Men Do: Crime and Transgression in Colonial Massachusetts. Ph.D., Columbia University, 1974. 453p. UMI# 7715282.

3262   Feiertag, Loretta C. American Public Opinion on the Diplomatic Relations Between the United States and the Papal States (1847-1867). Ph.D., Catholic University of America, 1933.

3263   Finlayson, Michael G. Independency in Old and New England, 1630-1660: An Historiographical and Historical Study. Ph.D., University of Toronto, 1968. 352p.

3264   Foster, F.M. Church and State; Their Relations Considered. Ph.D., New York University, 1899.

3265   Foster, Mary C. Hampshire County, Massachusetts, 1729-1754: A Covenant Society in Transition. Ph.D., University of Michigan, 1967. 337p. UMI# 6717759.

3266   Gildrie, Richard P. Salem, 1626-1668: History of a Covenant Community. Ph.D., University of Virginia, 1971. 399p. UMI# 72-07261.

3267   Gobbel, Luther L. Church-State Relationships in Education in North Carolina Since 1776. Ph.D., Yale University, 1934.

3268   Graham, Michael J. Lord Baltimore's Pious Enterprise: Toleration and Community in Colonial Maryland, 1634-1724. Ph.D., University of Michigan, 1983. 446p. UMI# 8402286.

3269   Greene, Maria L. Church and State in Connecticut to 1818. Ph.D., Yale University, 1895. 298p.

3270   Gribbin, William J. The War of 1812 and American Religion. Ed.D., Catholic University of America, 1968. 283p. UMI# 69-08880.

3271   Guenther, Scot M. The American Flag, 1777-1924: Cultural Shifts From Creation to Codification. Ph.D., University of Maryland, 1986. 381p. UMI# 8620782.

3272   Gunderson, Knut T. The Place of Religion in National Constitutions, 1787-1954. Ph.D., University of Southern California, 1958. 172p.

3273   Hall, Cline E. The Southern Dissenting Clergy and the American

Revolution. Ph.D., University of Tennessee, 1975. 346p. UMI# 76-11051.

3274   Hallman, Clive R., Jr. The Vestry as a Unit of Local Government in Colonial Virginia. Ph.D., University of Georgia, 1987. 257p. UMI# 8806793.

3275   Harris, Hendon M., Jr. A Short History of Religious Liberty. Ph.D., Northern Baptist Theological Seminary, 1953.

3276   Hatch, Nathan O. The Sacred Cause of Liberty: Political Religion in New England From the First to the Second Great Awakening. Ph.D., Washington University, 1974. 224p. UMI# 75-06598.

3277   Hertz, Karl H. Bible Commonwealth and Holy Experiment: A Study of the Relation Between Theology and Politics in the Puritan and Quaker Colonies. Ph.D., University of Chicago, 1949. 367p.

3278   Illick, Joseph E., II. William Penn's Relations With the British Government. Ph.D., University of Pennsylvania, 1963. 356p. UMI# 6307057.

3279   Isetti, Ronald E. The Constitution as an Experiment: A Study of Its Religious and Scientific Origins. Ph.D., University of California-Berkeley, 1972.

3280   Jacoby, Stewart O. The Religious Amendment Movement: God, People and Nation in the Gilded Age. Ph.D., University of Michigan, 1984. 544p. UMI# 8502849.

3281   Karraker, William A. The American Churches and the Spanish-American War. Ph.D., University of Colorado, 1941. 293p.

3282   Kay, Miryam N. Separation of Church and State in Jeffersonian Virginia. Ph.D., University of Kentucky, 1967. 407p. UMI# 89-19189.

3283   Kempainen, Michael D. The Salem Witch Trials and the Occult. Th.D., Dallas Theological Seminary, 1978. 229p.

3284   Krugler, John D. Puritan and Papist: Politics and Religion in Massachusetts and Maryland Before the Restoration of Charles II. Ph.D., University of Illinois at Urbana-Champaign, 1971. 353p. UMI# 7121161.

3285   Lauer, Paul E. Church and State in New England. Ph.D., Johns Hopkins University, 1892.

3286   Lenk, Barbara A. Foundations of American Civil Religion. Ph.D.,

Yale University, 1978. 281p. UMI# 7819508.

3287   Lomasney, Patrick J. The Relations Between Church and State in New France. Ph.D., Saint Louis University, 1932.

3288   Mantiply, Victor E. The Origin and Development in Virginia of the Concept of Separation of Church and State. Ph.D., Southern Baptist Theological Seminary, 1959.

3289   Markwyn, Daniel W. The Christian State and Public Order in Revolutionary Massachusetts, 1770-1780. Ph.D., Cornell University, 1970. 327p. UMI# 71-13811.

3290   McCord, David M. Sunday School and Public School: An Exploration of Their Relationship With Special Reference to Indiana, 1790-1860. Ph.D., Purdue University, 1976. 206p. UMI# 7701744.

3291   Meyer, Jacob C. The Relations of Church and State in Massachusetts, 1740-1853. Ph.D., Harvard University, 1924.

3292   Miller, Wallace E. Relations of Church and State in Georgia, 1732-1775. Ph.D., Northwestern University, 1938.

3293   Noll, Mark A. Church Membership and the American Revolution: An Aspect of Religion and Society in New England From the Revival to the War for Independence. Ph.D., Vanderbilt University, 1975. 379p. UMI# 75-21597.

3294   O'Brien Hanley, Thomas. The Impact of the American Revolution on Religion in Maryland: 1776-1800. Ph.D., Georgetown University, 1961.

3295   Ott, Edward R. The Influence of Church and Trade on French Colonial Policy as Seen in the History of Detroit, 1700-1752. Ph.D., Northwestern University, 1937.

3296   Owens, Oscar L. Earlier Diplomatic Negotiations of the United States in Matters Relating to Religion. Ph.D., Johns Hopkins University, 1916.

3297   Petrie, George. Church and State in Early Maryland. Ph.D., Johns Hopkins University, 1891.

3298   Pratt, John W. The Politics of Tolerance: A History of Church-State Relations in New York, 1624-1900. Ph.D., Harvard University, 1960.

3299   Quinlivan, Mary E. Ideological Controversy Over Religious

Establishment in Revolutionary Virginia. Ph.D., University of Wisconsin, 1971. 251p. UMI# 71-29009.

3300   Raine, Jesse E. The Tax Status of Religious Property in the United States With Special Emphasis on Nashville and Tennessee. Ph.D., University of Kentucky, 1967. 158p. UMI# 6920444.

3301   Reed, Susan M. Church and State in Massachusetts, 1691-1740. Ph.D., University of Illinois at Urbana-Champaign, 1913. 208p.

3302   Rhodes, Daniel D. The Struggle for Religious Liberty in Virginia, 1740-1802. Ph.D., Duke University, 1951.

3303   Rodgers, Jack W. The United States Constitution and Religious Liberty. Ph.D., University of Nebraska-Lincoln, 1953. 222p.

3304   Samson, Steven A. Crossed Swords: Entanglements Between Church and State in America. Ph.D., University of Oregon, 1984. 667p. UMI# 8422869.

3305   Schiavo, Bartholomew P. The Dissenter Connection: English Dissenters and Massachusetts Political Culture, 1630-1774. Ph.D., Brandeis University, 1976. 651p. UMI# 7625322.

3306   Scholes, France V. Church and State in New Mexico in the Seventeenth Century. Ph.D., Harvard University, 1943.

3307   Shradar, Victor L. Ethnic Politics, Religion, and the Public Schools of San Francisco, 1849-1933. Ph.D., Stanford University, 1974. 240p. UMI# 74-27113.

3308   Smylie, James H. American Clergymen and the Constitution of the United States of America, 1781-1796. Ph.D., Princeton Theological Seminary, 1958. 172p.

3309   Strickland, Reba C. Religion and the State in Georgia in the Eighteenth Century. Ph.D., Columbia University, 1940. 211p.

3310   Sweet, Douglas H. Church and Community: Town Life and Ministerial Ideals in Revolutionary New Hampshire. Ph.D., Columbia University, 1978. 350p. UMI# 80-28808.

3311   Thurow, Glen E. Abraham Lincoln and American Political Religion. Ph.D., Harvard University, 1968.

3312   Torpey, William G. Judicial Doctrines of Religious Freedom. Ph.D., New York University, 1941. 287p.

3313   Troutman, William F., Jr. Respecting the Establishment of Religion in Colonial America. Ph.D., Duke University, 1959. 593p. UMI# 60-00475.

3314   Turner, Eldon R. Law and Political Culture: A Functional Study of the Relation of Theology to Jurisprudence, Political Values and Legal Activity in Colonial Suffolk County, Massachusetts, 1671-1680. Ph.D., University of Kansas, 1973. UMI# 7330883.

3315   Unger, Daniel R. The Use of the Bible in Pennsylvania Public Schools: 1834-1963. Ph.D., University of Pittsburgh, 1969. 255p. UMI# 70-04545.

3316   Wessell, Lynn R. The Relation Between Religious Enlightenment and Politics in America: 1740-1840. Ph.D., Claremont Graduate School, 1976. 229p. UMI# 77-09333.

3317   West, Earl I. Religion and Politics in the Jacksonian Era. Ph.D., Indiana University, 1968. 241p. UMI# 68-15470.

3318   Williams, Rhys H. Cultural Power: Religion and Politics in an American City. Ph.D., University of Massachusetts, 1988. 275p. UMI# 8822683.[Springfield(MA)].

3319   Wright, Edward N. Conscientious Objectors in the Civil War. Ph.D., University of Pennsylvania, 1930.

3320   Zabel, Orville H. Church and State in Nebraska, 1854-1950: A Study of the Legal Relationship. Ph.D., University of Nebraska-Lincoln, 1954. 302p. UMI# 11234.

CLERGY

3321   Carey, Robert B. The Passing of the Parish Minister as a Learned Professional. Ph.D., Columbia University, 1984. 307p. UMI# 8505953.

3322   Carleton, Stephen P. Southern Church Leadership in the Emergence of Sectionalism and Schism, 1800-1850. Ph.D., University of Chicago, 1975.

3323   Dunham, Chester F. The Attitude of the Northern Clergy Toward the South, 1860-1865. Ph.D., University of Chicago, 1940. 239p.

3324   Ebinger, Warren R. The Role of the Clergy in the American Revolution. Ph.D., American University, 1976. 326p. UMI# 77-00773.

3325   Gambrell, Mary L. Ministerial Training in Eighteenth-Century New England. Ph.D., Columbia University, 1938. 171p.

3326   Hartney, Edwin A. The Clerical Contribution to the Revolutionary Mind in New England, 1763-1776. Ph.D., Drew University, 1935.

3327   Hudson, Roy F. The Theory of Communication of Colonial New England Preachers, 1620-1670. Ph.D., Cornell University, 1954.

3328   Lohrenz, Otto. The Virginia Clergy and the American Revolution, 1774-1799. Ph.D., University of Kansas, 1970. 436p. UMI# 70-25370.

3329   Phelps, Vergil V. The Pastor and Teacher, With Special Reference to the Pastor and Teacher in the New England Churches. Ph.D., Yale University, 1910.

3330   Schmotter, James W. Provincial Professionalism: The New England Ministry: 1692-1745. Ph.D., Northwestern University, 1973. 368p. UMI# 74-07814.

3331   Startup, Kenneth M. Strangers in the Land: The Southern Clergy and the Economic Mind of the Old South. Ph.D., Louisiana State University, 1983. 258p. UMI# 8409596.

3332   Stewart, Thomas H. The Minister and His Work: The Preacher in the Humor of the Old Southwest. Ph.D., University of Mississippi, 1987. 176p. UMI# 8804289.

3333   Stokes, Durward T. The Clergy of the Carolinas and the American Revolution. Ph.D., University of North Carolina-Chapel Hill, 1968. 352p. UMI# 69-01684.

3334   Thompson, J. Earl., Jr. A Perilous Experiment: New England Clergymen and American Destiny, 1796-1826. Ph.D., Princeton University, 1966. 341p. UMI# 66-09645.

3335   Watson, Patricia A. The Angelical Conjunction: The Preacher-Physicians of Colonial New England. Ph.D., Johns Hopkins University, 1987. 277p. UMI# 8716676.

3336   Williams, Eugene F. Soldiers of God: The Chaplains of the Revolutionary War. Ph.D., Texas Christian University, 1972. 176p. UMI# 72-27959.

DEATH

3337   Davidson, Glen W. Basic Images of Death in America: An Historical

Analysis. Ph.D., Claremont Graduate School, 1964. 284p. UMI# 66-03328.

3338   Dorr, Ronald F. Death Education in McGuffey's Readers, 1836-1896. Ph.D., University of Minnesota, 1979. 416p. UMI# 7926117.

3339   Elberfeld, Richard B., Jr. An Historical, Pastoral, and Liturgical Consideration of Fraternal and Military Burial Rites. D.Min., University of the South, 1987.

3340   Farrell, James J. The Dying of Death: The Meaning and Management of Death in America, 1830-1920. Ph.D., University of Illinois at Urbana-Champaign, 1980. 333p. UMI# 8017931.

3341   Krouse, Elizabeth A. The Treatment of Death in Selected Nineteenth Century Hymnals and Tunebooks From 1835 to 1870. D.M.A., University of Missouri-Kansas City, 1990. 181p. UMI# 9035064.

3342   LeMieux, Christine M. Living to Die: Nineteenth-Century Culture of Death and Dying in Delaware County, Pennsylvania. Ph.D., University of Pennsylvania, 1976. 364p. UMI# 7622725.

3343   Little, Margaret R. Sticks and Stones: A Profile of North Carolina Gravemarkers Through Three Centuries. Ph.D., University of North Carolina-Chapel Hill, 1984. 445p. UMI# 8415834.

3344   McDowell, Michael M. American Attitudes Towards Death, 1825-1865. Ph.D., Brandeis University, 1978. 510p. UMI# 7808639.

3345   Messer, Stephen C. Two Answers to the Riddle: A Comparison of Attitudes Toward Death in Colonial Massachusetts and South Carolina. Ph.D., Florida State University, 1987. 240p. UMI# 8713329.

3346   Shively, Charles A. A History of the Conception of Death in America, 1650-1860. Ph.D., Harvard University, 1969.

3347   Sloane, David C. The Living Among the Dead: New York State Cemetery Landscapes as Reflections of a Changing American Culture to 1949. Ph.D., Syracuse University, 1984. 370p. UMI# 85201723.

EDUCATION

3348   Aspinall, Richard. Some Legal Phases of Religious Education as Related to the Work of Public Instruction in the United States.

Ph.D., New York University, 1926. 97p. UMI# 7233464.

3349   Barr, Alfred T. The Lord's Prayer and Religious Education. Ph.D., Hartford Seminary Foundation, 1924.

3350   Beadie, Nancy E. Defining the Public: Congregation, Commerce, and Social Economy in the Formation of the Educational System, 1790-1840. Ph.D., Syracuse University, 1989. 384p. UMI# 9012744.

3351   Beck, Kenneth N. The American Institute of Sacred Literature: A Historical Analysis of an Adult Education Institution. Ph.D., University of Chicago, 1968.

3352   Bell, Arthur D. The Teaching Program of Religious Foundations at State Colleges and Universities. Ph.D., Southwestern Baptist Theological Seminary, 1949.

3353   Bertrand, Arthur L. The Religious Motive in Development of Education in Colonial Western Massachusetts. Ph.D., University of Connecticut, 1965. 208p. UMI# 66-00818.

3354   Bostrom, Harvey R. Contributions to Higher Education by the Society for the Promotion of Collegiate and Theological Education at the West, 1843-1874. Ph.D., New York University, 1960. 260p. UMI# 60-03736.

3355   Boyer, Edward S. The Development of Religious Education in Higher Institutions With Special Reference to Schools of Religion at State Universities and Colleges. Ph.D., Northwestern University, 1926.

3356   Brewer, Wallace. History of Advanced Church Education in Oklahoma. Ph.D., University of Oklahoma, 1945. 217p.

3357   Brill, Earl H. Religion and the Rise of the University: A Study of the Secularization of American Higher Education, 1870-1910. Ph.D., American University, 1969. 636p. UMI# 70-156693.

3358   Brown, Marianna C. Sunday-School Movements in America. Ph.D., Columbia University, 1902. 269p.

3359   Brown, Samuel W. The Secularization of American Education as Shown by State Legislation, State Constitutional Provisions, and State Supreme Court Decisions. Ph.D., Columbia University, 1912. 160p.

3360   Bryan, Daniel B. The History of the Secularization of Education in

North Carolina. Ed.D., New York University, 1915. 111p. UMI# 72-33487.

3361 Burnstein, Ira J. The American Movement to Develop Church Colleges for Men in Japan, 1868-1912. Ph.D., University of Michigan, 1964. 222p. UMI# 65-05278.

3362 Calam, John H. Parsons and Pedagogues: The SPG Adventure in American Education. Ph.D., Columbia University, 1969. 395p. UMI# 69-15664.

3363 Caldwell, Cleon C. The Development of Concepts Regarding the Use of Tax Funds for Public and Parochial Schools. Ph.D., University of Minnesota, 1956. 864p. UMI# 17841.

3364 Carrell, William D. Social, Political, and Religious Involvements of American College Professors, 1750-1800. Ph.D., George Peabody College for Teachers, 1968. 194p. UMI# 68-16341.

3365 Carson, Suzanne C. Samuel Chapman Armstrong: Missionary to the South. Ph.D., Johns Hopkins University, 1952.

3366 Cassidy, Ivan. The Calvinist Tradition in Education in France, Scotland and New England During the Sixteenth and Seventeenth Centuries. Ph.D., Queen's University-Belfast, 1966. 340p.

3367 Chirico, Joann. Defining America: The Religious Function of Education. Ph.D., University of Pittsburgh, 1984. 257p. UMI# 8511063.

3368 Clement, Stephen M., III. Aspects of Student Religion at Vassar College, 1861-1914. Ed.D., Harvard University, 1977. 293p. UMI# 77-32060.

3369 Confrey, Burton. Secularism in American Education, Its History. Ph.D., Catholic University of America, 1931. 153p.

3370 Cox, Joseph G. The Administration of Seminaries: Historical Synopsis and Commentary. Ph.D., Catholic University of America, 1931. 124p.

3371 Crawford, John O. The Impact of Puritanism on Education. Ph.D., University of Colorado, 1956. 180p. UMI# 22597.

3372 Davis, James M. Frontier and Religious Influences on Higher Education: 1796-1860. Ed.D., Northern Illinois University, 1975. 226p. UMI# 76-08909.

3373   Dawson, John H. A Survey of the Religious Content of American World History Textbooks Written Prior to 1900. Ph.D., University of Pittsburgh, 1954. 262p. UMI# 08886.

3374   Deschamps, Nello E. The Secularization of American Higher Education: The Relationship Between Religion and the University as Perceived by Selected University Presidents, 1867-1913. Ph.D., University of Southern California, 1976.

3375   Dimock, Hedley S. Educational Implications of the Scientific Understanding of Religion. Ph.D., University of Chicago, 1926.

3376   Donovan, Charles F. Education in American Social Thought, 1865-1900. Educational Ideas of Social Scientists and Social-Minded Clergymen. Ph.D., Yale University, 1948. 306p. UMI# 64-11368.

3377   Drakeman, Lisa N. Seminary Sisters: Mount Holyoke's First Students, 1837-1849. Ph.D., Princeton University, 1988. 330p. UMI# 8919195.

3378   Ebersole, Mark C. A History of the Christian Association of the University of Pennsylvania. Ph.D., Columbia University, 1952. 208p. UMI# 04176.

3379   Fink, Jerome S. The Purposes of the American Colonial Colleges. Ed.D., Stanford University, 1958. 224p. UMI# 5801272.

3380   Fiske, George W. The Sanction for Religious Education Based on the Function of Religion in Social Evolution. Ph.D., Boston University, 1919.

3381   Flynn, Luther. A Study of Moral, Spiritual, and Religious Values in the Public Schools of Virginia. Ed.D., University of Virginia, 1956. 236p. UMI# 0017631.

3382   Frank, Thomas E. Conserving a Rational World: Theology, Ethics, and the Nineteenth Century American College Ideal. Ph.D., Emory University, 1981. 366p. UMI# 81-24260.

3383   Gallagher, Thomas H. The History of the Sunday School Curriculum. Ph.D., New York University, 1914. 170p. UMI# 7403387.

3384   Godbold, Albea. Some Factors in the Rise and Character of the Church Colleges in the Ante-Bellum Seaboard South. Ph.D., Duke University, 1939.

3385   Goodman, Ruth P.W. Ideals of Life and Man and the Common

School Theories of Moral Education for the Public Schools From Horace Mann to John Dewey. Ph.D., Washington University, 1969. 332p. UMI# 7010955.

3386   Hall, Arthur J. Religious Education in the Public Schools of the State and City of New York, A Historical Study. Ph.D., University of Chicago, 1911. 111p.

3387   Hargis, Ronald I. Perspectives in Personalism: George Albert Coe, Pioneer in Religion. Th.D., Pacific School of Religion, 1962. 494p. UMI# 62-05727.

3388   Harker, John S. The Life and Contributions of Calvin Ellis Stowe. Ph.D., University of Pittsburgh, 1951. 134p.

3389   Harris, Yvonne B. The History of the Penn School Under Its Founders at St. Helena Island, Frogmore, South Carolina, 1862-1908. Ph.D., American University, 1979. 177p. UMI# 8000753.

3390   Hayes, Mary B. A Comparative Study of Public and Parochial Elementary Education in the Nineteenth Century in New York City. Ph.D., Fordham University, 1936.

3391   Hershey, C.B. The Church and Higher Education in the United States. Ed.D., Harvard University, 1923.

3392   Holtz, Adrian A. A Study of the Moral and Religious Elements in American Secondary Education up to 1800. Ph.D., University of Chicago, 1914. 86p.

3393   Howley, Mary C. The Treatment of Religion in American History Textbooks for Grades Seven and Eight From 1783-1956. Ph.D., Columbia University, 1960.

3394   Jeppson, Joseph H. The Secularization of the University of Utah to 1920. Ph.D., University of California-Berkeley, 1973. 357p. UMI# 73-19729.

3395   Kemp, William W. The Support of Schools in Colonial New York by the Society for the Propagation of the Gospel in Foreign Parts. Ph.D., Columbia University, 1914. 279p.

3396   Kilman, Gail A. Southern Collegiate Women Higher Education at Wesleyan Female College and Randolph-Macon Woman's College, 1893-1907. Ph.D., University of Delaware, 1984. 201p. UMI# 8420977.

3397   Kniker, Charles R. The Chautauqua Literary and Scientific Circle,

1878-1914: An Historical Interpretation of an Educational Piety in Industrial America. Ed.D., Columbia University, 1969. 419p. UMI# 71-14328.

3398   Knoff, Gerald E. The Yale Divinity School, 1858-1899. Ph.D., Yale University, 1936.

3399   Lankard, Frank G. A History of the American Sunday School Curriculum. Ph.D., Northwestern University, 1926.

3400   Le Duc, Thomas H.A. Piety and Intellect. The Relations of Religion and Learning at Amherst College, 1865-1912. Ph.D., Yale University, 1943.

3401   Lee, James W. The Development of Theology at Oberlin. Ph.D., Drew University, 1953.

3402   Luker, Richard M. The Western Reserve and a Legacy for Higher Education: Faculty Self-Governance at Oberlin College Under the Finney Compact, 1834-1846. Ed.D., University of Akron, 1985. 451p. UMI# 8514701.

3403   MacNaughton, Douglas. The Development of Secularism in Education, Particularly in the Northwest Territory, Prior to 1860. Ph.D., University of Chicago, 1956.

3404   Mahoney, Charles J. The Relation of the State to Religious Education in Early New York, 1633-1825. Ph.D., Catholic University of America, 1941. 233p.

3405   Maynard, Donald M. Influence on Religious Education of G. Stanley Hall's Theory of Recapitulation. Ph.D., Yale University, 1936.

3406   McDonald, Cleveland. The History of Cedarville College. Ph.D., Ohio State University, 1966. 235p. UMI# 6615114.

3407   McKinney, Larry J. An Historical Analysis of the Bible College Movement During Its Formative Years: 1881-1920. Ed.D., Temple University, 1986. 456p. UMI# 8627486.

3408   McPheeters, Alphonso A. The Origin and Development of Clark University and Gammon Theological Seminary, 1869-1944. Ph.D., University of Cincinnati, 1944. 67p.

3409   Medlin, Stuart B. The Founding of the Permanent Denominational Colleges in Virginia, 1776-1861. Ed.D., College of William and Mary, 1976. 143p. UMI# 76-11137.

3410   Moore, Jean S. Religious Education Among German Inhabitants of Colonial Pennsylvania. Ph.D., Hartford Seminary Foundation, 1925.

3411   Morris, William S. The Seminary Movement in the United States: Projects, Foundations, and Early Development, 1833-1866. Ph.D., Catholic University of America, 1932. 119p.

3412   Naylor, Natalie A. Raising a Learned Ministry: The American Education Society, 1815-1860. Ed.D., Columbia University, 1971. 430p. UMI# 72-12805.

3413   Ognibene, Richard T. Protestant and Catholic Views of Education, 1865-1900: National and Local Views Compared. Ed.D., University of Rochester, 1973. 265p. UMI# 73-25880.

3414   Perko, Francis M. A Time to Favor Zion: A Case Study of Religion as a Force in American Educational Development, 1830-1870. Ph.D., Stanford University, 1981. 255p. UMI# 8124131.

3415   Peterson, Charles E., Jr. Theron Baldwin and Higher Education in the Old Northwest. Ph.D., Johns Hopkins University, 1961.

3416   Pope, Christie F. Preparation for Pedestals: North Carolina Antebellum Female Seminaries. Ph.D., University of Chicago, 1977.

3417   Prickett, James R. Religious Practices in the Public Schools of Pittsburgh, Pennsylvania: 1834-1965. Ph.D., University of Pittsburgh, 1970. 182p. UMI# 71-16189.

3418   Rozeboom, Garrett G. The History of Christian Secondary Education in Iowa. Ed.D., University of Northern Colorado, 1958. 306p. UMI# 5900108.

3419   Schwalm, Vernon F. The Historical Development of the Denominational Colleges of the Old Northwest to 1870. Ph.D., University of Chicago, 1926.

3420   Seckinger, Richard K. Relation of the State to Religious Education in Pennsylvania, 1776-1874. Ph.D., Columbia University, 1953.

3421   Session, Mary J. Denominational Colleges of Michigan and the 1855 Act for Incorporation of Institutions of Learning. Ph.D., Wayne State University, 1989. 183p. UMI# 9022449.

3422   Sheehan, Patrick M. Harvard Alumni in Colonial America: Demographic, Theological, and Political Perspectives. Ph.D., Case Western Reserve University, 1972. 237p. UMI# 72-18736.

3423   Shepard, Robert S. The Science of Religion in American Universities: 1880-1930. A Comparison of Six Institutions. Ph.D., University of Chicago, 1988.

3424   Slavens, Thomas P. The Library of Union Theological Seminary in the City of New York, 1836 to the Present. Ph.D., University of Michigan, 1965. 368p. UMI# 66-06705.

3425   Smith, Sherman M. The Relation of the State to Religious Education in Massachusetts. Ph.D., Clark University, 1925. 350p.

3426   Spencer, Thomas E. Education and American Liberalism: A Comparison of the Views of Thomas Jefferson, Ralph Waldo Emerson, and John Dewey. Ph.D., University of Illinois at Urbana-Champaign, 1963. 262p. UMI# 6402972.

3427   Stevenson, Louise L. Scholarly Means to Evangelical Ends: The New Haven Scholars, 1840-1890. Ph.D., Boston University, 1981. 275p. UMI# 81-26812.

3428   Stewart, George. A History of Religious Education in Connecticut to the Middle of the Nineteenth Century. Ph.D., Yale University, 1921. 400p.

3429   Swiniarski, Louise B. A Comparative Study of Elizabeth Palmer Peabody and Susan Elizabeth Blow by Examination of Their Work and Writings. Ph.D., Boston College, 1976. 220p. UMI# 7618421.

3430   Tewksbury, Donald G. The Founding of American Colleges and Universities Before the Civil War, With Particular Reference to the Religious Influences Bearing Upon the College Movement. Ph.D., Columbia University Teachers College, 1932.

3431   Tingelstad, Oscar A. The Religious Element in American School Readers up to 1830: A Bibliographical and Statistical Study. Ph.D., University of Chicago, 1925.

3432   Van Brummelen, Harro W. Molding God's Children: The History of Curriculum in Christian Schools Rooted in Dutch Calvinism. Ed.D., University of British Columbia, 1984. UMI# 0557671.

3433   Vinie, Earl. The Treatment of the Principle of Religious Freedom and Other Religious Content in American History Textbooks for Elementary and Secondary Schools. Ph.D., Yale University, 1929.

3434   Wall, Margaret E. Puritanism in Education: An Analysis of the Transition From Religiosity to Secular Morality as Seen in Primary

Reading Materials 1620-1775. Ph.D., Washington University, 1979. 363p. UMI# 80-02468.

3435   Wayland, John T. The Theological Department in Yale College, 1822-1858. Ph.D., Yale University, 1933. 511p. UMI# 64-11903.

3436   Wilbee, Victor R. The Religious Dimensions of Three Presidencies in a State University: Presidents Tappan, Haven, and Angell at the University of Michigan. Ph.D., University of Michigan, 1967. 244p. UMI# 67-17858.

3437   Wilhoit, James C. An Examination of the Educational Principles of an Early Nineteenth Century Sunday School Curriculum: The "Union Questions". Ph.D., Northwestern University, 1983. 276p. UMI# 8400750.

3438   Williams, Lester A. Religious Education in the Public Schools of the United States in the Light of Its History. Ed.D., New York University, 1912. 134p. UMI# 72-33802.

3439   Wilson, Karl K. Historical Survey of the Religious Content of American Geography Textbooks From 1784 to 1895. Ph.D., University of Pittsburgh, 1951. 134p.

3440   Wittmer, Paul W. The Secularization of Geology Textbooks in the United States in the Nineteenth Century. Ph.D., New York University, 1967. 372p. UMI# 68-06174.

3441   Young, James R. Relation of the Church and Clergy to Education in the American Colonies. Ph.D., University of Chicago, 1916.

3442   Zimmer, Agatho P. Changing Concepts of Higher Education in America Since 1700. Ph.D., Catholic University of America, 1939.

ETHNIC GROUPS

3443   Bernard, Richard M. The Melting Pot and the Altar: Marital Assimilation in Wisconsin, 1850-1920. Ph.D., University of Wisconsin-Madison, 1977. 354p. UMI# 7725809.

3444   Brackman, Harold D. The Ebb and Flow of Conflict: A History of Black-Jewish Relations Through 1900. Ph.D., University of California-Los Angeles, 1977. 637p. UMI# 77-19625.

3445   Bukowozyk, John J. Steeples and Smokestacks: Class, Religion, and Ideology in the Polish Immigrant Settlements in Greenpoint and Williamsburg, Brooklyn, 1880-1929. Ph.D., Harvard University, 1980.

3446   Harkavy, Ira R. Reference Group Theory and Group Conflict and Cohesion in Advanced Capitalist Societies: Presbyterians, Workers, and Jews in Philadelphia, 1790-1968. Ph.D., University of Pennsylvania, 1979. 627p. UMI# 79-28138.

3447   Kuyper, Susan J. The Americanization of German Immigrants: Language, Religion and Schools in Nineteenth Century Rural Wisconsin. Ph.D., University of Wisconsin-Madison, 1980. 228p. UMI# 81-07844.

3448   Longenecker, Stephen L. Democracy's Pulpit: Religion and Egalitarianism Among Early Pennsylvania Germans. Ph.D., Johns Hopkins University, 1990. 303p. UMI# 9018602.

3449   Overmoehle, M. Hedwigis. The Anti-Clerical Activities of the Forty-Eighters in Wisconsin, 1848-1860: A Study in German-American Liberalism. Ph.D., St. Louis University, 1941. 377p. UMI# 00484.

3450   Puotinen, Arthur E. Finnish Radicals and Religion in Midwestern Mining Towns, 1865-1914. Ph.D., University of Chicago, 1974.

3451   Skavery, Stanley. A Case Study of the Irish of Detroit, 1850-1880. Ed.D., University of Michigan, 1986. 152p. UMI# 8612456.

3452   Spitzfaden, Thomas J. Irish Redemptorists in New Orleans, 1848-1878. Th.D., New Orleans Baptist Theological Seminary, 1977.

3453   White, Joseph M. Religion and Community: Cincinnati Germans, 1814-1870. Ph.D., University of Notre Dame, 1980. 391p. UMI# 80-20972.

3454   Yoshida, Ryo. A Socio-Historical Study of Racial/Ethnic Identity in the Inculturated Religious Expression of Japanese Christianity in San Francisco, 1877-1924. Ph.D., Graduate Theological Union, 1989. 566p. UMI# 9104379.

FRATERNAL ORDERS

3455   Blakeslee, George H. The History of the Anti-Masonic Party. Ph.D., Harvard University, 1903.

3456   Brackney, William H. Religious Antimasonry: The Genesis of a Political Party. Ph.D., Temple University, 1976. 393p. UMI# 76-22080.

3457   Bullock, Steven C. The Ancient and Honorable Society:

Freemasonry in America, 1730-1830. Ph.D., Brown University, 1986. 316p. UMI# 8617541.

3458   Carter, James D. Freemasonry in Texas: Background, History, and Influence to 1846. Ph.D., University of Texas-Austin, 1954.

3459   Fels, Anthony D. The Square and Compass: San Francisco's Freemasons and American Religion, 1870-1900. Ph.D., Stanford University, 1987. 806p. UMI# 8722992.

3460   Haigh, Elizabeth B. New York Antimasons 1826-1833. Ph.D., University of Rochester, 1980. 373p. UMI# 8028906.

3461   Hixson, Charles R., III. Antimasonry in Western New York: A Social and Political Analysis. Ph.D., University of California-Los Angeles, 1983. 304p. UMI# 8321987.

3462   Huss, Wayne A. Pennsylvania Freemasonry: An Intellectual and Social Analysis, 1727-1826. Ph.D., Temple University, 1985. 386p. UMI# 8509374.

3463   Lipson, Dorothy A. Freemasonry in Connecticut, 1789-1835. Ph.D., University of Connecticut, 1974. 523p. UMI# 7421794.

3464   Markham, Don C. Freemasonry and the Churches. D.Min., Colgate Rochester Divinity School/Bexley Hall/Crozer Theological Seminary, 1982.

3465   McCarthy, Charles. The Anti-Masonic Party. Ph.D., University of Wisconsin-Madison, 1901.

3466   Rupp, Robert O. Social Tension and Political Mobilization in Jacksonian Society: A Case Study of the Antimasonic Party in New York, Pennsylvania and Vermont, 1827-1840. Ph.D., Syracuse University, 1983. 314p. UMI# 8400786.

LITERATURE

3467   Aamodt, Terrie D. Righteous Armies, Holy Cause, Apocalyptic Imagery and the Civil War. Ph.D., Boston University, 1986. 331p. UMI# 8621407.

3468   Abel, Aaron D. The Immortal Pilgrim: An Ethical Interpretation of Hawthorne's Fiction. Ph.D., University of Michigan, 1949. 384p. UMI# 1182.

3469   Adams, Ann J. Sisters of the Light: The Importance of Spirituality in the Afra-American Novel. Ph.D., Indiana University, 1989. 382p. UMI# 9012147.

3470   Adams, Francis D. The Major Religious Poems of Christopher Smart. Ph.D., University of Southern California, 1965. 220p. UMI# 66-03815.

3471   Addison, Elizabeth H. Emerson, Quakerism, and an American Aesthetic. Ph.D., Duke University, 1985. 361p. UMI# 8614423.

3472   Ahrens, Katherine L. The Function of Religious Imagery in the Poetry of Emily Dickinson. Ph.D., Fordham University, 1973. 183p. UMI# 74-02773.

3473   Alaimo, Joseph P. A Natural History of American Virtue: Melville's Critique of the Transcendental Hero. Ph.D., University of Minnesota, 1974. 374p. UMI# 7502080.

3474   Alberti, John F. "Forms, Measured Forms": Relativism and the Moral Imagination of the Artist in the Works of Herman Melville. Ph.D., University of California-Los Angeles, 1989. 314p. UMI# 9006084.

3475   Alsen, Eberhard. Hawthorne: A Puritan Tieck, A Comparative Analysis of the Tales of Hawthorne and the *Marchen* of Tieck. Ph.D., Indiana University, 1967. 228p. UMI# 67-15061.

3476   Anderson, Marcia J. Devils and Divines: The New England Puritan in American Drama. Ph.D., Brandeis University, 1968. 428p. UMI# 69-02042.

3477   Andola, John A. Nathaniel Hawthorne's Use of Mesmerism in Four Major Works. Ed.D., Ball State University, 1977. 171p. UMI# 8122765.

3478   Anker, Roy M. Doubt and Faith in Late Nineteenth-Century American Fiction. Ph.D., Michigan State University, 1973. 425p. UMI# 74-05998.

3479   Armao, Agnes O. In the Matter of a New God: The Nineteenth-Century Literary Response to America's Deification of Law. Ph.D., Temple University, 1981. UMI# 81-15849.[Nathaniel Hawthorne, Herman Melville, Harriet Beecher Stowe, Henry David Thoreau].

3480   Askin, Denise T. Prophet of the Square Deific: Savior and Satan in the Works of Walt Whitman. Ph.D., University of Notre Dame, 1975. 258p. UMI# 74-13921.

3481   Auer, Michael J. Angels and Beasts: Gnosticism in American Literature. Ph.D., University of North Carolina-Chapel Hill, 1976. 232p. UMI# 77-02018.

3482   Baker, William D., Jr. The Influence of Mesmerism in Nineteenth Century American Literature. Ph.D., Northwestern University, 1950.

3483   Bakhsh, Jalaluddien K. Melville and Islam. Ph.D., Florida State University, 1988. 152p. UMI# 8814399.

3484   Baldwin, Lewis M., II. Moses and Mannerism: An Aesthetic for the Poetry of Colonial New England. Ph.D., Syracuse University, 1973. 156p. UMI# 7417559.

3485   Banta, Martha. The Two Worlds of Henry James: A Study in the Fiction of the Supernatural. Ph.D., Indiana University, 1964. 402p. UMI# 6503463.

3486   Benensohn-Sager, Karen M. American Abrahams: Some Antinomian Themes in American Literature. Ph.D., Northwestern University, 1977. 260p. UMI# 7805325.[C.B. Brown, Nathaniel Hawthorne, Anne Hutchinson, Soren Kierkegaard, Herman Melville, Jean-Paul Sartre, Henry David Thoreau].

3487   Benjamin, Nancy B. Traditional Enclosed Gardens in Nineteenth-Century American Fiction: The Constriction of Adamic Aspirations. Ph.D., University of Houston, 1984. 380p. UMI# 8426548.[James Fenimore Cooper, Nathaniel Hawthorne, Henry James].

3488   Bense, Charles J. Emerson and Hawthorne as Cultural Reporters: A Reevaluation of *English Traits* and *Our Old Home*. Ph.D., University of California-Davis, 1989. 394p. UMI# 9009231.

3489   Bensick, Carol M. La Nouvelle Beatrice: Renaissance Medicine and New England Theory in Hawthorne's *Rappaccini's Daughter*. Ph.D., Cornell University, 1982. 224p. UMI# 8228423.

3490   Bergquist, Bruce A. Walt Whitman and the Bible: Language Echoes, Images, Allusions, and Ideas. Ph.D., University of Nebraska-Lincoln, 1979. 322p. UMI# 79-26338.

3491   Bergstrom, Robert F. The Impulsive Counterchange: The Development and Artistic Expression of Melville's Religious Thought, 1846-1857. Ph.D., Duke University, 1968. 314p. UMI# 6911939.

3492   Bernstein, John A. Pacifism and Rebellion in the Writings of

Herman Melville. Ph.D., University of Pennsylvania, 1961. 290p. UMI# 6202821.

3493   Bloodgood, Melanie M. The Gnostic Nature of the World View and Fictional Themes of Herman Melville. Ph.D., Oklahoma State University, 1984. 434p. UMI# 8427645.

3494   Bloore, John S. The Jew in American Dramatic Literature, 1794-1930. Ph.D., New York University, 1950. 506p. UMI# 73-08434.

3495   Boland, Reed A. The Religious Dimensions of the Work of Edgar Allan Poe. Ph.D., Harvard University, 1977.

3496   Bowman, George W. Hawthorne and Religion. Ph.D., Indiana University, 1954. 180p. UMI# 10140.

3497   Braswell, William. Herman Melville and Christianity. Ph.D., University of Chicago, 1934.

3498   Breitwieser, Mitchell R. Plastic Economy: The Painful Birth of New Vision in the Writings of Cotton Mather and Walt Whitman. Ph.D., State University of New York-Buffalo, 1979. 227p. UMI# 8005641.

3499   Bretz, Ann C. Blossom of the Brain: Religious Experience in the Poetry of Emily Dickinson. Ph.D., University of Chicago, 1973. 237p.

3500   Britton, Wesley A. Mark Twain: "Cradle Skeptic". Ph.D., University of North Texas, 1990. 177p. UMI# 9105008.

3501   Bronstein, Zelda J. The Prophet of Art: Hawthorne and the Romance of American Democracy. Ph.D., University of California-Santa Cruz, 1981. 533p. UMI# 8302191.

3502   Bruce, Marjorie C. From a Theological Mode to a Biological Mode: Changing Psychological Assumptions in the American Novel: 1865-1900. Ph.D., University of California-Berkeley, 1972.

3503   Buschmann, Walter M. The Concept of Language in the Thought of George Herbert Mead and the Problem of Religious Language. Ph.D., University of Chicago, 1973. 176p.

3504   Calvert, Steven L. Christian Redemption From Chaos: The Religious Henry James in The Princess Casamassima. Ph.D., Rutgers University, 1975. 183p. UMI# 75-24668.

3505   Cappello, Mary C. Writing the Spirit/Reading the Mind: Representations of Illness and Health in Nineteenth Century

American Literature. Ph.D., State University of New York-Buffalo, 1988. 317p. UMI# 8905401.

3506   Carson, Sharon L. Ambiguous Tradition: Religious Language and Problems of Cultural Authority in Selected 19th-Century American Literature. Ph.D., University of Washington, 1990. 301p. UMI# 9104208.

3507   Carter, Stephen L. From the "Sacred Selfe" to the "Separate Self": A Study of the Mystical Elements in Five American Poets Prior to 1900. Ph.D., Texas Tech University, 1977. 369p. UMI# 7731140.[Emily Dickinson, Ralph Waldo Emerson, Edgar Allan Poe, Edward Taylor, Walt Whitman].

3508   Casale, Ottavio M. Edgar Allan Poe and Transcendentalism: Conflict and Affinity. Ph.D., University of Michigan, 1965. 160p. UMI# 66-05043.

3509   Chaffee, Patricia A. The Lee Shore: Volition, Time, and Death in the Fiction of Herman Melville. Ph.D., Indiana University, 1971. 180p. UMI# 7206757.

3510   Chang, Young-Hee. Journeys Between the Real and the Ideal. D.A., State University of New York-Albany, 1985. 151p. UMI# 8526835.[Ralph Waldo Emerson, Herman Melville, Henry David Thoreau, Mark Twain, Walt Whitman].

3511   Cherry, Joyce L. "Thoughts Unspeakable, but Full of Faith": Biblical Wisdom Concepts in Herman Melville's *Mardi* and *Pierre*. Ph.D., Emory University, 1987. 264p. UMI# 8803285.

3512   Church, Michael T. The Celibate Ideal: Transformation and the Process of Identity in Henry James's *The Ambassadors*. Ph.D., University of Kentucky, 1976. 238p. UMI# 7715940.

3513   Clark, James W., Jr. The Tradition of Salem Witchcraft in American Literature: 1820-1870. Ph.D., Duke University, 1970. 213p. UMI# 71-10361.

3514   Cleary, Barbara A.R. The Scarlet Amulet: The Woman's Limitations as Redeemer in Hawthorne's Major Fiction. Ph.D., University of Nebraska-Lincoln, 1975. 183p. UMI# 7604514.

3515   Cline, John. Hawthorne and the Bible. Ph.D., Duke University, 1948.

3516   Clouser, Marcia A.M. Mystic Gestures: Herman Melville's Images of the Body. Ph.D., University of Texas-Austin, 1979. 504p. UMI# 8009842.

3517   Cobb, Robert P. Society Versus Solitude: Studies in Emerson, Thoreau, Hawthorne, and Whitman. Ph.D., University of Michigan, 1955. 164p. UMI# 12556.

3518   Cody, Robert L. Providence in the Novels of Samuel Clemens. Ph.D., University of Florida, 1978. 162p. UMI# 78-17433.

3519   Collins, Christopher. The Uses of Observation: A Study of Correspondential Vision in the Writings of Emerson, Thoreau, and Whitman. Ph.D., Columbia University, 1964. 193p. UMI# 6502013.

3520   Collins, Frank M. The Religious and Ethical Ideas of James Fenimore Cooper. Ph.D., University of Wisconsin-Madison, 1954.

3521   Collins, John D. American Drama in Antislavery Agitation, 1792-1861. Ph.D., University of Iowa, 1963. 449p. UMI# 6304727.

3522   Conner, Frederick W. Cosmic Optimism: A Study of the Interpretation of the Idea of Evolution by American Poets From Ralph Waldo Emerson to Edwin Arlington Robinson. Ph.D., University of Pennsylvania, 1944.

3523   Connors, Donald F. Enchanted Wilderness: A Commentary on Thomas Morton's *New English Canaan*. Ph.D., Columbia University, 1961. 198p. UMI# 6102658.

3524   Cook, Dayton G. The Apocalyptic Novel: *Moby-Dick* and *Doktor Faustus*. Ph.D., University of Colorado-Boulder, 1974. 219p. UMI# 7422329.

3525   Couser, Griffith T. American Autobiography: The Prophetic Mode. Ph.D., Brown University, 1977. 410p. UMI# 8307965.[Jonathan Edwards, Ralph Waldo Emerson, Benjamin Franklin, Increase Mather, Thomas Shepard, Henry David Thoreau, John Woolman].

3526   Cross, Randy K. Religious Skepticism in Selected Novels of Mark Twain. Ph.D., University of Mississippi, 1982. 133p. UMI# 8217292.

3527   Cuni, Sandra L. Matthew Arnold and Walt Whitman: Objectivist and Transcendental Orientations in the Context of Self. Ph.D., University of Pittsburgh, 1972. 135p. UMI# 73-04100.

3528   Daigrepont, Lloyd M. Hawthorne's Conception of History: A Study of the Author's Response to Alienation From God and Man. Ph.D., Louisiana State University, 1979. 296p. UMI# 79-27521.

3529   Daniel, Stephen L. From Letter to Spirit: A Fourfold Hermeneutic and Its Application to Selected American Poems. Ph.D., Emory

University, 1974. 303p. UMI# 7423659.[Ralph Waldo Emerson, Edward Taylor, William Carlos Williams].

3530   Danielson, Susan S. Alternative Therapies: Spiritualism and Women's Rights in *Mary Lyndon; Or, Revelations of a Life*. Ph.D., University of Oregon, 1990. 259p. UMI# 9111101.

3531   Davies, James W. The Vision of Evil: An Inquiry Into the Dialogue Between Emerson, Melville, and Hawthorne and the Nineteenth Century. Ph.D., Union Theological Seminary, 1958.

3532   Davis, Frank M. Herman Melville and the Nineteenth-Century Church Community. Ph.D., Duke University, 1966. 337p. UMI# 67-06100.

3533   Davis, William P. The "Lords" and "Witnesses" of Creation: Mythologizing and Demythologizing Nature in American Literature. Ph.D., Case Western Reserve University, 1990. 235p. UMI# 9021370.[Annie Dillard, Ralph Waldo Emerson, Henry David Thoreau].

3534   De Saegher, William J. James Russell Lowell and the Bible. Ph.D., University of California-Los Angeles, 1964. 372p. UMI# 64-12215.

3535   Dean, Harold L. The *New England Courant*, 1721-1726: A Chapter in the History of American Culture. Ph.D., Brown University, 1943. 305p.

3536   Dew, Marjorie C. Herman Melville's Existential View of the Universe: Essays in Phenomenological Interpretation. Ph.D., Kent State University, 1966. 285p. UMI# 6709417.

3537   Doriani, Beth M. Emily Dickson: Daughter of Prophecy. Ph.D., University of Notre Dame, 1990. 290p. UMI# 9033095.

3538   Duban, James. Melville and Christianity: His Masquerade. Ph.D., Cornell University, 1976. 315p. UMI# 77-05738.

3539   Dula, Michael W. Laughter in the Dark: The Jester God in American Literature. Ph.D., University of Virginia, 1986. 285p. UMI# 8716970.

3540   Dussinger, Gloria R. The Romantic Concept of the Self, Applied to the Works of Emerson, Whitman, Hawthorne, and Melville. Ph.D., Lehigh University, 1973. 306p. UMI# 7406680.

3541   Early, Gerald L. "A Servant of Servants Shall He Be...": Paternalism and Millennialism in American Slavery Literature, 1850-1859. Ph.D.,

Cornell University, 1982. 231p. UMI# 8228437.

3542   Elder, Marjorie J. Nathaniel Hawthorne: Transcendental Symbolist. Ph.D., University of Chicago, 1963.

3543   Elliott, Patrick F. Melville's Tragic Vision: An Essay in Theological Criticism. Ph.D., University of Chicago, 1964.

3544   Ensor, Allison R., Jr. Mark Twain and the Bible. Ph.D., Indiana University, 1965. 320p. UMI# 66-01443.

3545   Fagan, David L. The Voyage to Easter: Melville's Resolution of Doubt and Belief. Ph.D., Florida State University, 1975. 191p. UMI# 7526768.

3546   Fairbanks, Henry G. Hawthorne's "Catholic" Critique. Ph.D., University of Notre Dame, 1954. 411p. UMI# 10724.

3547   Fayez, Ghulam M. Mystic Ideas and Images in Jalal Al-Din Rumi and Walt Whitman. Ph.D., University of Arizona, 1978. 179p. UMI# 79-9438.

3548   Felsen, Karl E. Toward a Redefinition of Metaphysical Poetry: Donne, Herbert, Crashaw, and Edward Taylor. Ph.D., State University of New York-Albany, 1975. 228p. UMI# 7519567.

3549   Ferguson, Helen M. Nathaniel Hawthorne and Charles Wentworth Upham: The Witchcraft Connection. Ph.D., University of Maryland, 1980. 358p. UMI# 8116473.

3550   Fick, Leonard J. The Theology of Nathaniel Hawthorne. Ph.D., Ohio State University, 1951. 184p.

3551   Finholt, Richard D. The Murder of Moby Dick: Mad Metaphysics and Salvation Psychology in American Fiction. Ph.D., Northern Illinois University, 1975. 218p. UMI# 74-09864.

3552   Fisher, Marilyn M. "If He Is Wicked and Cruel, as This Theology Makes Him, We Do Not Want His Heaven!": Women and Their Perceptions of Calvinism and Salvation in Selected Novels, 1850-1900. Ph.D., Indiana University of Pennsylvania, 1986. 396p. UMI# 8629041.

3553   Fitzgerald, A. Boylan, Jr. The Literary, Political and Religious Ideas of James Russell Lowell. Ph.D., Drew University, 1943. 363p.

3554   Flick, Robert G. Emily Dickinson: Mystic and Skeptic. Ph.D., University of Florida, 1967. 383p. UMI# 6809471.

3555   Foley, Marie L. The Key of Holy Sympathy: Hawthorne's Social Ideal. Ph.D., Tulane University, 1969. 185p. UMI# 70-06394.

3556   Ford, Thomas W. The Theme of Death in the Poetry of Emily Dickinson. Ph.D., University of Texas-Austin, 1959. 236p. UMI# 5904717.

3557   Foreman, Clifford W. Typology in the Fiction of Nathaniel Hawthorne. Ph.D., Boston University, 1987. 337p. UMI# 8629780.

3558   Frankel, Gusti W. Between Parent and Child in Colonial New England: An Analysis of the Religious Child-Oriented Literature and Selected Children's Works. Ph.D., University of Minnesota, 1976. 280p. UMI# 7718986.

3559   Friedman, George S. Reconstruction and Redemption in Selected American Novels, 1878-1915. Ph.D., Duke University, 1972. 433p. UMI# 7231570.

3560   Fulghum, Walter B., Jr. Quaker Influences on Whitman's Religious Thought. Ph.D., Northwestern University, 1943.

3561   Gallagher, Susan V.Z. "The Sane Madness of Vital Truth": Prophets and Prophecy in the Fiction of Herman Melville. Ph.D., Emory University, 1982. 301p. UMI# 8305958.

3562   Gamble, Richard H. The Figure of the Protestant Clergyman in American Fiction. Ph.D., University of Pittsburgh, 1972. 238p. UMI# 7301658.

3563   Garrett, William N. The Poems and Sermons of Thomas Coombe (1747-1822). Edited and With an Introduction and Annotation. Ph.D., Columbia University, 1965. 306p. UMI# 6601710.

3564   Gerlach, John C. The Kingdom of God and Nineteenth Century American Fiction. Ph.D., Arizona State University, 1969. 250p. UMI# 6916478.

3565   Gifford, Carey J. Space and Time as Religious Symbols in Ante-Bellum America. Ph.D., Claremont Graduate School, 1980. 253p. UMI# 80-05336.

3566   Gilmore, Michael T. The Middle Way: Puritanism and Ideology in American Literature. Ph.D., Harvard University, 1974.

3567   Goering, Wynn M. Pacifism and Heroism in American Fiction, 1770-1860. Ph.D., University of Chicago, 1984.

3568   Goldman, Maureen. American Women and the Puritan Heritage: Anne Hutchinson to Harriet Beecher Stowe. Ph.D., Boston University, 1975. 178p. UMI# 7520990.

3569   Goldman, Stanley A. Melville's *Clarel*: The Hiddenness and Silence of God. Ph.D., Emory University, 1987. 263p. UMI# 8716111.

3570   Grant, John A., Jr. The Nature of Spirituality in Walt Whitman's *Leaves of Grass*. Ph.D., Saint Louis University, 1984. 198p. UMI# 8520111.

3571   Gravett, Sharon L. "Freezes and Thaws": Romantic Irony in the Works of Thomas Carlyle, Ralph Waldo Emerson, Henry David Thoreau, and Walt Whitman. Ph.D., Duke University, 1989. 286p. UMI# 9001057.

3572   Greenbert, Robert M. Chasing the Leviathan: Religious and Philosophic Uncertainty in *Moby-Dick*. Ph.D., City University of New York, 1978. 192p. UMI# 78-16680.

3573   Grey, Robin S. The Complicity of Imagination: Seventeenth Century English Prose and the Ideology of Assimilation in Emerson, Thoreau, and Melville. Ph.D., University of California-Los Angeles, 1988. 263p. UMI# 8903650.

3574   Griffith, Frank C. Melville and the Quest for God. Ph.D., University of Iowa, 1952. 422p. UMI# 04064.

3575   Griffiths, C. Warren. The Religious Press and Labor, 1877-1896. Ph.D., University of Chicago, 1942.

3576   Grommon, Alfred H. James Russell Lowell's Writings on Liberty, Abolition and Public Affairs, 1836-1861. Ph.D., Cornell University, 1944.

3577   Hall, Mary L. The Relation of Love and Death in the Poetry of Emily Dickinson. Ph.D., Loyola University of Chicago, 1971. 412p. UMI# 7122737.

3578   Hallisey, Joan F. Walt Whitman, Hart Crane, and Denise Levertov: Poet/Prophets in the Tradition of Ralph Waldo Emerson. Ph.D., Brown University, 1978. 342p. UMI# 79-06557.

3579   Hamilton, James W. The Sidle Into Faith: Humanistic Nihilism in Melville, Conrad, Forster. Ph.D., Cornell University, 1983. 418p. UMI# 8309508.

3580   Harris, Helen L. The Theme of Death in Mark Twain's Fiction.

Ph.D., Florida State University, 1973. 249p. UMI# 7409485.

3581   Harvey, Bonnie C. A Movement Toward the Integrated Self: Antinomianism Reflected in the Poetry of Taylor, Emerson, Dickinson, and Frost. Ph.D., Georgia State University, 1990. 326p. UMI# 9032154.

3582   Hayes, Mary J.F. "And Warmth and Chill of Wedded Life and Death": New Hopes and Old Fears in Melville's Later Poetry. Ph.D., Florida State University, 1979. 251p. UMI# 8006271.

3583   Heeney, St. Agnes. The Cathedral in Four Major New England Authors: A Study in Symbolical Inspiration. Ph.D., University of Pennsylvania, 1957. 235p. UMI# 20803.

3584   Heidmann, Mark. Melville and the Bible: Leading Themes in the Marginalia and Major Fiction, 1850-1856. Ph.D., Yale University, 1979. 305p. UMI# 8121415.

3585   Helmeci, Hollis E. Hawthorne's Allusions and Ambiguous Characters in *Rappaccini's Daughter* and, Consuming Greatness: The Boa and the Belly in Emerson's *Representative Men*. Ph.D., University of Toledo, 1988. 57p. UMI# 8909908.

3586   Herbert, Thomas W., Jr. Spiritual Exploration in *Moby-Dick*: A Study of Theological Background. Ph.D., Princeton University, 1969. 313p. UMI# 70-14252.

3587   Hesser, Dale C. The Religion of Walt Whitman. Ph.D., University of Kansas, 1958.

3588   Hibler, David J. Sexual Rhetoric in Seventeenth-Century American Literature. Ph.D., University of Notre Dame, 1970. 187p. UMI# 7105539.

3589   Hodge, Bartow M. Unsound Believers: A Study of Three American Writers. Ph.D., State University of New York-Buffalo, 1977. 211p. UMI# 77-32667.[T.S. Eliot, Nathaniel Hawthorne, Cotton Mather].

3590   Hodges, Elizabeth L. The Bible as Novel: A Comparative Study of Two Modernized Versions of Biblical Stories: Zola's *La Faute de l'Abbe Mouret* and Faulkner's *A Fable*. Ph.D., University of Georgia, 1969. 164p. UMI# 7010196.

3591   Holland, Harold E. Religious Periodicals in the Development of Nashville, Tennessee, as a Regional Publishing Center, 1830-1880. D.L.S., Columbia University, 1976. 974p. UMI# 76-30387.

3592   Holland, Jeanne E. Refiguring Themselves: The Poetry of Anne Bradstreet and Emily Dickinson. Ph.D., State University of New York-Buffalo, 1989. 267p. UMI# 9013062.

3593   Holland, Jeffrey R. Mark Twain's Religious Sense: The Viable Years 1835-1883. Ph.D., Yale University, 1973. 286p. UMI# 73-26296.

3594   Hoover, Dwight W. The Religious Basis of the Thought of the Elder Henry James. Ph.D., University of Iowa, 1953. 287p. UMI# 05477.

3595   Howard, Ursula E. The Mystical Trends in the Poetry of Emily Dickinson and Annette von Droste-Hulshoff. Ph.D., University of Illinois at Urbana-Champaign, 1974. 216p. UMI# 7500328.

3596   Huffstetler, Edward W. The Voice From the Burning Bush: Spiritual Faith and the Religion of American Primitivism. Ph.D., University of Iowa, 1988. 270p. UMI# 8913271.[James Dickey, Ralph Waldo Emerson, William Faulkner, Herman Melville, Wallace Stevens].

3597   Hughes, James M. The Dialectic of Death in Poe, Dickinson, Emerson and Whitman. Ph.D., University of Pennsylvania, 1969. 249p. UMI# 7016163.

3598   Hume, Beverly A. The Framing of Evil: Romantic Visions and Revisions in American Fiction. Ph.D., University of California-Davis, 1983. 243p. UMI# 8407902.

3599   Hunt, Leigh. Review of American Literature: Biblical Diction. Ph.D., Syracuse University, 1889.

3600   Hutchinson, George B. American Shaman: Visionary Ecstasy and Poetic Function in Whitman's Verse. Ph.D., Indiana University, 1983. 315p. UMI# 8401570.

3601   Hutchinson, William H. Demonology in Melville's Vocabulary of Evil. Ph.D., Northwestern University, 1966. 388p. UMI# 6613998.

3602   Jackson, Frank M. An Application of the Principles of Aristotelean Rhetoric to Certain Early New England Prose. Ph.D., University of Texas-Austin, 1967. 199p. UMI# 6714847.

3603   Jensen, Howard E. The Rise of Religious Journalism in the United States. Ph.D., University of Chicago, 1920.

3604   Johnson, Evelyn C. Hawthorne and the Supernatural. Ph.D., Stanford University, 1938.

3605   Johnson, Julie M. Death in the Fiction of Henry James: A Formal and Thematic Study. Ph.D., Georgia State University, 1979. 297p. UMI# 8013057.

3606   Jolliff, William G. Harold Frederic: His Position in the Context of Modernism. Ph.D., Ohio State University, 1988. 365p. UMI# 8824534.

3607   Jones, Alexander E. Mark Twain and Religion. Ph.D., University of Minnesota, 1950. 199p.

3608   Jones, Betty H. "Experience Is the Angled Road": Patterns of Spiritual Experience in the Poetry of Emily Dickinson. Ph.D., Bryn Mawr College, 1972. 157p. UMI# 7309109.

3609   Jones, Eugene M. The Angel and the Machine: Hawthorne and the Conflict Between Mechanism and Idealism in Mid-Nineteenth-Century American Fiction. Ph.D., Temple University, 1979. 326p. UMI# 7923997.

3610   Jones, Harry L. Symbolism in the Mystical Poetry of Jones Very. Ph.D., Catholic University of America, 1967. 176p. UMI# 6715458.

3611   Jones, Henry B. The Death Song of the "Noble Savage": A Study in the Idealization of the American Indian. Ph.D., University of Chicago, 1924.

3612   Jones, Mary P. Elizabeth Margaret Chandler: Poet, Essayist, Abolitionist. Ph.D., University of Toledo, 1981. 277p. UMI# 8229784.

3613   Jones, Rowena R. Emily Dickinson's "Flood Subject": Immortality. Ph.D., Northwestern University, 1960. 285p. UMI# 6004766.

3614   Jones, Wayne A. The Divided Worlds: Studies of Hawthorne's Separation Between the Material and Spiritual Realms. Ph.D., Harvard University, 1974.

3615   Kaplan, Sidney. Herman Melville and the American National Sin. Ph.D., Harvard University, 1960.

3616   Keith, Philip M. The Idea of Quakerism in American Literature. Ph.D., University of Pennsylvania, 1971. 290p. UMI# 7217376.[St. John Crevecoeur, Ralph Waldo Emerson, Nathaniel Hawthorne, Herman Melville, William Penn, Walt Whitman, John Greenleaf Whittier, Roger Williams, John Woolman].

3617   Kelly, Robert A. The Prophetic Figure in Herman Melville's

Writing. Ph.D., Louisiana State University, 1976. 158p. UMI# 76-25270.

3618   Kerr, Howard H. Spiritualism in American Literature, 1851-1886. Ph.D., University of California-Los Angeles, 1968. 279p. UMI# 69-05323.

3619   Kimber, Thomas. The Treatment of the Quaker as a Character in American Fiction, 1825-1925. Ph.D., University of Southern California, 1954. 185p.

3620   Kinslow, Kenneth J. Quaker Doctrines and Ideas in the Novels of Charles Brockden Brown. Ph.D., University of Notre Dame, 1978. 228p. UMI# 78-21648.

3621   Kirby, Robert K. Melville's Attitude Toward the Historicity and Interpretation of the Bible. Ph.D., Indiana University, 1983. 181p. UMI# 8401605.

3622   Kolbenschiag, Madonna C. The Rhetoric of American Capitalism and Its Roots in Religious Ethos: A Study in Nineteenth-Century American Fiction and Prose Style. Ph.D., University of Notre Dame, 1973. 240p. UMI# 74-00057.

3623   Landstrom, Susan B. "Knotty Theames and Paynes": The Baroque Tradition in Early New England Poetry. Ph.D., University of North Carolina-Chapel Hill, 1986. 187p. UMI# 8711129.[Anne Bradstreet, Edward Johnson, Edward Taylor, Michael Wigglesworth].

3624   Lasseter, Janice M. Horrific Inspiration: The Dialogue of Faith and Reason in American Romanticism. Ph.D., University of Alabama, 1987. 231p. UMI# 8801918.

3625   Leverenz, Langmuir D. A Psychoanalysis of American Literature. Ph.D., University of California-Berkeley, 1969. 694p. UMI# 7013100.[John Cotton, Jonathan Edwards, Benjamin Franklin, Sigmund Freud, Thomas Hooker, Increase Mather, Thomas Shepard, Samuel Willard].

3626   Levy, Alfred J. Nathaniel Hawthorne's Attitude Toward Total Depravity and Evil. Ph.D., University of Wisconsin-Madison, 1957. 382p. UMI# 21857.

3627   Liedel, Donald E. The Antislavery Novel, 1836-1861. Ph.D., University of Michigan, 1961. 277p. UMI# 6106385.

3628   Lind, Mary J. They Summoned Death to Challenge Dread: The Function of Parable in the Poetry of Herman Melville, Emily

Dickinson and their Puritan Antecedents. Ph.D., University of Washington, 1979. 313p. UMI# 79-17598.

3629   Lind, Sidney E. The Supernatural Tales of Henry James: Conflict and Fantasy. Ph.D., New York University, 1949. 441p. UMI# 7318005.

3630   Lineback, Donald J. An Annotated Edition of the Diary of Johann Heinrich Mueller (1702-1782), Pietist and Printer of the American Revolution. Ph.D., University of North Carolina-Chapel Hill, 1975. 282p. UMI# 76-20052.

3631   Lobody, Diane H. Lost in the Ocean of Love: The Mystical Writings of Catherine Livingston Garrettson. Ph.D., Drew University, 1990. 335p. UMI# 9032135.

3632   Luisi, David R. The Religious Environment and the Role of Minister in the Novels of William Dean Howells. Ph.D., University of Notre Dame, 1974.

3633   Lyttle, Thomas J. An Examination of Poetic Justice in Three Selected Types of Nineteenth-Century Melodrama: The Indian Play, the Temperance Play, and the Civil War Play. Ph.D., Bowling Green State University, 1974. 259p. UMI# 75-10013.

3634   MacFarlane, Lisa W. The Mild Apocalypse: Domestic Millennialism in the Novels of Harriet Beecher Stowe. Ph.D., University of Michigan, 1987. 294p. UMI# 8720310.

3635   Magaw, Malcolm O. Melville and the Christian Myth: The Imagery of Ambiguity. Ph.D., Tulane University, 1964. 327p. UMI# 64-13708.

3636   Majdoubeh, Ahmad Y. Puritanic Idealism: The Body Controversy in the American Renaissance. Ph.D., Cornell University, 1984. 223p. UMI# 8427194.[Ralph Waldo Emerson, Henry David Thoreau, Walt Whitman].

3637   Malone, Walter K. Parallels to Hindu and Taoist Thought in Walt Whitman. Ph.D., Temple University, 1964. 327p. UMI# 6501411.

3638   Marino, Bert G. Melville and the Perfectionist Dilemma: A Study of Melville's Early Religious Thought. Ph.D., Fordham University, 1974. 218p. UMI# 74-25068.

3639   Marshall, Donald R. The Green Promise: Greenness as a Dominant Symbol in the Quest for Eden in American Fiction. Ph.D., University of Connecticut, 1971. 450p. UMI# 71-18428.

3640   Martin, John S. Social and Intellectual Patterns in the Thought of Cadwallader Colden, Benjamin Thompson (Count Rumford), Thomas Cooper, Fisher Ames, Timothy Dwight, David Humphreys, Benjamin Silliman, and Charles Brockden Brown. Ph.D., University of Wisconsin, 1965. 936p. UMI# 6510640.

3641   Martinez-Cruzado, America. The Philosopher-Mystic Aspects of Poe, Baudelaire and Cortazar. Ph.D., University of Illinois at Urbana-Champaign, 1976. 213p. UMI# 7709089.

3642   McConnell, Diane G. Individual Progress and Societal Reform: A Study of the Ideologies of Ralph Waldo Emerson and Nathaniel Hawthorne. Ph.D., University of Maryland, 1978. 201p. UMI# 7900917.

3643   McCrossan, Joseph M. The Role of the Church and the Folk in the Development of the Early Drama in New Mexico. Ph.D., University of Pennsylvania, 1945. 492p.

3644   McDonald, Lawrence L., Jr. Eden Revisited: Reflections of American West in Victorian Fiction. Ph.D., Arizona State University, 1976. 325p. UMI# 77-07555.

3645   McGregor, Elisabeth J. The Poet's Bible: Biblical Elements in the Poetry of Emily Dickinson, Stephen Crane, Edwin Arlington Robinson, and Robert Frost. Ph.D., Brown University, 1978. 298p. UMI# 79-06582.

3646   McIntosh, Margaret M. Emily Dickinson's Poems About Pain: A Study of Interrelated Moral, Theological, and Linguistic Freedoms. Ph.D., Harvard University, 1967.

3647   Meyer, Richard E. Colonial Values and the Development of the American Nation as Expressed in Almanacs, 1700-1790. Ph.D., University of Kansas, 1970. 321p. UMI# 7025377.

3648   Meyering, Sheryl L. Hawthorne and the Burden of Calvinism: Expiation, Gender, and Narrative Form. Ph.D., Michigan State University, 1986. 208p. UMI# 8700500.

3649   Mielke, Robert E. The Riddle of the Painful Earth: W.D. Howells' Explorations of Suffering in His Major Writings of the Early 1890's. Ph.D., Duke University, 1986. 225p. UMI# 8700028.

3650   Milder, Robert W. Herman Melville: A Prouder, Darker Faith. Ph.D., Harvard University, 1972.

3651   Millar, Albert E., Jr. Spiritual Autobiography in Selected Writings of Sewall, Edwards, Byrd, Woolman, and Franklin: A Comparison of Technique and Content. Ph.D., University of Delaware, 1968. 362p. UMI# 68-15542.

3652   Miller, Eleanor A. The Christian Philosophy in the New England Novels of Harriet Beecher Stowe. Ph.D., University of Nevada-Reno, 1970. 199p. UMI# 7118643.

3653   Mills, Bariss. Attitudes of Some Nineteenth Century American Writers Toward Puritanism. Ph.D., University of Wisconsin, 1942. 372p.

3654   Mills, Elizabeth M. Wording the Unspeakable: Emily Dickinson and A.R. Ammons. Ph.D., University of North Carolina-Chapel Hill, 1985. 205p. UMI# 8605615.

3655   Milner, Joseph O. The Social, Religious, Economic, and Political Implications of the Southwest Humor of Baldwin, Longstreet, Hooper, and G.W. Harris. Ph.D., University of North Carolina, 1971. 386p. UMI# 71-20987.

3656   Modder, Montagu F. A Study of the Jew as a Subject in Nineteenth Century Fiction. Ph.D., University of Michigan, 1935.

3657   Molson, Francis J. The "Forms" of God: A Study of Emily Dickinson's Search for and Test of God. Ph.D., University of Notre Dame, 1965. 385p. UMI# 65-14613.

3658   Monsell, Margaret E. The "Newborn Bard of the Holy Ghost": Spiritual Perfectionism in New England. Ph.D., Boston University, 1988. 192p. UMI# 8724728.

3659   Montgomery, Benilde. Emily Dickinson and the Meditative Tradition. Ph.D., State University of New York-Stony Brook, 1981. 442p. UMI# 8119241.

3660   Morehead, Martha H. George W. Cable's Use of the Bible in His Fiction and Major Polemical Essays. Ph.D., University of North Carolina-Greensboro, 1980. 362p. UMI# 8021779.

3661   Mott, Bertram L., Jr. The Residual Calvinism of Mark Twain: Its Evidence in His Post-1892 Work. Ph.D., University of Pennsylvania, 1968. 300p. UMI# 69-00150.

3662   Nathan, Rhoda B. The Soul at White Heat: Metaphysical Tradition in Thoreau's *Journal* and Dickinson's Poetry. Ph.D., City University of New York, 1973. 248p. UMI# 7314381.

3663   Nault, Clifford A., Jr. Melville's Two-Stranded Novel: An Interpretation of *Moby Dick* as an Enactment of Father Mapple's Sermon and the Lesser Prophecies, With an Essay on Melville Interpretation. Ph.D., Wayne State University, 1960. 286p. UMI# 6002332.

3664   Nelson, James A. Herman Melville's Use of the Bible in *Billy Budd*. Ph.D., University of Iowa, 1978. 213p. UMI# 79-02026.

3665   Nesaule, Valda. The Christ Figure and the Idea of Sacrifice in Herman Melville's *Billy Budd*, in Graham Greene's *The Potting Shed*, and in Fedor Dostoevski's *The Dream of a Ridiculous Man*. Ph.D., Indiana University, 1975. 129p. UMI# 602870.

3666   Nicholl, Grier. The Christian Social Novel in America, 1865-1918. Ph.D., University of Minnesota, 1964. 356p. UMI# 64-10844.

3667   Noel, Daniel C. The Portent Unwound: Religious and Psychological Development in the Imagery of Herman Melville, 1819-1851. Ph.D., Drew University, 1967. 512p. UMI# 67-14376.

3668   Nordin, Kenneth D. Consensus Religion: National Newspaper Coverage of Religious Life in America, 1849-1960. Ph.D., University of Michigan, 1975. 194p. UMI# 76-09477.

3669   O'Hara, Michael A. Utopian Community and Satiric Structure in *The Blithedale Romance*: Hawthorne's Alternatives to Alienation. Ph.D., University of California-San Diego, 1980. 192p. UMI# 8023110.

3670   O'Shaughnessey, Margaret E. The Middle Ages in the New World: American Views and Transformations of Medieval Art and Literature. Ph.D., Duke University, 1989. 296p. UMI# 9002058.

3671   Oberhaus, Dorothy H. The Religious Voice of Emily Dickinson. Ph.D., City University of New York, 1980. 289p. UMI# 8103951.

3672   Oliver, Lawrence J., Jr. Kinesthetic Imagery and the Nightmare of Falling in the Fiction of Brown, Cooper, Poe, and Melville. Ph.D., Pennsylvania State University, 1981. 190p. UMI# 8112829.

3673   Oliver, Virginia H. Apocalypse of Green: A Study of Emily Dickinson's Eschatology. Ph.D., University of Houston, 1982. 307p. UMI# 8224747.

3674   Otis, William B. American Verse, 1625-1807: A History. Ph.D., New York University, 1908. 303p.

3675   Pace, Janyce A. Elements of Prophecy in the Prose Fiction of Herman Melville. Ed.D., Oklahoma State University, 1974. 123p. UMI# 7609743.

3676   Pallante, Martha I. The Child and His Book: Children and Children's Moral and Religious Literature, 1700 to 1850. Ph.D., University of Pennsylvania, 1988. 205p. UMI# 8824781.

3677   Pankratz, John R. New Englanders, the Written Word, and the Errand Into Ohio, 1788-1830. Ph.D., Cornell University, 1988. 422p. UMI# 8821198.

3678   Parkhill, Lewis R. A Prophetic Fiction: Irony in the Novels of Herman Melville From *Typee* to *The Confidence-Man*. Ph.D., University of Texas-Austin, 1987. 361p. UMI# 8717507.

3679   Pass, Olivia M. Hawthorne's Complex Vision: The Growth of a New Consciousness as Revealed by the Female Characters in the Four Major Novels. Ph.D., University of Southwestern Louisiana, 1985. 158p. UMI# 8605674.[*Blithedale Romance, House of Seven Gables, Marble Faun, Scarlet Letter*].

3680   Patnode, Darwin N. Love and Death in the Jamesian Novel. Ph.D., University of Minnesota, 1974. 254p. UMI# 7426224.

3681   Pearce, Daniel M. "The Soul's Superior Instant": The Individual Psychology of Emily Dickinson's Poetry. Ph.D., University of California-Riverside, 1988. 213p. UMI# 8909880.

3682   Penrice, Daniel J. The Golden Key: Energy as Virtue in Emerson and Hawthorne. Ph.D., Harvard University, 1984. 234p. UMI# 8419394.

3683   Pettigrew, Richard C. Milton in the Works of Emerson, Lowell, and Holmes. Ph.D., Duke University, 1930.

3684   Pfeiffer, Benjamin. Religious, Moral, and Social Ideas in the Works of Mark Twain. Ph.D., University of Nebraska-Lincoln, 1964. 425p. UMI# 65-02763.

3685   Phelan, Joan D. Puritan Tradition and Emily Dickinson's Poetic Practice. Ph.D., Bryn Mawr College, 1972. 218p. UMI# 73-05898.

3686   Phillips, Emma J. Mysticism in the Poetry of Emily Dickinson. Ph.D., Indiana University, 1967. 345p. UMI# 6715149.

3687   Phinit-Akson, Helen. James Fenimore Cooper: A Critical Study of

His Religious Vision. Ph.D., University of Pittsburgh, 1972. 257p. UMI# 73-13254.

3688   Piercy, Josephine K. Studies in Literary Types in Seventeenth-Century America, With Particular Emphasis Upon the Beginnings of the Essay (1607-1710). Ph.D., Yale University, 1936. 529p.

3689   Pieschel, Bridget S. The Rhetoric of Degeneration From Bradford to Cooper. Ph.D., University of Alabama, 1989. 219p. UMI# 9000108.

3690   Pleticha, Susan E.M. The Enthusiasm of Love: Harriet Beecher Stowe's (1811-1896) Aspiring to the Presence of God. Ph.D., Drew University, 1989. 310p. UMI# 9014371.

3691   Pollock, Beth R. The Representation of Utopia: Hawthorne and the Female Medium. Ph.D., University of California-Berkeley, 1988. 257p. UMI# 8916835.

3692   Posey, Meredith N. Whitman's Debt to the Bible With Special Reference to the Origins of His Rhythm. Ph.D., University of Texas-Austin, 1938.

3693   Preussner, Alanna S. The Minister's Wooing: Temptation and the Sentimental Tradition in Five British and American Works of the Late Nineteenth Century. Ph.D., University of Colorado-Boulder, 1979. 217p. UMI# 80-03006.

3694   Raniszeski, Edward L. The Significance of the Christian Ethic in Herman Melville's *Pierre: or the Ambiguities*. Ph.D., Bowling Green State University, 1973. 267p. UMI# 73-18186.

3695   Rees, Robert A. Mark Twain and the Bible: Characters Who Use the Bible and Biblical Characters. Ph.D., University of Wisconsin, 1966. 261p. UMI# 66-09960.

3696   Reeves, John K. Religious Thought in Boston in the 1740's as Reflected in the Periodicals. Ph.D., Harvard University, 1938.

3697   Reimer, Earl A. Mark Twain and the Bible: An Inductive Study. Ph.D., Michigan State University, 1970. UMI# 71-02154.

3698   Reinitz, Richard M. Symbolism and Freedom: The Use of Biblical Typology as an Argument for Religious Toleration in Seventeenth Century England and America. Ph.D., University of Rochester, 1967. 407p. UMI# 6713643.

3699   Renner, Dennis K. Walt Whitman's Religion of the Republic: A Study of His Journalistic Writing and the First Editions of *Leaves of Grass* in Relation to Sectionalism and the Prospect of Civil War in America. Ph.D., University of Iowa, 1975. 300p. UMI# 75-23080.

3700   Reynolds, David S. Polishing God's Altar: The Emergence of Religious Fiction in America, 1785-1850. Ph.D., University of California-Berkeley, 1979. 507p. UMI# 8014857.

3701   Rhode, Robert T. Hankering, Gross, Mystical, Nude: The Persona in *Leaves of Grass*. Ph.D., Indiana University, 1981. 225p. UMI# 8128038.

3702   Rhorer, Donna A. Clothed and Housed in Eden: Female Characters as Redemptive Figures in Hawthorne's Longer Fiction. Ph.D., University of Southwestern Louisiana, 1990. 145p. UMI# 9032612.

3703   Rodman, Isaac P. Original Relations: Pantheism, Intertextuality, and an American Renaissance Aesthetic. Ph.D., University of Massachusetts, 1989. 343p. UMI# 9011786.[Ralph Waldo Emerson, Nathaniel Hawthorne, Herman Melville, Edgar Allan Poe, Henry David Thoreau, Walt Whitman].

3704   Roesler, Miriam C. The Sea and Death in Walt Whitman's *Leaves of Grass*. Ph.D., Catholic University of America, 1963. 148p. UMI# 6306824.

3705   Root, Robert W. The Religious Ideas of Some Major Early Writers of America. Ph.D., Syracuse University, 1959. 1001p. UMI# 60-00383.

3706   Rosenfeld, Alvin H. Emerson and Whitman: Their Personal and Literary Relationships. Ph.D., Brown University, 1967. 300p. UMI# 6801489.

3707   Rosenfeld, William. The Divided Burden: Common Elements in the Search for a Religious Synthesis in the Works of Theodore Parker, Horace Bushnell, Nathaniel Hawthorne, and Herman Melville. Ph.D., University of Minnesota, 1961. 245p. UMI# 62-01843.

3708   Rosenmeier, Rosamond R. The Evidence of Things Not Seen: Perspectives on History in the Writing of Anne Bradstreet, Thoreau, and Wallace Stevens. Ph.D., Harvard University, 1971. 332p.

3709   Ross, Virginia P. Nathaniel Hawthorne and the Irreverent Imagination. Ph.D., Emory University, 1985. 217p. UMI# 8516585.

3710   Russell, James T., Jr. Hawthorne's Martyrs: The Sacrificial Theme in His Tales and Novels. Ph.D., University of Alabama, 1972. 201p. UMI# 7308055.

3711 Salamon, Lynda B. Two Nineteenth Century American Views of History: James Fenimore Cooper and Francis Parkman. Ph.D., University of Maryland, 1989. 174p. UMI# 9021575.

3712 Samaan, Hanna. Spiritual Values in the Poetry of Emily Dickinson. Ph.D., University of Montreal, 1953.

3713 Schneider, Helen M. Three Views of Toleration: John Milton, Roger Williams, and Sir Henry Vane the Younger. Ph.D., State University of New York-Albany, 1977. 214p. UMI# 7805714.

3714 Schweninger, Lee F. "Between Fiction and Reality": The Motif of the Jeremiad in American Literature. Ph.D., University of North Carolina-Chapel Hill, 1984. 215p. UMI# 8508620.

3715 Scott, Graham S.J. Under Gentile Eyes: Images of the Jew in the Nineteenth-Century Novel of England and America. Ph.D., Brigham Young University, 1978. 164p. UMI# 70-01578.

3716 Sexton, Mark S. Vernacular Religious Figures in Nineteenth-Century Southern Fiction: A Study in Literary Tradition. Ph.D., University of North Carolina-Chapel Hill, 1987. 377p. UMI# 8728479.

3717 Sharma, Maya M. Poetry and Meditation: The Education of Emily Dickinson. Ed.D., Columbia University Teachers College, 1983. 250p. UMI# 8403284.

3718 Shaw, Nancy J. Speaking for the Spirit: Cotton, Shepard, Edwards, Emerson. Ph.D., Cornell University, 1988. 215p. UMI# 8900762.

3719 Shea, Daniel B. Spiritual Autobiography in Early America. Ph.D., Stanford University, 1966. 308p. UMI# 66-14718.

3720 Shea, Leo M. Lowell's Religious Outlook. Ph.D., Catholic University of America, 1926. 124p.

3721 Sheridan, James F. Paul Carus: A Study of the Thought and Work of the Editor of the Open Court Publishing Company. Ph.D., University of Illinois at Urbana-Champaign, 1957. 239p. UMI# 25282.

3722 Shuck, Emerson C. Clergymen in Representative American Novels, 1830-1930: A Study in Attitudes Toward Religion. Ph.D., University of Wisconsin, 1943.

3723   Siegfried, Regina. Conspicuous by Her Absence: Amherst's Religious Tradition and Emily Dickinson's Own Growth in Faith. Ph.D., Saint Louis University, 1982. 227p. UMI# 82-23729.

3724   Silverman, Kenneth E. Colonial American Poetry: An Anthology. Ph.D., Columbia University, 1964. 851p. UMI# 6502092.

3725   Sinclair, Susan D. Hawthorne's "New Revelation": The Female Christ. Ph.D., Duke University, 1981. 267p. UMI# 8207855.

3726   Slouka, Mark Z. American Triptych: The Millenial Theme in Melville's Works, 1850-1856. Ph.D., Columbia University, 1988. 133p. UMI# 8815699.

3727   Smith, Susan M. The Extension of Self-Culture: Margaret Fuller and Emily Dickinson. Ph.D., Texas A&M University, 1987. 297p. UMI# 8720947.

3728   Sneller, Delwyn L. Popular and Prophetic Traditions in the Poetry of John Greenleaf Whittier. Ph.D., Michigan State University, 1972. 236p. UMI# 73-05492.

3729   Snider, Harry R. Mark Twain as Theologian: A Perspective From a Selection of Posthumously Published Manuscripts. Ph.D., Kent State University, 1983. 412p. UMI# 8400097.

3730   Solomon, Jan K. The Puritan, the Gentleman, and the Artist: A Study of the Conflict Between Ethics and Aesthetics in the Novels of Henry James. Ph.D., University of Michigan, 1964. 191p. UMI# 65-05943.

3731   Song, Nina. Death in the Tragedies of William Shakespeare and Eugene O'Neill. D.A., State University of New York-Albany, 1988. 170p. UMI# 8814822.

3732   Sonneveldt, Nancy J. Analysis of an Early Nineteenth-Century American Periodical, the *Spirit of the Pilgrims*, With Emphasis on Religious Controversy, Revivalism, and Social Reform. Ph.D., Michigan State University, 1968. 343p. UMI# 6905956.

3733   Sousa, Raymond J. The Valley of the Shadow: Mark Twain's Dance With Death. Ph.D., University of Southwestern Louisiana, 1978. 266p. UMI# 7900132.

3734   Spencer, William D. Mysterium and Mystery: The Minister as Detective in the Clerical Crime Novel, 130 B.C./B.C.E. to the Present. Th.D., Boston University, 1986. 837p. UMI# 8616477.

3735 Staples, Katherine E. The American Pro-Slavery Novel: A Study in the Popular Fiction of the 1850's. Ph.D., University of Texas-Austin, 1977. 366p. UMI# 7729101.

3736 Steele, Betty J. Quaker Characters in Selected American Novels, 1823-1899. Ph.D., Duke University, 1974. 169p. UMI# 75-02427.

3737 Steinberg, Abraham H. Jewish Characters in the American Novel to 1900. Ph.D., New York University, 1956. 308p. UMI# 16778.

3738 Steiner, Donald L. August Strindberg and Edward Albee: The Dance of Death. Ph.D., University of Utah, 1972. 216p. UMI# 7221638.

3739 Sterner, Douglas W. Priests of Culture: A Study of Matthew Arnold and Henry James. Ph.D., Rutgers University, 1989. 363p. UMI# 8923615.

3740 Stewart, Veronica J. Emily Dickinson and the Rhetoric of Conversion. Ph.D., State University of New York-Stony Brook, 1990. 223p. UMI# 9109391.

3741 Stibitz, Edward E. The Treatment of Quakerism in American Historical and Literary Writing. Ph.D., University of Michigan, 1951. 290p. UMI# 02467.

3742 Stock, Ely. Studies in Hawthorne's Use of the Bible. Ph.D., Brown University, 1966. 238p. UMI# 67-02293.

3743 Stockton, Edwin L. The Influence of the Moravians Upon the Leather-Stocking Tales. Ph.D., Florida State University, 1960. 224p. UMI# 60-05506.

3744 Storlie, Erik F. Grace and Works, Enlightenment and Practice: Paradox and Poetry in John Cotton, Jonathan Edwards, and Dogen Zenji. Ph.D., University of Minnesota, 1976. 166p. UMI# 7627937.

3745 Stott, Graham S.J. Under Gentile Eyes: Images of the Jew in the Nineteenth-Century Novel of England and America. Ph.D., Brigham Young University, 1978. 164p. UMI# 7901578.

3746 Stout, Janis D. Sodoms in Eden: The City in American Fiction Before 1860. Ph.D., Rice University, 1973. 238p. UMI# 73-21604.

3747 Stroupe, Henry S. The Religious Press in the South Atlantic States, 1802-1865. Ph.D., Duke University, 1942. 312p.

3748 Stubbs, Mark N. The Scholar's Duty: A Comparative Analysis of

Emerson and Gandhi. Ed.D., University of Houston, 1989. 220p.
UMI# 8921597.

3749   Taylor, James W. The Swedenborgianism of W.D. Howells. Ph.D.,
University of Illinois at Urbana-Champaign, 1969. 178p. UMI#
70-13511.

3750   Taylor, John G. Hawthorne's Transmutations of Puritanism. Ph.D.,
University of Utah, 1958. 293p. UMI# 58-07957.

3751   Tegen, Charles R. The Religious Poetry of John Greenleaf Whittier.
Ph.D., University of Georgia, 1968. 242p. UMI# 69-09527.

3752   Theriault, William D. The Christian Captivity Motif in Early
American Literature. Ph.D., George Washington University, 1974.
260p. UMI# 75-05280.

3753   Thompson, Richard G. The Lovable Heathen of Happy Valley:
Mark Twain's Assault on the Christian Religion in *Huckleberry Finn*.
D.A., Middle Tennessee State University, 1984. 163p. UMI#
8413745.

3754   Tomlinson, Caroline D. The Search for God: Aspects of Mystical
Insight in Some North American Poets. Ph.D., University of Essex,
1978. 339p.

3755   Trimpi, Helen P. Romance Structure and Melville's Use of
Demonology and Witchcraft in *Moby Dick*. Ph.D., Harvard
University, 1966.

3756   Turner, Lorenzo D. Anti-Slavery Sentiment in American Literature
Prior to 1865. Ph.D., University of Chicago, 1926.

3757   Ullmer, R. John. The Quaker Influence in the Novels of Charles
Brockden Brown. Ph.D., Saint Louis University, 1969. 236p. UMI#
69-16053.

3758   Van Leer, David M. The Apocalypse of the Mind: Idealism and
Annihilation in the American Renaissance. Ph.D., Cornell
University, 1978. 762p. UMI# 7817813.[Ralph Waldo Emerson,
Nathaniel Hawthorne, Edgar Allan Poe].

3759   Vincent, John P. The Evolution of Ludic Fiction: Existential Play in
the Late Works of Henry Adams. Ph.D., Syracuse University, 1979.
354p. UMI# 7925646.

3760   Walhout, Clarence P. Religion in the Thought and Fiction of Three
Ante-Bellum Southerners: Kennedy, Caruthers, and Simms. Ph.D.,

Northwestern University, 1964. 280p. UMI# 65-03319.

3761   Wegener, Larry E. A Concordance to Herman Melville's *Clarel: A Poem and Pilgrimage in the Holy Land*. Ph.D., University of Nebraska-Lincoln, 1978. 1886p. UMI# 7916463.

3762   Wenska, Walter P., Jr. A Restless Temper: Toward a Definition of the "Puritan Tradition" in American Literature. Ph.D., Stanford University, 1975. 276p. UMI# 7525627.

3763   Werge, Thomas A. The Persistence of Adam: Puritan Concerns and Conflicts in Melville and Mark Twain. Ph.D., Cornell University, 1967. 211p. UMI# 68-03520.

3764   Whalen, Brian J. Home and Homelessness in the American Imagination. Ph.D., University of Dallas, 1988. 300p. UMI# 8827675.[Ralph Waldo Emerson, F. Scott Fitzgerald, Benjamin Franklin, Nathaniel Hawthorne, Arthur Miller].

3765   Wheatcroft, John S. Emily Dickinson and the Orthodox Tradition. Ph.D., Rutgers University, 1960. 390p. UMI# 60-04268.

3766   White, Isabelle B. The American Heroine, 1789-1899: Nonconformity and Death. Ph.D., University of Kentucky, 1978. 231p. UMI# 7918064.

3767   White, John W., Jr. Stephen Crane's Fascination With Man: A Study of Christian Themes in His Fiction. Ph.D., George Peabody College for Teachers, 1968. 309p. UMI# 69-13832.

3768   Willard, Malinda K. Jonathan Edwards and Nathaniel Hawthorne: Themes From the Common Consciousness. Ph.D., University of South Carolina, 1978. 240p. UMI# 7907640.

3769   Williams, James G. James Fenimore Cooper and Christianity: A Study of Religious Novels. Ph.D., Cornell University, 1973. 265p. UMI# 74-06364.

3770   Williams, John B. The Impact of Transcendentalism on the Novels of Herman Melville. Ph.D., University of Southern California, 1965. 269p. UMI# 65-08927.

3771   Williams, Joseph. Conditions Assigned by Providence: Proslavery Sentiment in American Fiction Before the Civil War. Ph.D., Harvard University, 1964.

3772   Williams, Louis P., Jr. Captives in Mystic Babylon: The Redeemer Figure in Late Nineteenth-Century American Culture. Ph.D.,

University of Minnesota, 1975. 275p. UMI# 7627845.

3773   Williams, Mentor L. Oliver Wendell Holmes: The Impact of Science Upon the Theology in the *Authentic Brahmin*. Ph.D., University of Michigan, 1938.

3774   Williams, Peter W. A Mirror for Unitarians: Catholicism and Culture in Nineteenth Century New England Literature. Ph.D., Yale University, 1970. 291p. UMI# 71-17165.

3775   Wilson, Charles E., Jr. The Antebellum Slave Narrative and American Literature. Ph.D., University of Georgia, 1988. 151p. UMI# 8903536.

3776   Wilson, Robert J. Poetics of the Sublime Poem in America, 1650-1860. Ph.D., University of California-Berkeley, 1976. 302p. UMI# 774653.

3777   Woodell, Charles H. The Preacher in Nineteenth-Century Southern Fiction. Ph.D., University of North Carolina-Chapel Hill, 1974. 303p. UMI# 7426952.

3778   Woolridge, Nancy B. The Negro Preacher in American Fiction Before 1900. Ph.D., University of Chicago, 1943.

3779   Wright, Nathalia. Melville and the Bible. Ph.D., Yale University, 1949.

3780   Wright, Robert G. The Social Christian Novel in the Gilded Age, 1865-1900. Ph.D., George Washington University, 1968. 404p. UMI# 69-00709.

3781   Wright, Thomas G. Aspects of Culture in New England During the First Century of Colonization, With Special Reference to Literary Culture and the Production of Literature. Ph.D., Yale University, 1917. 444p.

3782   Wyatt, Jennifer F. Portraits of Hester Prynne. Ph.D., University of Washington, 1985. 309p. UMI# 8521685.

3783   Yasuna, Edward C. The Power of the Lord in the Howling Wilderness: The Achievement of Thomas Cole and James Fenimore Cooper. Ph.D., Ohio State University, 1976. 397p. UMI# 76-24718.

3784   Yoder, John D. Melville, Manifest Destiny, and American Mission. Ph.D., University of Iowa, 1980. 457p. UMI# 8114320.

3785   York, Robert M. George Barrell Cheever: Puritan Protagonist. Ph.D., Clark University, 1941. 353p.

MISSIONS AND MISSIONARIES

3786   Atwood, Elmer B. Outlines of a History of Missions in China. Ph.D., Southern Baptist Theological Seminary, 1911.

3787   Baldwin, Alma F. The Impact of American Missionaries on the Bura People of Nigeria. Ph.D., Ball State University, 1973. 165p. UMI# 74-02932.

3788   Bass, Harold J. The Policy of the American State Department Toward Missionaries in the Far East. Ph.D., Washington State University, 1938.

3789   Beahm, William M. Factors in the Development of the Student Volunteer Movement for Foreign Missions. Ph.D., University of Chicago, 1942.

3790   Bennett, Adrian A., III. Missionary Journalism in Nineteenth-Century China: Young J. Allen and the Early *Wan-Kuo Kung-Pao*, 1868-1883. Ph.D., University of California-Davis, 1970. 417p. UMI# 71-15519.

3791   Beyan, Amos J. The American Colonization Society and the Formation of Political, Economic and Religious Institutions in Liberia, 1822-1900. Ph.D., West Virginia University, 1985. 186p. UMI# 8600811.

3792   Blankemeyer, Felix. Contribution of the Brothers of the Christian Schools to Education in Egypt. Ph.D., Fordham University, 1934.

3793   Bose, Anima. American Missionaries Involvement in Higher Education in India in the Nineteenth Century. Ph.D., University of Kansas, 1971. 445p. UMI# 71-27126.

3794   Branch, Ralph E., Jr. The American Missionary Association and Its Relationship to the Education of the Freedmen in Virginia. Ph.D., University of California-Berkeley, 1974.

3795   Brosnan, Cornelius J. Jason Lee: A Missionary's Part in the Founding of the Commonwealth of Oregon. Ph.D., University of California, 1930.

3796   Brown, Nettie T. The Missionary World of Ann Eliza Worcester Robertson. Ph.D., North Texas State University, 1978. 237p. UMI# 78-24635.

3797   Bultmann, William A. The Society for the Propagation of the Gospel in Foreign Parts and the Foreign Settler in the American Colonies. Ph.D., Brown University, 1952. 222p.

3798   Chaney, Charles L. God's Glorious Work: The Theological Foundations of the Early Missionary Societies in America, 1787-1817. Ph.D., University of Chicago, 1973. 475p.

3799   Chase, Thomas C. Christian Frederick Post, 1715-1785: Missionary and Diplomat to the Indians of America. Ed.D., Pennsylvania State University, 1982. 109p.

3800   Cheng, Chen W. The Educational Work of the Missionaries in China. Ph.D., University of Michigan, 1910.

3801   Cochran, Alice C. Miners, Merchants, and Missionaries: The Roles of Missionaries and Pioneer Churches in the Colorado Gold Rush and Its Aftermath, 1858-1870. Ph.D., Southern Methodist University, 1975. 398p. UMI# 75-22476.

3802   Daasvand, Paul O. The Norwegian Seaman's Mission: History, Analysis and Evaluation. D.Min., University of the South, 1982.

3803   Dawson, Deborah L. "Laboring in My Savior's Vineyard": The Mission of Eliza Hart Spalding. Ph.D., Bowling Green State University, 1988. 202p. UMI# 8906197.

3804   Dinnerstein, Myra. The American Board Mission to the Zulu, 1835-1900. Ph.D., Columbia University, 1971. 231p. UMI# 74-12702.

3805   Drake, Richard B. The American Missionary Association and the Southern Negro, 1861-1888. Ph.D., Emory University, 1957. 307p. UMI# 58-05136.

3806   Elsbree, Oliver W. The Rise of the Missionary Spirit in America, 1790-1815. Ph.D., Columbia University, 1928. 187p.

3807   Estes, Charles S. Christian Missions in China. Ph.D., Johns Hopkins University, 1895. 61p.

3808   Evearitt, Daniel J. Jewish-Christian Missions to Jews, 1820-1935. Ph.D., Drew University, 1988. 404p. UMI# 8906804.

3809   Fisher, James E. Democracy and Mission Education in Korea. Ph.D., Columbia University, 1928. 187p.

3810   Fleming, Daniel J. Devolution in Mission Administration, as Exemplified by the Legislative History of Five American Missionary

Societies in India. Ph.D., University of Chicago, 1914. 310p.

3811   Gelzer, David G. Mission to America: Being a History of the Work of the Basel Foreign Missions Society in America. Ph.D., Yale University, 1952. 390p. UMI# 68-01667.

3812   Goodykoontz, Colin B. The Home Missionary Movement and the West 1798-1861 With Particular Reference to the American Home Missionary Society. Ph.D., Harvard University, 1921.

3813   Hall, William W., Jr. The American Board Mission in Bulgaria, 1878-1918. A Study in Purpose and Procedure. Ph.D., Yale University, 1937.

3814   Haussmann, Carl F. Kunze's Seminarium and the Society for the Propagation of Christianity and Useful Knowledge Among the Germans in America. Ph.D., University of Pennsylvania, 1916. 141p.

3815   Hawkins, Dorine C. The Development and Influence of the Woman's Missionary Training Schools in Brazil. Ph.D., Southwestern Baptist Theological Seminary, 1958. 172p.

3816   Hawthorne, Bruce C. Industrial Massachusetts and the Foreign Missionary Movement, 1810-1820. Ph.D., Boston University, 1953. 323p.

3817   Haywood, Jacquelyn S. The American Missionary Association in Louisiana During Reconstruction. Ph.D., University of California-Los Angeles, 1974. 262p. UMI# 74-18773.

3818   Hendrix, Thomas C. "The Love of Liberty": A Study of the Religious Factor in the Nineteenth-Century Settlement of Afro-Americans in Liberia. Ph.D., University of Illinois-Chicago, 1985. 457p. UMI# 8518454.

3819   Hunter, Jane H. Imperial Evangelism: American Women Missionaries in Turn-of-the-Century China. Ph.D., Yale University, 1981.

3820   Hyatt, Irwin T., Jr. Patterns at Tengchow: Life Experiences of Three American Missionaries in East Shantung Province, China, 1864-1912. Ph.D., Harvard University, 1969.

3821   Johnson, Clifton H. The American Missionary Association, 1846-1861: A Study of Christian Abolitionism. Ph.D., University of North Carolina-Chapel Hill, 1959. 595p. UMI# 59-05561.

3822   Jones, Maxine D. "A Glorious Work": The American Missionary

Association and Black North Carolinians, 1863-1880. Ph.D., Florida State University, 1982. 341p. UMI# 8308673.

3823   Kuhns, Frederick I. The Operations of the American Home Missionary Society in the Old Northwest, 1826-1861. Ph.D., University of Chicago, 1947. 376p.

3824   Lindbeck, John M.H. American Missionaries and the Policies of the United States in China, 1898-1901. Ph.D., Yale University, 1948. 539p. UMI# 8329035.

3825   Loewe, Wolfgang E. The First American Foreign Missionaries: "The Students," 1810-1820. An Inquiry Into Their Theological Motives. Ph.D., Brown University, 1962. 219p. UMI# 63-01042.

3826   Mahaniah, Kimpianga, II. The Background of Prophetic Movements in the Belgian Congo: A Study of the Congolese Reaction to the Policies and Methods of Belgian Colonization and to the Evangelization of the Lower Congo by Catholic and Protestant Missionaries, From 1877 to 1921. Ph.D., Temple University, 1975. 422p. UMI# 75-28233.

3827   Mansoori, Ahmad. American Missionaries in Iran, 1834-1934. Ph.D., Ball State University, 1986. 194p. UMI# 8616731.

3828   McCutcheon, James M. The American and British Missionary Concept of Chinese Civilization in the Nineteenth Century. Ph.D., University of Wisconsin, 1959. 303p. UMI# 59-05796.

3829   Morris, Nancy J. Hawaiian Missionaries Abroad, 1852-1909. Ph.D., University of Hawaii, 1987. 454p. UMI# 8812144.

3830   Musser, Necia A. Home Missionaries on the Michigan Frontier. A Calendar of the Michigan Letters of the American Home Missionary Society, 1825-1846. Ph.D., University of Michigan, 1967. 836p. UMI# 6807679.

3831   Napier, Augustus Y. The Challenge of China to America. Ph.D., Southern Baptist Theological Seminary, 1922.

3832   Nestorova-Matejic, Tatyana K. American Missionaries in Bulgaria: (1858-1912). Ph.D., Ohio State University, 1985. 212p. UMI# 8603036.

3833   Nordmann, Bernhard F. American Missionary Work Among Armenians in Turkey (1830-1923). Ph.D., University of Illinois at Urbana-Champaign, 1927. 12p.

3834   Noricks, Ronald H. To Turn Them From Darkness: The Missionary Society of Connecticut on the Early Frontier, 1798-1814. Ph.D., University of California-Riverside, 1975. 295p. UMI# 76-12659.

3835   Osteraas, Gary L. Missionary Politics in Cameroon, 1844-1914. Ph.D., Columbia University, 1972. 332p. UMI# 76-15563.

3836   Perry, Alan F. The American Board of Commissioners for Foreign Missions and the London Missionary Society in the Nineteenth Century: A Study of Ideas. Ph.D., Washington University, 1974. 592p. UMI# 75-06615.

3837   Price, Allen T. American Missions and American Diplomacy in China 1830-1900. Ph.D., Harvard University, 1934.

3838   Rajapakse, Reginald L. Christian Missions: Theosophy and Trade: A History of American Relations With Ceylon 1815-1915. Ph.D., University of Pennsylvania, 1973. 469p. UMI# 74-14129.

3839   Rupert, Marybeth. The Emergence of the Independent Missionary Agency as an American Institution, 1860-1917. Ph.D., Yale University, 1974. 246p. UMI# 74-25769.

3840   Schneider, Robert A. The Senior Secretary: Rufus Anderson and the American Board of Commissioners for Foreign Missions, 1810-1880. Ph.D., Harvard University, 1980.

3841   Smith, Ralph R. "In Every Destitute Place": The Mission Program of the American Sunday School Union, 1817-1834. Ph.D., University of Southern California, 1973. 312p. UMI# 74-00944.

3842   Soleimani, Mansoor. The Educational Impact of American Church Missionaries on the Educational Programs of Iran (1834-1925 C.E.). Ed.D., University of the Pacific, 1980. 102p. UMI# 80-19378.

3843   Soremekun, Fola. A History of the American Board Missions in Angola 1880-1940. Ph.D., Northwestern University, 1965. 304p. UMI# 66-02744.

3844   Spalding, Arminta S. Cyrus Kingsbury: Missionary to the Choctaws. Ph.D., University of Oklahoma, 1975. 316p. UMI# 75-21197.

3845   Strevig, Jennie M. History of the Missionary Education Movement in the United States and Canada. Ph.D., New York University, 1930. 162p. UMI# 72-33765.

3846   Thrift, Charles T., Jr. The Operations of the American Home

Missionary Society in the South, 1826-61. Ph.D., University of Chicago, 1937.

3847   Todd, Gary L. American Perceptions of China, 1840-1860. Ph.D., University of Illinois at Urbana-Champaign, 1987. 304p. UMI# 8711894.

3848   Tollefson, Terry R. Schools for Cyprus: A History of the American Board's Mission (1834-1842). Ed.D., Harvard University, 1989. 249p. UMI# 9000887.

3849   Wagner, Sandra E. Sojourners Among Strangers: The First Two Companies of Missionaries to the Sandwich Islands. Ph.D., University of Hawaii, 1986. 242p. UMI# 8622105.

3850   White, Charles B. New England Merchants and Missionaries in Coastal Nineteenth-Century Portuguese East Africa. Ph.D., Boston University, 1974. 318p. UMI# 74-20409.

3851   Wickstrom, Werner T. The American Colonization Society and Liberia, 1817-1867. Ph.D., Hartford Seminary Foundation, 1958. 388p. UMI# 6203064.

3852   Wimberly, Ware W., II. Missionary Reforms in Indiana, 1826-1860: Education, Temperance, Antislavery. Ph.D., Indiana University, 1977. 321p. UMI# 77-22682.

3853   Wu, Chao-Kwang. The International Aspect of the Missionary Movement in China. Ph.D., Johns Hopkins University, 1930.

MUSIC

3854   Barr, John G. A Tonal History of Pipe Organs Built by M.P. Muller, Incorporated. S.M.D., Union Theological Seminary, 1977. 483p. UMI# 7803187.

3855   Bolton, Jacklin T. Religious Influences on American Secular Cantatas, 1850-1930. Ph.D., University of Michigan, 1964. 500p. UMI# 65-05879.

3856   Buechner, Alan C. Yankee Singing Schools and the Golden Age of Choral Music in New England, 1760-1800. Ph.D., Harvard University, 1960.

3857   Campbell, Douglas G. George Whitefield Chadwick, His Life and His Works. Ph.D., University of Rochester, 1957.

3858   Cappers, Paul K. The Anthems of Connecticut Composers

Contained in Connecticut Sacred Music Imprints From 1778 to 1801. D.M.A., University of Hartford, 1983.

3859   Carroll, Edward P. Daniel Brink Towner (1850-1919): Educator, Church Musician, Composer, and Editor-Compiler. Ed.D., New Orleans Baptist Theological Seminary, 1979. 364p. UMI# 80-12440.

3860   Carroll, Lucy E. Three Centuries of Song: Pennsylvania's Choral Composers 1681 to 1981. D.M.A., Combs College of Music, 1982. 351p. UMI# 8322500.

3861   Cooke, Nym. American Psalmodists in Contact and Collaboration, 1770-1820. Ph.D., University of Michigan, 1990. 668p. UMI# 9034406.[William Billings, Oliver Holden, Daniel Read].

3862   Covey, Cyclone. Religion and Music in Colonial America. Ph.D., Stanford University, 1942. 224p.

3863   Cross, Virginia A. The Development of Sunday School Hymnody in the United States of America, 1816-1869. D.M.A., New Orleans Baptist Theological Seminary, 1985. 701p. UMI# 8523087.

3864   Daniel, Ralph T. The Anthem in New England Before 1800. Ph.D., Harvard University, 1955. 930p.

3865   Danner, John H. The Hymns of Fanny Crosby and the Search for Assurance: Theology in a Different Key. Ph.D., Boston University, 1989. 376p. UMI# 8911546.

3866   DeVenney, David P. A Conductor's Study of the *Mass in D* by John Knowles Paine. D.M.A., University of Cincinnati, 1989. 118p. UMI# 9003198.

3867   Dooley, James E. Thomas Hastings: American Church Musician. Ph.D., Florida State University, 1963. 278p. UMI# 64-03594.

3868   Doran, Carol A. The Influence of Raynor Taylor and Benjamin Carr on the Church Music in Philadelphia at the Beginning of the Nineteenth Century. Ph.D., University of Rochester, 1970.

3869   Eskew, Harry L. Shape-Note Hymnody in the Shenandoah Valley, 1816-1860. Ph.D., Tulane University, 1966. 182p. UMI# 6703821.

3870   Gallo, William K. The Life and Church Music of Dudley Buck (1839-1909). Ph.D., Catholic University of America, 1968. 299p. UMI# 69-08886.

3871   Haussmann, William A. German-American Hymnology, 1683-1800.

Ph.D., Johns Hopkins University, 1895.

3872   Horne, Dorothy D. A Study of the Folk-Hymns of Southeastern America. Ph.D., University of Rochester, 1953. 336p.

3873   Hulan, Richard H. Camp-Meeting Spiritual Folksongs: Legacy of the "Great Revival in the West." Ph.D., University of Texas-Austin, 1978. 279p. UMI# 7910977.

3874   Klocko, David G. Jeremiah Ingalls's *The Christian Harmony: or, Songster's Companion* (1805). Ph.D., University of Michigan, 1978. 1332p. UMI# 7815962.

3875   Kroeger, Karl D. *The Worcester Collection of Sacred Harmony* and Sacred Music in America, 1786-1803. Ph.D., Brown University, 1976. 708p. UMI# 77-14148.

3876   Martinez, David M. Philip Phillips (1834-1895): Gospel Composer and Compiler. Ph.D., Northwestern University, 1987. 225p. UMI# 8729021.

3877   McDaniel, Stanley R. Church Song and the Cultivated Tradition in New England and New York. D.M.A., University of Southern California, 1983.

3878   Miller, David M. The Beginnings of Music in the Boston Public Schools: Decisions of the Boston School Committee in 1837 and 1845 in Light of Religious and Moral Concerns of the Time. Ph.D., University of North Texas, 1989. 405p. UMI# 9005345.

3879   Nelson, Carl L. The Sacred and Secular Music of the Swedish Settlers of the Midwest 1841-1917. Ph.D., New York University, 1950. 167p. UMI# 2190.

3880   Pappin, Gay G. The Organ Works of George Whitefield Chadwick. D.M.A., Louisiana State University, 1985. 122p. UMI# 8610658.

3881   Ruth, John L. English Hymn-Writing in America, 1640-1800. Ph.D., Harvard University, 1968.

3882   Sims, John N. The Hymnody of the Camp Meeting Tradition. Ph.D., Union Theological Seminary, 1960.

3883   Sizer, Sandra S. Revival Waves and Home Fires: The Rhetoric of Late Nineteenth-Century Gospel Hymns. Ph.D., University of Chicago, 1976.

3884   Smucker, David J. Philip Paul Bliss and the Musical, Cultural and

Religious Sources of the Gospel Music Tradition in the United States, 1850-1876. Ph.D., Boston University, 1981. 435p. UMI# 8126811.

3885   Steeves, Cynthia D. The Origin of Gospel Piano: People, Events, and Circumstances That Contributed to the Development of the Style; and Documentation of Graduate Piano Recitals. D.M.A., University of Washington, 1987. 136p. UMI# 8802341.

3886   Wilhoit, Melvin R. A Guide to the Principal Authors and Composers of Gospel Song of the Nineteenth Century. D.M.A., Southern Baptist Theological Seminary, 1982. 367p. UMI# 8217994.

3887   Worst, John W. New England Psalmody 1760-1810: Analysis of an American Idiom. Ph.D., University of Michigan, 1974. 564p. UMI# 75-00857.

3888   Yellin, Victor. The Life and Operatic Works of George Whitefield Chadwick. Ph.D., Harvard University, 1957.

NATIVISM

3889   Billington, Ray A. The Origins of Nativism in the United States, 1800-1844. Ph.D., Harvard University, 1933.

3890   Botein, Barbara. The Hennessy Case: An Episode in American Nativism, 1890. Ph.D., New York University, 1975. 246p. UMI# 7528507.[New Orleans(LA)].

3891   Fell, Marie L. Foundations of Nativism in American Textbooks, 1783-1860. Ph.D., Catholic University of America, 1941.

3892   Loucks, Emerson H. The Ku Klux Klan In Pennsylvania: A Study in Nativism. Ph.D., Columbia University, 1937.

3893   McGann, Agnes G. Nativism in Kentucky to 1860. Ph.D., Catholic University of America, 1944.

3894   McGrath, Paul Of The Cross. Political Nativism in Texas, 1825-1860. Ph.D., Catholic University of America, 1930.

3895   Noonan, Carroll J. Nativism in Connecticut, 1829-1860. Ph.D., Catholic University of America, 1938.

3896   Nugent, Walter T.K. Populism and Nativism in Kansas, 1888-1900. Ph.D., University of Chicago, 1961.

3897   Scisco, Louis D. Political Nativism in New York State. Ph.D., Columbia University, 1901.

3898   Weaver, John B. Nativism and the Birth of the Republican Party in Ohio, 1854-1860. Ph.D., Ohio State University, 1982. 238p. UMI# 8222197.

PHILOSOPHY OF RELIGION

3899   Boughton, Lynne C. The Concept of Virtue: The Influence of European Ethics, Metaphysics, and Theology on American Ideas of Virtue, 1670-1770. Ph.D., University of Illinois at Urbana-Champaign, 1982. 511p. UMI# 8218437.

3900   Cleland, Gail. The Relation of Bowne to Berkeley. Ph.D., Boston University, 1924.

3901   Come, Arnold B. Naturalism and the Religious Problem in America. Ph.D., Princeton Theological Seminary, 1946.

3902   French, Stanley G. Some Theological and Ethical Uses of Mental Philosophy in Early Nineteenth Century America. Ph.D., University of Wisconsin, 1967. 292p. UMI# 67-16941.

3903   Gaddis, Merrill E. Christian Perfectionism in America. Ph.D., University of Chicago, 1929.

3904   Gettys, Joseph M. The Philosophy of Life Contained in the Fourth Gospel Compared With the Philosophies of Plato and Dewey. Ph.D., New York University, 1938.

3905   Gillespie, Neal C. George Frederick Holmes and the Philosophy of Faith: A Study in the Religious Crisis of American Orthodoxy in the Nineteenth Century. Ph.D., Duke University, 1964. 320p. UMI# 64-07756.

3906   Gilmartin, Thomas V. Soul-Sickness: A Comparison of William James and Soeren Kierkegaard. Th.D., Graduate Theological Union, 1974. 321p. UMI# 7609152.

3907   Jacobs, Anton K. Evangelicalism and Capitalism: A Critical Study of the Doctrine of Atonement in the History of American Religion. Ph.D., University of Notre Dame, 1985. 250p. UMI# 8515218.

3908   Kelley, Jeffrey O. The Gospel of God's Grace as the Locus of Authority in the Free Church Tradition: A Critical Evaluation of the Thought of Peter Taylor Forsyth. D.Min., University of Chicago, 1987.

3909   Kessler, Sanford H. John Locke and the Founding of American Civil Religion. Ph.D., Boston College, 1979. 283p. UMI# 79-20490.

3910   Kleber, John E. The Magic of His Power: Robert G. Ingersoll and His Day. Ph.D., University of Kentucky, 1969. 345p. UMI# 7002581.

3911   Kloos, John M., Jr. Benjamin Rush, Revolutionary Physician: An Interpretation of Religion in the Republic. Ph.D., University of Chicago, 1984.

3912   Lazarus, Frederick K. The Metaphysics of Ramanuja and Bowne. Ph.D., Boston University, 1957. 488p. UMI# 21409.

3913   Lips, Roger C. The Spirit's Holy Errand: A Study of Continuities of Thought From Jonathan Edwards to Ralph Waldo Emerson. Ph.D., University of Wisconsin-Madison, 1976. 338p. UMI# 7610667.

3914   Moran, Jon S. Religious Selfhood in the Philosophies of Josiah Royce and G.H. Mead. Ph.D., Tulane University, 1972. 338p. UMI# 7224417.

3915   Moran, Vincent J. The Relation of Brownson to the Philosophy of Kant. Ph.D., University of Toronto, 1954.

3916   Parker, David L. The Application of Humiliation: Ramist Logic and the Rise of Preparationism in New England. Ph.D., University of Pennsylvania, 1972. 297p. UMI# 7225646.

3917   Russell, John M. The Idea of God in Peirce and James. Ph.D., Southern Illinois University-Carbondale, 1982. 180p. UMI# 8229310.

3918   Shin, Kee S. Paul Carus's *Positive Monism* and Critique of Other Types of Monism. Ph.D., Temple University, 1973. 491p. UMI# 7330173.

3919   Thomas, George B. The Religious Aspect of Pragmatism. Ph.D., Boston University, 1913.

3920   Zikmund, Barbara B. Asa Mahan and Oberlin Perfectionism. Ph.D., Duke University, 1969. 390p. UMI# 7011599.

POLITICS AND SOCIAL POLICY

3921   Alexander, Jon A. "The Disturbance of the Spring": The Attitude of Selected American Clergy Toward the Use of Violence Against British Authority, 1763-1776. Ph.D., Temple University, 1971. 296p. UMI# 71-19944.

3922   Allain, Mathe. French Colonial Policy in America and the Establishment of the Louisiana Colony. Ph.D., University of Southwestern Louisiana, 1984. 276p. UMI# 8416773.

3923   Bailey, David T. Slavery and the Churches: The Old Southwest. Ph.D., University of California-Berkeley, 1979. 258p. UMI# 80-00275.

3924   Bannan, Phyllis M. Arthur and Lewis Tappan: A Study of Religious and Reform Movements in New York City. Ph.D., Columbia University, 1950. 226p. UMI# 1829.

3925   Bard, David R. Gamaliel Bailey and the *National Era*: A Conservative Antislavery Editor in the Crisis Years, 1847-1859. Ph.D., University of Maine, 1974. 337p. UMI# 7512412.

3926   Barnes, Gilbert H. The Abolition Revival. Ph.D., University of Michigan, 1930.

3927   Bass, Dorothy C. "The Best Hopes of the Sexes": The Woman Question in Garrisonian Abolitionism. Ph.D., Brown University, 1980. 371p. UMI# 8111061.

3928   Bates, Jack W. John Quincy Adams and the Antislavery Movement. Ph.D., University of Southern California, 1953.

3929   Beattie, Donald W. Sons of Temperance: Pioneers in Total Abstinence and "Constitutional" Prohibition. Ph.D., Boston University, 1966. 517p. UMI# 611278.

3930   Beltz, Lynda A. Preachers of Social Discontent: The Rhetoric of the Muckrakers. Ph.D., Indiana University, 1968. 287p. UMI# 6815434.

3931   Bennett, John B. Albert Taylor Bledsoe: Social and Religious Controversialist of the Old South. Ph.D., Duke University, 1942.

3932   Berghorn, Donna E. "The Mother's Struggle": Harriet Beecher Stowe and the American Antislavery Debate. Ph.D., Rensselaer Polytechnic Institute, 1988. 293p. UMI# 8905504.

3933   Bernar, Joel C. From Theodicy to Ideology: The Origins of the American Temperance Movement. Ph.D., Yale University, 1983. 517p. UMI# 8619435.

3934   Berstein, Stanley B. Abolitionist Readings of the Constitution. Ph.D., Harvard University, 1970.

3935   Bissett, James S. Agrarian Socialism in America: Marx and Jesus in the Oklahoma Countryside. Ph.D., Duke University, 1989. 252p. UMI# 9002042.

3936   Blackmon, Dora M.E. The Care of the Mentally Ill in America, 1604-1812, in the Thirteen Original Colonies. Ph.D., University of Washington, 1964. 226p. UMI# 6505408.

3937   Brown, Daniel S., Jr. A Radical Republican in the United States Senate: The Antislavery Speaking of Benjamin Franklin Wade. Ph.D., Louisiana State University, 1987. 207p. UMI# 8719850.

3938   Bruland, Esther L.B. Great Debates: Ethical Reasoning and Social Change in Antebellum America: The Exchange Between Angelina Grimke and Catharine Beecher. Ph.D., Drew University, 1990. 464p. UMI# 9032118.

3939   Bruser, Lawrence. Political Antislavery in Connecticut, 1844-1858. Ph.D., Columbia University, 1974. 513p. UMI# 7507479.

3940   Bustami, Zaha B. American Foreign Policy and Question of Palestine, 1856-1939. Ph.D., Georgetown University, 1989. 508p. UMI# 9004732.

3941   Butler, Randall R., II. New England Journalism and the Questions of Slavery, the South, and Abolitionism: 1820-1861. Ph.D., Brigham Young University, 1979. 216p. UMI# 8017848.

3942   Camara, Evandro D. A Flight Into Utopia: The Proslavery Argument of the American South in Social-Hermeneutical Perspective. Ph.D., University of Notre Dame, 1986. 162p. UMI# 8616927.

3943   Carlson, Douglas W. Temperance Reform in the Cotton Kingdom. Ph.D., University of Illinois at Urbana-Champaign, 1982. 331p. UMI# 8209551.

3944   Carroll, Sharon A. Elitism and Reform: Some Antislavery Opinion Makers in the Era of Civil War and Reconstruction. Ph.D., Cornell University, 1970. 267p. UMI# 7014373.

3945   Carter, George E. The Use of the Doctrine of Higher Law in the American Anti-Slavery Crusade, 1830-1860. Ph.D., University of Oregon, 1970. 418p. UMI# 7021559.

3946   Cashdollar, Charles D. American Church Attitudes Toward Social Catastrophe: The Panic of 1873 as a Case Study. Ph.D., University of Pennsylvania, 1969. 257p. UMI# 6021330.

3947   Cavanagh, Helen M. Antislavery Sentiment and Politics in the Northwest, 1844-1860. Ph.D., University of Chicago, 1938.

3948   Christiano, Kevin J. Religious Diversity and Social Change in Turn-of-the-Century American Cities. Ph.D., Princeton University, 1983. 295p. UMI# 8402680.

3949   Cleland, John S. The Church and Social Service in Pittsburgh. Ph.D., University of Pittsburgh, 1914.

3950   Coffey, John J. A Political History of the Temperance Movement in New York State, 1808-1920. Ph.D., Pennsylvania State University, 1976. 371p. UMI# 7629622.

3951   Cohen, William. James Miller McKim: Pennsylvania Abolitionist. Ph.D., New York University, 1968. 326p. UMI# 6907942.

3952   Conroy, David W. The Culture and Politics of Drink in Colonial and Revolutionary Massachusetts, 1681-1790. Ph.D., University of Connecticut, 1987. 317p. UMI# 8800209.

3953   Cook, Lester H. Anti-Slavery Sentiment in the Culture of Chicago, 1844-1858. Ph.D., University of Chicago, 1953.

3954   Cormany, Clayton D. Ohio's Abolitionist Campaign: A Study in the Rhetoric of Conversion. Ph.D., Ohio State University, 1981. 187p. UMI# 8121778.

3955   Cox, Stephen L. Power, Oppression, and Liberation: New Hampshire Abolitionism and the Radical Critique of Slavery, 1825-1850. Ph.D., University of New Hampshire, 1980. 290p. UMI# 8108865.

3956   Curet, Jose. From Slave to Liberto: A Study on Slavery and Its Abolition in Puerto Rico, 1840-1880. Ph.D., Columbia University, 1980. 307p. UMI# 8016913.

3957   Davis, William G. Attacking "the Matchless Evil": Temperance and Prohibition in Mississippi, 1817-1908. Ph.D., Mississippi State University, 1975. 278p. UMI# 7611789.

3958   Del Porto, Joseph A. A Study of American Anti-Slavery Journals. Ph.D., Michigan State University, 1953. 308p. UMI# 6850.

3959   Dillon, Merton L. The Antislavery Movement in Illinois: 1809-1844. Ph.D., University of Michigan, 1951. 402p. UMI# 2582.

3960   Dixon, Frank J. Anti-Slavery Sentiment in the New York City Press,

1830-1850: A Consideration of Its Origin, Development, Extent and Quality. Ph.D., Fordham University, 1939.

3961   Doe, Seung J. Christian Perspectives on Poverty: An Ideological Foundation for Social Work, 1880-1920. Ph.D., Washington University, 1989. 266p. UMI# 9027395.

3962   Donnelly, Brenda W. Religious Ideology and Social Protest in America. Ph.D., University of Delaware, 1985. 254p. UMI# 8525289.

3963   Dwyer, Ellen. The Rhetoric of Reform: A Study of Verbal Persuasion and Belief Systems in the Anti-Masonic and Temperance Movements, 1825-1860. Ph.D., Yale University, 1977. 304p. UMI# 7727071.

3964   Eberly, Wayne J. The Pennsylvania Abolition Society, 1775-1830. Ph.D., Pennsylvania State University, 1973. 245p. UMI# 7416014.

3965   Edwards, John A. Social and Cultural Activities of Texans During Civil War and Reconstruction, 1861-1873. Ph.D., Texas Tech University, 1985. 366p. UMI# 8528579.

3966   Eisenstein, Ira. The Ethics of Tolerance Applied to Religious Groups in America. Ph.D., Columbia University, 1942. 87p.

3967   Ellsworth, Clayton S. Oberlin and the Anti-Slavery Movement up to the Civil War. Ph.D., Cornell University, 1930. 211p. UMI# 618.

3968   English, Philip W. John G. Fee: Kentucky Spokesman for Abolition and Educational Reform. Ph.D., Indiana University, 1973. 227p. UMI# 7400349.

3969   Essah, Patience. Slavery and Freedom in the First State: The History of Blacks in Delaware From the Colonial Period to 1865. Ph.D., University of California-Los Angeles, 1985. 251p. UMI# 8513110.

3970   Evans, Linda J. Abolitionism in the Illinois Churches, 1830-1865. Ph.D., Northwestern University, 1981. 530p. UMI# 8124881.

3971   Everson, Judith E.L. The Rhetoric of the Abolitionist Remnant, 1870-1877. Ph.D., Indiana University, 1973. 248p. UMI# 7314609.

3972   Ewing, George W. Some Verse of the Temperance Movement. Ph.D., University of Texas-Austin, 1962. 321p. UMI# 63-01655.

3973   Ferguson, Alfred R. Reflections on Transcendental Abolitionist Perfectionism in American Life, 1830-1860: Biography of a Fantasy. Ph.D., University of Minnesota, 1971. 262p. UMI# 71-22202.

3974   Finnie, Gordon E. The Antislavery Movement in the South, 1787-1836: Its Rise and Decline and Its Contribution to Abolitionism in the West. Ph.D., Duke University, 1962. 601p. UMI# 6303585.

3975   Fish, Andrew. Studies in the History of Christian Social Reform Doctrine in the United States. Ph.D., Clark University, 1923.

3976   Fliss, Matthew S. The Pilgrim's Progess: The Progressivism of Francis Wayland Parker (1837-1902). Ph.D., University of Pennsylvania, 1988. 182p. UMI# 8816128.

3977   Foster, Claudia C. Motive, Means, and Ends in Gradual Abolitionist Education, 1785 to 1830. Ph.D., Columbia University, 1977. 260p. UMI# 7714796.

3978   Frederick, Peter J. European Influences on the Awakening of the American Social Conscience, 1886-1904. Ph.D., University of California-Berkeley, 1966. 536p. UMI# 6708558.

3979   French, David C. The Conversion of an American Radical: Elizur Wright, Jr. and the Abolitionist Commitment. Ph.D., Case Western Reserve University, 1970. 238p. UMI# 7101690.

3980   Fulkerson, Raymond G. Frederick Douglass and the Anti-Slavery Crusade: His Career and Speeches, 1817-1861. Ph.D., University of Illinois at Urbana-Champaign, 1971. 1028p. UMI# 7212168.

3981   Fulmer, Hal W. The Defiant Legacy: Southern Clergy and a Rhetoric of Redemption for the Reconstruction South. Ph.D., Louisiana State University, 1985. 221p. UMI# 8517735.

3982   Gamble, Douglas A. Moral Suasion in the West: Garrisonian Abolitionism, 1831-1861. Ph.D., Ohio State University, 1973. 510p. UMI# 7410959.

3983   Garman, Mary V. "Altered Tone of Expression": The Anti-Slavery Rhetoric of Illinois Women, 1837-1847. Ph.D., Northwestern University, 1989. 224p. UMI# 9001800.

3984   Giele, Janet Z. Social Change in the Feminine Role: A Comparison of Woman's Suffrage and Women's Temperance, 1870-1920. Ph.D., Radcliffe College, 1961.

3985   Glasman, Paula. Zedina Eastman: Chicago Abolitionist. Ph.D., University of Chicago, 1969.

3986   Goerler, Raimund E. Family Self and Anti-Slavery: Sydney Howard Gay and the Abolitionist Commitment. Ph.D., Case Western

Reserve University, 1975. 298p. UMI# 7527912.

3987   Goldfarb, Joel. The Life of Gamaliel Bailey Prior to the Founding of the *National Era*; The Orientation of a Practical Abolitionist. Ph.D., University of California-Los Angeles, 1959.

3988   Goodheart, Lawrence B. Elizur Wright, Jr., and the Abolitionist Movement, 1820-1865. Ph.D., University of Connecticut, 1979. 219p. UMI# 7914153.

3989   Goodman, Gary S. "All About Me Forgotten": The Education of Caroline Healey Dall (1822-1912). Ph.D., Stanford University, 1987. 435p. UMI# 8720393.

3990   Grover, Norman L. The Church and Social Action: The Idea of the Church and Its Relation to Christian Social Strategy in Charles G. Finney, Horace Bushnell. Ph.D., Yale University, 1957. 588p. UMI# 67-03735.

3991   Gudelunas, William A., Jr. Before the Molly Maguires: The Emergence of the Ethno-Religious Factor in the Politics of the Lower Anthracite Region. Ph.D., Lehigh University, 1973. 208p. UMI# 73-23798.

3992   Hackett, David G. Religion and Society in Albany, New York, 1652-1836. Ph.D., Emory University, 1986. 466p. UMI# 8629849.

3993   Halker, Clark D. For Democracy, the Working Class, and God: Labor Song-Poems and Working-Class Consciousness, 1865-1895. Ph.D., University of Minnesota, 1984. 417p. UMI# 8424697.

3994   Hamand, Wendy F. Neither Ballots nor Bullets: Women Abolitionists and Emancipation During the Civil War. Ph.D., University of Illinois at Urbana-Champaign, 1985. 267p. UMI# 8521779.

3995   Hampel, Robert L. Influence and Respectability: Temperance and Prohibition in Massachusetts, 1813-1852. Ph.D., Cornell University, 1980. 446p. UMI# 8102895.

3996   Hamrogue, John M. John A. Andrew, Abolitionist Governor, 1861-1865. Ph.D., Fordham University, 1974. 288p. UMI# 7425052.[Massachusetts].

3997   Hansen, Debra G. Bluestockings and Bluenoses: Gender, Class, and Conflict in the Boston Female Anti-Slavery Society, 1833-1840. Ph.D., University of California-Irvine, 1988. 270p. UMI# 8907785.

3998   Harrold, Stanley C., Jr. Gamaliel Bailey, Abolitionist and Free Soiler. Ph.D., Kent State University, 1975. 541p. UMI# 7527811.

3999   Harwood, Thomas F. Great Britain and American Antislavery. Ph.D., University of Texas-Austin, 1959. 848p. UMI# 5904720.

4000   Henderson, Alice H. The History of the New York State Anti-Slavery Society. Ph.D., University of Michigan, 1963. 418p. UMI# 6408170.

4001   Hersh, Blanche G. "The Slavery of Sex": Feminist-Abolitionists in Nineteenth-Century America. Ph.D., University of Illinois-Chicago, 1975. 482p. UMI# 7602282.

4002   Heyrman, Christine L. A Model of Christian Charity: The Rich and the Poor in New England, 1630-1730. Ph.D., Yale University, 1977. 287p. UMI# 77-27077.

4003   Hickin, Patricia E.P. Antislavery in Virginia, 1831-1861. Ph.D., University of Virginia, 1968. 847p. UMI# 6818206.

4004   Hixson, William B., Jr. The Last Abolitionist: A Study of Moorfield Storey, 1845-1929. Ph.D., Columbia University, 1969. 444p. UMI# 7219128.

4005   Hovet, Theodore R. Harriet Beecher Stowe's Holiness Crusade Against Slavery. Ph.D., University of Kansas, 1970. 194p. UMI# 7025348.

4006   Hovey, Amos A. A History of the Religious Aspects of American Peace Movements. Ph.D., University of Chicago, 1930.

4007   Huff, Carolyn B. The Politics of Idealism: The Political Abolitionists of Ohio in Congress, 1840-1866. Ph.D., University of North Carolina-Chapel Hill, 1969. 185p. UMI# 7003255.

4008   Jarvis, Charles A. John Greenleaf Whittier and the Anti-Slavery Movement, 1828-1860. Ph.D., University of Missouri-Columbia, 1970. 278p. UMI# 7020789.

4009   Jentz, John B. Artisans, Evangelicals, and the City: A Social History of Abolition and Labor Reform in Jacksonian New York. Ph.D., City University of New York, 1977. 509p. UMI# 77-24890.

4010   Johnson, Reinhard O. The Liberty Party in New England, 1840-1848: The Forgotten Abolitionists. Ph.D., Syracuse University, 1976. 482p. UMI# 7724549.

4011   Kennicott, Patrick C. Negro Antislavery Speakers in America. Ph.D., Florida State University, 1967. 309p. UMI# 6800363.

4012   King, Keith L. Religious Dimensions of the Agrarian Protest in Texas, 1870-1908. Ph.D., University of Illinois at Urbana-Champaign, 1985. 342p. UMI# 8600239.

4013   Kirkpatrick, Jean R. The Temperance Movement and Temperance Fiction, 1820-1860. Ph.D., University of Pennsylvania, 1970. 225p. UMI# 71-07818.

4014   Kleiman, Jeffrey D. The Great Strike: Religion, Labor and Reform in Grand Rapids, Michigan, 1890-1916. Ph.D., Michigan State University, 1985. 207p. UMI# 8603437.

4015   Kooker, Arthur R. The Anti-Slavery Movement in Michigan, 1796-1840: A Study in Humanitarianism on an American Frontier. Ph.D., University of Michigan 1941.

4016   Kraut, Alan M. The Liberty Men of New York: Political Abolitionism in New York State, 1840-1848. Ph.D., Cornell University, 1975. 493p. UMI# 7608141.

4017   Lang, William L. Black Bootstraps: The Abolitionist Educators' Ideology and the Education of the Northern Free Negro, 1828-1860. Ph.D., University of Delaware, 1974. 256p. UMI# 7427858.

4018   Lehman, Neil B. The Life of John Murray Spear: Spiritualism and Reform in Antebellum America. Ph.D., Ohio State University, 1973. 480p. UMI# 7403230.

4019   Lengel, Leland L. The Righteous Cause: Some Religious Aspects of Kansas Populism. Ph.D., University of Oregon, 1968. 365p. UMI# 69-00033.

4020   Levine, Harry G. Demon of the Middle Class: Self-Control, Liquor, and the Ideology of Temperance in 19th Century America. Ph.D., University of California-Berkeley, 1978. 274p. UMI# 79-14672.

4021   Lewis, Caroline. The Antislavery Argument as Developed in the Literature From 1830-1840. Ph.D., Cornell University, 1917.

4022   Lobue, Wayne N. Religious Romanticism and Social Revitalization: The Oberlin Perfectionists. Ph.D., University of Kansas, 1972. 251p. UMI# 7311916.

4023   Ludlum, Robert P. Joshua R. Giddings, Antislavery Radical (1795-1844). Ph.D., Cornell University, 1936.

4024   Lumpkins, Josephine. Antislavery Opposition to the Annexation of Texas, With Special Reference to John Quincy Adams. Ph.D., Cornell University, 1941.

4025   Mandel, Bernard. The Northern Working Class and the Abolition of Slavery. Ph.D., Case Western Reserve University, 1952.

4026   Martin, Asa E. The Anti-Slavery Movement in Kentucky Prior to 1850. Ph.D., Cornell University, 1915.

4027   Martin, Bert E. Freedom and the Puritan Conscience: American Destiny and the Defenders of the "Amistad" African. Ph.D., Baylor University, 1979. 149p. UMI# 80-03329.

4028   Mathis, Richard S. Emancipation: A Study of Two Theories. Ph.D., Johns Hopkins University, 1986. 164p. UMI# 8707280.

4029   Matijasic, Thomas D. Conservative Reform in the West: The African Colonization Movement in Ohio, 1826-1839. Ph.D., Miami University, 1962. 406p. UMI# 6413179.

4030   McBride, Genevieve G. No "Season of Silence": Uses of "Public Relations" in Nineteenth and Early Twentieth Century Reform Movements in Wisconsin. Ph.D., University of Wisconsin-Madison, 1989. 438p. UMI# 9009570.

4031   McElroy, Frederick L. Prophets of Universal Redemption: Evangelical Antislavery Literature From John Woolman to Ottabah Cugoano. Ph.D., Indiana University, 1987. 412p. UMI# 8727516.

4032   McKivigan, John R. Abolitionism and the American Churches, 1830-1865: A Study of Attitudes and Tactics. Ph.D., Ohio State University, 1977. 572p. UMI# 78-05887.

4033   McMahon, Adrian M. The Concept of Freedom and the Radical Abolitionists, 1860-1870. Ph.D., University of Texas-Austin, 1970. 225p. UMI# 7018269.

4034   McPherson, James M. The Abolitionists and the Negro During the Civil War and Reconstruction. Ph.D., Johns Hopkins University, 1963.

4035   Merkel, Benjamin. The Antislavery Movement in Missouri, 1819-1865. Ph.D., Washington University, 1939.

4036   Meyer, Paul R., Jr. The Transformation of American Temperance: The Popularization and Radicalization of a Reform Movement, 1813-1860. Ph.D., University of Iowa, 1976. 282p. UMI# 7713114.

4037   Middleton, Stephen. Ohio and the Antislavery Activities of Attorney Salmon Portland Chase, 1830-1849. Ph.D., Miami University, 1987. 187p. UMI# 8709537.

4038   Miele, Frank J. The American Civil Religion in the 1890s: In Crisis and Revival. Ph.D., Tulane University, 1984. 229p. UMI# 8504823.

4039   Miller, Larry C. Dimensions of Mugwump Thought, 1880-1920; Sons of Massachusetts Abolitionists as Professional Pioneers. Ph.D., Northwestern University, 1969. 299p. UMI# 7000122.

4040   Miller, Marion C. The Antislavery Movement in Indiana. Ph.D., University of Michigan, 1938.

4041   Mooney, James E. Antislavery in Worcester County, Massachusetts: A Case Study. Ph.D., Clark University, 1971. 315p. UMI# 7203339.

4042   Moore, Wilbert E. Slavery, Abolition, and the Ethical Valuation of the Individual. Ph.D., Harvard University, 1940.

4043   Morris, Valarie Z. The Advocates of Peace: Theological Foundations of the Nineteenth-Century American Peace Movement. Ph.D., Emory University, 1987. 361p. UMI# 8716132.

4044   Morrison, Larry R. The Proslavery Argument in the Early Republic, 1790-1830. Ph.D., University of Virginia, 1975. 289p. UMI# 7522829.

4045   Mounger, Dwyn M. Bondage and Benevolence: An Evangelical Calvinist Approaches Slavery; Samuel Hanson Cox. Ph.D., Union Theological Seminary, 1976. 253p. UMI# 76-15739.

4046   Muhler, William M. Religion and Social Problems in Gold Rush California: 1849-1869. Ph.D., Graduate Theological Union, 1989. 472p. UMI# 8924371.

4047   Murphy, Teresa A. Labor, Religion and Moral Reform in Fall River, Massachusetts, 1800-1845. Ph.D., Yale University, 1982. 241p. UMI# 8310511.

4048   Myers, John L. The Agency System of the Anti-Slavery Movement, 1832-1837, and Its Antecedents in Other Benevolent and Reform Societies. Ph.D., University of Michigan, 1961. 750p. UMI# 6101895.

4049   Ndukwu, Maurice D. Antislavery in Michigan: A Study of Its Origin, Development, and Expression From Territorial Period to 1860. Ph.D., Michigan State University, 1979. 373p. UMI# 8001570.

4050   Newbold, Catharine. The Antislavery Background of the Principal

State Department Appointees in the Lincoln Administration. Ph.D., University of Michigan, 1962. 493p. UMI# 6301920.

4051   Norton, L. Wesley. The Religious Press and the Compromise of 1850: A Study of the Relationship of the Methodist, Baptist, and Presbyterian Press to the Slavery Controversy, 1846-1851. Ph.D., University of Illinois at Urbana-Champaign, 1959. 314p. UMI# 60-00222.

4052   O'Dell, Richard F. The Early Antislavery Movement in Ohio. Ph.D., University of Michigan, 1948. 431p. UMI# 1069.

4053   Parker, Russell D. "Higher Law": Its Development and Application to the American Antislavery Controversy. Ph.D., University of Tennessee, 1966. 239p. UMI# 6701373.

4054   Patterson, John S. The Structure of Commitment and the Survival of Fear: White Antislavery and Late-Nineteenth-Century Attitudes Toward Black Americans. Ph.D., Brown University, 1969. 259p. UMI# 7008775.

4055   Perry, Lewis C. Antislavery and Anarchy: A Study of the Ideas of Abolitionism Before the Civil War. Ph.D., Cornell University, 1967. 383p. UMI# 6800888.

4056   Petit, Mary L. Samuel Lewis, Educational Reformer Turned Abolitionist. Ed.D., Case Western Reserve University, 1966. 182p. UMI# 6704651.

4057   Pfister, Frederick W. In the Cause of Freedom: American Abolition Societies, 1775-1808. Ph.D., Miami University, 1980. 217p. UMI# 8023653.

4058   Pitman, Ursula W. Moncure Daniel Conway: The Development and Career of a Southern Abolitionist. Ph.D., Boston College, 1978. 695p. UMI# 7807243.

4059   Pivar, David J. The New Abolitionism: The Quest for Social Purity, 1876-1900. Ph.D., University of Pennsylvania, 1965. 393p. UMI# 6513371.

4060   Ratner, Lorman A. Northern Opposition to the Anti-Slavery Movement, 1831-1840. Ph.D., Cornell University, 1961. 263p. UMI# 6104888.

4061   Reep, Samuel N. Social Policy of Chicago Churches. Ph.D., University of Chicago, 1910.

4062   Reynolds, Todd A. The American Missionary Association's Anti-Slavery Campaign in Kentucky, 1848 to 1860. Ph.D., Ohio State University, 1979. 204p. UMI# 80-09334.

4063   Rice, Arthur H. Henry B. Stanton as a Political Abolitionist. Ed.D., Columbia University, 1968. 523p. UMI# 6906036.

4064   Richards, Leonard L. Gentlemen of Property and Standing: A Study of Northern Anti-Abolition Mobs. Ph.D., University of California-Davis, 1968. 233p. UMI# 6900822.

4065   Rothermund, Dietmar. Denominations and Political Behavior in Colonial Pennsylvania, 1740-1770. Ph.D., University of Pennsylvania, 1959. 231p. UMI# 5904655.

4066   Rumbarger, John J. The Social Origins and Function of the Political Temperance Movement in the Reconstruction of American Society 1825-1917. Ph.D., University of Pennsylvania, 1968. 370p. UMI# 6915112.

4067   Saillant, John D. Letters and Social Aims: Rhetoric and Virtue From Jefferson to Emerson. Ph.D., Brown University, 1989. 372p. UMI# 9002289.[Timothy Dwight, Ralph Waldo Emerson, Thomas Jefferson, James Madison, Thomas Paine].

4068   Sanders, Cheryl J. Slavery and Conversion: An Analysis of Ex-Slave Testimony. Th.D., Harvard University, 1985.

4069   Savage, William S. The Controversy Over the Distribution of Abolition Literature, 1830-1860. Ph.D., Ohio State University, 1935.

4070   Sayre, Robert D. The Evolution of Early American Abolitionism: The American Convention for Promoting the Abolition of Slavery and Improving the Condition of the African Race, 1794-1837. Ph.D., Ohio State University, 1987. 373p. UMI# 8710047.

4071   Schnell, Kempes Y. Court Cases Involving Slavery: A Study of the Application of Anti-Slavery Thought to Judicial Argument. Ph.D., University of Michigan, 1955. 359p. UMI# 12643.

4072   Schnitzer, Maxine M. A Rhetorical Analysis of the Anti-Slavery Speaking of Cassius M. Clay of Kentucky. Ph.D., Michigan State University, 1962. 284p. UMI# 6204460.

4073   Schor, Joel A. The Anti-Slavery and Civil Rights Role of Henry Highland Garnet, 1840-1865. Ph.D., Howard University, 1973. 389p. UMI# 7502188.

4074   Schriver, Edward O. The Antislavery Impulse in Maine, 1833-1855. Ph.D., University of Maine, 1967. 235p. UMI# 6809411.

4075   Seibert, Russell H. The Treatment of Conscientious Objectors in War Time, 1775-1920. Ph.D., Ohio State University, 1936.

4076   Sewell, Richard H. John P. Hale: Anti-Slavery Advocate, 1806-1861. Ph.D., Harvard University, 1962.

4077   Shain, Barry A. A Study in 18th-Century Political Theory: Liberty, Autonomy, Protestant Communalism and Slavery in Revolutionary America. Ph.D., Yale University, 1990. 571p. UMI# 9035367.

4078   Shay, John M. The Antislavery Movement in North Carolina. Ph.D., Princeton University, 1971. 546p. UMI# 7123383.

4079   Simmons, Adam D. Ideologies and Programs of the Negro Antislavery Movement, 1830-1861. Ph.D., Northwestern University, 1983. 330p. UMI# 8315967.

4080   Slavcheff, Peter D. The Temperate Republic: Liquor Control in Michigan, 1800-1860. Ph.D., Wayne State University, 1987. 392p. UMI# 8809139.

4081   Smith, Donald A. Legacy of Dissent: Religion and Politics in Revolutionary Vermont, 1749-1784. Ph.D., Clark University, 1981.

4082   Smith, Robert G. The Arguments Over Abolition Petitions in the House of Representatives in December 1835: A Toulmin Analysis. Ph.D., University of Minnesota, 1962. 297p. UMI# 6305043.

4083   Snay, Mitchell. Gospel of Disunion: Religion and the Rise of Southern Separatism, 1830-1861. Ph.D., Brandeis University, 1984. 305p. UMI# 8509834.

4084   Sokolow, Jayme A. Revivalism and Radicalism: William Lloyd Garrison, Henry Clarke Wright and the Ideology of Non-Resistance. Ph.D., New York University, 1972. 269p. UMI# 73-11773.

4085   Sorin, Gerald S. The Historical Theory of Political Radicalism: New York State Abolitionist Leaders as a Test Case. Ph.D., Columbia University, 1969. 240p. UMI# 6917616.

4086   Sparks, Robert V. Abolition in Silver Slippers: A Biography of Edmund Quincy. Ph.D., Boston College, 1978. 444p. UMI# 7814679.

4087   Spurlock, John C. Free Love: Marriage and Middle-Class Radicalism in America, 1825-1860. Ph.D., Rutgers University, 1987. 407p. UMI# 8723302.

4088   Steely, Will F. Antislavery in Kentucky, 1850-1860. Ph.D., University of Rochester, 1956.

4089   Steinsapir, Carol. The Ante-Bellum Total Abstinence Movement at the Local Level: A Case Study of Schenectady, New York. Ph.D., Rutgers University, 1983. 414p. UMI# 8406411.

4090   Stevenson, Robert C. Pacifism and Militarism: A History and Analysis of Ideas. Ph.D., University of California-Berkeley, 1929.

4091   Stock, Edwin W. The Role of the Church in the Inception and Survival of the Appalachian Regional Hospitals. Ph.D., Louisville Presbyterian Theological Seminary, 1979.

4092   Stout, Harry S., III. Remigration and Revival: Two Case Studies in the Social and Intellectual History of New England, 1630-1745. Ph.D., Kent State University, 1974. 426p. UMI# 757101.

4093   Strickland, John S. Across Space and Time: Conversion, Community and Cultural Change Among South Carolina Slaves. Ph.D., University of North Carolina-Chapel Hill, 1985. 477p. UMI# 8527327.

4094   Strong, Daniel G. Supreme Court Justice William Strong, 1808-1895: Jurisprudence, Christianity and Reform. Ph.D., Kent State University, 1985. 435p. UMI# 8604199.

4095   Strong, Douglas M. Organized Liberty: Evangelical Perfectionism, Political Abolitionism, and Ecclesiastical Reform in the Burned-Over District. Ph.D., Princeton Theological Seminary, 1990. 425p. UMI# 9030374.

4096   Sun, Tung-Hsun. Some Interpretations of the Abolition Movement. Ph.D., Michigan State University, 1972. 360p. UMI# 7305498.

4097   Tallant, Harold D., Jr. The Slavery Controversy in Kentucky, 1829-1859. Ph.D., Duke University, 1986. 468p. UMI# 8706840.

4098   Thomas, George M. Institutional Knowledge and Social Movements: Rational Exchange, Revival Religion, and Nation-Building in the U.S., 1870-1896. Ph.D., Stanford University, 1979. 202p. UMI# 79-12413.

4099   Thompson, Thomas C. The Failure of Jeffersonian Reform: Religious Groups and the Politics of Morality in Early National

Virginia. Ph.D., University of California-Riverside, 1990. 430p. UMI# 9034607.

4100   Thorning, Joseph F. Religious Liberty in Transition: A Study of the Removal of Constitutional Limitations on Religious Liberty as Part of the Social Progress in the Transition Period. Ph.D., Catholic University of America, 1931.

4101   Tise, Larry E. Proslavery Ideology: A Social and Intellectual History of the Defense of Slavery in America, 1790-1840. Ph.D., University of North Carolina-Chapel Hill, 1975. 770p. UMI# 7529088.

4102   Tolf, Robert W. Edmund Quincy: Aristocrat Abolitionist. Ph.D., University of Rochester, 1957.

4103   Trendel, Robert A., Jr. William Jay: Churchman, Public Servant and Reformer. Ph.D., Southern Illinois University-Carbondale, 1972. 465p. UMI# 73-06251.

4104   Tully, William A. William Penn's Legacy: Politics and Social Structure in Colonial Pennsylvania, 1726 to 1755. Ph.D., Johns Hopkins University, 1973. 571p. UMI# 7611233.

4105   Turner, Ian B. Antislavery Thought in the Border South, 1830-1860. Ph.D., University of Illinois at Urbana-Champaign, 1977. 627p. UMI# 7804182.

4106   Tyrrell, Ian R. Drink and the Process of Social Reform: From Temperance to Prohibition in the Ante-Bellum America, 1813-1860. Ph.D., Duke University, 1974. 266p. UMI# 7502436.

4107   Van Deburg, William L. Rejected of Men: The Changing Religious Views of William Lloyd Garrison and Frederick Douglass. Ph.D., Michigan State University, 1973. 361p. UMI# 74-06160.

4108   Vartanian, Pershing. The Puritan as a Symbol in American Thought: A Study of the New England Societies, 1820-1920. Ph.D., University of Michigan, 1971. 330p. UMI# 72-05003.

4109   Vigilante, Emil C. The Temperance Reform in New York State, 1829-1851. Ph.D., New York University, 1964. 291p. UMI# 6609539.

4110   Vogt, Allen R. "An Honest Fanatic": The Images of the Abolitionist in the Antebellum and Historical Minds. Ph.D., University of Houston, 1984. 423p. UMI# 8428104.

4111   Volpe, Vernon L. Forlorn Hope of Freedom: The Liberty Party in the Old Northwest 1838-1848. Ph.D., University of Nebraska-Lincoln, 1984. 416p. UMI# 8427915.

4112   Walters, Ronald G. The Antislavery Appeal: American Abolitionism After 1830. Ph.D., University of California-Berkeley, 1972.

4113   Wander, Philip C. The Image of the Negro in Three Movements: Abolitionist, Colonizationist, and Pro-Slavery. Ph.D., University of Pittsburgh, 1968. 216p. UMI# 6906414.

4114   Ward, James F. Consciousness and Community: American Idealist Social Thought From Puritanism to Social Science. Ph.D., Harvard University, 1975. 500p.

4115   Ward, William E. Charles Lenox Remond: Black Abolitionist, 1838-1873. Ph.D., Clark University, 1977. 345p. UMI# 7803414.

4116   Weisman, Richard M. Witchcraft in Seventeenth-Century Massachusetts: The Construction of a Category of Deviance. Ph.D., University of California-Berkeley, 1977. 438p. UMI# 78-12820.

4117   Welch, Eloise T. The Background and Development of the American Missionary Association's Decision to Educate Freedmen in the South, With Subsequent Repercussions for Higher Education. Ph.D., Bryn Mawr College, 1976. 205p. UMI# 7706542.

4118   Whelchel, Love H., Jr. The Case for Abolition in the Writings of William Wells Brown. Ph.D., Duke University, 1981. 204p. UMI# 8124816.

4119   Wilson, Renate. Halle and Ebenezer: Pietism, Agriculture and Commerce in Colonial Georgia. Ph.D., University of Maryland, 1988. 471p. UMI# 8827139.

4120   Wright, Conrad E. Christian Compassion and Corporate Beneficence: The Institutionalization of Charity in New England, 1720-1810. Ph.D., Brown University, 1980. 421p. UMI# 8111193.

4121   Wyatt-Brown, Bertram. Partners in Piety: Lewis and Arthur Tappan, Evangelical Abolitionists, 1828-1841. Ph.D., Johns Hopkins University, 1963.

4122   Yee, Shirley J. Black Women Abolitionists: A Study of Gender and Race in the American Antislavery Movement, 1828-1860. Ph.D., Ohio State University, 1987. 390p. UMI# 8726748.

4123   Young, Izola. The Development of the Narrator as Cultural Hero in the Anti-Slavery Writings of Frederick Douglass. Ph.D., Howard

University, 1987. 196p. UMI# 8818450.

4124   Zilversmit, Arthur. Slavery and Its Abolition in the Northern States. Ph.D., University of California-Berkeley, 1962. 383p. UMI# 6305469.

4125   Zorn, Roman J. Garrisonian Abolitionism, 1828-1839. Ph.D., University of Wisconsin-Madison, 1954.

PREACHING

4126   Adams, Douglas G. Humor in the American Pulpit From George Whitefield Through Henry Ward Beecher. Ph.D., Graduate Theological Union, 1974. 344p. UMI# 7423185.

4127   Anderson, Deyrol E. The Massachusetts Election Sermon: A Critical Analysis of a Social and Polemic Phenomenon. Ph.D., University of Denver, 1972. 328p. UMI# 7310167.

4128   Baxter, Batsell B. An Analysis of the Basic Elements of Persuasion in the Yale Lectures on Preaching. Ph.D., University of Southern California, 1944.

4129   Bell, James M. Preaching Among Representative Smaller Religious Groups of the United States: A Survey of Its Effectiveness. S.T.D., Temple University, 1954.

4130   Bradbury, Miles L. Adventure in Persuasion: John Witherspoon, Samuel Stanhope Smith, and Ashbel Green. Ph.D., Harvard University, 1967.

4131   Brewer, Robert S. The Convention Sermon in Boston 1722-1773. Ph.D., Louisiana State University, 1971. 248p. UMI# 72-03466.

4132   Brewster, Harold L. An Objective Study of the Oratory of Robert Green Ingersoll. Ph.D., University of Southern California, 1940.

4133   Carmack, William R., Jr. Invention in the Lyman Beecher Lectures on Preaching: The Lecturers' Advice on Gathering and Selecting Sermon Material. Ph.D., University of Illinois at Urbana-Champaign, 1958. 180p. UMI# 59-00485.

4134   Casteel, John L. Conceptions of Preaching in the Lyman Beecher Lectures, 1872-1941. Ph.D., Northwestern University, 1944.

4135   Counts, Martha L. The Political Views of the Eighteenth Century New England Clergy as Expressed in Their Election Sermons. Ph.D., Columbia University, 1956. 290p. UMI# 16894.

4136   Cox, Sherrill R. The Concept of Style in the Lyman Beecher Lectureship on Preaching. Ph.D., Ohio University, 1982. 236p. UMI# 8221899.

4137   Dalton, John V. Ministers, Metaphors, and the New England Wilderness, 1650-1700. Ph.D., University of New Hampshire, 1981. 226p. UMI# 82-12781.

4138   Fireoved, Joseph D. An Anthology of Colonial Sermons. Ph.D., University of Delaware, 1985. 468p. UMI# 8609048.[John Cotton, Jonathan Edwards, Thomas Hooker, Cotton Mather, Increase Mather, Jonathan Mayhews, Urian Oakes, Thomas Shepard, Gilbert Tennent, John Winthrop].

4139   Fischer, Raymond L. The Rhetorical Principles of Robert Green Ingersoll. Ph.D., University of Illinois at Urbana-Champaign, 1968. 213p. UMI# 6812115.

4140   Hiten, Stephen S. The Historical Background of the Election Sermon and a Rhetorical Analysis of Five Sermons Delivered in Massachusetts Between 1754 and 1775. Ph.D., University of Michigan, 1960. 290p. UMI# 60-01770.

4141   Hughes, John G. The American Contribution to Homiletic Theory. Ph.D., Southern Baptist Theological Seminary, 1907.

4142   Johnson, Louis R. American Preaching in the Seventeenth Century. Ph.D., Northern Baptist Theological Seminary, 1958.

4143   Jones, Phyllis M. A Literary Study of the Sermons of the First-Generation Preachers of New England. Ph.D., Harvard University, 1973.

4144   Kerr, Harry P. The Character of Political Sermons Preached at the Time of the American Revolution. Ph.D., Cornell University, 1962. 231p. UMI# 62-05986.

4145   Larson, Orvin P. Invention in Ingersoll's Lectures on Religion. Ph.D., University of Iowa, 1940.

4146   Lesser, Marvin X. "All for Profit": The Plain Style and the Massachusetts Election Sermons of the Seventeenth Century. Ph.D., Columbia University, 1967. 234p. UMI# 6715499.

4147   Loefflath-Ehly, Victor P. Religion as the Principal Component of World-Maintenance in the American South From the 1830's to 1900 With Special Emphasis on the Clergy and Their Sermons: A Case Study in the Dialectic of Religion and Culture. Ph.D., Florida State

University, 1978. 235p. UMI# 78-22185.

4148   McCants, David A. A Study of the Criticism of Preaching Published in America Between 1865 and 1930. Ph.D., Northwestern University, 1964. 416p. UMI# 6412317.

4149   Mixon, Harold D. The Artillery Election Sermon in New England, 1672-1774. Ph.D., Florida State University, 1964. 227p. UMI# 6505595.

4150   Smith, Donald G. Eighteenth Century American Preaching. Ph.D., Northern Baptist Theological Seminary, 1956.

4151   Stegmaier, Norma K. Mark Hopkins and His Baccalaureate Sermons. Ph.D., University of Illinois at Urbana-Champaign, 1965. 203p. UMI# 65-07166.

4152   Walhout, Mark D. Hermeneutical Patriotism: Interpretation and Culture in Antebellum America. Ph.D., Northwestern University, 1985. 293p. UMI# 8600933.

4153   Watters, Jack. A Historical Investigation of the Use of the Symbols Kingdom of God and Millennium in American Preaching From 1865 to 1914. Ph.D., Bob Jones University, 1977.

SABBATH

4154   Bronner, Frederick L. The Observance of the Sabbath in the United States, 1800-1865. Ph.D., Harvard University, 1937.

4155   Chamlee, Roy Z., Jr. The Sabbath Crusade: 1810-1920. Ph.D., George Washington University, 1968. 438p. UMI# 6900690.

4156   Jacoby, Harold S. Remember the Sabbath Day? The Nature and Causes of the Changes in Sunday Observance Since 1800. Ph.D., University of Pennsylvania, 1937.

4157   Pettibone, Dennis L. Caesar's Sabbath: The Sunday-Law Controversy in the United States, 1879-1892. Ph.D., University of California-Riverside, 1979. 412p. UMI# 7926485.

SCIENCE AND RELIGION

4158   Aparicio, George B. Transcendental Experience in Nature and in the City: A Study of Anglo-American Romanticism's Anti-Urban Attitude. Ph.D., Florida State University, 1988. 270p. UMI# 8906211.

4159   Ballantyne, Edmund C. After Darwin and the Reconciliation of Science and Religion in Nineteenth Century North America. Ph.D., University of Chicago, 1989.

4160   Boell, Margaret A. The History and Use of the Comparative Method in the Religious Sciences. Ph.D., University of Chicago, 1931.

4161   Bowden, Henry W. Studies in American Church Historiography, 1876-1918. Ph.D., Princeton University, 1966. 303p. UMI# 66-13291.

4162   Church, Avery M. The Reaction of the American Pulpit to the Modern Scientific Movement From 1850 to 1900. Ph.D., Southern Baptist Theological Seminary, 1944. 128p.

4163   Everett, John R. Religion in Economics: A Study of John Bates Clark, Richard T. Ely and Simon N. Patten. Ph.D., Columbia University, 1947. 160p.

4164   Fleming, Donald H. John William Draper and the Religion of Science. Ph.D., Harvard University, 1948.

4165   Gentle, Brian G. The Natural Theology of Newman Smyth: A Study of a Response of Late-Nineteenth Century New England Calvinism to Darwinian Evolutionary Science. Ph.D., Duke University, 1976. 415p. UMI# 7627973.

4166   Hanna, Willard A. Robert Elsmere: A Study in the Controversy Between Science and Religion in the Nineteenth Century. Ph.D., University of Michigan, 1940. 195p.

4167   Himrod, David K. Cosmic Order and Divine Activity: A Study in the Relation Between Science and Religion, 1850-1950. Ph.D., University of California-Los Angeles, 1977. 675p. UMI# 7716173.

4168   Hovenkamp, Herbert J. Science and Religion in America, 1800-1860. Ph.D., University of Texas-Austin, 1976. 424p. UMI# 76-26640.

4169   Jensen, John V. The Rhetoric of Thomas H. Huxley and Robert G. Ingersoll in Relation to the Conflict Between Science and Theology. Ph.D., University of Minnesota, 1959. 487p. UMI# 6000928.

4170   Johnson, Deryl F. The Attitudes of the Princeton Theologians Toward Darwinism and Evolution From 1859-1929. Ph.D., University of Iowa, 1968. 310p. UMI# 69-08753.

4171   Jorgensen, Stan W. A Passage of Faith: The Thought of John Bascom (1827-1911) and His Intellectual Successors. Ph.D.,

University of North Carolina-Chapel Hill, 1976. 413p. UMI# 77-17450.

4172   Lester, Jacob F. John Fiske's Philosophy of Science: The Union of Science and Religion Through the Principle of Evolution. Ph.D., Oregon State University, 1979. 291p. UMI# 7917998.

4173   Leventhal, Herbert A. In the Shadow of the Enlightenment: Occultism and Renaissance Science in Eighteenth-Century America. Ph.D., City University of New York, 1973. UMI# 73-21913.

4174   McElligott, John F. Before Darwin: Religion and Science as Presented in American Magazines, 1830-1860. Ph.D., New York University, 1973. 342p. UMI# 73-21129.

4175   McGiffert, Michael. Christian Darwinism: The Partnership of Asa Gray and George Frederick Wright, 1874-1881. Ph.D., Yale University, 1958.

4176   Neel, Samuel R., Jr. The Reaction of Certain Exponents of American Religious Thought to Darwin's Theory of Evolution. Ph.D., Duke University, 1942.

4177   Reuben, Julie A. In Search of Truth: Scientific Inquiry, Religion, and the Development of the American University, 1870-1920. Ph.D., Stanford University, 1990. 423p. UMI# 9024358.

4178   Saunders, William C. "Travel, Behold, and Wonder": Fashionable Images of the Wilderness in Upstate New York, 1800-1850. Ph.D., Columbia University, 1979. 515p. UMI# 8009698.

4179   Schoepflin, Gary L. Denison Olmsted (1791-1859), Scientist, Teacher, Christian: A Biographical Study of the Connection of Science With Religion in Antebellum America. Ph.D., Oregon State University, 1977. 437p. UMI# 77-29426.

4180   Simons, Kent S. Taming the Power of the Air: Science, Pseudoscience and Religion in Nineteenth-Century American Literature. Ph.D., Emory University, 1985. 207p. UMI# 8605746.

4181   Tachikawa, Akira. The Two Sciences and Religion in Ante-Bellum New England: The Founding of the Museum of Comparative Zoology and the Massachusetts Institute of Technology. Ph.D., University of Wisconsin, 1978. 300p. UMI# 78-23089.

4182   Trammell, Richard L. Charles S. Peirce's Understanding of Religion. Ph.D., Columbia University, 1971.

4183   Tyler, Glenn E. The Influence of Calvinism on the Development of Early Modern Science in England and America. Ph.D., University of Minnesota, 1951. 411p.

4184   Wells, John C. Charles Hodge's Critique of Darwinism: The Argument to Design. Ph.D., Yale University, 1986. 265p. UMI# 8629517.

4185   Zabilka, Ivan L. Nineteenth Century British and American Perspective on the Plurality of Worlds: A Consideration of Scientific and Christian Attitudes. Ph.D., University of Kentucky, 1980. 172p. UMI# 8028005.

THEOLOGY

4186   Blackwood, Russell T., II. Problems of Religious Knowledge in the Thought of Albrecht Ritschl, William James, and H. Richard Niebuhr. Ph.D., Columbia University, 1957. 230p. UMI# 21109.

4187   Block, Lawrence. Idea of God in American Reform. Ph.D., Hebrew Union College, 1960.

4188   Breitenbach, William K. New Divinity Theology and the Idea of Moral Accountability. Ph.D., Yale University, 1978. 416p. UMI# 7916631.

4189   Brown, George E. Catechists and Catechisms of Early New England. D.R.E., Boston University, 1934.

4190   Cato, Phillip C. The Evolutionary Theology of Joseph Leconte. Ph.D., Emory University, 1977. 300p. UMI# 7806904.

4191   Christian, Curtis W. The Concept of Life After Death in the Theology of Jonathan Edwards, Friedrich Schleiermacher and Paul Tillich. Ph.D., Vanderbilt University, 1965. 661p. UMI# 6510464.

4192   Clarke, Catherine K. The Nature and Destiny of Man in the Doctrine of Plotinus and H.P. Blavatsky. Ph.D., American University, 1987. 272p. UMI# 8806461.

4193   Conser, Walter H., Jr. Church and Confession: Conservative Theologians in Germany, England, and America, 1815-1866. Ph.D., Brown University, 1981. 676p. UMI# 82-09043.

4194   Downs, Perry G. Christian Nurture: A Comparative Analysis of the Theories of Horace Bushnell and Lawrence O. Richards. Ph.D., New York University, 1982. 260p. UMI# 8226750.

4195   Gardner, Edward C. Man as a Sinner in Nineteenth Century New England Theology. Ph.D., Yale University, 1952. 175p.

4196   Gay, Ralph G. A Study of the American Liturgical Revival, 1825-1860. Ph.D., Emory University, 1977. 255p. UMI# 77-25313.

4197   Goldman, Irvin. The Beginnings of Theories of Natural Ethics and Theology in Seventeenth Century America. Ph.D., University of Michigan, 1938.

4198   Gustafson, James W. Causality and Freedom in Jonathan Edwards, Samuel Alexander, and Brand Blanshard. Ph.D., Boston University, 1967. 384p. UMI# 6713314.

4199   Hand, James A. Teleological Aspects of Creation: A Comparison of the Concepts of Being and Meaning in the Theologies of Jonathan Edwards and Paul Tillich. Ph.D., Vanderbilt University, 1969. 488p. UMI# 6913456.

4200   Harpole, Ralph O. The Development of the Doctrine of Atonement in American Thought From Jonathan Edwards to Horace Bushnell. Ph.D., Yale University, 1924. 267p. UMI# 6706903.

4201   Hein, Charles D. Abraham Lincoln's Theological Outlook. Ph.D., University of Virginia, 1982. 281p. UMI# 8302594.

4202   Hewitt, Glenn A. Regeneration and Morality: A Study of Four Nineteenth-Century American Theologians. Ph.D., University of Chicago, 1986. UMI# 0374974.[Horace Bushnell, Charles G. Finney, Charles Hodge, John W. Nevin].

4203   Hopkins, Mark T.E. Baptists, Congregationalists, and Theological Change: Some Late Nineteenth Century Leaders and Controversies. D.Phil., University of Oxford, 1988. 318p. UMI# 91735.[James B. Brown, John Clifford, Robert W. Dale, Charles H. Spurgeon].

4204   Hunsaker, Orvil G. Calvinistic Election and Arminian Reparation: A Striking Contrast in the Works of Roger Williams and John Milton. Ph.D., University of Illinois at Urbana-Champaign, 1970. 220p. UMI# 7114804.

4205   Janzen, Kenneth L. The Transformation of the New England Religious Tradition in California, 1849-1869. Ph.D., Claremont Graduate School, 1964. 269p. UMI# 66-03340.

4206   Owen, Dennis E. Satan's Fiery Darts: Explorations in the Experience and Concept of the Demonic in Seventeenth-Century New England. Ph.D., Princeton University, 1974. 324p. UMI# 750666.

4207   Richards, Walter W. A Study of the Influence of Princeton Theology Upon the Theology of James Petigru Boyce and His Followers With Special Reference to the Work of Charles Hodge. Ph.D., New Orleans Baptist Theological Seminary, 1964.

4208   Schattschneider, David A. "Souls for the Lamb": A Theology for the Christian Mission According to Count Nicolaus von Zinzendorf and Bishop Augustus Gottlieb Spangenberg. Ph.D., University of Chicago, 1975.

4209   Simundson, Daniel N. John Ballou Newbrough and the Oahspe Bible. Ph.D., University of New Mexico, 1972. 314p. UMI# 7316581.

4210   Steele, Richard B. "Gracious Affection" and "True Virtue" in the Experimental Theologies of Jonathan Edwards and John Wesley. Ph.D., Marquette University, 1990. 517p. UMI# 9101425.

4211   Vanden Burgt, Robert J. Philosophical Roots of the Finite God Theories of William James and Edgar Sheffield Brightman. Ph.D., Marquette University, 1968. 208p. UMI# 6903332.

4212   Weddle, David L. The New Man: A Study of the Significance of Conversion for the Theological Definition of the Self in Jonathan Edwards and Charles G. Finney. Ph.D., Harvard University, 1973.

4213   Weeks, John S. A Comparison of Calvin and Edwards on the Doctrine of Election. Ph.D., University of Chicago, 1963.

4214   Westermeyer, Paul. What Shall We Sing in a Foreign Land? Theology and Cultic Song in the German Reformed and Lutheran Churches of Pennsylvania, 1830-1900. Ph.D., University of Chicago, 1978.

4215   Whitaker, Daniel C. Historiographical Presupposition in American Study of Jesus, 1865-1965. Ph.D., Southern Baptist Theological Seminary, 1969. 317p. UMI# 69-04448.

4216   Wilson, Robert J., III. Ebenezer Gay: New England's Arminian Patriarch, 1696-1787. Ph.D., University of Massachusetts, 1980. 614p. UMI# 8012650.

4217   Winter, Robert M. American Churches and the Holy Communion: A Comparative Study in Sacramental Theology, Practice, and Piety in the Episcopal, Presbyterian, Methodist, and German Reformed Traditions, 1607-1875. Ph.D., Union Theological Seminary in Virginia, 1988. 880p. UMI# 8827690.

WOMEN

4218   Andolsen, Barbara H. Racism in the Nineteenth and Twentieth Century Women's Movements: An Ethical Appraisal. Ph.D., Vanderbilt University, 1981. 350p. UMI# 8120186.

4219   Behnke, Donna A. Created in God's Image: Religious Issues in the Woman's Rights Movement of the Nineteenth Century. Ph.D., Northwestern University, 1975. 338p. UMI# 75-29575.

4220   Clark, Elizabeth B. The Politics of God and the Woman's Vote: Religion in the American Suffrage Movement, 1848-1895. Ph.D., Princeton University, 1989. 361p. UMI# 9024522.

4221   Dillon, Mary E. The Influence of Frances Willard on the Woman's Movement of the Nineteenth Century. Ph.D., Northwestern University, 1940.

4222   Gay, Dorothy A. The Tangled Skein of Romanticism and Violence in the Old South: The Southern Response to Abolitionism and Feminism, 1830-1861. Ph.D., University of North Carolina-Chapel Hill, 1975. 193p. UMI# 7609247.

4223   Gordon, Lynn D. Women With Missions: Varieties of College Life in the Progressive Era. Ph.D., University of Chicago, 1980. [University of California(CA), University of Chicago(IL), Sophie Newcomb College(LA), Vassar College(NY)].

4224   Gusfield, Joseph. Organizational Change: A Study of the Women's Christian Temperance Union. Ph.D., University of Chicago, 1955.

4225   Hogeland, Ronald W. Femininity and the Nineteenth Century Post Puritan Mind. Ph.D., University of California-Los Angeles, 1968. 286p. UMI# 68-16538.

4226   Isenberg, Nancy G. "Coequality of the Sexes": The Feminist Discourse of the Antebellum Women's Rights Movement in America. Ph.D., University of Wisconsin-Madison, 1990. 446p. UMI# 9030795.

4227   Johnson, Robert L. Frances Willard From Five Thousand Feet. Ph.D., University of Oregon, 1973. 81p. UMI# 7406921.

4228   Kennon, Donald R. "A Knit of Identity," Marriage and Reform in Mid-Victorian America. Ph.D., University of Maryland 1981. 536p. UMI# 8202609.

4229   Kimball, Gayle H. The Religious Ideas of Harriet Beecher Stowe:

Her Gospel of Womanhood. Ph.D., University of California-Santa Barbara, 1976. 282p. UMI# 77-22221.

4230   Lee, Susan E.D. Evangelical Domesticity: The Origins of the Woman's National Christian Temperance Union Under Frances E. Willard. Ph.D., Northwestern University, 1980. 463p. UMI# 8026851.

4231   Lindley, Susan H. Woman's Profession in the Life and Thought of Catharine Beecher: A Study of Religion and Reform. Ph.D., Duke University, 1974. 374p. UMI# 75-02400.

4232   Malmsheimer, Lonna M. New England Funeral Sermons and Changing Attitudes Toward Woman, 1672-1792. Ph.D., University of Minnesota, 1973. 217p. UMI# 7400773.

4233   Martenas, Sharleen J. America's Third Egalitarian Crisis: Sex Equality in the Mid-Nineteenth Century, 1848-1869. Ph.D., Claremont Graduate School, 1979. 379p. UMI# 7922025.

4234   Miller, Ida T. Frances Elizabeth Willard: Religious Leader and Social Reformer. Ph.D., Boston University, 1978. 242p. UMI# 7819818.

4235   Newell, Jane I. The Woman's Christian Temperance Union in America. Ph.D., University of Wisconsin, 1919.

4236   Pellauer, Mary D. The Religious Social Thought of Three U.S. Women Suffrage Leaders: Towards a Tradition of Feminist Theology. Ph.D., University of Chicago, 1980.

4237   Porterfield, E. Amanda. Maidens, Missionaries, and Mothers: American Women as Subjects and Objects of Religiousness. Ph.D., Stanford University, 1975. 208p. UMI# 7525590.

4238   Sklar, Kathryn K. Household Divinity: A Life of Catharine Beecher. Ph.D., University of Michigan, 1969. 427p. UMI# 70-04194.

4239   Szelag, Sandra A. Elizabeth Cady Stanton: Prophetic Theologian of the Women's Rights Movement, a Model for Being Human Religiously. D.Min., Meadville/Lombard Theological School, 1984.

4240   Whitaker, Francis M. A History of the Ohio Woman's Christian Temperance Union, 1874-1920. Ph.D., Ohio State University, 1971. 499p. UMI# 71-27581.

AUTHOR INDEX

Conner, Frederick W., 3522
Connors, Donald F., 3523
Connors, Joseph M., 745
Conrad, Flavius L., Jr., 1339
Conroy, David W., 3952
Conroy, Paul R., 491
Conry, Thomas P., 3246
Conser, Walter H., Jr., 4193
Cooey-Nichols, Paula M., 1085
Cook, Dayton G., 3524
Cook, George A., 891
Cook, Harold, 2740
Cook, Lester H., 3953
Cook, Thomas H., 1268
Cooke, M. Francis, 750
Cooke, Nym, 3861
Cooksey, Ronald L., 99
Cooper, James F., Jr., 1511
Cooper, Rex E., 1778
Copeland, Edwin L., 2465
Corcoran, Mary A., 3219
Corkern, Randall A., 246
Cormany, Clayton D., 3954
Cornelius, Janet D., 1442
Corrigan, John A., Jr., 892
Corrigan, M. Felicia, 492
Cory, Earl W., Jr., 3041
Costello, William J., 581
Coughlin, Margaret M., 276
Counts, Martha L., 4135
Couser, Griffith T., 3525
Covey, Cyclone, 3862
Covington, Robert C., 1044
Cox, James L., 3247
Cox, Joseph G., 3370
Cox, Sherrill R., 4136
Cox, Stephen L., 3955
Coy, Gerald W., 33
Coyle, Edward W., 199
Cragun, Leann, 1754
Craig, Raymond A., 2632
Crandall, Robert A., 2434
Crawford, Benjamin F., 2034
Crawford, John O., 3371
Crawford, Michael J., 1402
Crawley, James W., 277
Creasy, William C., 1260
Creed, John B., 200

Creel, Margaret W., 2030
Creelan, Paul G., 2527
Crichton, Robert J., 201
Criswell, Paul D., 1332
Crocco, Stephen D., 893
Croce, Paul J., 2168
Crocker, Richard R., 3147
Cromwell, Paul F., 2833
Cronk, Sandra L., 1873
Crook, Roger H., 297
Crosby, Donald A., 827
Cross, Arthur L., 125
Cross, Barbara M., 894
Cross, Lawrence J., 667
Cross, Randy K., 3526
Cross, Robert D., 407
Cross, Virginia A., 3863
Cross, Wilford O., 2528
Crouse, Moses C., 1086
Crouse, Russel J., 1839
Crowe, Charles R., 383
Crowther, Edward R., 2371
Croy, Hazel M., 1743
Crummey, David C., 2053
Crumpacker, Laurie, 1368
Culver, Mearl P., 1950
Culver, Raymond B., 3069
Cummings, Melbourne S., 1951
Cummins, Roger W., 2912
Cuni, Sandra L., 3527
Cunningham, Homer F., 2611
Cunningham, James L., 202
Curet, Jose, 3956
Curley, Michael J., 3248
Curran, Robert E., 493
Curry, Catherine A., 582
Curry, Thomas J., 3249
Curtis, Richard K., 1452
Curzon, Gordon A., 3107
Cushman, Joseph D., Jr., 1276

Daasvand, Paul O., 3802
Dahlquist, John T., 895
Daigrepont, Lloyd M., 3528
Dailey, Barbara R., 828
Daily, Maria R., 408

Goode, Gloria D., 76
Goodell, John, 917
Gooden, Rosemary D., 2737
Goodheart, Lawrence B., 3988
Goodliffe, Wilford L., 1682
Goodloe, Robert W., 2041
Goodman, Avram V., 1557
Goodman, Dana R., 1102
Goodman, Gary S., 3989
Goodman, Ruth P.W., 3385
Goodrow, Esther M., 420
Goodwin, Gerald J., 101
Goodykoontz, Colin B., 3812
Gordon, Albert I., 1558
Gordon, Lynn D., 4223
Gordon-McCutchan, R.C., 3029
Gordon, Morton L., 1559
Goris, George, 804
Gorka, Ronald R., 599
Gorrell, Donald K., 3157
Gossard, John H., 918
Gossett, Edward F., 2468
Gottfredson, Montchesney, 1758
Gottschalk, Stephen, 813
Goudie, Andrea K., 2872
Gougeon, Leonard G., 2915
Gough, Deborah M., 102
Gould, Timothy D., 999
Gould, William D., 1191
Goulding, James A., 833
Gower, Joseph F., Jr., 686
Grabner, John D., 2027
Grabo, Norman S., 1103
Gradie, Charlotte M., 705
Graebner, Norman B., 2376
Graffam, Alan E., 1371
Gragg, Larry D., 2761
Graham, Gael N., 2469
Graham, George P., 2172
Graham, Judith, 2727
Graham, Michael J., 3268
Graham, Stephen R., 2344
Grant, John A., Jr., 3570
Gravely, William B., 1959
Gravett, Sharon L., 3571
Gray, Harry B., 2079
Gray, Henry D., 2873
Graybill, Ronald D., 19

Grayson, John T., 3158
Grazier, James L., 1053
Greatwood, Richard N., 1294
Green, James J., 421
Green, Judith A., 3014
Greenbert, Robert M., 3572
Greene, Maria L., 3269
Greenholt, Homer R., 1814
Greenwell, James R., 1776
Greenwood, Douglas M., 919
Greer, Harold E., Jr., 278
Gregerson, Edna J., 1744
Gregg, Alice H., 2470
Gregory, Christopher W., 1535
Greising, Jack H., 1864
Gresham, Charles R., 1220
Grey, Robin S., 3573
Gribbin, William J., 3270
Grice, Stephen E., 2967
Griffen, Clyde, 1277
Griffin, Charles J.G., 1454
Griffin, Edward M., 920
Griffin, Joseph A., 422
Griffin, Paul R., 1999
Griffioen, Arie J., 790
Griffith, Frank C., 3574
Griffith, Lee E., 2762
Griffiths, C. Warren, 3575
Grim, John A., 2122
Grimmelmann, Jan E.L., 1192
Grinstein, Hyman B., 1560
Grishman, Lee H., 1745
Grollmes, Eugene E., 600
Grommon, Alfred H., 3576
Grosjean, Paul E., 2496
Grossbart, Stephen R., 834
Grossberg, Sidney H., 1561
Groth, John H.C., 2940
Grover, Norman L., 3990
Grozier, Richard J., 509
Grummer, James E., 668
Grundy, Martha P., 2763
Grusin, Richard A., 2874
Guarneri, Carl J., 3089
Gudelunas, William A., Jr., 3991
Gueguen, John A., Jr., 2534
Guelzo, Allen C., 835
Guenther, Scot M., 3271

Thomas, Bill C., 350
Thomas, Cecil K., 1218
Thomas, Frank H., Jr., 318
Thomas, George B., 3919
Thomas, George L., 726
Thomas, George M., 4098
Thomas, Herman E., 74
Thomas, John W., 3063
Thomas, Lavens M., Jr., 2014
Thomas, M. Evangeline, 471
Thomas, M. Ursula, 472
Thomas, Nathan G., 2084
Thomas, Reid S., 2263
Thomas, Robert D., Jr., 2160
Thomas, Samuel J., 733
Thomas, Trudy C., 2141
Thompson, Christa M., 1171
Thompson, J. Earl, Jr., 3334
Thompson, Luther J., 351
Thompson, Richard G., 3753
Thompson, Stephen J., 1711
Thompson, Thomas C., 4099
Thompson, William O., Jr., 1421
Thompson, William P., 13
Thorning, Joseph F., 4100
Thorp, Daniel B., 2095
Thrift, Charles T., Jr., 3846
Thrift, Ronald E., 3100
Thurau, Robert H., 1835
Thurin, Erik I., 2900
Thurow, Glen E., 3311
Thurston, Burton B., 1254
Tibbetts, Joel W., 2427
Tickemyer, Garland E., 1751
Tidwell, Donavon D., 319
Tietjan, John H., 1867
Tiffany, Henry W., 185
Tiffin, Gerald C., 1244
Tingelstad, Oscar A., 3431
Tingle, Larry O., 2015
Tise, Larry E., 4101
Titus, Mathew P., 2505
Tlochenska, Mary S., 656
Todd, Gary L., 3847
Todd, Margo F., 2573
Todd, Willie G., 320
Todes, David U., 1629
Toews, Jacob J., 1898

Tolf, Robert W., 4102
Tollefson, Terry R., 3848
Tolles, Frederick B., 2788
Tomas, Martha M., 1172
Tomasi, Silvano M., 676
Tomlinson, Caroline D., 3754
Toms, Deella V., 1818
Tonks, Alfred R., 291
Torbet, Robert G., 321
Torpey, William G., 3312
Touchstone, Donald B., 63
Toulouse, Teresa A., 1060
Towell, Sherman E., 186
Tracy, Patricia J., 964
Trammell, Richard L., 4182
Tranquilla, Ronald E., 2933
Trechock, Mark A., 2512
Tredway, John T., 2513
Trefz, Edward K., 2676
Trendel, Robert A., Jr., 4103
Tresch, John W., Jr., 187
Treutlein, Theodore E., 769
Trimble, John C., 1255
Trimmer, Edward A., 1980
Trimpey, John E., 2656
Trimpi, Helen P., 3755
Trotter, Frederick T., 2075
Troutman, William F., Jr., 3313
Trowbridge, John E., 2300
Tucker, Edward B., 2574
Tucker, Robert L., 2044
Tucker, William E., 1226
Tull, James E., 188
Tully, William A., 4104
Tumangday, Miriam S., 12
Tumblin, John A., Jr., 292
Tunnell, Gene V., 293
Turner, Charles C., 2183
Turner, Eldon R., 3314
Turner, Elizabeth H., 2413
Turner, Ian B., 4105
Turner, James B., 189
Turner, Lorenzo D., 3756
Turner, Maxine T., 2663
Turner, R. Edward, 41
Turner, Robert C., 3004
Turpie, Mary C., 2901
Tuttle, Robert B., 3132

SUBJECT INDEX

Alexander, Charles M., 1440, 3885

Alexander, Samuel, 4198

Alexanderwohl Mennonites, 1881

Alexian Brothers, 785

Algonquian Indians, 706

Alice Doane's Appeal, 3549

Allegheny Brethren Conference, 362

Allegheny County(PA), 2408

Allegheny(PA), 533

Allen, Ethan, 1189, 1190

Allen, Richard, 69

Allen, T.M., 1425

Allen, Young J., 3790

Allston, Washington, 3217

Almanacs, 359, 3647, 3688

Almira College(IL), 2005

Alpaca Revisited, 3106

Altes und Neues, 1869

Alton Observer, 2236

Alton(IL), 2236

Amana Church Society(IA), 89-92, 3092

Ambassadors, 3512

American Anti-Slavery Association, 2265

American Anti-Slavery Society, 1422

American Baptist, 157, 189, 208, 274, 285, 305, 316, 338, 352

American Baptist Foreign Missions Society, 280

American Baptist Home Mission Society, 258, 273

American Baptist Publication Society, 346

American Bible Society, 1271, 2862

American Board of Commissioners for Foreign Missions, 2145, 2467, 2471, 2475, 2477, 3796, 3804, 3813, 3836, 3840, 3843, 3848, 3849

American Christian Missionary Society, 2708, 2711

American Colonization Society, 1374, 3791, 3851

American Hebrew, 1646

American Home Missionary Society, 3415, 3812, 3823, 3830, 3846, 4205

American Institute of Sacred Literature, 3351

American Jewish Committee, 1613

American Missionary Association, 79, 81, 379, 2441, 3794, 3805, 3817, 3821, 3822, 4062, 4117

American National Covenant, 2584

American Peace Society, 4043

American Prayer Book, 1333

American Protective Association, 474

American Revolution, *Denominations and Movements*: African American, 53; Anglican, 103, 111; Baptist, 161, 164; Catholic, 399; Congregational, 834, 863, 864, 877, 955; Deist, 1189, 1196; Episcopal, 1289, 1336; German Reformed, 1476; Great Awakening, 1524; Methodist, 1906, 1917; Presbyterian, 2194, 2217, 2272, 2273; Puritan, 2542; Restoration Movement, 2713; Shaker, 2726; Society of Friends, 2780, 2784; *Topical Studies*: General, 3168, 3176, 3210; Church and State, 3230, 3239, 3240, 3253, 3273, 3289, 3293, 3294, 3299, 3310; Clergy, 3324, 3326, 3328, 3333, 3336; Fraternal Orders, 3457; Literature, 3630; Philosophy of Religion, 3911; Politics and Social Policy, 3921, 3952, 4077, 4081, 4099; Preaching, 4127, 4144

American Scholar, 2938

American Society for the Propagation of the Gospel, 1030

American Society of Church

Breckinridge, Robert J., 2251
Brent, Linda, 3469
Brethren, 269, 354-382, 1391,
    1897, 1898, 1991
Brewster, William, 3781
Brick Presbyterian Church(NY),
    2346
Bridge, William, 831
*Brief Retrospect of the Eighteenth
    Century*, 2305
Brief Rule against Small Pocks,
    3688
Briggs, Charles A., 1296, 1309,
    1310, 1345, 2244, 2358
Brigham Young University(UT),
    1750
Brigham's Daughters, 1760
Brightman, Edgar S., 4211
Brisbane, Albert, 3089
Bristol County(MA), 824
British Americans, 1668
Broadus, John A., 194, 216, 322
Brook Farm(MA), 383-386, 3089,
    3091
Brooklyn(NY), 567, 968, 3445
Brooks, Phillips, 1295, 1304, 1331,
    1340, 1342, 1344, 1346, 3243,
    4133
Brotherhood of New Life, 2116
Brothers of the Christian
    Schools, 3792
Brown, Brockden, 3624
Brown, Charles B., 3117, 3486,
    3505, 3598, 3620, 3640, 3672,
    3757
Brown, James B., 4203
Brown, John, 2333, 3967
Brown University(RI), 240
Brown, William A., 2264, 2350,
    2368
Brown, William G., 3766
Brown, William W., 4118
Brownson, Orestes A., 404, 437,
    445, 486, 489, 491, 492, 494,
    497-499, 506, 507, 513, 523,
    529, 531, 543-547, 557, 621,
    644, 682, 684, 687, 689, 788,

790, 791, 794-796, 798, 799,
    2933, 3030, 3915
Brownsville(TX), 1562
Brute de Remur, Simon W.G.,
    508
Bryant, William Cullen, 2080
Buck, Dudley, 3870
Bucks County(PA), 2763, 2794
Buddhist, 387, 388, 2903, 3721
Bulgaria, 3813, 3832
Bulkeley, Peter, 1178, 2656, 2688,
    2698
Bullard, Isaac, 2417
Bunyan, John, 2640, 2651, 2655,
    3689
Bura(Nigeria), 3787
Burdens of the Earth, 1761
Burial, 2126, 2142, 2589, 2657,
    2668, 2671
Burke, Thomas N., 746
Burlington(IA), 1553
Burlington(NJ), 2836
Burma, 196
Burned Over District, 10, 389,
    390, 1502, 4095
Burns, James A., 514
Burr, Aaron, 1368
Burr, Esther, 1368, 3568
Burroughs, Jeremiah, 831
Burroughs, John, 2114, 3533
Burton, Asa, 1501
Bush, George, 2856
Bushnell, Horace, 827, 857, 859,
    866, 894, 896, 927, 947, 983,
    984, 987, 988, 1048, 1068, 1073,
    1077, 1097, 1107, 1111, 1118,
    1125, 1141, 1144, 1147, 1148,
    1159, 1162, 1177, 1185, 1401,
    2368, 2447, 3143, 3198, 3707,
    3990, 4194, 4200, 4202, 4225
Butler County(KA), 1879
Butler, Joseph, 132
Butler, Mann, 3014
Byars, Noah T., 212
Byrd, Robert E., 3651
Cabell, James B., 3539
Cabet, Etienne, 3091

Cable, George W., 3660
Cache Valley(UT), 1712
Caesar's Column, 3128
California, 7, 154, 155, 413, 504,
    536, 582, 586, 589, 601, 608,
    623, 625, 638, 699, 701, 703,
    708, 716, 802, 836, 1337, 1577,
    1667, 1673, 1717, 1743, 1919,
    2132, 2409, 2454, 2507, 2774,
    3260, 3307, 3354, 3454, 3459,
    4046, 4205, 4223
Calvert, George (Lord
    Baltimore), 753, 3268
Calvin, John, 3916, 4213
Calvinism, *Denominations and
    Movements*: Baptist, 185, 189,
    301; Congregational, 824, 841,
    855, 860, 863, 864, 967, 988,
    998, 1067, 1086, 1110, 1138,
    1165, 1176; Evangelism, 1433,
    1457; Great Awakening, 1500,
    1524; Methodist, 1957; Pres-
    byterian, 2214, 2224, 2245,
    2256, 2271, 2333, 2335, 2347,
    2351, 2361; Protestant, 2414,
    2492; Puritan, 2665; Restora-
    tion Movement, 2713; Society
    of Friends, 2797; *Topical
    Studies*: Education, 3366, 3432;
    Literature, 3552, 3648, 3661;
    Missions and Missionaries,
    3849; Philosophy of Religion,
    3916; Politics and Social
    Policy, 4045, 4092, 4094;
    Science and Religion, 4165,
    4183; Theology, 4200, 4203,
    4204, 4210, 4213; Women,
    4238
Calvinistic Methodist Society,
    1457
Cambridge Platform, 824, 1511,
    2515, 2681
Cambridge Press, 1021
Cambridge Synod(MA), 2683
Cambridge(England), 1176
Cambridge(MA), 1021, 2585,
    2597, 2617, 2629, 2663

Cameroon, 3835
Camp meetings, 1398, 1403, 1456,
    1519, 1943, 2022, 2023, 3873,
    3882
Campbell, Alexander, 801, 1207,
    1208, 1211, 1215, 1216, 1218,
    1219, 1222, 1223, 1225, 1228,
    1231, 1232, 1236, 1237, 1239-
    1243, 1245, 1248-1252, 1254,
    1256, 1259, 1262-1266, 1730,
    1746, 1922, 2708, 2711, 2713
Campbell, George, 1249, 1250
Campbell-Stone Movement, 801,
    2708
Campus Crusade for Christ, 1376
Canada, 391, 399, 1549, 1710,
    1767, 1892, 1930, 3845
Cane Hill College(AR), 2274
Cannon, George Q., 1669, 1724
Canon law, 392, 748, 3252
Canon of the Old Testament, 483
Cantatas, 3855
Canterbury(NH), 2723
Canticles, 1032, 1143
Canton(China), 2475
Capitalism, 795, 1846, 1924, 1957,
    2392, 3167, 3190, 3446, 3506,
    3622, 3907
Capuchins, 770
Caribbean, 67
Carlyle, Thomas, 2902, 3473,
    3571
Carmelites, 742
Carr, Benjamin, 3868
Carroll, B.H., 198, 289, 329, 349
Carroll, Charles, 613
Carroll, John, 398, 480, 613
Carrollton(MD), 613
Carson, Hannah, 76
Cartwright, Peter, 1401, 1948
Carus, Paul, 3721, 3918
Caruthers, William A., 3760
Case Western Reserve
    University(OH), 3402
Catechism, 696, 2286, 4189
Cathedral of Saint John the
    Divine(NY), 479

Clark, John B., 4163
Clark University(GA), 3408
Clarke, James F., 2903, 2933,
  3014, 3015, 3052, 3057, 3063,
  3078
Clarke, William N., 335, 337
Clay, Cassius M., 4072
Clay County(MO), 1698
Cleage, Albert B., 68
Clear Creek(IL), 2818
Clergy, *Denominations and Movements*: Adventist, 14; African
  American, 67, 69-72, 75-77;
  Anglican, 97, 111, 114-116,
  128, 132; Baptist, 193, 194,
  200, 207, 216, 222, 224, 225,
  229, 239, 245-247, 250; Brethren, 365, 371; Catholic, 398,
  425, 431, 441, 445, 480-487,
  489-499, 502, 504, 506-513,
  515-520, 522-526, 528-531, 533-
  537, 541-551, 554-558, 561-565,
  600, 611, 612, 620, 633, 650,
  713, 735, 739, 741, 743, 763,
  791, 793, 797, 800; Congregational, 826, 838-840, 859-869,
  871-874, 876-878, 880-886, 889,
  891, 893, 894, 896, 897, 898-
  901, 903-910, 912, 915-918,
  921, 922, 924, 925, 927-932,
  935, 936, 938-943, 945-953,
  957-959, 961-966, 968-972, 976,
  978-981, 987, 1006, 1023, 1046,
  1052, 1053, 1061, 1067, 1070,
  1078, 1080, 1088, 1090, 1092,
  1093, 1098, 1099, 1104, 1106,
  1109, 1110, 1112, 1114, 1117,
  1125, 1128, 1129, 1131, 1135,
  1137, 1140, 1141, 1144, 1147,
  1149, 1156, 1158-1160, 1163,
  1167, 1169, 1170, 1174, 1175,
  1179, 1186, 1187; Disciples of
  Christ, 1219, 1222, 1223, 1225,
  1228, 1231-1233, 1243, 1253,
  1260, 1265; Episcopal, 1284,
  1290, 1292-1294, 1296-1301,
  1303, 1304, 1306-1311, 1313-
  1319, 1334, 1345, 1349; Evangelical, 1372; Evangelism,
  1422-1424, 1426, 1427, 1430,
  1431, 1432, 1434, 1436, 1439,
  1443, 1450; Great Awakening,
  1510-1515, 1520; Hopedale,
  1534, 1535; Judaism, 1606,
  1610, 1616, 1618; Latter-Day
  Saints, 1665, 1692, 1721, 1722,
  1725, 1729, 1730, 1732, 1739,
  1740, 1762, 1781, 1783, 1786,
  1789; Lutheran, 1797, 1807,
  1810-1812, 1822, 1823; Mennonite, 1877; Methodist, 1914,
  1941, 1948, 1950, 1951, 1954,
  1955, 1959, 1962-1965, 1967,
  1969, 1970, 1973, 1977, 1980,
  1983, 1984-1988, 1990, 2002,
  2015, 2017, 2038, 2041, 2043,
  2046, 2049, 2069; Moravian,
  2101, 2107; Native American,
  2137; Presbyterian, 2221, 2226,
  2227, 2230, 2233, 2239, 2241,
  2243, 2244, 2247, 2252-2254,
  2260, 2261, 2263, 2265, 2266,
  2268, 2269-2273, 2308, 2319,
  2329, 2330, 2333, 2334, 2345,
  2358, 2359; Protestant, 2377,
  2424, 2428, 2429, 2439, 2446;
  Puritan, 2515, 2537, 2542, 2548,
  2571, 2585, 2591-2593, 2595,
  2598, 2602, 2607-2610, 2643,
  2648, 2674, 2687, 2690; Society
  of Friends, 2801, 2810; Transcendentalism, 2906, 2917,
  2919, 3018-3020; Unitarian,
  3047, 3051, 3053-3056, 3058-
  3061, 3063, 3064, 3066, 3067,
  3073, 3079; *Topical Studies*:
  General, 3149, 3170, 3177,
  3210, 3214; Church and State,
  3230, 3243, 3253, 3265, 3273,
  3305, 3308, 3310; Clergy, 3321-
  3336; Education, 3362, 3376,
  3412, 3436, 3441; Ethnic
  Groups, 3449; Literature, 3532,
  3562, 3631, 3632, 3663, 3693,

North West Indiana Conference,
2009
Northampton Church(MA), 1084
Northampton(MA), 838, 1023,
1084, 1104
Northwest Territory, 471, 2749,
3403, 3415, 3419, 3823
Norton, Charles E., 401
Norton, Herman, 1401
Norton, John, 2616, 2681
Norway, 1769
Norwegian Americans, 1833,
1838, 1841-1844, 1846, 1855
Norwegian Seaman's Mission,
3802
Norwegian Synod, 1838
Norwood, 3736
Notes on the Apocalypse, 1022
Notes on the State of Virginia,
3689
Noyes, John H., 2155, 2157-2160,
2417, 3099, 3103, 3920
Noyes, Nicholas, 2656
Nuns, 397, 502, 538, 549, 571,
574, 619, 642, 647, 663, 702,
719, 742, 748-751, 754-762,
765, 767, 768, 783, 785
Nursing, 761, 783
Nyack College(NY), 1371
Nyack Missionary Training
College(NY), 2218
Nye, Philip, 831
O'Brien, Fitz-James, 4180
O'Connell, Denis J., 453, 501
O'Connell, William H., 539
O'Connor, Michael, 555
O'Kelly, James, 1922, 2403
O'Neill, Eugene, 3731
O'Reilly, John B., 442
Oahspe, 4209
Oak Park(IL), 3085
Oakes, Urian, 3602, 3674, 4138
Oberlin College(OH), 940, 982,
1374, 1437, 2449, 3382, 3401,
3402, 3920, 3967
Oblate Sisters, 742
Observer, 2226

*Occident and American Jewish
Advocate*, 1605
Occult, 3283, 4173
Ocean Grove(NJ), 1456
Odin, John M., 550
*Of Atoms and Perfectly Solid
Bodies*, 1176
Of Being, 1176, 3744
Of Plymouth Plantation, 1008,
2621, 2648, 3602
Of Poetry and Style, 3688
*Of the Laws of Ecclesiastical
Polity*, 1007
Ohio, 269, 302, 403, 495, 510,
530, 580, 626, 631, 636, 982,
1316, 1361, 1370, 1374, 1389,
1417, 1540, 1546, 1581, 1654,
1706, 1813, 1825, 1911, 1991,
2006, 2104, 2188, 2193, 2394,
2739, 2741, 2749, 2783, 3246,
3354, 3401, 3402, 3406, 3453,
3677, 3898, 3954, 3967, 4007,
4029, 4037, 4052, 4226, 4240
Ohio Baptist Convention, 302
Ohio Conference, 1885
Ohio River(OH), 1581
Ohio Valley(NY), 1389
Okinawa, 2481
Oklahoma, 282, 472, 758, 1274,
2144, 3356, 3935
Olcott, Henry S., 387
Old Order Amish, 94, 1873
Old Order Amish-Beachy, 93
Old Order Mennonites, 1873,
1876
Old School Presbyterian
Church(GA), 2249
Old South Church(MA), 2601,
2690
Old Testament, 1120, 1203, 2299,
3224, 3227, 3675
Oldham, Herbert, 374
Oldtown Folks, 3552, 3652
Oliver, Henry K., 3071
Olmsted, Denison, 4179
On Slavery, 3688
On That Shaded Day, 2983

About the Compilers

ARTHUR P. YOUNG is Dean of Libraries at the University of South Carolina. He has published several bibliographies of dissertations and is the author of *Academic Libraries: Research Perspectives* (1990). His many articles and reviews have appeared in such journals as *Collection Management, College & Research Libraries, Libraries & Culture,* and *Library Quarterly.*

E. JENS HOLLEY is the interlibrary loan librarian at the University of South Carolina. He also serves as the religion bibliographer and editor of the *Fellowship of Christian Librarians and Information Specialists Newsletter.* He has published two bibliographies for the South Carolina Library Association and contributed several entries to the *Dictionary of American Literary Characters* (1990).

ANNETTE BLUM is a Catalog Librarian at the Charleston County Library, Charleston, South Carolina.